The Genesis of Debussy's
Pelléas et Mélisande

Studies in Musicology, No. 88

George Buelow, Series Editor

Professor of Music
Indiana University

Other Titles in This Series

The Genesis of Debussy's
Pelléas et Mélisande

by
David A. Grayson

UMI RESEARCH PRESS
Ann Arbor, Michigan

Produced and distributed by
UMI Research Press
an imprint of
University Microfilms, Inc.
Ann Arbor, Michigan 48106

Library of Congress Cataloging in Publication Data

Grayson, David A.
  The genesis of Debussy's Pelléas et Mélisande.

  (Studies in musicology ; no. 88)
  Revision of thesis (Ph.D.)—Harvard University, 1983.
  Bibliography: p.
  Includes index.
  1. Debussy, Claude, 1862-1918. Pelléas et Melisande.
I. Title II. Series.
ML410.D28G7 1986   782.1'092'4   85-24530
ISBN 0-8357-1674-0 (alk. paper)

Contents

vi   *Contents*

Acknowledgments

The current vitality of Debussy research is in no small part owing to the efforts of two people to whom I am enormously indebted. François Lesure, in his dual capacity as Director of the Département de la Musique of the Bibliothèque Nationale and President of the Centre de Documentation Claude Debussy, is apparently tireless in disseminating information and laying the groundwork for the field. Also indispensable is Margaret G. Cobb, another tremendous source of documentary information, who has done much to promote a spirit of good will and generous exchange of discoveries within the growing network of Debussy scholars. Of this group, I am most indebted to Robert Orledge, who kindly advanced me materials he was planning to use in his own *Debussy and the Theatre* (1982). Carolyn Abbate and Marie Rolf also made helpful suggestions.

Since so much of this book involved the study of manuscript materials in both private and public collections in the U.S. and in Europe, my work would have been impossible without the cooperation and generosity of many people. I am most grateful to those who invited me into their homes and gave me free access to the precious materials in their possesion: the late Mme Gaston de Tinan (Debussy's stepdaughter, née Dolly Bardac), who also graciously shared her personal memories of Debussy; Mme Henry Goüin, who inherited the library of her late brother, François Lang, and exhibited a kindness and sympathy that I will never forget; François Meyer, who gave me a tour of the collection which belonged to his late father, André Meyer, and permitted me to study the *Pelléas* sketches in that collection; Françoise Prudhomme, marvelously considerate of the scholar's needs; and a collector in Basel, who maintains a lively musical and scholarly interest in the items in his impressive collection. In addition to these, Maurice Gendron, Roy Rawlins, and Gary and Naomi Graffman kindly sent me copies of Debussy letters in their possession. Through Mme Goüin, I was able to meet Gendron, as extraordinary a person as he is an interpreter of the Debussy Cello Sonata; he shared with me some of his insights into *Pelléas*.

The initial stages of my work would not have been possible without the assistance of Larry Mowers of the Isham Memorial Library at Harvard. In a gallant gesture towards the French repertory, Larry stepped outside of his preferred German mainstream and secured for me microfilm copies of many of the materials I needed. Throughout my research, library staffs have been unfailingly helpful, and I wish to thank those of the New England Conservatory Library (especially Geraldine Ostrove), the Humanities Research Center of the University of Texas at Austin (especially Ellen S. Dunlap), The Pierpont Morgan Library (especially J. Rigbie Turner), the Houghton Library, the Lincoln Center branch of the New York Public Library, the Bibliothèque Nationale, the Centre de Documentation Claude Debussy, the Bibliothèque de l'Arsenal, the Bibliothèque de l'Association de la Régie Théâtrale, the Bibliothèque de l'Opéra, the Bibliothèque Littéraire Jacques Doucet, the library of the Société des Auteurs et Compositeurs Dramatiques, the Archives Nationales, and the British Library. Margaret Groesbeck and Sally Evans, respectively of the Frost Library and the Vincent Morgan Music Library of Amherst College, also provided cheerful and prompt assistance with often difficult reference questions.

Publishing and opera house staffs were no less cooperative, though unaccustomed to the requests I made of them. I would like especially to thank Guy Kaufmann of Editions Durand et Cie and Mme Jobert-Georges of Editions Jobert for allowing me to consult materials in their archives (and in the case of Mme Jobert-Georges, items in her personal collection). Jean Bouvier, régisseur général of the Salle Favart, granted me access to part of the Opéra-Comique archives, and Hugues R. Gall, administrateur adjoint of the Paris Opéra, granted me permission to examine the *Pelléas* score housed in the Service de la Copie. My friends Terry and Janet Wallstein arranged for me to attend rehearsals and a performance of *Pelléas* at the New York City Opera and to examine the performance materials used there.

I would also like to thank four friends and colleagues who performed various research missions for me: Fred Gajewski, Lowell Lindgren, Peter Lurye, and Martin Marks. My own travel to Europe was facilitated through generous grants from the Wesley Weyman Fund.

The spark for this project was kindled in the Harvard seminars of Louise Litterick, whose own interest in source studies engendered a group of Harvard studies along those lines. Throughout my work, Christoph Wolff, Lewis Lockwood, and Elliot Forbes of Harvard provided encouragement and advice. Lowell Lindgren and Edward Olleson suggested many improvements which I gratefully incorporated into chapter 6, a version of which was published in *Music and Letters* 66 (January 1985), 34–50. William Rothstein made helpful remarks relative to a preliminary version of chapter 9, and I received invaluable assistance with the French translations from Evelyne and

Ron Tiersky. A portion of the musical examples were prepared by Rudolf Haken using the Interactive Music System developed by Lippold Haken at the University of Illinois at Urbana-Champaign.

Finally, I would like to dedicate this work to my own Mélisande, my wife Lydia.

Abbreviations

Recurring Sources*:

AND   Andrieux, Georges, sale catalogue (30 November–8 December 1933).

BAR   Debussy, Claude, *Lettres de Claude Debussy à sa femme Emma* (1957).

BNexp   Lesure, François, *Claude Debussy* (Bibliothèque Nationale exposition, 1962).

CAP   Debussy, Claude, *Lettres inédites à André Caplet* (1957).

CHA1   Debussy, Claude, and Ernest Chausson, "Correspondance inédite de Claude Debussy et Ernest Chausson" (1925).

CHA2   Debussy, Claude, "Deux lettres de Debussy à Ernest Chausson" (1926).

CHA3   Chausson, Ernest, "Dix lettres d'Ernest Chausson à C. Debussy" (1962).

DIE   Dietschy, Marcel, *La Passion de Claude Debussy* (1962).

DUR   Debussy, Claude, *Lettres de Claude Debussy à son éditeur* (Durand) (1927).

GOD   Debussy, Claude, *Lettres à deux amis* (Godet and Jean-Aubry) (1942).

---

* Since Robert Orledge, in his *Debussy and the Theatre* (1982), has already created a system of abbreviations for many of the sources I have used, it seemed sensible to adopt (or adapt) his, rather than invent new ones.

HAR   Debussy, Claude, "Lettres de Debussy à l'éditeur Hartmann" (1964).

LAL   Debussy, Claude, "Correspondance de Claude Debussy et de Louis Laloy" (1962).

LCat   Lesure, François, *Catalogue de l'oeuvre de Claude Debussy* (1977).

LCD   Lesure, François, *Claude Debussy* (iconography) (1975).

LCr   Debussy, Claude, *Monsieur Croche et autres écrits,* ed. François Lesure (1971).

LER   Denis, Maurice, *Henry Lerolle et ses amis* (1932).

LL   Debussy, Claude, *Lettres 1884–1918,* ed. François Lesure (1980).

LOC   Lockspeiser, Edward, *Debussy: His Life and Mind,* 2nd ed. (1978).

LOU1   Debussy, Claude, and Pierre Louÿs, *Correspondance de Claude Debussy et Pierre Louÿs* (1945).

LOU2   Louÿs, Pierre, "Neuf lettres de Pierre Louÿs à Debussy" (1962).

LOU3   Debussy, Claude, "Lettres inédites de Claude Debussy à Pierre Louÿs" (1971).

LPm   Debussy, Claude, *Esquisses de "Pelléas et Mélisande,"* ed. François Lesure (1977).

MES   Debussy, Claude, *L'Enfance de Pelléas. Lettres de Claude Debussy à André Messager* (1938).

OCexp   Martin, Auguste, *Claude Debussy* (exposition at the Opéra-Comique, 1942).

ORL   Orledge, Robert, *Debussy and the Theatre* (1982).

PET   Peter, René, *Claude Debussy*, 2nd ed. (1944).

RLS   Debussy, Claude, *Debussy on Music*, ed. and trans. Richard Langham Smith (1977).

TIE   Tiénot, Yvonne, and Oswald d'Estrade-Guerra, *Debussy: l'homme, son oeuvre, son milieu* (1962).

TOU   Debussy, Claude, and Paul-Jean Toulet, *Correspondance de Claude Debussy et P.-J. Toulet* (1929).

VAL   Vallas, Léon, *Claude Debussy et son temps*, 2nd ed. (1958).

YSA   Debussy, Claude, "Claude Debussy à Eugène Isaye. Lettres inédites" (1933).

Other Abbreviations

OS   orchestra (full) score of *Pelléas*; if not qualified by date or publisher, refers to current Durand score.

VS   vocal score of *Pelléas*; if not qualified by date or publisher (DVS for Durand vocal score, FVS for Fromont vocal score), refers to current Durand score.

Libraries and Collections*

CH-B   Private collection, Basel, Switzerland

F-ASO   Bibliothèque François Lang, Asnières-sur-Oise, France

F-Pdurand   Durand et Cie archives, Paris

F-Pmeyer   Private collection, André Meyer, Paris

F-Pn   Bibliothèque Nationale (Département de la Musique), Paris

F-Po   Bibliothèque de l'Opéra, Paris

F-Ptinan   Private collection, Mme Gaston de Tinan, Paris

* Identified by R.I.L.M. sigla

GB-Lbm   British Library, London

US-AUS   Humanities Research Center, University of Texas at Austin

US-CAh   Houghton Library, Harvard University, Cambridge, Massachusetts

US-NYp   New York Public Library (Lincoln Center)

US-NYpm   The Pierpont Morgan Library, New York

US-Wc   Library of Congress, Washington, D.C.

Introduction

This book started out several years ago as a study of the *Pelléas* manuscript in the library of the New England Conservatory of Music, Boston. Today, that manuscript is no longer owned by the Conservatory, nor is it the principal focus of this book. A close examination of the manuscript revealed it to be a link, though probably the most important link, in a complex compositional chain, and it quickly became apparent that its significance could only be fully understood in relation to those sources which preceded it and those which it generated. Since the sources of *Pelléas* have never been systematically investigated, my next task was to examine as many of them as I could locate. François Lesure's invaluable *Catalogue de l'oeuvre de Claude Debussy* (1977) had not yet been published, so I was guided by references in books, articles, and exhibition catalogues, especially those of the 1942 and 1962 Debussy exhibitions in Paris.[1] The search took me to libraries, publishing houses, opera houses, and private collections in the United States and in Europe, and it resulted in several "finds"—the discovery of important materials previously unknown to scholars. A suggestion from the French conductor Jean-Pierre Marty led to a private collection containing corrected proofs of the *Pelléas* vocal score with additional annotations by Jean Périer, the original Pelléas, and also part of the *Stichvorlage* of the vocal score. The final proofs of the full score turned up in a hallway closet of the late Mme de Tinan, Debussy's stepdaughter (along with corrected proofs of *Masques, Suite Bergamasque,* and the first movement of *La Mer*; editions of Debussy's music with autograph dedications to his second wife, Emma; printed editions of works by various composers with autograph dedications to Debussy or to Emma, including Stravinsky's *Le Sacre du Printemps* and *Zvezdoliki*; and a Fauré manuscript). All of these "discovered" *Pelléas* materials are now in the Bibliothèque Nationale—the vocal score *Stichvorlage* and proofs since 1978 and the full score proofs since 1980—too recently to be included in the Lesure catalogue. Since other *Pelléas* manuscripts and proofs have also just come to light in the past few years, the Appendix of this book is a catalogue of the *Pelléas* sources, arranged in a format somewhat different from that used by Lesure.

In order to evaluate these musical sources, it was essential first to place them in a chronological context, relating them, not only to Debussy's compositional schedule, but to the early performances and the publication history of the work, since it became apparent that the opera's eventual form was influenced by the composer's relationship with his publishers and his response to the practical requirements of the opera house—its conductor, producer, cast, audience, and even the censors. The first part of the book (chapters 1–5) is therefore a critical, narrative account of the opera's history, recounting Debussy's initial contact with Maeterlinck's *Pelléas et Mélisande*, his composition of the opera based on that play, his efforts to get the work performed, its eventual acceptance by the Opéra-Comique, the rehearsals and performances by that company, and the publication of the vocal and full scores. This narrative is based largely on documentary evidence—letters, published interviews, and memoirs of witnesses and participants, as well as archival records. The story of Debussy's work on *Pelléas*, an important part of the composer's biography, has been told numerous times, and many of these accounts rely on the same well-known documents and testimony. This fact has not deterred me from quoting them, but rather challenged me to find new meaning in them while uncovering new information to fill in some remaining gaps. Indeed, many documents in this section appear for the first time.

Debussy's correspondence, much of which is still unpublished, remains the richest source of biographical data, and the recovery and publication of the composer's letters (and of letters written to him) are a high priority for the Debussy scholar. Even those letters which have been published, however, pose serious problems. In many cases, presumably at the insistence of the composer's heirs, proper names or entire sentences or paragraphs containing proper names were suppressed (often with no signal that an omission had been made), generally to remove unflattering references to people who were still alive (and who might sue), and perhaps to conceal the darker, ironical side of Debussy's personality, which often emerged on such occasions. The collections of letters to Chausson, Messager, and Durand, crucial to a study of *Pelléas*, fall into this category. Another problem with the published letters is that the locations of the originals are rarely indicated. Admittedly, letters in private collections often change hands and their owners may desire anonymity, but it would certainly be useful to know when letters are rather securely housed and readily available in public collections. The physical appearance of a letter (the type of stationery, handwriting characteristics, etc.) could help to date it, if it is undated, or provide evidence for the dating of other, undated letters. Also, a comparison of the original letters with the published transcriptions is important, not only to restore suppressed passages, but to evaluate the editorial procedures and, in all too many cases, to correct the editor's work.

Debussy's notoriously poor spelling (especially when it came to verb endings) has traditionally been corrected without comment, surely an advisable policy; the misspellings could be of interest to only the most probing of psychoanalytic biographers. But the composer's idiomatic, and often expressive, punctuation and capitalization are rather more problematic. Sometimes, it is true, Debussy's punctuation is ambiguous or confused and needs to be edited for the sake of clarity (unless, of course, one's intent in transcription is to produce a facsimile, in which case a photographic reproduction is more to the point), but the routine "correction" and modernization of punctuation and capitalization can result in considerable loss in terms of the spirit, if not the meaning, of the original. Even the most responsible of editors have taken different approaches to this problem. Edward Lockspeiser, in his 1957 edition of the letters to André Caplet, corrected spelling errors but "scrupulously preserved" the punctuation (CAP, p. 25). François Lesure, in his recent anthology of the composer's correspondence, *Lettres: 1884–1918* (1980), exercised slightly greater editorial freedom, explaining in his preface that "the relatively fanciful orthography of the musician has been corrected, as well as the punctuation in the most troublesome cases."[2]

Another problem concerns the dating of the letters, many of which the composer sent undated. In cases where a date has been assigned by an editor, one would ideally like to see it be signalled as such and moreover, to know the rationale for the assignment, whether it came from a postmark, from internal evidence, or from a relationship to dated events or letters. In some cases where the letter's postmark apparently provided the date, incongruities could nevertheless result, such as "Sunday (6 September 1893)" (CHA1, p. 117); in fact, 6 September was a Wednesday in 1893, not a Sunday, and the discrepancy should be explained. Even when Debussy himself supplied the dates, these sometimes need to be questioned. For example, in his January 1907 letters to Jacques Durand concerning the Brussels première of *Pelléas*, the composer carefully dated the letters, but as is true for many of us at the beginnings of years, when old habits are slow to break, he wrote the wrong year, 1906 instead of 1907; these letters were consequently published out of sequence (DUR, pp. 37–38).

My purpose in this lengthy digression was not to criticize any particular editor, but to illustrate some of the difficulties the Debussy scholar must confront in interpreting the composer's published letters and in arriving at an appropriate editorial policy for the transcription of his unpublished ones. Because of the documentary focus of my account of the compositional history of *Pelléas,* I would have preferred to cite the quoted documents in their original language, but I was persuaded to translate them for the benefit of those who might be interested in this subject but do not read French.

The second part of the book (chapters 6–9) turns to the sources of *Pelléas* and begins with a discussion of the libretto and its precise—heretofore unclear—relationship to the Maeterlinck play from which it was drawn. This topic, which has been treated only rather superficially in the literature, is actually a rather complex one, complicated by the fact that both play and libretto underwent a series of concurrent revisions, and those of the latter were sometimes dependent and sometimes independent of those of the former. This study rather unexpectedly yielded valuable clues to the dating of several music manuscript sources of *Pelléas*.

Chapter 7 examines the manuscript and printed sources of *Pelléas* in roughly chronological order, grouping them according to the compositional stage that they represent. This chapter turned out to be rather long, a result of both the large number of sources and the variety of topics that seemed important. My intention was to describe the documents and place them in the context of Debussy's compositional schedule and procedures in order, first, to establish the precise relationship among the sources and to document the genesis of the opera; second, to make observations about Debussy's working habits and methods; and third, to point out and discuss specific revisions of the piece. Because the *Pelléas* sources are so numerous and complicated, my remarks in this section have been necessarily quite selective. The discussion encompasses the various editions and annotated scores of the opera in a further attempt to chronicle Debussy's refinements of the work following the publication of the first edition and also in order to determine the basis for a critical edition of the opera.

The need for such an edition was one of the conclusions of my research, and this need seemed so compelling to me that my work often became torn between two objectives: on the one hand, to study and analyze the compositional process, and on the other, to point out errors in the currently available scores and suggest guidelines for a critical edition. In addition to the many errors which the current full and vocal scores continue to perpetuate, there are many places where the two offer different readings. Furthermore, Debussy made numerous post-publication revisions which were not consistently adopted by the published scores. There was a time not too long ago when *Pelléas* was regularly conducted by men who were aware of some of these editorial problems (conductors like Ansermet, Inghelbrecht, Monteux, and Désormière), and they adjusted their performances accordingly. Today this is no longer the case. Most conductors simply accept the current score and parts, unaware that Debussy continued to revise the score long after its publication. The place for a thorough, detailed treatment of this complex and crucial topic is in conjunction with a critical edition of the opera, which I am preparing as part of the recently announced critical edition of Debussy's collected works, to be published jointly by Durand and Costallat, with the indefatigable François Lesure serving as General Editor. Nevertheless, I have raised in this chapter some of the issues which that edition will consider, and I have suggested certain solutions or procedures which I plan to utilize. Debussy's apparently unceasing, and in some cases, perhaps provisional, retouching of his orchestration makes a definitive edition an impossibility. This same editorial problem exists as well for certain orchestral works of Debussy, but in the case of the opera, there is the added complication of the vocal lines, which were also extensively revised. Chapter 8 discusses some of these changes in the voice parts, and shares the dual thrust of chapter 7, considering aspects of both compositional process and textual authority.

The *Pelléas* manuscripts have been described and discussed by a number of writers and for a variety of purposes. Oswald d'Estrade-Guerra's "Les Manuscrits de *Pelléas et Mélisande*" (1957) is a description of four manuscripts then located in Paris—the Meyer, Legouix, and Bréval MSS, and the manuscript full score—with a view toward pointing out some ways in which the preliminary versions differ from the final one. Edward Lockspeiser, in *Debussy: His Life and Mind,* vol. 1 (1962), listed the *Pelléas* manuscripts known to him and tried to use their dates to reconstruct the compositional schedule (pp. 221–22); he also (p. 194) made some observations about the manuscript short score (the NEC MS), an important manuscript which Estrade-Guerra did not discuss. The 1977 facsimile publication of two *Pelléas* manuscripts in *Esquisses de 'Pelléas et Mélisande,'* ed. François Lesure—the Meyer and Bréval MSS only, the Legouix MS having disappeared (it has since resurfaced)—drew attention to these sources and elicited some commentary in the form of reviews of the volume. Two dissertations in progress are also concerned with the *Pelléas* sketches: James R. McKay, "*Pelléas et Mélisande*: The Bréval Manuscript" (Univ. of Chicago) and Clà Vital, "Studien zu Debussys Skizzen zu *Rodrigue et Chimène* und *Pelléas*" (Zurich). McKay's 1977 article "The Bréval Manuscript: New Interpretations" previewed some of the conclusions of his dissertation; comparing the successive layers of the Bréval MS, he observed that Debussy "is moving from a situation in which the structural symmetry of the accompaniment dominated the text and melody to a situation in which the text and melody informs the shape of the whole musical structure which of necessity, becomes much more asymmetrical" (p. 12).

The *Pelléas* chapter of Robert Orledge, *Debussy and the Theatre* (1982), makes substantial reference to the manuscript revisions, and a recent master's thesis by Marian Liebowitz, "Debussy's *Pelléas et Mélisande.* Monteux Score #40" (Smith College, 1980), discusses Debussy's postpublication changes of the orchestration as they were copied into a study score formerly owned by Pierre Monteux. Finally, Carolyn Abbate's 1981 article, "*Tristan* in the Composition of *Pelléas,*" offers a comprehensive overview of the manuscript sources before focusing on the earliest sketches, the Meyer MS, and the evidence she finds in them that, in the earliest compositional stage, Debussy used "a system of text-generated tonal organization, borrowed from... Wagnerian models" (p. 136). She pursues other Wagnerian connections as well, including the identification of hidden quotations from *Tristan* and *Die Meistersinger* which appear to function as musical "puns." Debussy's revisions are interpreted as an effort "to disguise the indebtedness" to Wagner, "though without disguising all traces of his presence" (p. 141).

The final chapter of this book (chapter 9) also takes "Debussy and Wagner" as a point of departure. The issue of a Wagnerian influence on *Pelléas* has been raised since the time of the opera's première, and critical opinion on this subject has run the full gamut from "There is nothing, or almost nothing of Wagner in *Pelléas*..." to the view that Debussy is "a veritable disciple of Wagner" or that "though the music itself is avowedly anti-Wagnerian, it constitutes a more advanced step towards the complete realization of Wagner's own theories than any step taken by Wagner himself."[3]

Chapter 9 begins by examining Debussy's own views both on Wagner and on his influence on the composition of *Pelléas*, opinions recorded in Debussy's critical writings, letters, and interviews. His objections to what he called the "Wagnerian formula" ("la formule wagnérienne")—the use of a system of leitmotifs and the application of symphonic developments to dramatic action—then serve as a reference point for studying a particular type of revision in the *Pelléas* drafts: thematic revisions in the orchestra part. One purely practical consideration suggested this particular area of investigation: Debussy's first sketches for a given scene were generally so hastily written that it is often impossible to read the notation with complete certainty; however, while individual notes may be unclear or ambiguous, the presence of an identifiable theme (and even some idea of its setting and use) is often obvious, putting thematic analysis on much more secure ground than, say, harmonic analysis, which would of necessity be dependent on many questionable readings and myriad bracketed accidentals. This practical consideration aside, the question of thematic usage, which concerns the use of leitmotifs and, to borrow another Wagnerian term, "orchestral melody," raises issues of fundamental importance to the compositional choices in post-Wagnerian opera. It was a question which concerned Debussy and which was of prime importance to his contemporaries, both composers and critics. In Debussy's case, the general topics of thematic usage and Wagnerian influence have not only aesthetic, but biographical (and psychological) significance as well, since the composer's actual practice appears to be somewhat at variance with his stated aesthetic principles.

The book thus falls into two basic sections: a documentary narrative of the opera's genesis, followed by a study of its sources and comments on the compositional process; the latter section culminates in the selection of a crucial aesthetic question and an analysis of the successive revisions with respect to that question. The logic of this plan is evident: the "documentary history" is necessary background for an evaluation of the musical sources and compositional procedures, which in turn provides the groundwork that makes the last chapter possible. Needless to say, this hardly exhausts the subject. The precious manuscripts, proofs, and editions of *Pelléas* will doubtless continue to be studied and many more conclusions will be drawn from them. Analysts have not satisfactorily dealt with the question of musical form in *Pelléas*, nor have they offered a precise definition of its vocal style, which runs the gamut from "recitativelike" to "arialike." These are topics which the sketches and drafts might help to illuminate, and I hope, at some future date, to pursue them through studies of the successive drafts of Act IV, scene 1 (style and form in "recitative") and Act IV, scene 3 ("aria").

The proper relationship between analysis and source studies is a subject which has recently aroused considerable debate in the musicological community. The nature of the controversy and an overview of the debate are discussed in Joseph Kerman's provocative article, "Sketch Studies" (1982). While the contributions of source studies to biography and compositional process are undeniable, certain scholars and critics feel that such investigations are irrelevant to analysis, which should, they say, be concerned only with the work itself, the final product, and not what went into it, the sketches and preliminary drafts. In grappling with this question, Kerman defends the role of sketch studies in criticism (the broader topic of which analysis is a part): "Sketch studies focus our understanding of a work of art by alerting us to certain specific points about it, certain points about it that worried the composer" (p. 179). They may tell us what questions we should ask of a piece and may even suggest an analytic approach. An analytic approach which is suggested by the composer, either explicitly expounded in writings and reported statements or implicitly inferred through a study of his own criticism (revisions) of his work, would not exclude other approaches, nor would it even necessarily take precedence over them. Nevertheless, help is certainly needed in this direction for a composer like Debussy, whose music has often proved elusive, or at least resistant, to analysis. With widely varying success, a broad range of analytic techniques has been applied to this music—from traditional harmonic analysis to techniques based on Schenkerian, serialist, or semiological premises. Arthur Wenk, in the *Pelléas* chapter of his *Claude Debussy and Twentieth-Century Music* (1983), pages 35–50, has suggested an approach to the opera originating in the symbolist aspects of its text, which "provides the basis for a global, rather than a linear, conception of musical structure"; Wenk thus associates symbolic or expressive meanings with the work's various melodic, rhythmic, harmonic, timbral, and tonal elements and shows how they contribute to the organization of the work.[4] His analytic observations suggest new ways of examining the sources, just as studying the sources can point to fresh analytic approaches. In this way, analysis and source studies can coexist in a symbiotic relationship.

But source studies need not seek to justify themselves in terms of analysis. Within Debussy research, both source studies and analysis are still relatively young and rapidly growing fields. The enormous recent growth in the former area is perhaps a manifestation of a current musicological preoccupation finding its way into a new part of the repertory, and it has been greatly encouraged by the activities and publications of the Centre de Documentation Claude Debussy, which was inaugurated in 1973. Of chief importance is the Centre's collection of reproductions of autograph manuscripts and its publication (through Minkoff) of some fundamental research tools (a facsimile of some of the *Pelléas* sketches, a catalogue of the composer's works, and a discography of historic recordings) and an annual bulletin, *Cahiers Debussy,* which prints articles and announcements, including lists of recent publications and theses pertaining to the field. One of the principal contributions of the new catalogue, compiled by François Lesure with the assistance of Margaret G. Cobb, is the information it provides concerning the existence and locations of manuscripts, corrected proofs, and annotated scores of the composer's works—an invaluable updating of the listings given by Léon Vallas in the catalogue supplement to his *Claude Debussy et son temps* of 1932. Such information is especially important for a composer such as Debussy, who left many unpublished compositions in unique manuscript copies. The composer's practice of giving manuscripts (or detached pages of manuscripts) to friends, a habit which his second wife inherited, is also responsible for the dispersal of this material, and a Debussy scholar today must keep a careful watch over the auction showrooms of Europe and the United States, as these items are frequently coming up for sale (and at rapidly escalating prices). Even in the few years since the 1977 publication of the Lesure catalogue, a number of manuscripts have changed hands and others, which had disappeared into unknown private collections, have resurfaced. The most recent listings, which update and in some cases supplement and correct the Lesure catalogue, are, for vocal works, Margaret G. Cobb, *The Poetic Debussy: A Collection of His Song Texts and Selected Letters* (1982), and, for theater works, Robert Orledge, *Debussy and the Theatre.* Mrs. Cobb's refusal to name private collectors (she identifies them only by country) is perhaps excessively discreet when these same collectors were named (presumably with their knowledge and permission) by Lesure.

Scholarly interest in the manuscripts has been about evenly divided between studies of unpublished and published compositions. The former activity has been considerably inhibited by the general refusal of Debussy's heirs, until quite recently, to permit the publication of works which the composer either left unfinished or did not publish in his lifetime. Of the many works in this inheritorial limbo, the most important is probably the opera *Rodrigue et Chimène* of 1890–92, nearly complete, which Debussy worked on in the years just before he started *Pelléas*; several studies of this work are currently underway. Of the completed, published works, *Pelléas* seems to be the ideal one with which to begin a study of Debussy's compositional process, not only because of the survival of source materials representing every stage of composition, but because of the importance of the work itself, both in the history of opera and, more to the point, in Debussy's output. It is the largest and most ambitious work of his career, the piece on which he spent the longest period of time, and the only operatic project he carried through to completion. The fact that opera is the most complex of musical genres only supports the choice of *Pelléas* as a case study of Debussy's compositional procedures.

Part One

A Documentary History of the Circumstances Surrounding the Composition, Publication, and Early Performances of *Pelléas et Mélisande*

1

From Maeterlinck's Play to Debussy's Opera (1892–95)

In 1910 Debussy told an interviewer: "I returned to France [from Rome in 1887] and didn't know exactly what to do with myself, until I came across 'Pelléas et Mélisande.' Since then you know what I have done."[1] The discovery of *Pelléas* in 1893 was indeed a major turning point in Debussy's career, and, as his remarks imply, it was the production of his opera in 1902 that brought him international celebrity. From that point on, everybody did indeed know what he had done.

Maeterlinck's *Pélléas*

Maurice Maeterlinck's play *Pélléas et Mélisande*[2] was published in Brussels by Paul Lacomblez in May 1892[3] and was first performed a year later in Paris on 17 May 1893 through the initiative and persistence of the young actor and director Aurélien-François Lugné-Poe, who had to overcome a series of obstacles before he could finally bring the symbolist play to the Parisian audience. After reading the play, Lugné-Poe proposed that the "Cercle des Escholiers," a theater company with which he was associated, present it on a double bill with another Belgian play, Camille Lemonnier's *Madame Lupar*.[4] The Committee of the Escholiers met on 21 December 1892 to discuss this proposal, but since Lugné-Poe was unable to attend the meeting, the play was read to them by Georges Bourdon. The Committee found it incomprehensible without the scenery and felt that it was impossible to do justice to it at the moment. Therefore, out of respect for the play itself, they decided to defer its presentation for the time being.[5] Despite the rejection by the Committee, *Le Mercure de France* of January 1893 announced a forthcoming performance of *Pelléas* by the Escholiers.[6] Although the announcement was in error, it nevertheless served to bring some public attention to the Maeterlinck play.

Despite this setback, Lugné-Poe remained loyal to the play and began rehearsing it, even though he had no idea how or where he would be able to present it. His cast consisted largely of actors with whom he had just appeared in the Escholiers production of Ibsen's *La Dame de la mer* (16 December 1892).[7]

Almost simultaneous with these events, Paul Fort and Tola Dorian were planning to reinstate Fort's Théâtre d'Art, and for their first production, announced in January 1893, they selected Villiers de l'Isle-Adam's *Axël*. (Coincidentally, Debussy had begun to set this play as an opera in 1887–89, though by this time he had long abandoned the project.)[8] Lugné-Poe was invited to assist in the production. When the company was forced to abandon *Axël*, it was decided, in mid-February, to replace it with *Pelléas*, a substitution which Lugné-Poe eagerly endorsed. The rehearsals must have progressed rapidly, for on 7 March *L'Echo de Paris* announced the dress rehearsal for 9 March and the première for the following day.[9] However, for unknown reasons, the performance did not take place, and Lugné-Poe once again found himself without the means of presenting *Pelléas*.

With the assistance of the writer Camille Mauclair and the encouragement of Maeterlinck, Lugné-Poe decided to mount the play by himself, and not under the aegis of an established company. He thought he had found a receptive theater in the Théâtre du Vaudeville, of which Albert Carré was director, and the 25 April issue of *Entretiens politiques et littéraires* even announced that *Pelléas* was to be presented at the Vaudeville, independently of the Théâtre d'Art.[10] But if Carré had indeed agreed to cooperate, he soon withdrew his offer.[11] Therefore, with money borrowed from his father, Lugné-Poe rented the Théâtre des Bouffes-Parisiens for a single performance, the matinee of 17 May. To publicize the performance, Mauclair wrote a laudatory article, which appeared in *L'Echo de Paris* of 9 May under the name of Octave Mirbeau, the dedicatee of the play. The article, which promoted the performance as an important artistic event, described Maeterlinck as one of the "princes of letters" among the new generation and proclaimed the forthcoming performance a milestone in the dramatic renaissance.[12] Other articles appearing in the Paris press the day of the performance, including an interview with Maeterlinck in *Le Figaro*, helped to arouse interest in the production.[13]

On 12 May, Maeterlinck arrived in Paris to offer his assistance and encouragement in the final days before the performance.[14] In general, the Belgian playwright did not enjoy supervising rehearsals of his plays,[15] although he gladly offered advice by mail; his letters to Lugné-Poe communicated changes in the play itself, discussed the motivations of the characters, requested a particular actress for a certain role, and even offered suggestions concerning the design and colors of the costumes.[16] But the playwright preferred to place responsibility for the production in the hands of a director he trusted. He obviously felt he had found one in Lugné-Poe, and, in a letter of 22 February, described him as a "wonderful artist" in whom he had the "utmost confidence."[17]

The cast of the production included Lugné-Poe himself as Golaud, and Marie Aubry (Pelléas), Eugénie Meuris (Mélisande), Emile Raymond (Arkel), Georgette Camée (Geneviève), Georgette Loyer (Yniold), Louise France (old servant), Boulay (Physician), Grange (porter), and Mmes Poraye, Inès-Netza, Millet, Lemarié, and Arnold (servants). The décors were painted by Paul Vogler, and the costumes were designed by Lugné-Poe. The music for Mélisande's song in Act III, scene 2 was written by Gabriel Fabre.[18]

A distinguished audience was in attendance at this important première. Among those present, Lugné-Poe noted Lucien Muhlfeld, Henry Lerolle, Henri de Régnier, Comtesse Greffulhe, Tristan Bernard, Léon Blum, Georges Clemenceau, Léonide Leblanc, Romain Coolus, Rachilde, Robert Dreyfus, Robert de Rothschild, Jacques-Emile Blanche, and Claude Debussy.[19] In addition, an article which appeared in *Le Journal* the day after the performance recorded the presence of Stéphane Mallarmé, James McNeill Whistler, Maurice Barrès, Henry Bauër, Henry Céard, Paul Hervieu, and Paul Adam.[20]

The reviews were mixed and included criticisms of the actors and the scene changes, which were judged too frequent and too slow.[21] One prophetic review, by Henry Céard in *L'Evénement* (19 May 1893), seemed almost to anticipate Debussy's opera in judging the play an opera scenario awaiting music, since the musicality of the text "lacked the power to completely satisfy the listener's yearnings."[22]

Debussy's Contact with *Pelléas*

According to the memoirs of Lugné-Poe, it was Mauclair who suggested to Debussy the possibility of a musical composition based on the Maeterlinck play.[23] In a prepublication excerpt from the same memoires, Lugné-Poe even claimed partial credit for the suggestion.[24] The discrepancy between the two accounts casts doubt on the truth of either version, but, even if Mauclair or Lugné-Poe had proposed the idea to the composer, it had probably already occurred to him. In fact, that idea may well have accounted for his presence in the audience.

Louis Laloy, the composer's friend and biographer, thought that Debussy's interest in *Pelléas* was the result of his having read the play before seeing it on the stage, but that his decision to set it became definitive only after his experience of the live performance had demonstrated the play's theatrical viability.[25] Robert Godet, another friend, attached even less significance to the performance at the Bouffes-Parisiens, claiming that both the composer's decision to write the opera and his first musical sketches predated the play's première.[26] Curiously, the composer's own recorded recollections of these events omit any mention of his having seen the play, but rather stress his contact with the printed word. In an interview edited by Louis Schneider for the *Revue d'histoire et de critique musicale* of April 1902, the very question was put to him: "How did the young musician get the idea to set the Maeterlinck play to music? One fine day he bought the slim volume, set about reading it, and saw in it a fine subject for an opera" (LCr, pp. 267–68). And in an article entitled "Why I wrote 'Pelléas,'" also written in April 1902, Debussy explained: "My acquaintance with *Pelléas* dates from 1893. Despite the enthusiasm of a first reading, and perhaps a few secret ideas about possible music, I did not begin to think seriously about it until the end of that year (1893)" (RLS, p. 74; LCr, p. 61). And finally, there is a slip of paper on which the composer wrote simply: "Purchased and read Pelléas in 1893."[27] Nowhere is there any mention of the performance by Lugné-Poe's troupe. But even if Debussy had not read the play by the time he heard about the upcoming production of it, which, after all, had been announced in the press as early as January 1893, he would probably have done so before attending the performance. Therefore, his initial contact with the play would have been from reading, and not seeing it. Indeed, he owned a deluxe copy of the first edition of the play.[28]

Debussy must have had more than a casual interest in the new Maeterlinck play. Two years before, in 1891, he had requested the playwright's authorization to do a musical setting of the latter's play *La Princesse Maleine,* which had been published in 1889 and had not yet been performed. The request was denied. As Maeterlinck explained in a letter of 23 June 1891 to Jules Huret, editor of *L'Echo de Paris,* who was acting as an intermediary in the matter, the musical rights had already been promised to Vincent d'Indy, who had expressed the "vague intention" of doing a setting of it some day.[29] Having been attracted to *Princesse Maleine,* Debussy would naturally have been curious about *Pelléas.*

Although he may immediately have become aware of the operatic potential of *Pelléas* (according to Laloy, his decision to set the play was made the day after he read it!),[30] he did not immediately seek the playwright's authorization. As an interviewer reported in 1902, "he did not get in contact with Maeterlinck until his plans had ripened" (LCr, p. 268). In thinking it over, Debussy apparently shared his idea of writing an opera based on *Pelléas* with several friends, the writer Pierre Louÿs among them. Each read the play in turn, and each tried to dissuade him from the project.[31]

Debussy's Works in Progress (Summer 1893)

But besides the desire to ponder the play and to seek the counsel of his friends, Debussy had another reason to postpone his plans for *Pelléas*: during the late spring and early summer of 1893, he was already in the midst of several compositional projects. First, he had to complete an orchestration of his 1891 *Marche écossaise,* which the Belgian violinist Eugène Ysaÿe was to conduct. On 4 June Debussy reported in a letter to Ernest Chausson that it was practically completed.[32] He was also reworking his String Quartet, a piece whose completion had been prematurely announced in February 1893 (LCat, p. 85). Debussy wrote to Chausson on 2 July that, even after starting the finale of the Quartet three times, he was still dissatisfied (LL, p. 45). During these summer months he also completed the *Proses lyriques,* a group of four songs to his own texts that he had begun in 1892; the third, "De fleurs," was written in June (its completion was announced in the 2 July letter to Chausson) and the fourth, "De soir," was sketched in July and completed in August or early September.[33]

In addition to these three compositions, the *Marche écossaise,* the String Quartet, and the *Proses lyriques,* there was also the matter of his largest work in progress, the opera *Rodrigue et Chimène,* with a libretto by Catulle Mendès based on *Le Cid,* which Debussy had begun by April 1890 (the date of the manuscript's dedication to his mistress, Gabrielle Dupont). During the summer of 1893 Debussy played what he had so far completed of the opera for Paul Dukas, who praised the work lavishly in a letter to Vincent d'Indy dated 1 October.[34] Dukas described the opera as being nearly complete and expressed surprise at the "dramatic breadth of certain scenes." He found all of the episodic scenes "exquisite" and displaying a "harmonic finesse" reminiscent of Debussy's early songs. His only reservation was the libretto, which he found "uninteresting": "a mixture of Parnassian bric-à-brac and Spanish barbarism."

Despite Dukas's enthusiasm, Debussy himself appears to have felt little sympathy for the opera. He wrote to Robert Godet (30 January 1892) that his life was "sadly feverish because of this opera, where everything is against me. . . . I am anxious to see you in order to have you hear the two completed acts, for I fear that I have won victories over myself" (GOD, pp. 97–98). He complained similarly to Gustave Charpentier that *Rodrigue* was "contrary to everything I wished to express. The traditional aspects of the subject call for music which is not my own" (VAL, p. 136).

Debussy thus evidently viewed the work as a concession to popular taste and felt that he was being forced to compromise his artistic aspirations. He had undertaken the project in response to parental pressure to achieve fame and, more practically, in exchange for the librettist's assistance in facilitating the publication of his works, in particular, the latter's underwriting the engraving costs of the *Fantaisie* for piano and orchestra, another "conventional" work aimed at the general audience.[35] Although the dates entered into the manuscript of *Rodrigue* suggest that Debussy stopped work on it in 1892,[36] he obviously left Dukas with the impression that the opera was, in the summer of 1893, still a work in progress which he had every intention of completing. This is surely what he must have told his librettist in May 1893 when he provided musical illustrations for Mendès's lectures on *Das Rheingold* and *Die Walküre*. Indeed, the very fact that Debussy was willing to play *Rodrigue* for Dukas suggests that he did not really dislike the work as much as one would suppose on the basis of the letters to Godet and Charpentier. Debussy valued Dukas's opinion and would not have shown him music with which he was dissatisfied. It is significant, for example, that at their summer meeting Debussy played only the first three movements of his Quartet, withholding the last, which was then undergoing revision. And a few months later he refused to show Dukas the early drafts of *Pelléas*, explaining in a letter of 11 January 1894 that he placed so much value on his friend's criticism that he preferred to wait until he could give a more complete impression of the work by playing one or two entire acts. [37]

Even if Debussy stopped working on *Rodrigue* in 1892, it is by no means certain that this represented a complete abandonment of the opera. However, the work's status may well have changed once the composer had discovered the more congenial text of *Pelléas*. This was not, after all, the first time that a Maeterlinck play had threatened the future of the Mendès collaboration. In 1891, presumably in the midst of his work on *Rodrigue,* Debussy solicited but was refused Maeterlinck's permission to set the latter's *Princesse Maleine.* Had the permission been granted, would Debussy have postponed or quit work on *Rodrigue* in favor of the Maeterlinck text? One can only guess. It does seem, though, that Debussy was on the lookout for an operatic alternative to the unappealing project in which he was engaged and that in mid-1893 *Pelléas* was a serious candidate. This thought may well have been in the back of his mind when he played *Rodrigue* for Dukas. Was Debussy secretly hoping to elicit a negative response from this audition, a confirmation of his own doubts and a justification for setting the work aside permanently? If so, he was disappointed, and Dukas's enthusiastic reaction may have made the ultimate abandonment of *Rodrigue* all the more difficult.

What made the eventual abandonment possible was Debussy's decision to proceed with *Pelléas*, a decision which itself was dependent on both his own serious commitment to the work and the authorization of its playwright. (After the experience of *Princesse Maleine* he certainly would not have embarked on *Pelléas* without that authorization.) Only when these conditions had been met could he feel justified in terminating a project that may have been ungratifying, but had nonetheless occupied more than two years of his life. To save face with Mendès, Debussy pretended that the manuscript of *Rodrigue* had been accidentally destroyed in a fire. In fact, Debussy did not destroy it, but kept it among his papers, where it was discovered by Alfred Cortot after the composer's death. [38]

Maeterlinck's Authorization and Debussy's Composition of *Pelléas* Act IV, Scene 4 (August–October 1893)

When Debussy eventually decided to contact Maeterlinck, he did so through an intermediary, Henri de Régnier. This was the same procedure he had used two years before relative to *Princesse Maleine* when he asked Jules Huret to contact Maeterlinck on his behalf. In early August 1893 Maeterlinck received the following letter from Régnier:

> My friend, Achille Debussy, who is a musician of the most clever and delicate talent, has begun some charming music for *Pelléas et Mélisande*, which deliciously garlands the text while scrupulously respecting it. Before going further with this work, which is not inconsiderable, he would like authorization to continue.[39]

Maeterlinck posted his affirmative response on 8 August:

> My dear Poet,
> Please tell Monsieur Debussy that I very gladly give him the necessary authorization for *Pelléas et Mélisande*, and since you approve of what he has done so far, I thank him already for all that he will be willing to do.
> To you too, my dear poet, most cordial thanks for your friendly intervention.... [40]

Régnier's statement that Debussy had already begun writing music for *Pelléas* was probably nothing more than a piece of diplomatic strategy, and judging from Maeterlinck's reply, the tactic was successful. The only indication that any composition had taken place by this date is the recollection of Robert Godet that, almost immediately after reading the play, Debussy jotted down a few musical ideas ("impressions musicales"): the rhythm representing the ponderous walk of Golaud, the five-note "arabesque" of Mélisande, and the theme to accompany Pelléas's words, "On dirait que ta voix a passé sur la mer au printemps" (Act IV, scene 4).[41] Even overlooking the dubious aspects of Godet's testimony (to be discussed in chapter 9), one can hardly imagine that these few jottings were sufficient to justify Régnier's considerable praise. It is most likely that the composition of *Pelléas* did not really begin until Maeterlinck's authorization had been secured. Debussy himself later recalled that "as regards *Pelléas*, I actually began it in September 1893...."[42] Elsewhere, he referred to his prior involvement with the opera as being nothing more than "the secret thought of some possible music" (LCr, p. 61).

Now, however, having secured Maeterlinck's authorization, Debussy began to think seriously about starting work on *Pelléas*. His early progress on the opera can be chronicled through his correspondence with Chausson, who served at this time as a kind of musical mentor and senior colleague to the young composer. At first, Debussy's compositional activity was delayed by an unhappy state of mind. As he explained to Chausson in a letter dated 26 August, he had not written to him recently because he had been sick ("an awful fever, which kept me in bed, dejected, dazed, and made my fingers run like hares on my coverlet") and depressed ("I perceived a succession of long days, like an avenue lined with dead trees") (LL, p. 46). Chausson replied two days later, hopeful that this bad period would soon be over: "I am so glad to know that it was only a passing indisposition; I hope that you are now rid of it and that you can begin again to think about *Pelléas et Mélisande*" (CHA3, p. 53).

Debussy was indeed thinking about *Pelléas*, but when he next addressed Chausson, on 3 September,[43] serious self-doubt was added to his depression. He was nonetheless hard at work:

> I have tried in vain, but I have not succeeded in brightening up the sadness of my surroundings: sometimes my days are fuliginous, gloomy, and silent, like those of a hero of Edgar Allan Poe, and my Romantic soul is like a Ballade of Chopin! My solitude is populated by too many memories which I still cannot expel. Finally, I must live and wait!...
>
> And now the hour of my thirty-first birthday has just rung, and I am not yet very sure of my aesthetics, and there are things which I still do not know! (how to write masterpieces, for example, or how to be very serious, among other things, having the fault of thinking too much about my life and of not seeing realities until they become insuperable). Perhaps I am more to be pitied than blamed. In any case, in writing you this, I depend upon your forgiveness, and your patience.
>
> ...As for me, I am working furiously, but (is it the misanthropy of my existence?) nevertheless, I am unhappy with what I am doing. I wish that you were here for a while. I am afraid of working in a vacuum.... (LL, pp. 51–52)

In sharp contrast to the depressed tone of the body of the letter, a jubilant postscript was added, perhaps a few days later, announcing his "Latest News":

> I have just finished the last of the *Proses lyriques,* dedicated to H. Lerolle, first, to please myself, then to prevent breaking a circle of friends....
>
> C.A. Debussy is finishing a scene from *Pelléas et Mélisande*, "A fountain in the park" (Act IV, scene IV), about which he would like the opinion of E. Chausson. I wonder if there isn't some way to arrange excursion trains between Paris and Royan on behalf of this event, whose great interest needs no further explanation. (LL, p. 52)

These achievements obviously gave the composer a tremendous sense of accomplishment. In reply, Chausson sent his congratulations:

> At last, here is a good, long letter which convinces me that you are no longer ill. This makes me rejoice. The scene from *Pelléas et Mélisande* finished! And the fourth *Prose lyrique!* You are really going now! I would very much like to hear all of this. I know in advance that I will love it. (CHA1, p. 119)[44]

The surprise that Chausson expressed over the rapidity with which Debussy had accomplished so much, suggests that the scene from *Pelléas* may in fact have been written in a matter of days. As has been noted, its composition was probably not begun before mid-August and perhaps was started as late as the end of that month.

In interviews given sixteen and seventeen years later, Debussy discussed his work habits and attitudes towards his compositional projects. Although distanced in time and subject to journalistic misquotation, his remarks are entirely consistent with this reconstructed sequence of events:

> I can only write when I am in the mood for it, and then I can only write on the work to which my mood directs me.[45]
>
> No, . . . I do not know how I compose. At the piano? No, I can't say I do. I don't know how to explain it exactly. It always seems to me that we musicians are only instruments, very complicated ones it is true, but instruments which merely reproduce the harmonies which spring up within us. I don't think any composer knows how he does it. If he says he does, it seems to me he must be deluding himself. I know I could never describe the process.
>
> Of course, in the first place, I must have a subject. Then I concentrate on that subject, as it were—no, not musically, in an ordinary way, just as anybody would think of a subject. Then gradually after these thoughts have simmered for a certain length of time music begins to centre around them and I feel that I must give expression to the harmonies which haunt me. And then I work unceasingly.
>
> There are days and weeks and often months that no ideas come to me. No matter how much I try I cannot produce work that I am satisfied with. They say some composers can write, regularly, so much music a day—I admit I cannot comprehend it. Of course, I can work out the instrumentation of a piece of music at almost any time, but as for getting the theme itself—that I cannot do.
>
> I have tried it. I have forced myself to work when I felt least like it, and I have done things which did not seem so bad at the time. I would let those compositions lie for a couple of days. Then I would find they were only fit for the waste basket.[46]

Though made well over a decade later, these remarks seem to apply as well to Debussy's work schedule of the 1890's, where periods of inactivity were suddenly interrupted by bursts of compositional activity, and where achievement was often followed by rejection and revision.

About two weeks after learning that Debussy had completed a scene from *Pelléas*, Chausson again wrote to his young colleague, wondering why he had not heard from him in such a long time:

> I haven't had news from you in a very long time. I miss it. No doubt you are working ferociously. On what? Everything that I knew you to be working on is finished. Send me lots of details: you are always sure to give me pleasure. (CHA3, p. 54)

In asking what compositions Debussy was working on, Chausson was evidently assuming that the former was not proceeding with other scenes from

Pelléas. Could it be that Debussy's original intention was to set but a single scene from the play? This is exactly what Raymond Bonheur believed. Bonheur, a fellow student from Debussy's Conservatoire days, was one of the first to hear the newly composed scene, and he claimed that

> it was not with the preconceived intention of writing a theater work that, in the beginning, he allowed himself to be captivated by the Maeterlinck play. It was for no purpose other than his own pleasure that he first tried to set the great scene at the fountain, a first version which was quite different from what it was to become.... [47]

Perhaps Debussy chose to set the dramatic climax of the play as an experiment, in order to test the feasibility of an opera based on the Maeterlinck play, but it is certainly hard to imagine that he could have conceived of this scene as a complete and performable dramatic entity. [48] Where Bonheur is undoubtedly correct, however, is in noting the vast differences between the first version of the "Scène de la fontaine" and its ultimate form. This first scene to be written was also the one most frequently revised, and its first revision was undertaken less than a month after its original completion. [49] In a letter of 2 October, Debussy confided to Chausson his reasons for discarding the original draft:

> My only excuse for not writing in so many days is that I have been working too much!...
> I was too hasty in crying victory for *Pelléas et Mélisande*, because, after a sleepless night, the kind that offers counsel, I had to admit to myself that it wasn't that at all. It was like a duo by Mr. So-and-so, or no matter who, and then, above all, the ghost of old Klingsor, alias R. Wagner, appeared at the turning of a certain measure, so I tore it all up and set out again in search of a little formula of phrases that were more personal. I have forced myself to be both Pelléas and Mélisande and have gone in search of the music behind all of the veils which she gathers to hide even from her most ardent worshippers! I have come up with something which may perhaps please you. As for the others, I simply don't care. Quite spontaneously, I came up with a technique which seems to me quite extraordinary, that is to say, Silence (don't laugh!) as a means of expression! Perhaps it is the only way to set off the emotional content of a phrase. If Wagner used silence, it seems to me that it was only in a completely dramatic way, a little bit like the way it is used in certain other dubious dramas in the style of Bouchardy, Ennery, and others! (LL, p. 55; US-AUS)

Traces of a Wagnerian influence would have seemed especially abhorrent to Debussy since he was reported at the time to be writing an article entitled "On the Uselessness of Wagnerism" ("De l'inutilité du wagnérisme"). The article was first announced in the September 1893 issue of *L'Idée Libre,* and the announcement was repeated in each issue until February 1894. [50] The article never appeared and was presumably never written, but its title reflects an opinion that was to recur like a leitmotif throughout Debussy's critical writings.

Debussy must have finished his revision of the "Scene at the Fountain" before 19 October: it has survived as the earliest known fair-copy short score of the scene, the Legouix MS, which is dated "September–October 1893." Debussy habitually tried out newly composed scenes by playing them for privileged friends, and it was probably this revised version of the scene, still different from its ultimate form, that he played for Raymond Bonheur and Henry Lerolle on separate occasions in mid-October. Chausson reported Bonheur's enthusiasm in a letter to Debussy of 19 October: "Bonheur is absolutely enamored of your scene from *Pelléas et Mélisandre* [sic]. I would certainly like to hear it. I know very well that I will love it" (CHA3, p. 57). In answering Chausson's letter on 23 October,[51] Debussy mentioned Lerolle's visit:

> I meant to write to you Saturday [21 October], but I had a visit from Lerolle, which gave me great pleasure. He must have written you some extraordinary things about *Pelléas*! But he is so full of sympathy for me that you should probably believe only half of what he says.... (LL, p. 59; US-AUS)

Lerolle himself wrote to Chausson the very day of his visit with Debussy:

> It occurred to me to go to Debussy's.... He just played me ... a scene from *Pelléas et Mélisande*.... It is marvelous.... and then it makes my spine tingle. Really, it is very well done. Besides, he seems to be satisfied with it.... (LPm, p. 11)

The composer's manner of performing on such occasions can be inferred from Henry Lerolle's account, in a letter of 5 February 1894 to Chausson, of the way Debussy played and sang through Act I of *Parsifal* at a private society gathering:

> A reading of Act I of *Parsifal* by Debussy. It went very well, and I believe that all were satisfied, although some found that they couldn't hear the words clearly enough. I don't doubt it! You know how he enunciates when he sings. It's even lucky if he doesn't just say: "Tra ta ra ta ta."
> ... poor Debussy was exhausted. I thought he wouldn't make it to the end. As soon as he finished, I took him secretly to the back room and gave him something hot.... I thought he was going to topple over. The fact is that he played and sang with such spirit! He assured me that if I hadn't been beside him, turning the pages, he would have closed the score at some point and left. It is agreed that next time we will take a cigarette break in the middle of the second act, and I think that everybody will be happy....[52]

One imagines that when singing *Pelléas* he would have been more attentive to the text (he knew it by heart), but his performances were surely no less intense and energetic. Bonheur wrote vividly of Debussy's special qualities as a performer of his own works:

> One knows what an incomparable interpreter he was of his own works, creating the illusion of an orchestra and giving an extraordinary impression of life and movement. His hollow voice was exact in accent and expression, and whoever has not heard him in the terrible

hair-pulling scene [scene 2] from the fourth act of *Pelléas* cannot imagine its tragic power. But it was when he played from a sketch still in progress and practically in the fever of improvisation that he was truly wonderful. He used to say, "How I envy painters, who can carry through in their dreams the freshness of a sketch...."[53]

And Gustave Doret recorded the indelible impression made on him by Debussy's piano performance of the *Prélude à L'Après-midi d'un faune,* which he heard in 1894:

> Whoever had not heard Debussy himself play his works on the piano in private cannot completely do justice to the Debussyist art, an art so incorporeal, so subtle that only the composer, with his extraordinary hands, guided by his profound sensibility, could give it its ideal interpretation.
>
> What force the violent accents took under his grip! With what extraordinary gifts he was able at the keyboard to give his scores the colors of his orchestra, with the most perfect balance, even with the precise instrumental nuances.[54]

Visits with Maeterlinck and Ysaÿe in Belgium (November 1893)

For the moment, then, Debussy was satisfied with his work—he had written and revised the "Scene at the Fountain," and the friends for whom he had played it responded with enthusiasm. He was now sufficiently committed to the opera that he wished to consult personally with his librettist. Thus, in early November 1893, Debussy journeyed to Belgium with Pierre Louÿs, his poet friend, who, though of French parentage, was born in Ghent. The composer actually had two scheduled missions, which were reported in the 12 November issue of the Brussels journal *L'Art Moderne*:

> M. A.-C. Debussy . . . spent two days in Brussels before going off to Ghent, where he went to play for Maurice Maeterlinck the musical setting of *Pelléas et Mélisande*, which he has just written.
>
> He showed M. Eugène Ysaÿe a string quartet which he has just completed and which will be given its première at the concerts of the *Libre Esthétique.*[55]

The Libre Esthétique (meaning "Independent" or "Free Aesthetics") was a recently formed Belgian society whose aim was the promotion of avant-garde art, and violinist-conductor Ysaÿe served as its director of concerts.[56] The purpose and goals of the Libre Esthétique were outlined in an article which appeared in the 29 October 1893 issue of *L'Art Moderne*. The following excerpts from that article will suggest the nature of the organization:

> The LIBRE ESTHÉTIQUE: this is the name of the new association which intends to create in Belgium a new forum for art.
>
> Its plan? To give independent art the place which, from now on, it has the right to occupy, by offering independent artists, both native and foreign, the opportunity to make themselves known to the Belgian public by being presented under the best possible conditions.

Therefore, every year, the LIBRE ESTHÉTIQUE will invite painters and sculptors chosen in Belgium and abroad, from among those who evince individuality and who point toward new horizons; we will assemble their works in an eclectic Salon, in which the various tendencies which contribute to the evolution of art will be represented....

The LIBRE ESTHÉTIQUE will also invite musicians belonging to the new schools of art to have their works heard, and, towards this end, it will put at their disposal the resources which it has at its command.[57]

Debussy's discussions with Ysaÿe during this November meeting were not limited to his String Quartet. He had also brought along several other works to play for the violinist-conductor, no doubt with the hope of future performances. *Pelléas* was among them. According to the violinist's son, "Debussy had read through the opera, he and Théophile [Ysaÿe] at two pianos and [Eugène] Ysaÿe singing each part in turn. 'We saw it through our ears,' said Ysaÿe afterwards."[58] Since Debussy probably had a single score, a duet rather than a two-piano performance is more likely. Debussy himself described the "audition" in an undated letter to Chausson, written shortly after his return to Paris:

As a result of my friendship with Pierre Louÿs, whom you know, I believe, I took a short trip to Brussels; since that city held no other interest for me except that it contained Ysaÿe, my first visit was with him, and I will not surprise you very much in telling you that he let out real shouts of joy when he saw me and hugged me to his wide chest, addressing me as familiarly as he would his younger brother; after which, I had to give him news of everybody, particularly about you, which, alas, I could only speak of on the basis of correspondence; then, music, wild music, and in one memorable evening, I played in succession the *Cinq poèmes* [*de Baudelaire*], *La Damoiselle élue, Pelléas et Mélisande*; I was as hoarse as if I had been selling newspapers on the boulevard. *Pelléas* had the distinction of moving some young people, English girls, I believe; as for Ysaÿe, he was delirious, and I really cannot repeat what he said to me! Your "quartet" [Debussy's String Quartet, originally dedicated to Chausson] pleased him just as much, and he is having it studied. (LL, p. 60)

Although seemingly added as an afterthought, the Quartet was the main object of the conference with Ysaÿe, for, according to the 12 November notice in *L'Art Moderne,* the work was to receive its première at the Libre Esthétique concerts. Debussy left the manuscript with the violinist so that the Ysaÿe Quartet could work on it. The composer, anxious to learn if the other members of the group (Mathieu Crickboom, Léon Van Hout, and Joseph Jacob) shared the first violinist's enthusiasm, wrote to Ysaÿe, presumably in late November, and may have been trying to hurry a decision by telling him that Durand, to whom he had sold the work, needed the manuscript. The letter also mentioned *Pelléas* and his intention of dedicating the opera to Ysaÿe:

I am anxious to learn your opinion of my quartet and to know what fate Your Eminence intends for it? Besides, all of the employees of Maison Durand et Fils are on my back, and they show up each morning demanding my manuscript. "What shall I do, O Lord? What shall I do?" as Saint Paul said in a celebrated verse.[59]

I have been so pushed around since my return to Paris that it was not until today that I find a moment to write and tell you once again how very sorry I was to have been obliged to leave so quickly! Because I can hardly tell you how much I enjoyed the few hours spent with you. I assure you that your approval of *Pelléas et Mélisande* has given me absolutely unparalleled encouragement, and I only hope that receiving the dedication of this work gives you as much pleasure as I had in bestowing it upon you. Now, would you do me the kindness of returning *the manuscript and parts of the quartet* as quickly as possible! I will have them recopied immediately if you still need them!

I am still hoping that you will come to Paris in December, and I await you impatiently.[60]

Ysaÿe reportedly had difficulty convincing his colleagues in the Quartet of the value of Debussy's String Quartet, but he was ultimately successful.[61] The Ysaÿe Quartet gave the première performance of the work on 29 December 1893 at a Société Nationale concert (Salle Pleyel, Paris), and Ysaÿe planned to include it in an all-Debussy program to be presented by the Libre Esthétique in Brussels on 1 March 1894.

Debussy's second mission during his November trip to Belgium was to meet with Maeterlinck. According to the 12 November news item in *L'Art Moderne,* the composer's purpose was to play for Maeterlinck the music he had written so far for *Pelléas* (i.e., Act IV, scene 4). There must have been other reasons. There was no doubt a purely social motivation, to establish personal contact with the man who had supplied his libretto, but Debussy probably had another and more practical objective—to secure the playwright's permission to make cuts in the play. Since he already had Maeterlinck's authorization to set *Pelléas* (and perhaps knew of the playwright's disinterest in music), there was no real necessity to play the music for him. However, Debussy did need the dramatist's approval for any cuts or changes he may have wished to make in the text, and it seems that this is what he sought. Debussy described the visit, the first meeting of playwright and composer, in the same letter to Chausson that detailed his visit with Ysaÿe:

I saw Maeterlinck, with whom I spent a day in Ghent; at first he acted like a young girl being introduced to her future husband, then he thawed and became charming; he talked theater to me truly like an absolutely remarkable man; regarding *Pelléas,* he gives me complete authorization to make cuts, and even indicated some which are very important, *even very useful!* Now, from the point of view of music, he says that he understands nothing about it, and, faced with a Beethoven Symphony, he is like a blind man in a museum; but really, he is very nice and speaks of the extraordinary things that he discovers with an exquisite simplicity of the soul: at one point I thanked him for having entrusted *Pelléas* to me, and he did everything he could to prove to me that it was he who should be indebted to me for having been willing to put it to music! Since my opinion is diametrically opposed, I had to use all of my diplomacy, which nature has not, after all, given me in abundance.

In the end, you see that it was a more profitable voyage than that of [Gide's] Urien![62]

Maeterlinck's claim that he had no understanding of music was one that he consistently repeated,[63] and Debussy's letter does not mention whether or not he actually played any of his music for Maeterlinck, again suggesting that this was not really the point of the visit.

What prompted Debussy to seek permission to make cuts in the play? An examination of the September–October 1893 drafts of Act IV, scene 4 (part of the Meyer MS, the Legouix MS, and the pages of the Bréval MS that were once part of Legouix) reveals that Debussy originally set Maeterlinck's text complete, with only two tiny changes in wording and not a single cut. Perhaps he was considering some cuts for this scene.[64] More likely he was looking ahead to other scenes. Having successfully tested his affinity for the play by completing to his satisfaction (at least temporarily) the scene which was probably at the center of his attraction to the play, Debussy was thinking about the opera as a whole and the form he wished it to take. Such thoughts might have led him to consider the omission of certain lines or even entire scenes. To carry this out he needed the playwright's approval, which he obtained in the course of their meeting. In fact, he obtained more than approval—Maeterlinck even suggested some cuts which the composer found "very important, even very useful."

Work on *Pelléas* Resumes: Act I (December 1893–February 1894)

In December 1893, not long after his return from Belgium, Debussy began to work again on *Pelléas*, shifting his attention from the climax of the play to its beginning. He did not set the first scene of Maeterlinck's play—no sketches survive for this scene or for the other three that he cut (Act II, scene 4; Act III, scene 1; and Act V, scene 1), suggesting that their omission was probably a precompositional decision, perhaps at Maeterlinck's suggestion. Debussy's Act I thus consists of scenes 2, 3, and 4 of Maeterlinck's first act. Debussy seems to have composed the three scenes of Act I in sequence, one each month, working relatively continuously throughout the three-month period, from December 1893 through February 1894. These dates were inscribed on the final folio of the short score draft of Act I (NEC MS, I, fol. 23): "Dec. 93/Jan./Feb. 94."

The composition of Act I gave Debussy considerable trouble, which he described in an undated letter to Chausson, probably written in late December or early January in reply to one from the latter of 18 December.[65] Debussy explained why he had not written in so long:

> It is Mélisande's fault!
> *and will you forgive us both?*
>
> I have spent days in pursuit of the "nothingness" that she (Mélisande) is made of [Act I, scene 1?] and I sometimes lacked the courage to tell you all of this—besides, these are battles that you understand, but I don't know if, like me, you go to bed with a vague desire to cry, feeling a little bit like someone who has spent the day without seeing a dearly beloved friend.

> Now it is Arkel who torments me [Act I, scene 2?]; he is from *beyond the grave,* and he has that impartial and prophetic tenderness of those who will soon disappear, and all of this must be expressed with do, re, mi, fa, sol, la, si, do!!! Some profession!

> I will write to you at greater length tomorrow. Today, just a simple hello to say that I am thinking of you. (CHA2, pp. 183–84)

One implication to be drawn from this letter is that Debussy composed Act I, scene 1 in December and subsequently worked on scene 2. Since we know that he was setting Act I at this time, his mention of Mélisande and Arkel most likely refers to scenes 1 and 2 respectively; Arkel appears only in the second scene of this act, and, although Mélisande appears in both the first and third scenes, Debussy's remarks seem more appropriate to her characterization in the first. After completing the first two scenes, he turned his attention to the third, finishing his draft of Act I before the end of February 1894. In that month he inscribed a Japanese fan to the daughter of Henry Lerolle, writing the opening measures of Act I, scene 3 and a dedication dated February 1894: "to Mademoiselle Yvonne Lerolle, a souvenir of her little sister Mélisande."[66]

Debussy announced his completion of Act I in an undated letter to an unidentified friend (Chausson?):

> Sunday:
> Dear Friend!
>   Just two words to beseech you not to bear me a grudge; and if only you knew how much I miss your friendship, especially among so many men with narrow principles and oversized frock-coats.
>   Finally: I have finished Act I of *Pelléas*; and I have been able to pay my rent, which was not as easy.
>   Until tomorrow, at greater length,
>
> Your devoted
Claude[67]

Two important points can be inferred from this letter: first, that Debussy intended his opera to adhere to the structure of Maeterlinck's play (i.e., to retain the playwright's division into acts, even if some scenes were cut), and second, that the composer considered each act a separate and integral musical unit. The latter point is substantiated by a letter that Debussy wrote to Paul Dukas on 11 January 1894, while in the midst of his work on Act I:

> Dear friend,
> You are the one who is being difficult!
> and that is why I will not play you *Pelléas*! Let me explain myself:
> The various performances which I have given until now have been necessarily fragmentary, and the impression they produced seems to me somewhat confused, not to say contradictory; I would therefore much prefer to wait until I have an act or two finished, in order to give you a more nearly complete impression of it; I hope that you will be moved by

feelings of self-denial and will see in my refusal only a desire to please you more, because it is practically unnecessary for me to tell you what great value I place on your criticisms as well as on your encouragement. (LL, p. 63)

While Dukas was eager to hear Debussy's music for *Pelléas*, Chausson was not. An element of jealousy, perhaps previously latent, had surfaced in the relationship between Debussy and Chausson. The latter, encountering considerable difficulty with the composition of his own opera, *Le Roi Arthus,* could not tolerate comparison with the achievement of his younger colleague. On 28 November 1893 he wrote to Henry Lerolle that, though he sees Debussy often, he refuses to listen to *Pelléas*: he is sure that his inevitable admiration for the music will interfere with his ability to complete his own opera.[68]

Among the "various performances" of *Pelléas* given while Debussy was working on Act I was an after-dinner performance at the home of Mme Fontaine (CHA3, p. 58), and another, on 18 December 1893, at the home of Henry Lerolle, who described the "petite réunion" in some detail in a letter to Chausson written the following day.[69] Lerolle had invited a distinguished group: Debussy, Vincent d'Indy, Paul Poujaud, Camille Benoît, Charles Bordes,[70] Maurice Denis and his wife, and Arthur Fontaine and his wife. The principal musical entertainment was the third act of d'Indy's opera *Fervaal,* but Lerolle had also asked Debussy to bring *Pelléas*. Upon arriving, Debussy "said that he hadn't brought it—that it would have been too much music." After dinner, "cigars and cigarettes," and d'Indy's presentation, the Fontaines and Denises departed. Lerolle's account continued:

> Then, at a quarter to twelve . . . Debussy was doodling at the piano, acting like his mind was somewhere else. Someone said, "Go ahead, then." "But I have nothing to play." And I see that he wants badly to play something. A suspicious thought occurs to me—I tell him that perhaps he has deceived me, and in fact, I find *Pelléas* in his briefcase—and he goes at it. We gather around the piano while Benoît, furious, goes to lie down on the divan. And Debussy gets carried away, and d'Indy twirls his mustache while turning the pages, and Poujaud looks quite amazed while Benoît rolls over in boredom, yawns loudly, winds his watch noisily, turns around, finds that the divan isn't big enough for his legs, then, on the last note, before Debussy can mop his brow or remove his hands from the keys, he disappears without saying a word to anyone . . . and we hear the front door slam loudly. Then, praise for *Pelléas*, which, I think, really astonished them. Then, speaking of Benoît, Debussy says simply that he just didn't want to tell him that it was very good. Poujaud says that he shouldn't be angry with him, that that's just the way Benoît is, and I say that he's a skunk. . . . And they left at eleven-thirty, very cheerfully and, I think, very pleased. . . . (LPm, p. 15)[71]

In February 1894, the composer also played portions of *Pelléas* for Mme Marguerite Baugnies de Saint-Marceaux, hostess of an illustrious salon during this period. She recorded the event in her diary, calling the work "a revelation" and commenting on its novelty.[72]

The Brussels Concert (1 March 1894) and Georges Hartmann

Towards the end of the month, Debussy was doubtless preoccupied with his forthcoming concert for the Libre Esthétique in Brussels, the first concert to be devoted exclusively to his own compositions. The program, under the direction of Ysaÿe, was scheduled for 1 March, and, as announced in the 4 February issue of *L'Art Moderne,* was to consist largely of those works that Debussy had played for Ysaÿe during the "memorable evening" in November 1893: the String Quartet, *La Damoiselle élue, Poèmes de Baudelaire,* and *L'Après-midi d'un faune* (elsewhere announced as "un *Prélude,* des *Interludes* et une *Paraphrase finale* pour '*L'Après-midi d'un faune*'"[73]). Shortly before the scheduled date, the program was changed: *L'Après-midi d'un faune* was probably not ready and was dropped, and the two Baudelaire songs, "Recueillement" and "Le Jet d'eau," were replaced by "De fleurs" and "De soir" (two of the *Proses lyriques*), which Debussy had just performed at the Société Nationale concert of 17 February with soprano Thérèse Roger, the composer's fiancée.[74] Mlle Roger's participation in the concert surely contributed to the program change. Originally, Angèle Delhaye had been announced as the soprano for *La Damoiselle élue,* and Désiré Demest was to be accompanied by the composer in the Baudelaire songs.[75] When Delhaye became ill at the last moment, Mlle Roger was called in to replace her, and it was probably a natural consequence to substitute as well the songs which the composer and his fiancée had so recently rehearsed and performed. While in Brussels to participate in this concert, Debussy gave another informal performance of portions of his opera. Among those present were Ysaÿe, Octave Maus, Guillaume Guidé, and Maurice Kufferath, and reportedly all were "extremely impressed."[76]

In a review of the Brussels concert, the critic for *L'Art Moderne* noted that Debussy was at work on two new compositions—a second string quartet and *Pelléas.* He also commented that during the breaks between rehearsals Debussy was correcting the proofs of the *Proses lyriques,* which were being published by Georges Hartmann.[77]

According to Vallas, Debussy met Hartmann soon after the February 1890 publication of his *Cinq poèmes de Baudelaire.* Generous and foresighted, Hartmann had promoted numerous young French composers, discovering or taking on Bizet, Franck, Lalo, Saint-Saëns, Massenet, and Charpentier, among others. He not only published their music, but provided a forum for it by helping to found in 1873 the *Concert national de l'Odéon,* later to become the *Concerts Colonne.* Following the bankruptcy of his publishing house, he continued to publish music under the imprint of Eugène Fromont.[78] It must have been around the time of the Brussels concert that Hartmann "discovered" Debussy, easing, though not eliminating, the composer's financial burdens by offering him a grant of 500 francs per month in exchange for exclusive publishing rights to future compositions.[79] This arrangement was to last until Hartmann's death in the spring of 1900.

Pelléas Resumed: Act III and Act IV, Scene 3 (May–September 1894)

The next indication of Debussy's progress with the composition of *Pelléas* comes from the announcement of another informal performance of scenes from the opera, this time at the home of Pierre Louÿs. On 31 May 1894, Louÿs wrote to Debussy, reminding him of the soirée planned for that evening:

> I am inviting some people *to hear Pelléas.*
> Don't forget.
> You will dine with the Natansons and [Paul] Robert. After dinner five or six friends will come, invited especially, I remind you, for *Pelléas.*
> Please be good enough to bring: 1) the first act, 2) the "scène de la fontaine," 3) a third scene if it is finished (the "scène des cheveux," even incomplete).
> The piano has arrived. (LOUI, p. 32)[80]

From a telegram sent the same day by Louÿs to Léon Blum (one of the five or six invited friends—another was Ferdinand Hérold), we learn that the musical portion of the evening was to begin at ten o'clock (BNexp, p. 43, no. 130).

In assembling his calendar of Debussy's work on *Pelléas*, François Lesure (LPm, p. 8) assumed that Louÿs was referring to Act II, scene 1 when he asked the composer to bring "la scène de la fontaine" to the 31 May soirée. It would certainly make sense that, having completed Act I, Debussy would continue directly with the next consecutive scene, the first scene of Act II, but certain evidence suggests that Louÿs was instead referring to the original "scène de la fontaine," Act IV, scene 4, which Debussy had completed the previous October. The problem arises from the fact that the two scenes share the same setting (décor), and although the fountain may figure more prominently in Act II, scene 1, Debussy did refer to Act IV, scene 4 as the "scène de la fontaine," as in his letter to Chausson of 3 September 1893.

As has been pointed out, Debussy accepted the dramatic unity of Maeterlinck's acts and conceived his setting of each act as an integral musical unit. Despite a few exceptions, his tendency was to concentrate on one act at a time and to set its scenes consecutively, but he did not necessarily undertake the acts in sequence, and there is no firm evidence that he proceeded with the second act upon completing the first. In fact, all dated references to Act II, in letters and in manuscript drafts, point to the summer of 1895. It seems probable that Debussy bypassed the second act (he wrote to Raymond Bonheur on 9 August 1895 that he thought Act II would be "child's play"[LL, p. 74]) and turned his attention to the third; at the time of Louÿs's soirée he was apparently working on its first scene.

Louÿs's request then, was for the composer to bring along *everything* that he had written so far for *Pelléas*: the completed Act I and Act IV, scene 4, and the scene in progress, "la scène des cheveux" (Act III, scene 1).

During the month of June, Debussy continued to work on *Pelléas*. At least that was the excuse he gave Durand for the extended delay in his correction of the proofs of his String Quartet and for the fact that he had not written a promised violin sonata (DUR, p. 5). A letter to Pierre Louÿs of 17 June also shows the composer to be preoccupied with his opera: "Could you meet me tomorrow (Monday), seven o'clock, at Durand's, since I will not go out during the day. Pelléas and Mélisande send you their kindest regards" (LOU3, p. 30). Was Debussy still working on Act III, scene 1? The earliest indication that he had moved on to scene 2 appears in a letter of 20 July to Louÿs, who had just left Paris to spend two months in Algeria:

> As for me, my sole companions have been Pelléas and Mélisande, who remain very accomplished, humble young people. I have decided to set the scene in the underground vaults [Act III, scene 2], but in a way which you will give me the pleasure of finding strange ("curieux") when you see it.... (LOU3, p. 30)

Afraid that his letter had gotten lost in the mail ("or has perhaps ended up as a curl-paper for the postmaster's mistress"), Debussy wrote to Louÿs a week later (27 July) and again told his friend of his continued work on *Pelléas*:

> Here are a few lines to reassure you of the fate of your little friend, still on holiday on rue Gustave Doré, shaded solely by the black foliage of sixteenth notes in the midst of which Pelléas and Mélisande toss about. (LOU1, p. 39)

In the month that followed, Debussy worked hard and accomplished a great deal: he completed the second and third scenes of Act III and, briefly interrupting his work on that act, set the third scene of Act IV. This was announced in a letter to Louÿs dated 20 August:

> I have been working so hard wielding sixteenth notes these days that I lacked the strength to recite the various anecdotes appropriate to these same sixteenths; I have thus worked like a horse: finished the scene in the underground vaults [Act III, scene 2], at the exit from the vaults [Act III, scene 3], the scene with the sheep [Act IV, scene 3]... (LOU1, p. 40)

Debussy's inspiration continued unabated. It even seemed to increase. On 28 August, just a week after his letter to Louÿs, Debussy reported to Henry Lerolle that he was at work on the final scene of the third act, had begun a set of *Nocturnes* for violin and orchestra, and was even beginning to think about the fifth act of *Pelléas*. If his thirty-first birthday had found him unsure of his aesthetic principles, his thirty-second (22 August 1894) found him self-assured and flourishing. The letter to Lerolle, unusually rich in descriptive detail, contains news of at least the past month:

Pelléas and Mélisande began to sulk and were no longer willing to come down from their tapestry, and I was therefore forced to play with other ideas; then, a bit jealous, they came back to bend over me and Mélisande, with the soft, sickly voice which you know she has, said to me: "Abandon those little follies, favorites of the cosmopolitan public, and save your dreams for my hair; you know well that no tenderness is as dear as ours."

And the scene in the underground vaults was finished, full of furtive terror, and so mysterious as to make the most temperate souls giddy; also the scene at the exit from those same vaults, filled with sunlight, but a sun suffused by our good mother, the sea. This, I hope, will make a good impression. . . . I have also completed the scene with the little sheep, in which I have tried to put something of the compassion of a child, to whom a sheep at first is perceived as a toy which he may not touch, and also a pity which is no longer felt by people anxious to be comfortable. Now I am working on the scene between the father and son [Act III, scene 4], and I am afraid: I need things which are so profound and so sure! There is a "little father" ("petit père") there that gives me a nightmare.

An idea came to me for the death of Mélisande [Act V], which is to put an orchestral group on the stage, to have some sort of death of all resonance. What do you think of this? I have begun some pieces for violin and orchestra which will be entitled *Nocturnes,* in which I will use separate orchestral groups to try to find nuances with these groups by themselves, because one truly does not dare to do enough in music, fearful of that sort of divinity which is called "common sense" and which is in fact the most miserable thing I know, because it is, after all, only a religion founded to excuse the imbeciles for being so numerous! In short, let us cultivate the gardens of our own instincts, and let us walk without regard over the flower beds where ideas in white neckties are symmetrically lined up.

My life here is simple as a blade of grass and my only joy is to work (which is certainly sufficient, poor wretch!).[81]

Given the composer's inclination and tendency to conceive acts as integral units and to write them continuously, one wonders why he interrupted work on Act III to set the scene with the little sheep ("scène des petits moutons") of Act IV. Of course, it could have been nothing more than a matter of getting a particular idea at a particular time. Debussy's letter to Lerolle, however, reveals considerable anxiety concerning the closing scene of Act III, the climax of the act, in which Golaud forces his son, Yniold, to spy on Pelléas and Mélisande. This scene has a special and powerful emotional content and lacks the obvious scenic or pictorial imagery of the three previous scenes. There is also the added problem of writing for a child (for Debussy seems always to have considered Yniold a child's role). These difficulties may have caused Debussy to pause, and it was perhaps while wondering what to do here with Yniold that he decided to set that character's other scene—the more obvious "scène des petits moutons," Act IV, scene 3. After composing that scene he returned to Act III, presumably completing it in September, within a few weeks following his letter to Lerolle. Pierre Louÿs presented the composer with a copy of his translation of Lucien de Samosate's *Scènes de la vie des courtisanes* in which he inscribed: "To Claude Achille Debussy, to remind him that in 1894 he worked on the third act of *Pelléas.*"[82]

Work on Other Compositions (September–December 1894)

There is no indication that Debussy worked further on Act V or any other part of *Pelléas* during the balance of 1894. Following an October visit with the composer, Lerolle reported to Chausson that he had heard no new music and was content to rehear sections with which he was already familiar (LPm, p. 14). Although Debussy did not compose Act V until the following year, it is significant that his first thoughts about it concerned the instrumentation, even if the particular idea (an orchestra on stage) did not figure in his drafts or final version of that act.[83] The composer's interest in orchestrational experimentation was to find expression in the two compositional projects to which he immediately turned—the three *Nocturnes* for violin and orchestra and the *Prélude à L'Après-midi d'un faune,* the orchestration of which remained to be completed.

The *Nocturnes,* already begun at the time of the 28 August letter to Lerolle, were the subject of a letter that Debussy wrote on 22 September to Ysaÿe, the violinist for whom they were being composed. After alluding to his recent industriousness, Debussy gave a detailed description of his orchestrational scheme for the *Nocturnes* and explained why he had temporarily set *Pelléas* aside:

> I am not abandoning *Pelléas* for them, and besides, the further I advance the more gloomy doubts I have. Then, this pursuit of an ideal expression which vanishes into nothingness and also the willful suppression of all extraneous happenstance end up wearing me out like a stone over which too many carriages have been driven. (LL, p. 69)

It was also in September that Debussy completed the orchestration of his *Prélude à L'Après-midi d'un faune,* inscribing that date on the final folio of the manuscript full score.[84] On 23 October he sold all rights to the piece to Georges Hartmann for 200 francs.[85] Begun in 1892, the work had been scheduled as part of Debussy's Brussels program of 1 March 1894, but it was not to receive its première performance until 22 December 1894, when it was presented by the Société Nationale in the Salle d'Harcourt, Paris, with Gustave Doret conducting.

During the winter of 1894, Debussy also composed a set of three *Images* for piano; the title page of the manuscript is dated "Winter 1894."[86] Of these pieces, dedicated to Henry Lerolle's daughter Yvonne, only the second was published in the composer's lifetime.[87] According to Vallas, a fourth piece, a "Valse," was also announced (on 10 December), but it never appeared.[88] On 11 December Debussy may have provided music for a soirée at the home of Pierre Louÿs, and *Pelléas* may have been among the offerings.[89]

Pelléas Resumed? (January–February 1895)

In January 1895 Debussy returned to work on his opera, and, with six (of fifteen) scenes remaining to be written (the three scenes of Act II, the first two of Act IV, and the single scene of Act V), the composer was already projecting the opera's completion. He wrote to Pierre Louÿs on 22 January:

> Pelléas and Mélisande are my only little friends at the moment; perhaps we are beginning to know each other too well and only tell tales whose outcome we know perfectly well; then, to finish a work: isn't it a little like the death of someone one loves?... (LOUI, p. 42)

Debussy did not specify what part of the opera he was working on—perhaps the opening scenes of Act IV, the only scenes whose chronology cannot otherwise be accounted for. A literal interpretation of the composer's words ("Pelléas and Mélisande are my only little friends at the moment") might point to Act IV, scene 1, a scene involving only the opera's title roles (though Act II, scenes 1 and 3 also satisfy this condition). Debussy's comment about "stories whose outcome we know perfectly well" could refer both to his own feeling about the work and to the plot of this particular scene, in which Pelléas and Mélisande make arrangements to meet that evening near the fountain in the park, knowing that it will be for the last time.

When he wrote to Louÿs on 23 February 1895, Debussy may still have been working on *Pelléas*—and, with a characteristic pessimism tempered by irony and a sense of ultimate vindication, wondering how his work would eventually be received:

> I am working on things which will be understood only by the little children of the twentieth century; they alone will see that "the clothes do not make the musician" and will tear off the masks of the idols, beneath which there is nothing but a sad skeleton. . . . (LL, p. 73)

Another Interruption: *Cendrelune*

Debussy was anticipating the completion of *Pelléas* to such an extent that he was soon willing to devote considerable thought to plans for a new theatrical project, a children's Christmas play which Léon Carvalho, Director of the Opéra-Comique, commissioned Pierre Louÿs to write for performance on Christmas 1895. During April and May, Debussy's correspondence with Louÿs was largely concerned with the scenario for that play, for which Debussy was to provide music. Discussion of the project must have begun shortly after 1 April, when the writer returned to Paris from a three-month trip abroad.[90] The first hint of the collaboration was in a visiting card note dated "Thursday" [4 April], in which Debussy asked Louÿs to bring some Christmas stories to their lunch meeting the following day (LOU3, p. 31). About a week later, on 12 April, Louÿs was able to inform his brother that they had decided on the story of the Erl King: "It is the story which by far moved me the most when I was little" (LOU1, p. 49). On the same day, Louÿs sent Debussy an outline for the first act of the story. The accompanying letter suggests that the two had discussed the project previously, and in some detail.[91] There were to be many such discussions in the course of the next seven weeks, one of which was unexpectedly cancelled by the composer, who described his sudden impulse to work on Act V of *Pelléas* in a letter to Louÿs:

> I truly thought that I would see you today, but I was surprised by the death of Mélisande [Act V], which makes me anxious and which I work on, trembling....
>
> [I will do something very good with the heroine that you propose], and I love her so much already that the sad Mélisande dolefully came between me and this little intruder.... (LOU1, p. 50)[92]

Debussy's collaboration with Louÿs on the scenario of *Cendrelune,* as the story was soon titled, contrasts strikingly with the way he acquired the libretto for *Pelléas.* In the case of his opera, he simply accepted a published play as his libretto, making only a number of cuts and minimal changes. With *Cendrelune,* he took a very active role in the fashioning of the scenario, making suggestions and insisting on changes. Letters exchanged by the collaborators in mid-May reveal a failure to reach an agreement on aspects of the scenario. Louÿs finally became so exasperated by the criticisms made, not only by the composer, but by his editor Georges Hartmann, that he threatened to renounce the project, writing to Debussy on 12 May: "Write *Cendrelune* YOURSELF. You are perfectly capable of it. By dint of the changes you have made in this little libretto, it has become a complete stranger to me. As it is, I could no longer develop it" (LOU1, p. 54). But Debussy wanted very badly to preserve the collaboration, and he was apparently willing to make any compromise necessary to do so. On 16 May he answered Louÿs in conciliatory, even entreating terms, and agreed, if necessary, to go back to the previous version. He even promised to stifle Hartmann's objections.[93] Louÿs must have been appeased, as on 31 May, he announced to his brother, no doubt with great relief: "Hartmann has accepted my scenario. This business is now settled. I am pretty happy about it" (LOU1, p. 20).

Pelléas Completed: Act IV Revised, Acts II and V Composed (April–August 1895)

Though the scenario was settled, the libretto of *Cendrelune* remained to be written. Debussy, however, was in no particular rush to have it; once again his attention had returned to *Pelléas*. During May he undertook an extensive revision of Act IV, scene 4, the scene that was the first to be composed and the first to undergo a revision. By this time, Debussy had written music for all four scenes of Act IV—scene 4 in September–October 1893, scene 3 in August 1894, and scenes 1 and 2, possibly in January–February 1895, but certainly by May. The decision to rework scene 4 may have resulted from a consideration of the act as a totality.

Debussy next turned in earnest to Act V. This act had previously occupied the composer's thoughts: in August 1894 he had had an idea for a particular orchestral sonority appropriate to the scene, and he may actually have begun setting it in April 1895. By 20 June 1895 his draft of the act was complete; on that date he sent Lerolle an express letter whose message consisted of the final five measures of the opera (with "End." written beneath the concluding double bar) and the words: "Here, for the voyage of Mélisande's soul."[94]

It was probably in June (and after the 20th, by which time he had completed Act V) that Debussy began work on Act II, the only part of the opera remaining to be written. The manuscript short score of this act (NEC MS) is dated "June/17 August 95,"[95] and the Meyer MS, which consists principally of the complete preliminary drafts of Acts II and V, is dated "June–July 95." Debussy apparently anticipated little difficulty with the second act, which may explain why he put it off until the last. (Of course, the opposite may also be true—that he secretly dreaded writing it.) He wrote to Bonheur on 9 August about the unexpected problems it was giving him:

> I believed that the second act of *Pelléas* would be child's play ("jeu d'enfant") for me, but it is a hellish game ("jeu d'enfer") instead!...
> Truly, music hardly allows anything that resembles a conversation, and he who hits upon the "interview in music" will be worthy of the highest rewards. (LL, p. 74)

These difficulties likely contributed to Debussy's decision to decline Lerolle's suggestion that he present Act II at a private gathering: "It is a kind of fare which could be of interest to the two of us, but which, like all laboratory products, is not ready for the public" (LER, p. 31).[96] In fact, Debussy sometimes had so many doubts about his work that a piece would no sooner be declared finished than it would find its way back to his work table. Robert Godet recalled just such a turn of events with respect to *Pelléas*, when on a "springlike" evening in 1895 the composer prematurely announced the completion of his opera, and fifteen days later, began to work on it again.[97]

On 17 August, five days before Debussy's thirty-third birthday, *Pelléas* was finally completed, almost exactly two years after he had begun work on it. To mark the event, he inscribed that date on the final folio of the short score of Act II (NEC MS)—the only precise date to appear on any manuscript of *Pelléas*. On the same day he wrote to Lerolle:

Good heavens! yes, my dear Lerolle, I have found myself sadly obliged to finish *Pelléas* while you are so far from me! In addition, it has not been without some foot stamping, especially the scene between Golaud and Mélisande [Act II, scene 2]! Because it is there that one begins to sense forebodings of catastrophes, there where Mélisande begins to lie to Golaud and to become enlightened about herself, aided in this way by the same Golaud, an honest fellow just the same, who proves that one should not be completely frank, even with young girls; I believe that the scene before the grotto [Act II, scene 3] will please you, it tries to capture all of the mystery of the night, where, amidst so much silence, a blade of grass stirred from its sleep makes a most disturbing noise; then it is the approaching sea which shares its grievances with the moon, and Pelléas and Mélisande who are a little afraid to speak amid so much mystery.

I will not go on about this any longer, out of fear that it will become like the descriptions of a foreign land made after a period of time has elapsed, in which one reheats the reveries which reality has wiped away with a cruel sponge....

But for Debussy, the completion of *Pelléas* was cause less for celebration than for misgivings and uncertainty. The letter to Lerolle continued:

... Now, all of my anxiety begins; how will the world act towards these two poor little beings?—I hate crowds, universal suffrage, and tricolored phrases!—Look, there is Hartmann, who is certainly a representative of a good, average intelligence. Well! the death of Mélisande, such as it is done, hardly moves him at all! For him, it makes no effect! Besides, in France, every time a woman dies in the theater, it has to be as in "La Dame aux camélias," and one merely replaces the camelias with other flowers and the Lady with a lower-class princess ("princesse de bazar")! People cannot concede that one departs discreetly like someone who has had enough of this planet Earth and vanishes to where the flowers of tranquility bloom!

Then, in the end, everything which is an attempt to familiarize one's contemporaries with the sublime is sheer deception, except to oneself. (LER, p. 32)

Following his custom, Debussy soon played the recently composed scenes for his close friends, and Lerolle, who had followed every stage of the composition with great interest, was anxious to be among the first. However, it seems that he did not return from his vacation in time to earn that privilege, and Debussy had to assuage his disappointment in a letter of 23 September: "To appease your jealousy towards those who have heard the ending of *Pelléas*, realize that only [Raymond] Bonheur and [Etienne] Dupin have had that honor! (interpret the word honor any way you like)" (LPm, p. 16). Lerolle's loyalty was rewarded in another way: Debussy presented him with a collection of his sketches and drafts of *Pelléas* (Meyer MS), surely ample compensation.

2

Finding a Stage for the Opera (1895–1901)

Shortly after he had completed the short score draft of *Pelléas*, Debussy received a letter from his friend Pierre Louÿs. Writing from Lapras (Ardèche) on 21 August 1895, the poet inquired: "How do things stand with *Pelléas*? . . . And *Cendrelune?* When do you want me to begin it?"[1] In reply, Debussy must have announced the completion of his opera and probably expressed a willingness to begin working at once on *Cendrelune*, the children's story the two had been discussing since the spring. In his answer of 29 August, Louÿs explained that his work on the novel *L'Esclavage* (the first version of *Aphrodite*), which was serialized in *Mercure de France* and whose installments were therefore bound by very strict deadlines, would occupy him for the next fifteen days, and that, while he could devote three of those fifteen days to the first scene of *Cendrelune*, he would prefer it if Debussy would spend a month on the *Nocturnes* and on eight piano pieces before turning to the new work. Louÿs, after showing some uncertainty or confusion over his schedule, concluded that he would be free on 15 October, in "exactly six weeks."[2] Debussy did indeed seem eager to work on a new piece, especially a theater piece, now that *Pelléas* was finished, but he was also apparently exhausted after the concentrated creative work of the previous months. In a letter to Henry Lerolle of 23 September, he commented on this fatigue: "I was tired from having extracted so much music from a single head" (LL, p. 76). Nevertheless, he was obliged, under pressure from Hartmann, to work "day and night" on the Fantasy for piano and orchestra, which Raoul Pugno was to perform with Edouard Colonne during the coming winter. (The performance did not actually take place.) He also had the three *Nocturnes* to complete and had even begun preparing a libretto for an opera based on Balzac's *La Grande Bretèche*. Like *Cendrelune*, the latter project was never realized.

Unsuccessful Attempts to Find a Stage for *Pelléas*

Debussy may have been eager to begin some new compositional projects, but he was certainly not ready to set *Pelléas* aside. To see his opera performed must surely have been his greatest wish, although part of him seems to have feared exposure to the general public. Two years earlier, on 3 September 1893, when he had just begun working on *Pelléas*, he had written to Chausson about his misgivings in this direction: "Instead of seeking to disseminate art to the public, I propose the formation of a Society of Musical Esotericism. . . ."[3] Curiously, when several performance possibilities soon materialized, they came, not from the opera companies of Paris, but from its avant-garde theater. Paul Larochelle of the Théâtre Libre approached the composer shortly after the announced completion of *Pelléas* with an offer to produce the opera.[4] Larochelle's interest in Debussy's score may have been stimulated by a desire to capitalize on Maeterlinck's name and increasing reputation. Among the greatest successes of Paul Fort's Théâtre d'Art had been the premières of Maeterlinck plays: *L'Intruse* on 20-21 May 1891 and *Les Aveugles* on 11 December 1891, and Lugné-Poe's Théâtre de l'Oeuvre, the successor to the Théâtre d'Art, had scored triumphs, albeit controversial ones, with *Pelléas et Mélisande* on 17 May 1893 and *L'Intérieur* on 15 March 1895.[5] Also, *Annabella,* Maeterlinck's translation and adaptation of John Ford's *'Tis Pity She's a Whore,* had been presented by the Théâtre de l'Oeuvre on 6 November 1894.[6] Larochelle had only recently assumed the directorship of the Théâtre Libre—André Antoine, the previous director, had turned the company over to him in the spring of 1894, though performances did not resume until 14 February 1895[7]—and the new director may have considered Debussy's opera a way of breaking the monopoly that the rival company seemed to have on the dramas of Maeterlinck. Perhaps he recalled Antoine's remark, published in an interview in *Le Figaro* on 25 November 1893, that his major mistake had been not to produce any Maeterlinck.[8] While opera had not previously figured in the programs of the Théâtre Libre, Larochelle's announcement of his plans for the 1895-96 season, printed in the *Mercure de France* of August 1895, indicated his intention of utilizing musical resources sufficient for highly elaborate incidental music, and even operatic production:

> The Théâtre Libre, under the new direction of M. Larochelle, declares itself prepared to make substantial sacrifices in order to become, at the same time, a lyric as well as a dramatic theater: "The orchestra will comprise 70 instrumentalists, the chorus, 50 voices."[9]

Since Debussy had not given Larochelle a definite answer to his offer, the following announcement, which appeared in *Le Figaro* on 11 October 1895, was rather premature: "*Pelléas et Mélisande,* opera in 4 [sic] acts by M. de

Bussy on the play of Maeterlinck is in rehearsal" at the Théâtre Libre.[10] A similar notice appeared in *L'Echo de Paris* the following day.[11]

It seems that, having completed *Pelléas* and having received Larochelle's offer, Debussy wrote to Maeterlinck, probably in August, requesting the playwright's authorization of his setting and his approval of the production by Larochelle's company. Maeterlinck apparently sought the advice of Camille Mauclair, who recalled the incident:

> Maeterlinck wrote to me one day: "I have received a letter from a French composer telling me that he has composed a score based on my *Pelléas* and that he would like my authorization. Would you go to hear it and tell me what this music might be worth? The composer is named Claude Debussy. You know that I hear nothing in music."...I answered immediately: "Debussy is an admirable, but underrated harmonist. I will go to see him."[12]

Mauclair had previously met Debussy, first "chez Mallarmé" and later "chez Pierre Louÿs,"[13] and he was acquainted at the time with some of Debussy's music: *L'Après-midi d'un faune* and the Baudelaire and Verlaine songs.[14]

As cofounder and advisor of the Théâtre de l'Oeuvre, Mauclair was surely representing Lugné-Poe's, and not just Maeterlinck's, interests in carrying out this mission for the playwright. Larochelle's announcement no doubt caused Lugné-Poe some concern, as the latter's association with Maeterlinck's *Pelléas* probably led him to regard the work as his exclusive property, at least for performance in Paris. The première of the play had been the production that prompted the formation of the Théâtre de l'Oeuvre, and Lugné-Poe had included *Pelléas* in the group of four plays (the others being Maeterlinck's *L'Intruse* and Ibsen's *Rosmersholm* and *Master Builder*) that his company brought to London 25–30 March 1895 under the auspices of the Independent Theatre.[15] His interest in continuing this monopoly on the works of Maeterlinck was evident in his plans for the 1895–96 season, which included the Belgian playwright's *La Mort de Tintagiles* (a production which, however, never actually took place).[16] Surely Lugné-Poe was curious about the reports that Debussy's setting of *Pelléas* was complete and entering rehearsals at the rival Théâtre Libre, and surely Mauclair's investigatory visit to Debussy was as much on behalf of Lugné-Poe as on behalf of Maeterlinck.

Mauclair left a brief description of this visit, which must have taken place on or shortly before 14 October 1895:

> I saw a singularly sarcastic being, at once cold and violent, with his arched brow, frizzy black hair, sensual mouth, and strange eyes. He said to me: "I am going to play you my score. You will write to Maeterlinck what you wish." And I heard *Pelléas*, played as only Debussy himself knew how to play. When it was finished, I replied with intense emotion: "I will tell Maeterlinck that I have just heard a masterpiece!"[17]

Presumably acting on Mauclair's recommendation, Maeterlinck sent his authorization to Debussy in a letter postmarked 17 October 1895:

> My dear Debussy,
>   Regarding *Pelléas*, it goes without saying that it belongs to you entirely, and that you may have it performed when and how it will be agreeable to you. I will confess only that personally I would feel extremely reluctant to renew connections with the directors mentioned. They have not treated me any too nicely and if given in their theater I would prefer to stay away completely ... provided, of course, this would not be harmful to you, for I put you far above all those petty little things. Unfortunately, I have been unable to come to Paris in August, for very humble reasons; and at the present writing the same reasons persist, but I hope they will soon fade away. I would be so happy to see you, to shake your hand and to talk of our *Pelléas!*[18]

Despite Maeterlinck's reservations about the proposed production, Debussy got the authorization he desired—the playwright's *carte blanche* to pursue any performance opportunity he desired. But though he had found a willing (or at least interested) company in the Théâtre Libre, Debussy, it seems, had no intention of accepting Larochelle's offer. At least that is what he told Mauclair, who recalled asking the composer where he hoped to present *Pelléas.* Debussy replied "nonchalantly":

> I don't know. ... I wrote it out of admiration for the work. Nobody will want it. I have been led to hope that [Robert de] Montesquiou will arrange a performance of it in his home, in his "Pavillon des Muses," when I have orchestrated it. ... [19]

On 14 October 1895 Mauclair sent Lugné-Poe a summary of his meeting with Debussy, assuring him that Larochelle's announcement was premature for two reasons: though the piano score of *Pelléas* was indeed complete the orchestration would not be ready for another three months, and furthermore, Debussy had no intention of offering his opera to Larochelle.[20] The precise nature of Lugné-Poe's interest in Debussy's opera is not certain. Years later, Debussy recalled that Lugné-Poe had planned a Paris revival of *Pelléas* in 1895 and had abandoned the plan upon learning that Debussy had completed his opera based on that play.[21] But if Lugné-Poe initially wanted only reassurance that a competing production of *Pelléas* was not in the offing, it seems that he soon became interested in Debussy's opera as a possible production for his own company. At the end of the year Debussy wrote to the soprano Julia Robert, who had sung in the première of *La Damoiselle élue* on 8 April 1893 and whom he may have selected for the role of Mélisande: "There is talk of mounting *Pelléas et Mélisande* at the Théâtre de l'Oeuvre, and they seem to me to be quite serious. ... "[22] Like the Théâtre Libre, the Théâtre de l'Oeuvre was not in the habit of presenting opera. However, it had offered plays with substantial incidental music, such as *La Belle au bois dormant* by

Henry Bataille and Robert d'Humières, with music by Georges Hüe (24–25 May 1894),[23] and projected for performance during the 1895–96 season was Ibsen's *Peer Gynt* with music by Grieg; when this play was finally presented (12 November 1896), an orchestra of approximately sixty musicians performed Grieg's music.[24] Lugné-Poe may have considered, rather than a full production of Debussy's opera, a performance of the play with incidental music adapted from the opera. Debussy recalled (in a letter of 9 August 1898 to Hartmann [LL, p. 92]) that such a request had been made of him in late 1895, when Mauclair approached him "on behalf of Maeterlinck," and that he had rejected the suggestion with the explanation that, having conceived the work as an opera, he refused to do anything that would have seemed like a denegation of it.

Writing to Debussy on 27 November 1895, Pierre Louÿs protested the composer's rejection of an offer to write a "symphonic suite" based on the music from *Pelléas* for performance in London:

> Why do you refuse the propositions to write a symphonic suite ("suite symphonique") from *Pelléas* for London? It is none of my business, but do you really believe that it is such a bad idea?
>
> If you refuse, of course you have the right to prevent it from being done by somebody else, but if I were you, I wouldn't care at all. Remember that the old wretch [Wagner] sold the scenario of the *Flying Dutchman* to Mr. So-and-so, and you can be sure that nobody today could stop your ploy if you were to do the same.
>
> Let's talk about it again.... (LOU I, p. 65)

The nature of Louÿs's argument suggests that he was probably referring to incidental music, and it is possible that Lugné-Poe, having performed *Pelléas* in London the previous spring (March 1895), was hoping to return to that city with the play, but with the added attraction of music by Debussy. Or perhaps an English company, intrigued by the Théâtre de l'Oeuvre performance, envisioned an independent production featuring Debussy's music. In any case, a performance of the play with incidental music by Debussy was out of the question, and the Théâtre de l'Oeuvre must have abandoned whatever plans it may have had for producing the opera, perhaps due to a lack of money.[25] This episode brought an end to Debussy's negotiations with the Paris avant-garde theater.

It may be, however, that Louÿs's reference to a "symphonic suite" really did refer to an orchestral suite or potpourri drawn from the opera, which might have been requested by a London orchestra. *Pelléas* was certainly not well suited to such treatment since it is conspicuously lacking in discrete orchestral numbers (or even passages of extended melody) which could easily be extracted. In 1895 the score did not even include the expanded interludes which might have served this purpose.[26]

Debussy was consistently adamant, however, that the sense of his music could only be understood in the context of a complete, staged performance of the opera. This position emerged in the course of his correspondence with Ysaÿe over what was presumably a less objectionable compromise. Ysaÿe, it will be recalled, had heard some of the early drafts of *Pelléas* during Debussy's November 1893 visit to Belgium, and his friendship and professional association with the composer had continued: the Ysaÿe Quartet had performed Debussy's String Quartet and Debussy had been working on a new work for the violinist, *Three Nocturnes* for violin and orchestra. In 1896, after Ysaÿe was unsuccessful in his attempts to arrange for performances of *Pelléas* at the Théâtre de la Monnaie in Brussels,[27] he proposed the performance of scenes from the opera in one of the orchestral concerts he was to conduct in Brussels during the coming season. So sure was he of the composer's approval that he sent notices to the press; an announcement in the 11 October 1896 issue of *L'Art Moderne* listed the following as the program for the second "Concert Ysaÿe": "For the second concert, on 13 December, cellist Joseph Jacob will perform a concerto of his own composition. M. Demest and Mlle Duthil will sing excerpts from *Pelléas et Mélisande*, the new score of C.-A. Debussy for the play of Maeterlincke."[28] This announcement, like so many others, proved to be premature. Debussy promptly wrote to Ysaÿe explaining his objections to the program in a letter dated 13 October 1896:

> I am deeply touched by your kind letter with its friendly concern for *Pelléas et Mélisande*, poor little beings so difficult to introduce into the world, since, even with a godfather like you, the world does not want to allow itself to be convinced.
>
> Now, I will humbly give you the reasons which make me unable to be of your opinion regarding a performance of excerpts from *Pelléas*. First, if this work has any merit, it is above all in the connection between its scenic and musical aspects. Hence it is obvious and indubitable that this connection would be lost in a concert performance, and one could not reproach anyone for completely failing to comprehend the special eloquence of the "silences" which abound in this work; besides, the simplicity of means employed acquires its true significance only on the stage; in concert, one would immediately throw in my face the American opulence of Wagner, and I would seem like a poor man who couldn't afford to pay for "contrabass-tubas"! In my opinion, *Pelléas et Mélisande* must be performed *as they are,* and then people can either take them or leave them, and if we have to fight, it will then have been worth the trouble.... (YSA, p. 226)

Debussy proposed replacing the scenes from *Pelléas* with several pieces that he expected to complete by the time of the December concert. Diplomatically, he offered something for each of the artists engaged for the concert: *La Saulaie* for baritone and orchestra, a setting of a poem by Dante Gabriel Rossetti, to be sung by Demest; orchestral versions of two of the *Proses lyriques* for Mlle Duthil; and the *Three Nocturnes* for violin and orchestra to be played by Ysaÿe. Hoping to win his point with flattery, Debussy continued: "...these

Nocturnes could only be played by him [Ysaÿe]: even if Apollo himself were to ask me for them I would be forced to refuse him!" Nevertheless, Ysaÿe was persistent and repeated his request in passionate and persuasive terms. He wrote to Debussy:

> My dear old Brother, I am not entirely of your opinion. Your reasoning leaves no part to the practical side. No doubt I would much prefer telling you "we put on your work in a theater"! But I realize how impossible this is when people are without the first indispensable tool, not to speak of the others. It seems probable that sooner or later, some theater will open its doors to your work. But it is to be feared that this may come only after your style has transformed itself. Youthful productions must be presented in the age, the time, the atmosphere in which they are born. If one does not see the possibility of realizing this dream to its full extent, it is perhaps a mistake to turn down a partial performance. Successful or not, it brings a work out of the darkness where it lies whining, aging, shrivelling up, waiting until it loses its teeth to appear more beautiful. Badly presented, fragments of a work can harm the life of the work itself. But performed with care, by a youthful, vibrant orchestra, which plays *con amore,* and with intelligent, well-trained singers, I confess that even without the make-up of the stage, these fragments can draw keener attention from those who hold in their hands the means of producing the work in its entirety and in its frame. May I point out to you, that the theater of Wagner started in the concert hall. As regrettable as it may be that these conditions have not changed, especially in France, who could contend seriously that it ever hurt the prestige of Wagner? We could almost say, that no one would have wanted to mount his works on the stage if the fragments, repeated over and over in concert form, had not aroused attention. Concerning *Pelléas,* I'll add this: whether it turns out to be a fiasco or a triumph, it will not matter in the least. The important thing is to stir public attention by the fact that a young institution [Association des Concerts-Ysaÿe] known as daring and forward, dedicating itself to discoveries, whose programs demonstrate a spirit of curiosity, has seen in your work something that attracts us—us—and which we want to disclose to all. Write to me.[29]

Debussy did write. Unmoved by Ysaÿe's arguments, he reiterated his firm decision in a letter postmarked 17 November 1896:

> Regarding the *Pelléas* project, I have thought it over carefully, and despite all of the joy it would give me to see you conduct this work, and all of the great passion which you would put into it, I think that we must not do it; even if you, with your magnanimity, would understand it despite everything, the others will not understand, and you would go to the trouble for nothing. . . . I am very proud of your concern for me, and I am quite sure that everything will fall into place some day.[30]

By this time Ysaÿe had already revised his schedule, which was printed in the 15 November issue of *L'Art Moderne*: the 13 December concert was moved to 10 January 1897 and was to feature the "Netherlands A Cappella Quartet." There was no mention of *Pelléas* or any other work by Debussy.

Unable to reach an agreement with the Parisian avant-garde theater, rejected by the opera house of Brussels, and unwilling to extract incidental music or to accept the compromise offers of the concert platform, either in the form of a "symphonic suite" or of excerpts from the opera, Debussy found himself temporarily without prospects for a public performance of *Pelléas*.[31] Denied this, he continued to offer informal private performances of scenes from his opera for small groups of friends, singing the vocal parts from the piano, just as he had done while composing the work. One such gathering took place at the home of Robert Godet on 19 April 1897. On 11 April Debussy wrote to Godet: "As for *Pelléas,* if you like, it could certainly blossom into a performance at your house during Easter week."[32] A date was set, and on 15 April Debussy wrote: "Count on me for this Monday [19 April], only I won't be free until around seven o'clock; we could, then, just like at Bayreuth, have a light dinner, and after emotions are stirred, sup seriously. Arrange all of this as you like."[33] Jules de Brayer, Edouard Rist, and Francis de Pressensé joined Godet[34] as the composer played Act V.[35] Also in 1897, Debussy gave a private performance, which Gustave Samazeuilh attended, of *La Damoiselle élue,* the *Prélude à L'Après-midi d'un faune,* and several scenes from *Pelléas*: Act III, scene 1; Act IV, scene 4; and Act V.[36]

A Period of Inactivity and Depression

Such occasions were no substitute for the public exposure the composer must have desired, and his inability to find an appropriate stage for his opera doubtless contributed to the depression he was experiencing. Pierre Louÿs attempted to lift his spirits by proposing a "musical soirée" for the end of June 1897, one that would feature Debussy as both composer and performer. With the participation of the Quartet Crickboom (and an organist to be chosen), the program was to consist of works by Debussy (String Quartet and a scene from *Pelléas*), Bach (keyboard works), and Beethoven (Quartet No. 15, "Grosse Fuge," and the "Archduke" Trio). Louÿs planned a small gathering, with no more than ten friends, and the evening seems to have been calculated to boost the composer's self-esteem by presenting his works in a context that would demonstrate them to be worthy of sharing the stage with those of the masters. The letter proposing the musicale acknowledged the composer's difficult state. Enclosing a copy of his poem "La Chevelure" (from the *Chansons de Bilitis*) for Debussy to set, Louÿs wrote:

> Here is the chanson.
> Try to do it anyway, old friend; you are not working because your life is tough, and you have a tough life because you are not working. It's a vicious circle. But one must immediately break away via some tangent when one gets caught in such a trap.
> If in fifteen days, and after a good, hard effort, you suddenly show up at Hartmann's, as if by accident, with a manuscript under your arm, that would be enough to break your string of misfortune, and you would not have the miserable summer that you see coming.
> Just promise me that you will work four hours a day for one week. (LOU1, p. 95)

This inability to work and lack of productivity haunted Debussy throughout the year. He commented on it in a letter to Hartmann dated 31 December 1897: "I cannot keep from being exceedingly sad by this dreary end of the year, a year in which I accomplished practically nothing of what I wanted to do" (LL, p. 88). In fact, since the August 1895 completion of *Pelléas*, Debussy had composed relatively little. Completed works included only "La Flûte de Pan" and "La Chevelure," two of the three *Chansons de Bilitis*, and the orchestration of two *Gymnopédies*, piano pieces by Erik Satie. During this period he reported working on *La Saulaie* and the three *Nocturnes* for violin and orchestra, but of the former, only one page of music survives, and of the latter, nothing at all.[37] He toyed with numerous theater projects—*La Grande Bretèche* (Balzac), *Daphnis et Chloé* (Louÿs), *Cendrelune* (Louÿs), *Les Uns et les autres* (Verlaine), *Aphrodite* (Louÿs), and *Le Chevalier d'Or* (Mme Forain)—but nothing came of them.[38] It was not until December 1897 that he began work on a major composition that he was eventually able to bring to completion, the *Nocturnes* for orchestra. Still, these were not completed until two years later (December 1899), the composer commenting in a letter to Hartmann of 16 September 1898: "The three *Nocturnes* . . . have given me more trouble, just the three of them, than the five acts of *Pelléas*" (LL, p. 93). It was also in December 1897 that Debussy began his setting of "Le Tombeau des Naïades," the third of the *Chansons de Bilitis*, which was drafted by the end of the month but not completed until March 1898.[39] In April 1898 he composed two *Chansons de Charles d'Orléans* for four-part chorus, which remained unpublished until 1908, when the set was completed with the composition of a third.[40]

A combination of factors contributed to Debussy's low morale in the spring of 1898. His relative nonproductiveness and inability to find an opera house willing to present *Pelléas* only added to a series of personal disappointments and setbacks during the previous few years: the estrangement from his closest friends (Chausson, Lerolle, and Ysaÿe), the termination of two engagements, first to Thérèse Roger and later to Catherine Stevens, and the recent departure of his mistress, Gabrielle Dupont.[41] He expressed his depressed state of mind in a letter, probably written in April 1898, to his friend Pierre Louÿs, who was visiting his brother in Egypt:

> I assure you that I need your affection, I feel so alone and hopeless. Nothing has changed in the black sky which forms the background of my life, and I hardly know where I am headed except towards suicide, a stupid denouement to something which perhaps deserved better; this comes, above all, from weariness at struggling against impossibilities which are idiotic, besides being despicable. You know me better than anyone, and you alone can take it upon yourself to tell me that I am not entirely an old fool. (LOU1, pp. 110–11)

Louÿs's reply of 5 May communicated, not only empathy and reassurance, but encouragement and practical advice:

> You, old friend, you do not have the slightest excuse for having such nightmares, because YOU ARE A GREAT MAN.... You must continue your work and make it known, two things which you dispense with equally and which must be entirely for yourself. It is not in giving music lessons that you will achieve security in your life, but it is in doing everything to have *Pelléas* performed. You consider practical steps unworthy of you, and perhaps you are mistaken; because the main point is that you be able to work, and you will only work if you have the basic necessities at home.
> Think about it. (LOU2, pp. 68–69)

Louÿs lent more than moral support: he told his secretary Robert Cardinne-Petit that at one point he had prevented the depressed composer from destroying the complete manuscript of *Pelléas*.[42] With the urging of Louÿs, Debussy renewed efforts to arrange a performance of his opera, and through the initiative of his publisher Georges Hartmann, *Pelléas* was soon brought to the attention of the new administration of the Paris Opéra-Comique.

The Opéra-Comique

Léon Carvalho, director of the Opéra-Comique, died on 29 December 1897, and, in response to his passing, Jules Huret of *Le Figaro* asked various composers what direction they thought the Opéra-Comique should take. Debussy's response, in a letter of 19 January 1898 not intended for publication, reflected his prevailing cynicism and bitterness as well as the fact that he had in his portfolio an unperformed opera, one which he evidently did not expect would soon be accepted by the Opéra-Comique; he wrote:

> Nobody in France loves music enough, neither those who make it nor those who listen to it, in order for a lyric theater to sustain itself, and one will always return to schemes whereby music takes on the unexpected aspects of a matchmaker.
> The moral of all this is in the transformation that Art in general has undergone: it is no longer so proudly idealistic, but indeed a means of making a fortune, put within reach of men who are fond of the proper trades; in defense of my contemporaries, I must say that this has already been going on for a long time, and there is nothing to suggest that it won't also continue for quite a while. (LL, p. 89)

Things were in fact soon to change at the Opéra-Comique, at least as far as Debussy was concerned, and a combination of factors—a new initiative on the part of the composer, the help of his publisher, and the favorable disposition of the new administration, which had already been appointed by the time of Debussy's letter—was to result in the eventual acceptance of *Pelléas* by that company.

On 13 January 1898, Albert Carré was appointed the new director of the Opéra-Comique. He assumed his responsibilities on 14 January, relieving the Baron des Chapelles, who, in his fifteen days as interim director, was responsible for a deficit of 30,000 francs.[43] In an interview published at the time of his appointment, Carré expressed his intention to produce new works, specifically new French works. Speaking with Jules Huret of *Le Figaro*, Carré mentioned his plans:

> ... to present new works and new composers as often as possible, which seems to me the only way to make a ranking, to know where we are in France and to find out if, as is wrongly claimed, our young musicians have really given themselves entirely over to this or that foreign tendency. I believe that there are individual personalities among them which need only to be revealed. For that, they must be given the means—and that is to perform them. This I shall do.[44]

This certainly seemed like a propitious moment to submit *Pelléas* to the Opéra-Comique.

What made the situation even more favorable was the fact that André Messager had just been appointed music director and conductor of the Opéra-Comique. Messager was long familiar with Debussy and his music, having attended the première of *La Damoiselle élue* at the Société Nationale concert of 8 April 1893[45] and having conducted the *Prélude à L'Après-midi d'un faune* at the Vaudeville concerts shortly after its première in December 1894.[46] On 24 May 1895 he played Debussy's *Proses lyriques* at the salon of Mme de Saint-Marceaux.[47] In a letter to Chausson of 2 October 1893, Debussy described meeting Messager: "I met Messager, who, by virtue of I don't know what sudden sense of friendship, invited me to dinner! and there talked about music quite bizarrely...."[48] In his reply of 19 October, Chausson urged Debussy, who was then seeking a conducting post, to cultivate his new friendship:

> Since you are his friend all of a sudden, take advantage of it by speaking to him about yourself, without false modesty. He could be very useful to you. (Here I go again with my sermons!) He knows all of the people that one could know, in the press and in the theaters, in France and in the whole world. It is inconceivable that he couldn't help you to secure the position that you need. It's very tiresome, I know, to ask a favor of someone who is not really a friend. But after all, it is necessary and there is nothing dishonorable about it. Please do it. (CHA3, p. 56)

This was prophetic advice. Messager may not have helped Debussy find a conducting job in 1893, but he performed a far more valuable service in 1898 with respect to *Pelléas*.

Hartmann, perhaps aware of Carré's declared commitment to contemporary French opera, may have formulated the strategy of approaching him through Messager, a rather well placed intermediary known to be sympathetic to Debussy and his music. At Hartmann's urging, Debussy played parts of his opera for Messager. Taken by what he heard, Messager in turn asked Carré to listen to the work. Carré responded to this recommendation with great interest: "I would be delighted to hear it. Bring him to me."[49] He remembered going to Debussy's apartment for the audition, and, after hearing "fragments" of the opera, was, in his own words, "struck by the novelty, the originality of this music which traces every inflection of the text and releases such great emotion, and I proclaimed to Debussy that his work had been accepted by the Opéra-Comique."[50]

Although Carré assigned these events to "1899 or 1900," they must have taken place in the spring of 1898, during his first season at the Opéra-Comique. This is indicated by a letter from Debussy to Hartmann dated 15 May 1898, in which a rendezvous (or audition) with the director is discussed: apparently Carré had proposed a time for the meeting which was inconvenient for both Debussy and Hartmann; the composer had no objection to changing the time if doing so would not jeopardize the meeting, but he felt that the audition was so important and urgent that perhaps they should accept the appointment despite the "barbarity of the hour."[51] This meeting, in which Hartmann seems to have taken an active part, must have ended to the composer's satisfaction, as a few days later he received a letter from Louÿs, dated 21 May, congratulating him on the acceptance of his opera by the Opéra-Comique.[52]

Although given a promise "in principle" that *Pelléas* would be produced at the Opéra-Comique, Debussy was anxious for a more concrete commitment and a definite date. On 14 July he wrote to Hartmann:

> Do you think it would be possible, when we next see Carré and Messager, to draft an agreement so that they can't keep us waiting forever? It seems to me that this coming winter would really be the right time; many people have already spoken of *Pelléas*, and we should neither lose nor lessen the effect that its artistic novelty would have to stimulate the contemporary sensibility; but you handle these "explosives" with more skill than I, and, as usual, I rely upon your know-how. Only, we must not let too much "fluff" accumulate in the ears of our precious dilettantes.[53]

Hartmann, in turn, was worried that Gabriel Fauré's recently composed incidental music for *Pelléas*, written in the spring of 1898 for a production of the play in London (21 June-1 July 1898 at the Prince of Wales' Theatre),[54] might have an adverse effect on interest in Debussy's opera, a fear that Debussy forcefully dismissed in a letter of 9 August (LL, pp. 92–93): the effect of Fauré's music, he pointed out, was limited to the particular production for which it was composed, and, frankly, he didn't see how anybody could confuse his setting with Fauré's.

In fact, negotiations with the Opéra-Comique seemed to be proceeding favorably for Debussy's opera, as a notice in the 30 October 1898 issue of *L'Art Moderne* announced: "It has been decided that *Pelléas et Mélisande*, the moving drama of Maurice Maeterlinck, set to music by C.-A. Debussy, will be presented in the course of the season at the Opéra-Comique in Paris."[55]

Despite this announcement, *Pelléas* was not programmed during the 1898–99 season, nor was it even listed, a year later, among the offerings for 1899–1900. Debussy wrote, with obvious disappointment, to Hartmann on 3 July 1899:

> Have you seen the list of works that Mr. A. Carré plans to produce next season? There is *Louise*, something by Pierné, *Le Juif polonais*, etc. I can hardly wait to hear these works! But what becomes of poor little Pelléas and Mélisande? Mr. A. Carré must have very little heart not to adopt two such amiable children immediately. Their future is really beginning to worry me, and before long I will no longer be able to nourish them. . . . You who are also somewhat their father, don't you think there is something that can be done? Me, I am not very good at asking unless I know in advance that I won't be refused—it's a position that is rather difficult to take and full of contradictions. (LL, p. 98)

Once again Debussy had to remain content with the private, informal readings of *Pelléas* with which he entertained his friends: on 2 February 1899 at the home of Arthur Fontaine and in 1900 for Maurice Ravel, Raoul Bardac, and Lucien Garban.[56] His compositional activities during these years include the completion of the *Berceuse pour 'La Tragédie de la mort'* (April 1899) and the *Nocturnes* for orchestra (December 1899) as well as work on *La Saulaie* and on a collection of songs called *Nuits blanches*.[57] Debussy's personal life also took a positive turn when, on 19 October 1899, he married Rosalie (Lilly) Texier.[58]

In January 1900 Debussy turned his attention once more to *Pelléas* and again revised its fourth act,[59] perhaps in response to renewed talk of scheduling it at the Opéra-Comique. Although this revision represents the first datable recomposition of any part of the opera since August 1895, there were surely intervening retouchings. As early as 24 June 1896, Debussy expressed his dissatisfaction with some parts of the opera when he wrote to Paul Dukas that the score of *Pelléas* had just returned from being stitched, and he commented: "I don't know if it is because of the stitching, but too many things no longer please me sufficiently!" (LPm, p. 16). *Pelléas* did not just sit on a shelf during these years. It was often on his piano rack and, we may assume, on his work table as well.[60]

In April 1900 it appeared as if plans to mount *Pelléas* were nearly definite. Hartmann wrote to Debussy:

> Yesterday I saw Messager. Carré is still in a good disposition for next season. From every angle, it is important not to place ourselves in wrong; therefore I urge you to give me without fail, before April 30th, latest delay, the completed reduction of "Pelléas." May and June will not be too much for the engraving, July for correcting, and August for printing; and we must be ready so that the scores can be distributed to the artists on September first.[61]

Regrettably, these plans were rather suddenly and unexpectedly thwarted by the publisher's death on 22 April, just eight days short of the deadline he had imposed on Debussy. The composer lost, not only a publisher, but a patron and friend. He wrote of Hartmann's passing in a letter to Louÿs of 25 April:

> ... I could not see Hartmann, neither in his final moments nor at his funeral; this death truly grieved me—he was someone providential for me, and he brought to this role a good grace and a kind smile, quite rare among the philanthropists of art.
>
> I have no idea what will happen with *Pelléas*; however, it appears that Hartmann settled his affairs very carefully; the executor of his estate is Général Bourjat [Bourgeat, Hartmann's nephew]. (LOUI, p. 144)

As it turned out, Bourgeat not only lacked Hartmann's interest in and generosity towards Debussy, but came to regard the monthly subsidy of 500 francs which his uncle had granted the composer since 1894 as unearned "advances" which had to be repaid.[62]

With Hartmann's death, plans to publish *Pelléas* were suspended and the composer once again faced financial hardship. The opera was not forgotten, though. *Le Ménestrel* of 5 August 1900 announced Carré's program for the upcoming season, and although *Pelléas* was not one of the four new works listed as definitely planned (they were *William Ratcliff* by Xavier Leroux, *L'Ouragan* by Alfred Bruneau, *La Fille de Tabarin* by Gabriel Pierné, and *La Troupe Jolicoeur* by Arthur Coquard),[63] it was included in the list of eighteen works "which were to follow in a sequence which had not yet been fixed." (*Le Ménestrel* misspelled the opera's name and inaccurately described it as "*Péléas et Mélisande,* six tableaux by M. Maeterlinck, music by M. Debussy.") *L'Art Moderne* of 16 September 1900, making a similar announcement, was more specific and less optimistic concerning the status of *Pelléas*, including it among those new works which would be presented when the "repertory permitted."

Pelléas was in the news again at the end of the year. On 9 December 1900 the Concerts Lamoureux presented the première of "Nuages" and "Fêtes" from Debussy's *Nocturnes,* conducted by Camille Chevillard; in his review for *La Liberté,* critic Gaston Carraud "deplored the fact that *Pelléas et Mélisande* was not to be produced at once at the Opéra-Comique as it had been announced two years previously" (i.e., in 1898).[64]

According to Dietschy (p. 137), in April 1901 Debussy once again played his opera for Carré at Messager's urging, and, perhaps as a consequence, the composer received on 3 May Carré's written promise that *Pelléas* would definitely be included in the Opéra-Comique's next season. Debussy was surely happy to have this promise in writing: "I accept for performance at the Opéra-Comique in 1902, the opera *Péléas* [sic] *et Mélisande* by M. Claude Debussy."[65] Two days later, on 5 May, Debussy wrote to Pierre Louÿs, telling him his good news. Almost three years had passed since Debussy had informed his friend of the opera's acceptance "in principle." Now he wrote: "I don't want you to hear about it from a stranger: *I have the written promise of M. A. Carré* that he will produce *Pelléas et Mélisande* next season" (LOU1, p. 160). Louÿs immediately replied, on 7 May:

> It is kind of you to send me a really good piece of news right away. Bravo that you get played; bravo to those who decided finally to give us some music. You can be sure that I will not be off in the Indies the winter when *Pelléas* will be performed. (LOU1, p. 160)

Debussy's immediate reaction to the definite acceptance of *Pelléas* was once again to redo the final scene of Act IV, a revision which, according to a letter of 25 July 1907 to Louis Laloy, was accomplished in May.[66]

The inclusion of *Pelléas* in the Opéra-Comique schedule for the 1901–2 season was soon announced in the "Nouvelles diverses" column of *Le Ménestrel* of 2 June, with the opera's title now misspelled as *Pelléas et Mélisandre*. The same information was repeated with the correct spelling in the issue of 23 June, and newly misspelled and misdescribed, as "*Peléas et Mélisande* (6 tableaux)," on 8 September.[67]

Negotiations with Publishers

But before these public announcements, in fact only ten days after Carré's written promise of 3 May, the music publisher Paul Choudens wrote to Debussy, making an offer to publish *Pelléas*. Choudens pointed out that he had long had confidence in the young composer (his firm had published several of Debussy's piano pieces in 1890–91),[68] and he asked the composer to name his terms.[69] Debussy's immediate response to this offer is unknown, but it was Fromont and not Choudens who was to publish *Pelléas*. Debussy's works had appeared exclusively under Fromont's imprint during the years he was sponsored by Hartmann, and after the latter's death, Fromont continued to publish some of his works.[70] (Others were brought out by Durand, who was to become the composer's exclusive publisher in the fall of 1905.)[71]

With performances projected for the coming season, Debussy was obviously anxious to have his opera published as soon as possible—certainly in advance of the first rehearsals. The principals would need scores in order to learn their parts, and the availability of printed scores would constitute a considerable savings in copyist fees. According to Vallas, the manuscript of the vocal score was given to Fromont's engraver, A. Gulon, sometime during the summer of 1901.[72] The composer, vacationing in Bichain during August and early September, wrote to Fromont expressing his deep concern over the progress of the publication. A letter of 28 August, chiefly concerned with the edition of *Pour le piano,* closed with the plea: "Talk to me about *Pelléas.* . . . "[73] And again, on 2 September, he voiced a more urgent expression of his anxiety:

I am very worried regarding *Pelléas*? . . . You don't give me any news about it, as I begged you to do, and once again, that worries me.

Aren't you convinced that we haven't a day to lose?

Send word, as quickly as possible, *I beg of you.* (Coll. Jobert-Georges)

Fromont was not alone in holding up the publication, for, even at this late date, Debussy was still not satisfied with his score; the final folio of the fourth act in the short score manuscript (NEC MS) bears several dates of composition, the latest being September 1901, suggesting that the composer was once again revising that act. It would seem, then, that Fromont could not have received the last two acts of the vocal score before September. A letter of 2 September to Pierre Louÿs also appears to indicate current work on the opera, though here Debussy seems to be preoccupied with the orchestration of the score, another crucial task that evidently remained to be done: "I have walked for a long time in the company of that little neurasthenic Mélisande, who can only put up with the violins if they are divided into eighteen parts (she is so weak)" (LOU1, p. 165). Although the published vocal score was not actually ready until May 1902, at the time of the opera's première, the plates were engraved in time to allow uncorrected proof pages to be printed for the benefit of the singers and the assistant conductors: the vocal coach ("chef du chant") and the choral director ("chef des choeurs").

The Controversy between Playwright and Composer (1901–2)

While negotiations with the publisher were taking place, other arrangements were also being made to bring *Pelléas* to the public. Soon after receiving Carré's written promise, Debussy must have notified Maeterlinck of the plans to produce *Pelléas* at the Opéra-Comique in the upcoming season. On 30 May 1901, Maeterlinck wrote to Debussy that he would be in Paris until 6 June and would be happy to meet with him: "I will be happy to shake your hand and to talk about our *Pelléas*."[1] A meeting apparently took place, and Maeterlinck, who in October 1895 had written to Debussy that "regarding *Pelléas*, it goes without saying that it belongs to you entirely, and that you may have it performed where and how it will be agreeable to you," and who had confessed to a reporter, "I do not hear music . . . for me it is noise . . . useless,"[2] now had a suggestion to make regarding the opera's production: he wanted the role of Mélisande to be sung by his mistress Georgette Leblanc.

Georgette Leblanc

The soprano Georgette Leblanc had made her Opéra-Comique debut on 23 November 1893, creating the role of Françoise in the première of Alfred Bruneau's *L'Attaque du moulin*.[3] According to her memoirs, she appeared there again in 1897, when she sang the part of Fanny Legrand in Massenet's *Sapho*,[4] and on 8 December 1898, she appeared in the title role of Bizet's *Carmen* on the occasion of the inauguration of the Salle Favart, the new home of the Opéra-Comique.[5] No doubt she had long considered the role of Mélisande to be hers. In anticipation of that honor, she often sang Gabriel Fabre's setting of "Les Trois Soeurs aveugles," Mélisande's Act III song from the original 1893 stage production of *Pelléas*; her photograph adorns the cover of the 1898 edition of that song.[6] She was mentioned in connection with the part as early as February 1899, when an article in *Le Théâtre* described her as "one of those rare singers who are truly suitable to create a modern work.

She is to give us the proof of this one of these days in Saint-Saëns's *Proserpine*[7] and Claude Debussy's *Pelléas et Mélisande*."[8]

According to Leblanc's memoirs, she and Maeterlinck were living on the rue Raynouard in Passy when, late in 1901, Debussy came to play *Pelléas* for them.[9] Maeterlinck was completely uninterested in the music:

> The position of the piano [against the wall] forced him to turn his back to us and permitted Maeterlinck to make desperate signs to me. Not understanding music in the least, the time seemed long to him. Several times he wanted to escape but I held him back. Resigned, he lit his pipe.[10]

By the end of the performance, Maeterlinck was "half asleep" in his armchair, but before Debussy left, the subject of casting was raised. As Leblanc recalled: "I longed to play the rôle. Maeterlinck urged it."[11] "We shall see," was the reply that Debussy remembered giving, and Maeterlinck's version of the conversation was consistent with the composer's: "M. Debussy did not reject this request but was of the opinion that we should not press M. Carré, but should wait."[12]

Leblanc remembered that the composer had expressed reservations about her suitability for the role: "He told me that after seeing me so violent in *Carmen* he had at first doubted me, and that he had not known to what an extent I could adapt myself."[13] To prove herself capable, Leblanc asked to be allowed to study the part. After she had worked on it for a while by herself, she felt ready to audition for the composer. Hoping to gain his sympathy, some coaching sessions, and eventually the role, she wrote him the following letter:

> You cannot imagine to what point I am passionately in love with your work. It realizes all that I have dreamed! The result of my lone practice will of course be most imperfect, and I feel that only with you and under your direction I will be able to work efficiently, for in this musical form that you are creating, everything is so admirably "measured"! Still, after your own will has been heeded, I do not think that the part of the interpreter remains so small. You certainly trace for him a circle of marvelous precision; but your work is so human that there seem to be more interesting elements, more color and more life in the reduced space which you reserve for the interpreter than in the large ground where other musical forms allow him to evolve.
>
> ... do not wrong me in thinking any longer that I would perhaps not be "supple"; on the contrary, I am happy to yield to what is true and beautiful.
>
> ... I have sung several phrases of Mélisande for Maurice, and he understood perfectly! He found the words "prettier that way." It is the triumph of your logic! ...
>
> I remain so astounded, so delighted to find at last a lyric work which is completely satisfying intellectually. ...[14]

Leblanc recalled rehearsing with the composer two or three times at her home and twice in Debussy's rue Cardinet apartment.[15] She was sure that everything was going well: "Debussy approved of my interpretation. ... While we worked our understanding was perfect.... My diction gave him a pleasure that he constantly commented upon."[16]

Under the impression that Debussy was delighted with her and that he approved of her interpretation, the soprano had every reason to believe that she was to create the role of Mélisande, but the intervention of Albert Carré prevented her from realizing her ambition. As soon as he learned that Debussy was being pressured to accept her as Mélisande, Carré vetoed the idea categorically and assumed all responsibility for the decision. As he explained in his memoirs:

> I did not call into question the talent of Mme Leblanc.... But I had already made a casting error in having her play Carmen, and I did not want to make another; I considered that this singer, with her mature beauty, did not possess the physical qualities of the woman-child character who was Mélisande: the voice, the movement, the natural grace, the melancholy smile, the winged walk.... [17]

Assembling the *Pelléas* Cast

With his background in the spoken theater, Carré always insisted that singers be the right physical types for the characters that they were to portray. Thus, when Debussy met with Carré and Messager to discuss the casting of the opera, the three reviewed the entire company and even considered singers outside of the Opéra-Comique in an effort to find a soprano who was both physically and vocally suited to the part of Mélisande. Carré finally proposed Mary Garden, a young Scottish soprano who had been a complete unknown at the Opéra-Comique when she made her sensational debut on 10 April 1900, replacing without benefit of rehearsal the ailing lead, Marthe Rioton, in the third act of a performance of Charpentier's *Louise*.[18] She may still be inexperienced, Carré reasoned, but he judged that an asset for the role of Mélisande.[19] Debussy and Messager were persuaded to give her a chance.

René Peter recalled that, for the part of Pelléas, Debussy wanted someone youthful: "For him, the character was incomprehensible without this quality." He even (jokingly?) considered Peter for the part, although the latter was not a professional singer: "Your voice is true and *young*—but—can you sing?... you wouldn't be bad—as Pelléas!"[20] Carré had thought of assigning the role to the tenor Edmond Clément, but, as he explained, "Clément was not very enthusiastic, and, as far as I was concerned, it was not so much the voice that mattered in this very special role, but rather the acting ability and the physical appearance."[21] Carré preferred in this case to sacrifice musical for visual qualities and favored the *baryton Martin* Jean Périer, because of his appearance: "With his tall, slim profile, his sad, handsome look, Jean Périer seemed to me to be Pelléas himself.... And the part was adapted to his *baryton Martin* range."[22] Périer was already familiar with *Pelléas* and its composer. As the singer later recalled: "I was very friendly with the Stevenses; at their home I met Debussy often, and we had many friends in common. It was in this manner, in chance performances in the private salons, in small fragments, that I discovered *Pelléas*."[23] The other roles were also assigned: Hector Dufranne[24] as Golaud, Félix Vieuille as Arkel, Jeanne Gerville-Réache as Geneviève, and Viguié as the doctor. The part of Yniold was not cast until after rehearsals had begun.

A lengthy notice in the 29 December 1901 issue of *Le Ménestrel* discussed the forthcoming production of *Pelléas*, focusing on the anticipated difficulties of this "long cherished project."

> During January we will have the première of *La Troupe Jolicoeur*, the new work by M. Arthur Coquard, based on a novel by Henri Cain. M. Albert Carré will then proceed with a long cherished project: the rehearsal of *Péléas* [sic] *et Mélisande*, by M. Debussy, to a libretto by Maeterlinck. This will be a lot of work, as much because of the importance of the work as because of the care that it requires; it will need many rehearsals and a long, delicate, and meticulous mise-en-scène, and until now, the Director of the Opéra-Comique could not find the necessary time to carry it out. But now, with the enormous success of [Massenet's] *Grisélidis,* the great favor that the current repertory enjoys, the approaching première of *La Troupe Jolicoeur,* on whose success he is counting, in short, a very favorable general situation will allow M. Albert Carré to apply himself calmly to M. Debussy's opera, which will require two or three months of rehearsals. This long and laborious work is indispensable, not only because the piece is by a young composer who, in a superior manner, has already made his mark on the musical world, but also because it consists of no fewer than fifteen scenes.

The article concluded with a list of the cast, and noted that "remaining to be cast is a very important child's role, for which the Director of the Opéra-Comique seeks a little prodigy, boy or girl, eleven or twelve years old."[25]

Much thought was given to the manner of presenting *Pelléas* to the public. According to Messager, he and Carré

> had frequent discussions on this subject: he [Carré] thought that *Pelléas* should be reserved for nonsubscription performances or for matinees intended especially for habitués of the Sunday concerts, and I felt that it would be better to attack the problem head-on and to appeal right away to the ordinary public, without stressing the exceptional aspects of the work. It was my opinion which prevailed.... [26]

On 30 December the "bulletin de réception," the document indicating the authors' agreement to the work's acceptance by the theater, was deposited at the Société des Auteurs.[27] Carré had sent it to the composer for his signature in late December, and, in an accompanying letter, asked him to antedate the bulletin 3 May 1901 (the date of his written promise to produce *Pelléas*) and to return it to him as quickly as possible.[28] The reason for this somewhat mysterious request probably pertained to fears over the playwright's possible interference with the production, for it was exactly in this context that the apparently routine document was soon to have great significance.

Everything now seemed to be in order, and, with rehearsals about to begin, the principals were invited to the home of André Messager to hear the composer play through his opera. This reading, which probably took place during the second week of January,[29] was described by Messager:

> Debussy played his score at the piano, singing all of the roles in that deep and hollow voice, which often forced him to transpose down an octave, but whose expression became, little by little, irresistible. The impression which this music produced that day was, I believe, unique. There was at first a certain suspicion and resistance, then more and more, respect was maintained, with emotion rising little by little until the final notes of the "Death of Mélisande," which fell amidst silence and tears. At the end, all were transported, enraptured, and burned with the desire to get to work as soon as possible.[30]

Jean Périer, who had previously heard portions of the opera, recalled: "I was not surprised in hearing it complete one fine day at the home of André Messager, boulevard Malesherbes, and I was able to give in to my astonishment."[31] Mary Garden left a rather more detailed and vivid account of the event:

> Then one afternoon we were all invited to M. Messager's home. We were there only a short while when the door opened and in came Debussy. We were all presented to him, and he spoke the usual words of greeting. Without another word, he sat at the piano and sang the whole thing from beginning to end.
>
> There we sat in the drawing room—M. Carré, and M. and Mme Messager, and the whole cast—each of us with a score, heads bowed as if we were all at prayer. While Debussy played I had the most extraordinary emotions I have ever experienced in my life. Listening to that music I seemed to become someone else, someone inside of me whose language and soul were akin to mine. When Debussy got to the fourth act I could no longer look at my score for the tears. It was all very strange and unbearable. I closed my book and just listened to him, and as he played the death of Mélisande, I burst into the most awful sobbing, and Mme Messager began to sob along with me, and both of us fled into the next room. I shall never forget it. There we were crying as if we had just lost our best friend, crying as if nothing would console us again.
>
> Mme Messager and I returned to the drawing room just as Debussy stopped. Before anyone could say or do anything, he faced us all and said:
>
> "*Mesdames et messieurs,* that is my *Pelléas et Mélisande.* Everyone must forget that he is a singer before he can sing the music of Debussy. *Oubliez, je vous prie, que vous êtes chanteurs!*"
>
> Then he murmured a quick "*Au revoir*" and, without another word, was gone.[32]

Félix Vieuille's recollections differ from those of his colleagues in two important details:

> That day the scores were lacking and we followed after a fashion the score on the piano, from which Messager, imperturbably, continued to play. Debussy watched us very attentively.... We left the audition, taking away a strange, indefinable impression of a music which broke with everything that we had performed up until that time.[33]

Contrary to the accounts of Messager and Garden, Vieuille remembered Messager, and not Debussy, at the piano. In all likelihood it was Debussy who performed on this occasion; in fact, he probably played through his score several times during this period for the benefit of Messager and Carré, prompting him to write to Godet on Friday evening, 10 January: "As for *Pelléas*, I really have played it a bit too much these days!" (GOD, p. 103).

A second difference concerns the score: while Vieuille recalled that the principals followed a single score at the piano, Mary Garden claimed that each had a score. Since the vocal score was not published until the première (and the full score not until more than two years later), whatever scores were present (in addition to Debussy's manuscript) must have been early, uncorrected printings from the engraved plates of the vocal score. Such proofs were used by the singers to learn their parts, and those belonging to Jean Périer have survived. This use of proofs for preparing the Opéra-Comique production is confirmed by the memoirs of Henri Busser, the "chef des choeurs," who recorded that on 4 March he asked the "chef du chant" Louis Landry to entrust him with the proofs of the score.[34]

The rehearsals for *Pelléas* began on Monday, 13 January, a few days after the "lecture aux artistes." The rehearsal schedule was meticulously entered into the *livre de bord,* the register in which the daily activities of the Opéra-Comique, both rehearsals and performances, were recorded.[35] At first the rehearsals took the form of private lessons ("leçons"), usually about an hour in length, in which the principals were individually coached by Louis Landry. On the first afternoon, the composer was also present, hearing successively Périer, Dufranne, Garden, and Vieuille; Gerville-Réache did not join the rehearsals until 23 January and Viguié, not until 6 February. For about a week, Debussy entrusted the daily lessons to Landry, returning on Tuesday, 21 January to supervise these coaching sessions—he was present at nearly every subsequent rehearsal. Since the definitive acceptance of the cast was subject to the composer's approval, Carré was especially concerned that Garden make a good impression. He thus had her study her part with both Landry and Messager.[36] When she had learned the role, Debussy was asked to hear her.[37] The audition took place in one of the small rehearsal rooms of the Salle Favart, the same rooms that were used for the lessons. Debussy accompanied her at the piano, singing all of the other parts. During the tower scene (Act III, scene 1)—approximately one hour after the session began—Debussy suddenly stopped playing and abruptly left the room. He burst into Carré's office and asked the director: "Where is this woman from?" "I believe that she was born in northern Scotland," replied Carré. Debussy was obviously pleased: "She's the one!... She is my Mélisande!"[38] Mary Garden, who had been left behind, without explanation, in the rehearsal room, didn't know what to do. As she recalled:

> I stayed there for a little while and waited, quite bewildered. I had a feeling I had offended him in some mysterious way and I began to prepare myself for the shock of not singing Mélisande. I put on my hat and was about to leave the rehearsal room when a boy came in and said: "Miss Garden, M. Carré would like to see you in the office." When I walked in, there sat Debussy with M. Carré. Rising from his chair, he came right up to me and took both my hands in his.
>
> "Where were you born?" he asked.
>
> "Aberdeen, Scotland."
>
> "To think that you had to come from the cold far North to create my Mélisande—because that's what you're going to do, Mademoiselle."
>
> Then he turned to M. Carré, and I remember he put up his hands, and said: "*Je n'ai rien à lui dire.* I have nothing to tell her."
>
> He paused, as if embarrassed, and, still looking at M. Carré, added: "What a strange person, this child!"[39]

After this audition Mary Garden was definitively accepted for the role of Mélisande, and, as far as Debussy was concerned, there was no further question of Georgette Leblanc.

Maeterlinck Intervenes

But Maeterlinck was of a different opinion. It was probably in early January, perhaps just before rehearsals began, that Maeterlinck learned from a newspaper article that Mary Garden, and not Georgette Leblanc, had been engaged for the role of Mélisande.[40] Maeterlinck immediately went to the Opéra-Comique and accosted Debussy and Carré in an effort to persuade them to accept his mistress for the role, but he was told that his protest was too late: the production had already been registered with the Société des Auteurs and the rehearsals had already begun.[41] Since his personal entreaties proved unsuccessful, Maeterlinck decided to take a more legalistic approach. On 14 January, only the second day of rehearsals, he ascertained that the "bulletin de réception" had been deposited on 30 December 1901, but was antedated 3 May 1901, and he thus wrote to Carré on 15 January, charging that the "bulletin" was doubly void: first, because of the antedating, and second, because he had not signed it. Furthermore, he had no intention of giving his signature unless the role of Mélisande went to Leblanc. Rather than exercise the author's privilege of insisting on, either his choice of singer or the withdrawal of the work, he still hoped that Carré would show the civility of granting the "natural and legitimate desire" which he had long before asked

Debussy to convey to him.[42] In response to this argument, Carré and Debussy produced the letter which Maeterlinck had sent the composer on 19 October 1895, which contained the following crucial sentence: "Regarding *Pelléas*, it goes without saying that it belongs to you entirely, and that you may have it performed when and how it will be agreeable to you." They argued that this document sufficed to validate the "bulletin" and that the playwright's signature was therefore unnecessary.[43]

Mary Garden maintained that Debussy nevertheless made a concession to Maeterlinck's demand by allowing Leblanc to sing an act of *Pelléas* before a jury of musicians. As Garden explained: "They were to decide whether she could or could not sing Mélisande. Their verdict was quick and emphatic."[44] In any case, by the end of the month, Debussy was convinced that the matter was settled—in his favor. On 27 January he wrote to René Peter: "Maeterlinck is in the bag and Carré agrees with me that he is a real pathological case. But there are still some mental hospitals in France" (PET, p. 175; LL, p. 113). A similar letter was sent to his pupil Nicolas Coronio on the same day: "Maeterlinck is in the bag and his case appears to me to show up the most curious of pathologies. But, there are still some mental hospitals in France. Carré has calmed down about it, and I will try to do the same" (F-Pn, l.a. Debussy (C), 8).

But Maeterlinck was not ready to accept defeat. On Friday, 7 February, he brought his complaint against Debussy and Carré before the Société des Auteurs at its weekly meeting. His protest hinged on his letter to Debussy of 19 October 1895, and he asked that the letter be presented in its entirety. He claimed that the crucial sentence extracted by Debussy and Carré pertained to particular circumstances, which would be explained by the rest of the letter. He questioned their use of it in this instance because the letter was neither part of his original authorization for the composition of the opera (this had been given more than two years previously), nor did it pertain to the production at the Opéra-Comique. Therefore, Debussy and Carré had no right to regard the letter as a "blank check." Furthermore, Maeterlinck went on, he had not signed the "bulletin de réception," which, he thought, should invalidate it. The document was further suspect, he pointed out, because, though dated 3 May 1901, it was not deposited until 30 December, that is, long after he had expressed to both Debussy and Carré his wish to have Leblanc create the female lead. He had, after all, made this request as early as the spring of 1901, when Debussy informed him that Carré had accepted their work for the Opéra-Comique, and, at that time, Debussy did not reject his request. After hearing this testimony, the Committee of the Société, presided over by its president, Victorien Sardou, agreed to take up the complaint in the presence of the two parties at their next meeting, the following week.[45]

At the meeting on 14 February, Debussy was called in first: Sardou read him Maeterlinck's testimony from the previous meeting and asked him for his version of the story. Debussy did not produce the 1895 letter, as Maeterlinck had requested, and described only rather sketchily the circumstances that had prompted it: he said only that there had been a possibility for a performance of the opera and that he believed the letter gave him complete authority to have the work performed where and when he wished. He did not challenge Maeterlinck's allegations regarding the "bulletin de réception" but disputed his account of their discussion regarding Leblanc. Debussy recalled that it was in the middle of the summer, not in the spring, that Maeterlinck absolutely insisted that the role of Mélisande be played by Leblanc, but that, having heard her sing a few years before, the composer did not believe at the time that he could possibly entrust her with the role. Nevertheless, faced with Maeterlinck's formal request, he merely said, "We shall see," and made no promises.

Having completed his testimony, Debussy was asked to withdraw and Maeterlinck was brought in. Sardou asked him if he was willing to submit to arbitration and if he would agree to accept the decision of the Committee. Maeterlinck wanted time to think this over and promised an answer by the next meeting. When the same question was put to Debussy, he immediately agreed to abide by their decision.

On 21 February, with Vice President Georges Ohnet presiding, Maeterlinck announced his decision to drop his complaint before the Société des Auteurs and to appeal instead to the courts in order to bring his case against both Debussy *and* Carré: he considered the latter largely responsible for the rejection of Leblanc and, being a director, Carré was not subject to the arbitration of the Société des Auteurs.[46] If Maeterlinck subsequently consulted any lawyers, they must have urged him to drop the case. His legal battle had come to an end.[47]

Maeterlinck's extreme emotional involvement in this matter has already been suggested by Debussy's letters to Peter and Coronio. Leblanc recalled his crazed reaction to the frustration brought on by his inability to gain juridical satisfaction:

> Justly annoyed to find himself stripped before the law, Maeterlinck brandished his cane and announced to me that he was going to "give Debussy a drubbing to teach him what was what."
>
> My love had none of the stoic quality of the heroines of antiquity. This threat of a beating terrified me and I clung to Maeterlinck who jumped briskly out of the window. (. . . We often went out through the window.) . . .
>
> The story was pitiable. As soon as he entered the salon he had threatened Debussy who dropped into a chair while Madame Debussy distractedly ran toward her husband with a bottle of smelling salts. She had begged the poet to go away and, my word, there was nothing else to do.
>
> Maeterlinck, who did not like musicians any more than music, kept saying as he laughed, "They're all crazy, all off their heads, these musicians!"[48]

The impresario Henry Russell gave a similar account of the incident in his book, *The Passing Show*:

> Maeterlinck arrived at his [Debussy's] attic, armed with a cane. Being a man of few words, he realized that a stick might be more effective than an eloquent speech. The door was opened by Madame Debussy, who asked what he wanted. The reply was short: "You see this stick, Madame? I have brought it to beat your husband because he refuses to allow Georgette to sing in 'Pelléas.'" Madame Debussy began to cry, and swore that her husband was ill. This silenced the poet's wrath, and he left the house, saying that musicians were useless and troublesome members of society.[49]

Maeterlinck verified the essential accuracy of this account. In answer to a query from Henry Russell, made while the latter was writing his book, the playwright replied:

> The Debussy story is practically correct, but if I had a large stick, it was only my usual cane. Besides, I didn't have to use it to threaten him because, when Debussy saw that I was so ill-tempered, he was eager to promise me anything that I wished in order to get rid of me.[50]

Debussy, looking back on this unpleasant episode, simply said: "I can hardly believe that it happened."[51]

Maeterlinck's threatening attack on the composer failed to discharge his fury, which finally grew to the point where there was even talk of a duel. Duels were nothing new to Maeterlinck, who, one or two years earlier, had accused George Stockhausen of pirating his works and proposed to meet him "sword in hand."[52] Debussy, however, was inexperienced in such matters, and Carré and Robert de Flers offered to stand in for him.[53] The playwright went so far as to rehearse the confrontation. Lugné-Poe's recollection of the incident shows that Carré, and not Debussy, was the anticipated adversary:

> I don't understand why Maurice thirsts so for vengeance and blood!... Since eight o'clock in the morning he is in such a state of excitement that he wants to smash the whole world to pieces. This lasted awhile... Then, he wanted to kill... whom?...
>
> Albert Carré was among the first that he identified in confidence.... Often, when I arrived, he pushed me towards the garden, gave me a sword, and shouted: "Stand there, in place of Carré!..."[54]

Maeterlinck also practiced with a revolver. Lucie Delarue-Mardrus, who lived in the same house occupied by the playwright, recounted:

> It was just before the première of *Pelléas et Mélisande* at the Opéra-Comique. Debussy and Maeterlinck were involved in a quarrel to the death. The latter practiced with a revolver in order to kill Debussy. One morning in the park he chose as a living target his black cat, which came towards him, purring, and he killed it without hesitation.[55]

The duel never took place, but Maeterlinck consulted a clairvoyant in an effort to learn how the dispute with Carré would finally be settled, and the session was recounted in his book *Le Temple enseveli,* published in 1902.[56] The clairvoyant, a middle-aged woman, spoke to him through the spirit of a young girl named Julia. She asked him, "You want to know everything that will happen? That is very difficult."

"How will it end? Will I be the victor?" asked Maeterlinck.

"Yes, yes, I see; don't be afraid; I will help you; you will receive satisfaction."

"But the enemy that you spoke of, who resists me and wishes me ill . . . "

"No, no, he wants nothing of you: it is because of another person. I don't see why. He detests her. Oh, he hates her, he hates her! And it is because you love her that he does not want you to do for her what you wish to do."

Maeterlinck noted that she was telling the truth, probably because he believed Leblanc's claim, insinuated in her memoirs, that Carré opposed her because she had repulsed his amorous advances in 1898.[57] Maeterlinck pressed further, "But will he go to the extreme? Won't he concede at all?"

"Oh, don't worry about him. I see that he is ill; he will not live long."

"You are wrong Julia," Maeterlinck protested. "I saw him the day before yesterday and he looked perfectly well."

"No, no, that makes no difference; he is sick. It does not show, but he is very sick. He is going to die soon."

"But when, and how?"

"He has blood on him, around him, everywhere. . . . "

"Blood? Is it a duel?" he asked, noting that he had at one time considered finding some pretext for battling his adversary. "Is it an accident, murder, vengeance?" After all, he commented, his opponent was an unjust man without scruples, who had done much harm to many people.

"No, no, don't question me further; I am very tired. Let me go. Be good; I will help you . . . "

Maeterlinck's campaign against Debussy, which continued throughout the three-and-a-half months of rehearsals, must have taken its toll on the composer, who thought at one point of withdrawing his opera. In an undated letter to René Peter he explained the cancellation of an appointment:

> Forgive me this latest in a series of habitual disappointments, but something quite painful has happened to me: I have just withdrawn *Pelléas* from the Opéra-Comique! . . . (Don't speak to anybody about this for the time being. . . .) I am thus in no condition to go out, at least not today.
> Forgive me, and understand all that I leave unsaid. (PET, pp. 221–22)

Maeterlinck seems to have steered clear of the *Pelléas* rehearsals although, for reasons which have never been explained, he did attend one, on the afternoon of 19 March. Debussy was also present, and Messager first rehearsed the orchestra in the music of Act III (starting at 1 p.m.) and was later (2:45) joined by the principals to go over the same act. Provided he stayed, Maeterlinck would have heard Mary Garden in the "Tower scene," which opens that act. If he had an opinion of Leblanc's rival, he apparently did not express it. The rehearsal evidently proceeded without incident, though one can well imagine a chill in the hall. Oddly enough, Debussy seems never to have commented on this remarkable reunion.[58]

Having failed to impose his mistress on the production and unable to achieve satisfaction through threatened physical attacks on the composer and director, Maeterlinck next tried to undermine the production by bringing his case to the public and denouncing Debussy's opera. This denunciation took the form of a letter to *Le Figaro*, written on 13 April and printed the following day. Maeterlinck probably intended his letter to appear on the eve of the première. *Le Ménestrel* of 23 March had estimated that the first performance of *Pelléas* would take place between 10 and 15 April, and on 6 April, the same journal had projected the première "around the 16th of the month." Had the second estimate been accurate, the letter could not have been more strategically timed. As it turned out, the première was further postponed for another two weeks. Maeterlinck's letter read as follows:

> The management of the Opéra-Comique announces the forthcoming production of *Pelléas et Mélisande*. This production will take place against my wishes, because MM. Carré and Debussy have disregarded the most legitimate of my rights. I would have had the dispute settled by the courts which, yet one more time, would probably have proclaimed that the poem belongs to the poet, if an extraordinary circumstance had not "altered the case," as they say at the Palace [of Justice].
>
> Indeed, M. Debussy, after having agreed with me as to the choice of the interpreter whom I considered uniquely capable of creating the role of Mélisande according to my intentions and wishes, thought fit, in the face of M. Carré's unjustifiable opposition to this choice, to deny me the right to intervene in the casting, by misusing an extremely confidential letter which I wrote to him nearly six years ago. This inelegant gesture was joined by strange practices, as is proved by the "bulletin de réception" of the work, manifestly antedated in an attempt to establish that my protestations had been too late. Thus they succeeded in excluding me from my own work, which, from then on, was treated like conquered territory. Arbitrary and absurd cuts have been imposed which have rendered it incomprehensible; [material] has been kept that I intended to suppress or improve, as I have done in the edition that has just been published, in which it can be seen how much the text adopted by the Opéra-Comique differs from the authentic text. In a word, the *Pelléas* in question is a play that has become foreign to me, almost inimical; and, stripped of all control over my work, I am reduced to wishing that its failure be prompt and resounding. (PET, pp. 175–76)

Maeterlinck's claims were mostly factual, though he somewhat colored the truth to make his point—most conspicuously, he omitted specific mention of Georgette Leblanc and his relationship with her. And while the casting of

Mélisande was originally his essential, even sole, complaint against the production of *Pelléas*, he now raised an objection to the opera itself, one which, though having a legitimate basis, had not been previously voiced. Debussy had indeed made cuts in Maeterlinck's play, but these were sanctioned and some were even suggested by the playwright in November 1893. To call them "arbitrary and absurd" was unfair. It is true, though, that Debussy had essentially based his opera on the original 1892 text of the play, one which Maeterlinck had subsequently revised three times: in 1893 for the first stage performance, in 1898 for the sixth edition, and again in 1901–2 as part of his collected theater works. Given other circumstances, one could sympathize with the playwright, who, having just published an extensive revision of his play, suddenly encountered a musical setting of a version he had rejected nine years before. In the present case, however, one cannot help but feel that this charge was manufactured. [59]

Georgette Leblanc recalled Maeterlinck's mood on the day he wrote the letter, which she begged him not to send: "The same day I wrote to a friend, 'I can't write to you, I am so tormented by Maeterlinck's belligerence—he wants to smite everyone on earth.' "[60] The day Maeterlinck's letter was published in *Le Figaro*, Debussy sent a telegram to Robert Godet: "Would like to see you to respond to Maeterlinck letter...." (GOD, p. 104). Godet advised him not to respond, advice which the composer took. [61]

In an effort to counter the damaging effect of Maeterlinck's letter, Carré formulated the plan of inviting Octave Mirbeau, Maeterlinck's longtime friend and the dedicatee of the play *Pelléas*, to a rehearsal of the opera, hoping, no doubt, that a favorable impression might move him to placate the enraged playwright or to write an article favorable to the production. On 18 April, Mirbeau responded to the offer in a letter to Carré:

> A thousand thanks for the charming notion that you have had. I will certainly go tomorrow, Saturday, at the time that you have invited me, to the rehearsal of *Pelléas*.
>
> I don't need to tell you how much I regret the attitude taken by Maeterlinck and how I wish that my friendship were strong and persuasive enough to enlighten him regarding this attitude, especially as to how ridiculous it is! But I can hope for nothing in the face of such blindness. I cannot appeal to his reason; he does not reason anymore. And everything that I would venture to do about it, at this moment at least, would only exasperate even further a sentiment which is already at such a point of exasperation that it has become, in this kindly, extremely sensible man, a truly raging madness. I do not believe that even the resounding success that I expect for this work will mollify him—quite the opposite. I have never seen a man possessed to this point by the evil genius of a woman. But rest assured that if I can find a way to bring poor Maeterlinck back to a truer understanding of things, I will not let the opportunity escape, because this distresses me, as it does all of his true friends. (PET, pp. 176–77) [62]

Carré's plan was only partially successful. Although unable to pacify Maeterlinck, Mirbeau attempted to offset the negative publicity resulting from Maeterlinck's public denunciation by writing enthusiastically about the opera in an article which appeared in *Le Journal* on 27 April, one day before the public dress rehearsal ("répétition générale") and three days before the première. Mirbeau took the playwright, and not the opera, as his point of departure, and discussed the three Maeterlinck works which were currently before the Parisian public: his recent book *Le Temple enseveli*, the opera *Pelléas et Mélisande*, and the play *Monna Vanna*, which was to have its première on 17 May by Lugné-Poe's Théâtre de l'Oeuvre at the Nouveau-Théâtre with Georgette Leblanc in the title role.[63] The paragraph relative to *Pelléas* reads in part:

> Wednesday at the Opéra-Comique we will have *Pelléas et Mélisande*, a beautiful and sad legend, like that of Paolo and Francesca, a poem with a lyrical tone so new, so moving, and so simple, which M. Debussy expresses in exquisite music, and which M. Albert Carré frames in a mise-en-scène which is the ultimate in most picturesquely and most artistically uniting the comprehension of and the respect for a work—which is a masterpiece twice over! I was able to attend a rehearsal of *Pelléas et Mélisande*, and after three days I retain an overwhelming impression of it—like an obsession. I also retain [the impression of] a light, very vivid and very soft, which, far from dissipating, enters into me more each minute, bathes me and penetrates me. I hope that Maurice Maeterlinck will permit me, out of friendship and a desire for his happiness as well as his glory, to defend him against himself, and against the letters published recently, to tell him, with the easily prophetic tranquility which comes from the overwhelming knowledge of the beauty which has been achieved— that *Pelléas et Mélisande* will be a great and proper triumph.... Leaving this rehearsal, dazzled, so proud to be your friend and proud that you have done me the honor of dedicating this work to me, I said to myself: "How sad it is that Maurice Maeterlinck is obliged to disown publicly his genius, which is so peaceably pure, so harmoniously beautiful!" And I was tempted to cry out, like one of the characters in your play, and in loving you more: "If I were God, I would have pity on the poor hearts of men!"[64]

Although the article seemed tailor-made to Carré's purposes, it is impossible to calculate its effect in countering Maeterlinck's letter. There were numerous audience disturbances during the public dress rehearsal, which took place the following day, but these were attributable less to Maeterlinck's letter than to a satiric "Sélect-Programme," sold outside the theater, which cruelly and salaciously parodied the plot of the opera.[65] This pamphlet may have been the playwright's final act of revenge; though responsibility for it has never been determined, rumors circulated that Maeterlinck himself was its author. Mary Garden certainly believed it,[66] and there is no doubt that the playwright would gladly have ridiculed his own play in order to contribute to the failure of Debussy's opera. The day after the public dress rehearsal, Carré announced to the press his intention of filing suit against the publisher of the fake program, but it seems that this was never pursued.[67]

Maeterlinck seems to have learned something from the entire experience and made certain not to duplicate his strategic errors in his next dealing with the Opéra-Comique when, a few years later, he was successful in securing for Leblanc the title role in his *Ariane et Barbe-Bleue,* set by Paul Dukas and performed at the Opéra-Comique in the spring of 1907.[68]

In 1912, on the occasion of the hundredth performance of Debussy's *Pelléas,* Maeterlinck rather evasively told the press:

> I have no interesting recollection of *Pelléas* from 1893. As for the performances at the Opéra-Comique, I'd rather not talk about them. Besides, I value enormously the prerogative and good fortune to forget a work totally the moment that it is handed over to the public.[69]

In the same year, Leblanc finally sang the role of her dreams, in Henry Russell's Boston production of *Pelléas,* but Maeterlinck did not attend the performances.[70] He actually did not hear Debussy's opera until 1920, after both the death of the composer and the end of his relationship with Leblanc. At Mary Garden's invitation, he attended a performance given on 27 January 1920 by the Chicago Opera Company in New York's Lexington Theatre, a performance in which Garden sang the role of Mélisande.[71] The following day he wrote to the soprano:

> I had sworn to myself never to see the lyric drama, *Pelléas et Mélisande.* Yesterday I violated my vow and I am a happy man. For the first time I have entirely understood my own play, and because of you.
>
> I saw there many things which I had never perceived or which I had forgotten. Like every great artist, more than any other perhaps, you have the genius to add to a work or to vivify in it those things which I omitted or had left in a state of sleep.[72]

Maeterlinck later told a Paris reporter he had only stayed for the first act.[73] During intermission he spoke with reporters. It seems that the wounds had finally healed—he had broken his vow never to attend a performance of the opera, and he even permitted himself a few favorable comments about Debussy's music. To a reporter for the *New York Sun* "he confessed a musical deafness, but said that even this did not hinder his realization that the spirit of the play had been enhanced, explained and beautified by the musical setting of Debussy...."[74]

About five years later he reflected on his conflict with Debussy and noted: "I find today that all of the fault was on my side and that he was right a thousand times over."[75]

4

Rehearsals and Performances at the Opéra-Comique (1902)

Rehearsals Begin and an Yniold is Found

The *Pelléas* rehearsals, which began on 13 January 1902, took place nearly every afternoon, except on Sundays, until the première.[1] Initially individual coaching sessions for the principals, these rehearsals were run by "chef de chant" Louis Landry, who was joined in this activity by Debussy starting 21 January, and by conductor André Messager starting 27 January. Beginning 23 January, the "lessons" sometimes included two or three singers, suggesting that they were starting to put scenes together.

The first ensemble rehearsal took place on 6 February, after three-and-a-half weeks of "lessons," and involved all six adult principals: Vieuille, Dufranne, Périer, Viguié, Garden, and Gerville-Réache. (This was apparently the first rehearsal attended by Viguié, who had the minor role of the Doctor.) Although individual and small group rehearsals still continued, they became relatively infrequent and were merely supplements to the daily ensemble rehearsals. In principle, all of the singers were now present at all rehearsals. Of course, there were some absences due to illness, and, since the Opéra-Comique was a repertory company, some singers occasionally had responsibilities in other productions. The operas being given that spring which involved members of the *Pelléas* cast were: *La Troupe Jolicoeur* (Périer), *Grisélidis* (Dufranne, Viguié), *Le Roi d'Ys* (Dufranne, Vieuille, Viguié), *Le Domino noir* (Périer), *Louise* (Garden, Vieuille, Viguié), *Mireille* (Vieuille), *Manon* (Garden), *La Basoche* (Périer), and *Lakmé* (Vieuille). According to Messager, the rehearsals progressed in an atmosphere of ever-increasing "ardor and enthusiasm," "each scene recommenced twenty times without a single performer ever showing the slightest temper when faced with the demands of a composer who was often difficult to satisfy...."[2] After weeks of studying their individual parts, the singers finally had a chance to experience their roles in the context of a musical and dramatic totality.

On 3 March the staging rehearsals ("répétitions en scène") began. Since 6 February, there had been nineteen ensemble rehearsals (and there were to be two more, on 4 and 5 March, making a total of twenty-one). The staging was rehearsed either on the main stage or in the "little theater" ("petit théâtre") on the fifth floor of the Salle Favart,[3] and followed the mise-en-scène which had been scrupulously prepared by Albert Carré.[4] On many days they worked on just a single scene.[5] Debussy was always in attendance. As Carré noted, the composer supervised every aspect of the production: "Nothing was done which wasn't desired, chosen, or conceived by him or with him."[6]

Rehearsals were well under way before a child was located for the part of Yniold. As noted above, this was the last role to be cast. The name of Blondin, the boy who eventually got the part, did not appear in the *livre de bord* until 5 March, the date of the third staging rehearsal and the final ensemble rehearsal. Blondin must have had private coaching before this date, but there is no record of it in the *livre de bord*. It is not known exactly when Blondin was chosen, but since the part is so important, one may assume that Debussy and Messager would have wanted the relatively inexperienced child to be at rehearsals as soon as possible. And since the ensemble rehearsals had already been in progress for about a month, it seems probable that Blondin was not discovered until shortly before the 5 March rehearsal in which he made his first appearance. After that date, the boy did not miss a single rehearsal.

In light of the evidence in the *livre de bord,* it is surprising to read in Busser's "diary" entry of 24 March (nearly three weeks after Blondin had joined the rehearsals) that Carré sent him to the solfège classes of the Paris Conservatoire to find a child for the part.[7] Busser thought he had found the "rare bird" he sought in Noël Gallon (at the time a ten-and-a-half-year-old student, later to become a professor of fugue), but the boy's voice had a mezzo soprano timbre rather than the soprano quality upon which Debussy insisted. Busser claims that Blondin was eventually discovered in the children's chorus from *Carmen.*[8] Although his dates are obviously in error, Busser's account of the events in question may well be accurate.

Meanwhile Busser satisfied his responsibilities as "chef des choeurs" in rehearsing the chorus, which had a small but important part in Act I, scene 3. In his diary under 4 March, Busser noted that he had the chorus read through its part;[9] the first chorus rehearsal recorded in the *livre de bord* was on 7 March, three days later.

The Orchestration of the Score and the Orchestra Rehearsals

At the same time that he was rehearsing the singers, Debussy was attending to another important musical responsibility: he had to complete the orchestra score and see that the parts were copied in time for the first orchestra rehearsal on 8 March. The earliest mention of an orchestra score of *Pelléas* was in a letter of 24 June 1896 from the composer to Paul Dukas, but the score in question was probably the short score with instrumental indications (NEC MS) rather than a full score. Besides, any full score from this period would have been rendered obsolete by subsequent revisions of the opera, and the last revision undertaken while the work was in manuscript apparently took place in September 1901. At that time, as we have seen, Debussy was probably completing the vocal score of *Pelléas* and may have been working on the orchestration.

Dietschy may be right in theorizing that Debussy decided to reorchestrate *Pelléas* as a result of attending the rehearsals of the *Nocturnes,* which were performed complete for the first time on 27 October 1901. Shortly after that performance he wrote to Louÿs: "I have set my mind to reorchestrating *Pelléas* (don't breathe a word of this to anyone). . . . "[10] And in January 1902, the composer commented on his preoccupation with *Pelléas* in another letter to the same friend: "As for me, I have no excuse for not having gone to see you, other than that I am working on an inspection of the cogwheels of the *Pelléas et Mélisande* machine. . . . Without appearing to be this way, it consumes my days and nights" (LOU1, p. 169). If his days were already occupied by rehearsals, his nights must have been devoted to the full score, still unfinished.

In an interview given years later, Debussy remarked that he could "work out the instrumentation of a piece of music at almost any time,"[11] and Godet has given testimony that the composer did indeed write out the full score speedily and efficiently, doing most of the job while rehearsals were in progress,[12] in three or four weeks early in 1902, "harrassed, of course, by telegrams from M. Messager."[13] Godet actually witnessed the writing of the full score since he assisted the composer by ruling "the pages of music paper which Debussy filled, night after night, with an imperturbable regularity, mostly without rough drafts to guide him."[14] He commented that Debussy worked "with a calm and steady movement" and "hardly paused while writing, except now and then to 'sketch' in the air, for example, a harp figure, to make sure of its playability" (LCat, p. 13). This job of ruling the paper was probably the assistance that the composer solicited in a letter to Godet of 14 February 1902: "Would you be kind enough to come to see me as soon as possible. I have a big favor to ask of you regarding *Pelléas!*" (GOD, p. 103). Debussy was so pressed, according to Godet, that another friend was called upon to enter the text and vocal lines, after which the instrumental staves were filled in by the composer.[15] Thus assisted, Debussy finished the full score and delivered the completed acts to a piano student, who copied out the orchestra parts.

On 8 March the orchestra was assembled for the first time to read through the opera. Messager conducted and the composer was present. The results were worse than anyone could have predicted. As Messager recalled:

The first reading of the orchestra was the start of a series of gloomy days and disheartening sessions. Debussy had had the generous but unfortunate idea of having his orchestra parts copied by a comrade down on his luck, but a mediocre copyist and a bit elementary as a musician. The calligraphy of this good man was distressing; his musical education made him unable to account for rather unusual harmonies, and the copying errors were scattered throughout the orchestra parts with a disconcerting abundance. One can get a clear idea of what it must have been like to have a reading under such conditions! We had to devote three or four rehearsals for corrections alone.[16]

Godet's reminiscences give further details about the copyist and the nature of his mistakes:

...an ignorant copyist (he was a piano student who used to reel off his scales on the floor above, while on the floor below a singer spun out her trills) played the dirtiest trick on him, without intending any harm: in conscientiously calculating the rests for each instrument, notated en bloc, he neglected to indicate the changes of meter or key signature which occurred during the duration, gloriously producing a first act which was irreproachable to the eye, but which needed innumerable scratchings out to satisfy the ear. This was a business for which Debussy was always unfit, and the occasion seemed badly chosen to prove the point.[17]

The copying mistakes alone must have tested the patience of the players, but according to Maurice Emmanuel, "The worst of it was that the composer, upon whom the questions poured—'Is that a sharp here, a flat there?'— sometimes answered, 'I don't know anything anymore!' "[18] There is no way of knowing how long the composer submitted to this torture, since the *livre de bord* entry for 8 March indicates his presence at an ensemble rehearsal that began forty-five minutes after the start of the orchestra reading. The frustrations of the situation may well have prompted an early departure.

An attempt was made to correct the parts before the next orchestra rehearsal. According to Busser, Messager assigned him the task of proofreading the string parts while Debussy took care of the winds. This still did not remedy the situation. As Busser recalled: "The errors were innumerable and, despite our combined efforts, they cropped up anew at each rehearsal, which exasperated Messager."[19] Before it was joined by the singers, the orchestra met twice more (on 13 and 15 March) in further attempts to weed out the errors and to become more familiar with the music. Messager paid tribute to his colleagues in the pit:

...they were admirable in their patience and good will despite the completely natural irritation caused by the rather tedious work, and they never ceased to show the most touching respect towards Debussy, even though the majority of them declared the work incomprehensible and destined for failure.[20]

The seventeenth of March was the date of the first "répétition a l'italienne" *(Sitzprobe)*—the first meeting of orchestra and singers, who remained seated instead of acting their parts. For the next few weeks, rehearsals essentially alternated between staging rehearsals with piano and rehearsals with orchestra, most often with stage action but sometimes with the singers seated. The orchestra still needed some rehearsals of its own and met on 19, 21, and 24 March. These sessions must have sufficed to correct the many mistakes that continued to crop up, for Busser remarked of the next rehearsal involving the orchestra, on 26 March, that they were finally able to go through the work without having to stop to make corrections.[21] Busser took advantage of the Easter holiday, during which rehearsals were suspended, in order to go over the parts, adding the "nuances" that Messager and Debussy had requested during the rehearsals.[22]

The Sets and the Interlude Expansions

It was also on 17 March, while the first *Sitzprobe* was taking place in the "petit théâtre," that the décors (sets) of *Pelléas* were first brought out on the main stage. These décors, like every other aspect of the production, were designed in accordance with the composer's wishes. Even before rehearsals began, Debussy, together with Carré and Messager, met with the designers ("décorateurs") of the Opéra-Comique: set designers Lucien Jusseaume and Eugène Ronsin and costume designer Charles Bianchini.[23] To speed up the process, the eight décors were divided between the two set designers, who proceeded to sketch the sets they were assigned: Jusseaume was responsible for the forest (I:1),[24] a fountain in the park (II:1, IV:3–4), and a room in the castle (II:2, V); Ronsin designed the gallery (I:2, IV:1–2), the terrace (I:3), the tower (III: 1, 3–4), the vaults beneath the castle (III:2), and the grotto (II:3).[25] First the sketches, then the models ("maquettes") of the décors had to meet with Debussy's approval, and, as the following undated letter to an unidentified friend (probably Carré) reveals, the composer had very definite ideas about what he wanted and was not satisfied with less: "Jusseaume, after making a great fuss, has decided to understand what I want, which would not be too bad. Today I am going to see the other models at M. Ronsin's; may God help me in this new struggle...."[26] The designers were probably not accustomed to taking orders from composers, but it seems that Debussy got his way. As Carré noted: "Debussy was not just a musician; he was a poet who was as sensitive to lines and colors as he was to sounds and words. The 'look' of the première was as much his work as it was mine or Jusseaume's or Bianchini's."[27] According to René Peter, Debussy was finally very happy with the décors and found them ravishing.[28] He presented Peter with a sketch of one that particularly "amused" him—the "tower"—but found it necessary to label the tower ("tour") and linden tree ("tilleul") in order to identify the ambiguous shapes in his crude drawing.[29]

The first trial of the décors may not have included all eight; the *livre de bord* entry for the morning of 27 March indicates another such session, this time with Ronsin supervising (only Jusseaume was present on the 17th).[30] On 29 March the décors of the vaults beneath the castle and the grotto, both designed by Ronsin, were brought on stage. The main stage was reserved for the scene-shifters and stagehands ("machinistes") on both 2 April and the morning of the following day, perhaps to put the décors in place and to practice changing them. On the afternoon of 3 April, there was a run-through of all the décors, except the "terrace."

Even before these last two days of work with the décors, Messager knew that some of the interludes that Debussy had composed to link the scenes did not give the scene-shifters enough time to change the sets. On 2 April, Debussy wrote to his friend Paul-Jean Toulet:

> Claude Debussy proposes and M. Messager disposes.... Last night around ten o'clock the latter came to ask me for 75 measures of linking-up music for the second act of *Pelléas*.... Naturally he needed it right away, and that is what killed the lovely evening that I had allowed myself to hope for. (TOU, p. 11)

As rehearsals proceeded it became evident that the interludes in the first and fourth acts also had to be extended to accommodate the set changes. The insufficiency of the interludes was less a miscalculation on the part of the composer than a shortcoming in the design of the Salle Favart, which made scene changes awkward and time-consuming. The wings, scarcely two meters wide, were so narrow that performers—singers, chorus members, dancers, and extras—had to line up practically single file to await their entries.[31] Storage space was also severely limited. Most of the scenery and props had to be kept at the back of the stage rather than in the wings, making it more difficult to transport them on and off the stage. Furthermore, the hall, though built in 1898, was not equipped with the most recent automatic machinery to facilitate scene-shifting. Everything had to be done by hand.[32] Debussy's original conception of very rapid scene changes (or even perhaps of scene changes without lowering the curtain)[33] was simply impossible to achieve with the inadequate and antiquated facilities of the Opéra-Comique. Given this situation, the composer had no choice but to lengthen the interludes, which he did with great reluctance. As Messager recalled: "He had to get back to work, ill-tempered and raving, and I had to go each day to wrest from him the pages which he filled between one rehearsal and another, because it was in this fashion that he composed the admirable interludes which comment on the action in such a moving manner."[34]

On the issue of when the interlude extensions were composed, Messager is contradicted by the often unreliable Henri Busser, whose diary-memoirs chronicled the history of the interludes.[35] Busser wrote that during the rehearsal of 6 April the orchestra had to stop repeatedly between scenes because the scene-shifters needed more time to change the sets; according to the *livre de bord*, *Pelléas* was not even rehearsed on that date. In connection with the rehearsals of 7 and 9 April, Busser noted that Carré asked Debussy to compose interludes long enough to avoid these halts, but that Debussy refused, saying, "That is impossible for me. I can't just grind them out. I will add them during the vacation." Busser registered some astonishment that they were prepared to stop the orchestra in performance if the set changes were not ready![36] He continued to note such pauses in rehearsals on the 17th and 25th and reported visiting Debussy on the morning of 1 May, the day following the première: the composer was writing the interludes and played Busser some of his sketches for them. Nearly two months later, on 26 June (the date of the final *Pelléas* performance of the season), Busser recorded being told by Mme Debussy that her husband was still working hard on the interludes, which, he noted, were not incorporated into the score until 30 October, the first performance of the 1902–3 season.

Debussy himself did not settle the matter in favor of either Messager, who claimed the interludes were finished before the first performance, or Busser, who wrote that they were not ready until the following fall. The composer's only reference to the dating of the interludes was in a letter of 25 July 1907 to Louis Laloy, in which he simply stated: "The interludes are from 1902!!!" (LAL, p. 26). However, Gustave Samazeuilh, who made the piano reduction of the interlude interpolations, supported Messager's memory over Busser's diary. He wrote: "At Debussy's request, I immediately made piano transcriptions of the orchestral interludes, so rich in substance, which he composed, even while the rehearsals were in progress, to facilitate the set changes...."[37] Samazeuilh stressed the speed with which Debussy worked, remarking how some of the interpolations were written in a single night and orchestrated in a few hours.

The reviews of the première support this recollection. Not a single review mentioned any pauses between the tableaux. Rather, one finds remarks such as those made by Raymond Bouyer in *La Nouvelle Revue* of 15 May 1902:

This musical *Pelléas* is a succession of scenes, like Shakespeare, linked by plaintive interludes: between two décors, between two fugitive visions, the curtain falls again, and the orchestra, uninterrupted, escorts us from the autumnal forest to the old manor, from the manor to the terrace, from the terrace at twilight to the magical fountain, and so on, always one after the other, in morose halls or under centenarian trees, with the only repose during the intermissions.[38]

Michel-Dimitri Calvocoressi's review for the 4 May 1902 issue of *L'Art Moderne,* not only mentioned the musical continuity created by the interludes, but lamented the fact that Debussy had been forced to make interpolations in the interludes to achieve that result. He specifically commented that the additions (which he heard at the première) did not appear in the original piano score, thus proving that the expanded interludes were part of the first performance:

> The thirteen tableaux are linked by interludes so short that they had to be intercalated afterwards by symphonic links which do not appear in the score and which prolong the lengths of the acts quite needlessly. It is regrettable that they hadn't found a way to change the décors more rapidly, even at the cost of certain sacrifices: but concern for the reputation of the mise-en-scène at the Opéra-Comique seems to override all musical considerations.[39]

The fact that these independent, first-hand sources contradict the precise and precisely dated recollections of Busser, unfortunately forces one to doubt the accuracy of his diary and makes one wonder if the entries actually are the "daily notes, taken on the quick,"[40] as he would have us believe they are.

Final Rehearsals and the Public Dress Rehearsal ("Répétition Générale") of 28 April 1902

Practically the entire month of April was devoted to putting the final touches on the musical and especially the visual aspects of the production—rehearsing the extras, fitting the costumes, and adjusting the sets and lights. On Friday, 4 April, while the principals worked with the orchestra upstairs in the little theater, Landry directed a rehearsal on stage of the extras (including the servants of the fifth act and the pigeons of the third) with the décors; they were apparently joined by the singers later in the afternoon. Starting the following week, all rehearsals took place on the main stage, and the chorus and extras were almost always present. On Tuesday, 8 April, there was evidently a complete run-through of the opera, without orchestra, but with servants and sets; after rehearsing two scenes (the subterranean vaults and the tower scenes) they went through the entire opera. It took several rehearsals to get the décors properly lighted and in place. The 10th and 14th of April were devoted exclusively to the sets, first a "rehearsal of the décors," with all of the décors presented in order, then the "dress rehearsal of the décors in order—complete décors, changes of backdrops, gauzes, furniture, props, complete lighting, projections, front curtain and double curtain," all overseen by Landry. Even after the first dress rehearsal on 17 April, Debussy was still dissatisfied with aspects of the lighting; Carré responded to his complaints in a letter dated Friday, 18 April:

All of your observations relative to the lighting are quite accurate, but I will respond to them en bloc by repeating to you that I have not finally adjusted the lighting of the work, but have only been experimenting with it. This is why I require tomorrow's rehearsal *with the performers*. It would be better to get this indispensable work out of the way before returning them to rehearsals with the music.

I could give them to you on Tuesday in the little theater for the work that you speak of.

I have arranged the terrace (third tableau) in a way which will now surely give pleasure. (F-Pn, l.a. Carré (A), 52)

On the 18th the stage had been reserved for the machinists and painters, specifically Ronsin, who worked on the décor of the terrace, finally achieving the result that pleased Carré so much. Another rehearsal of the décors took place on the 23rd, and Jusseaume reserved the stage for his work on the mornings of the 24th and 25th.

On 11 April, the singers rehearsed in costume for the first time. At this and at subsequent rehearsals, including the dress rehearsals on 17, 19, and 21 April, one or another element was missing (either décors, costumes, or orchestra), so the "final dress rehearsal for the house" on 25 April was evidently the first opportunity to get a complete impression of the entire production. Carré was reportedly pleased, sure of a huge success.[41] For the sake of security, however, a cover cast was concurrently being trained by Landry.

The date of the première had been postponed a number of times. On 23 March it was anticipated between 10 and 15 April, and on 6 April, estimated around the 16th.[42] On the 13th, it was announced for the 23rd, and on the 18th for the 29th, and finally, on the 22nd, the day after what was probably a successful dress rehearsal, fixed for the 30th, with the "public dress rehearsal" scheduled on the 28th.[43]

By the time of this public dress rehearsal, the production had been in rehearsal for about three-and-a-half months, including about 78 coaching sessions for the principals, 21 ensemble rehearsals, 36 staging rehearsals (12 with orchestra and 24 without), 2 *Sitzproben* (with orchestra), and 6 rehearsals for the orchestra alone.[44] There were 6 rehearsals in costume, and the chorus, which sings for only 27 measures in the third tableau, attended about 11 rehearsals. There were also additional rehearsals for the extras, the décors, the set painters, and the stagehands. Mary Garden was not exaggerating when she recalled: " . . . we had months of scenic rehearsals and rehearsals of the light. . . . So much depends upon lighting and mise-en-scène in *Pelléas*. . . . "[45] She commented on the thoroughness and intensity of those rehearsals: "Oh, how often we went over those tableaux, always with the greatest concentration on every single detail! I don't remember ever seeing anything so thoroughly worked out to the highest perfection. . . . Those were four complicated months we went through. No opera I know of, at least of our time, was given such infinite study and attention."[46] Debussy later said of these rehearsals: "These were my most precious moments in the theater; it was there that I met the boundless devotion of really great artists" (RLS, p. 227; LCr, p. 196).

The public dress rehearsal on the afternoon of 28 April 1902 started at 1:15. This first public exposure of his opera was a moment which Debussy had long both cherished and feared. This ambivalence, which characterized his attitude toward public performance, was even expressed in a definition of music that he once gave: "Music is the art of gathering sounds and of gathering together people who only hear them quite seldom."[47] Deep concerns over the public reception of his music repeatedly arose in the course of his correspondence with Chausson around the time he began composing *Pelléas*. In a letter of 26 August 1893 he wrote:

> The artist in modern civilization will always be someone whose usefulness is understood only after his death.... Therefore, it would be better if he never had to mingle with his contemporaries; and what is the use even, of having them through a mediocre performance, to experience joys for which so few are fit! It would suffice that one be "discovered" much later, because certain recent glories will surely have terrible responsibilities to assume with regard to the future. (CHA1, p. 117)

A week later, on 3 September, he proposed the formation of a "Society of Musical Esotericism" as an alternative to public performance. And in January 1894, when he dreamt of popular success and thought that *Pelléas* was his only possibility for financial security, his hopes were mixed with fear: "I have no other hope than *Pelléas et Mélisande,* and God alone knows if that hope won't go up in smoke!" (CHA2, p. 183). Even upon completing his first version of the work, on 17 August 1895, his jubilation immediately turned into apprehension ("Now, all of my anxiety begins"), as he wondered how his work would be received ("How will the world act towards these two poor little beings [Pelléas and Mélisande]?"), and once again voiced his distaste for the general public ("I hate crowds, universal suffrage, and tricolored phrases!") (LER, p. 32). If, in the years that followed, he did not always pursue possibilities for public performance with unflagging vigor, it may have been due to such misgivings. These feelings even surfaced after *Pelléas* had been accepted "in principle" by the Opéra-Comique. On 1 February 1900 he attended the dress rehearsal there of Charpentier's *Louise,* a work for which he expressed an intense dislike, and he bitterly resented its enormous success with both audience and critics. On 6 February he wrote to Louÿs: "It seems to me that it was necessary for this work to be written, performed, and acclaimed. It satisfies too well the need for base beauty and imbecile art which so many people crave." He seemed to regret that his own opera was to be presented on the same stage, commenting ironically that even success would be a kind of failure: "I assure you that I would much prefer that *Pelléas* be performed in Japan, because, in the name of an elegant eclecticism, people (the same ones) will surely want to yield to it, and I declare that that would make me quite ashamed" (LOU1, pp. 136–37).

Less than a month before the première of *Pelléas*, Debussy seemed to be prepared for a hostile and bewildered audience reaction to his opera. He expressed this fear in a note written for Georges Ricou, secretary general of the Opéra-Comique, in which he explained how he came to write *Pelléas* and commented on the prevailing attitude of the theater-going public:

> The people who go to listen to music in the theater are really like those crowds whom one sees gathered around street musicians! There you can have your emotions-in-melody for a couple of sous! You can also be sure of a greater degree of attention than is usually found among the patrons of our state theaters, and you will even find a greater wish to understand—something totally lacking in the above-mentioned public.
>
> By a unique stroke of irony, this public which demands "something new" is the same one that is bewildered by, and which jeers at, anything new or unusual, whenever someone is trying to break away from making the customary hullabaloo. This may seem hard to understand, but one must not forget that with a work of art an attempt at beauty is always taken as a personal insult by some people. (RLS, p. 75; LCr, p. 62)

The audience that attended the public dress rehearsal of *Pelléas* easily justified the composer's essential fear, that of not being understood. As an institution, the public dress rehearsal was the very antithesis of the "Society of Musical Esotericism" that he had proposed nine years before.

For over thirty years it had been the custom in Paris to invite the critics to the final dress rehearsal of a play or opera. The purpose was to give the critics, whose reviews usually had to appear the morning after the première, some additional time to formulate their judgments—it gave them at least an additional day to study the work and write their reviews and also the opportunity to refine their opinions after a second hearing at the première. In order to create the atmosphere of a performance at this final dress rehearsal, the management invited an audience to sit with the thirty or forty critics who might be expected to review the production. In addition to the friends of the author, cast, and theater management, the audience on such occasions generally consisted of a rather bizarre assortment of people. According to a contemporary account, one might encounter "stockholders in the theater, creditors, speculators, outside brokers, deputies, senators, unemployed actors and actresses, authors whose plays had failed, police commissioners, fire chiefs, floozies both young and old (mostly old), tradesmen, dressmakers, tailors, hairdressers, and shoemakers."[48] This was the audience that judged the new production—a handful of well-wishing friends, a small group of professional critics, whose more or less reliable opinions would appear in the newspapers, and a theater full of amateurs and incompetents, whose views spread by word of mouth from the theater corridors into the streets.

Debussy had his group of well-wishers at the dress rehearsal of *Pelléas*. Naturally his wife Lilly was there, and he reserved a *baignoire* for his old friend Pierre Louÿs, stressing in a letter how important the latter's support was: "I don't need to tell you how necessary it is to our friendship that you be there" (LOU1, p. 170). In reply, Louÿs assured his friend that he had even enlisted some additional supporters: "Count on me, Claude. I am inviting five people to fill the *baignoire* with applause. I have hardly seen you since the nineteenth century, but that does not change my opinion of *Pelléas*. Thank you and good luck!" (LOU1, p. 170). Also among the invited were Robert Godet, Raymond Bonheur and his sister, Paul Valéry, Léon Blum, Paul Robert, Paul-Jean Toulet, Jacques de Montesquieu, Curnonsky (Maurice Sailland), René de Castéra, Henri de Régnier, André Lebey, Vincent d'Indy, René Peter, and Pierre de Bréville.[49] The house was packed, and this sympathetic enclave unfortunately could not offset the hostile mood created by Maeterlinck's publicly announced wish for a swift and resounding failure and by the satiric "Sélect-Programme," which was sold on the streets for six sous and ridiculed, sometimes scurrilously, the opera's plot (and, in a closing note, even its librettist). If the former predisposed the audience to boo, the latter predisposed it to mock.

Accounts of the dress rehearsal may vary in detail, but all are in essential agreement that it was a controversial occasion, marked at times by commotion and outbursts from the audience. In Busser's version, the turbulence was initially restricted to the corridors:

> House packed. The first two acts are a bit surprising to the audience, which listens religiously. Corridors are very spirited, excited conversations. Among the detractors: Hüe, Xavier Leroux, and the Hillemacher brothers; the admirers: Gabriel Pierné, Paul Dukas. As for Pierre Lalo, he reserves judgment.[50]

From his position in the pit, however, Messager was aware of some disturbances in the hall, beginning in the second act:

> The first act unfolded...in relative calm; the house, nervous, manifestly hostile, nevertheless remained silent. It was in the second tableau of the second act, at Mélisande's reply, "I am not happy!" that the storm burst forth.[51]

Carré described a gradual change in the audience reaction:

> The reception was restrained at first. The general impression of desultoriness, irresolution, and boredom was little by little transformed, by a phenomenon frequent in such circumstances, to gentle mockery and inopportune mirth, which became, towards the end of the second act, a veritable uproar.[52]

The laughter and commotion continued in the first scene of the third act, especially, as René Peter recalled, when Pelléas began to play tenderly with Mélisande's hair,[53] but it was in the act's final scene that audience interruptions reached a peak. As Busser reported:

> The scene...stirs up general hilarity at the words "Petit père, petit père...", so often repeated. The young Blondin...loses his head and gets confused. When the curtain drops there are multifarious protests, which drown out the applause.[54]

Messager also commented on the impact of the expression "petit père":

> All of those who were only waiting for an excuse to show their hostility used the text as a pretext for assaulting the music; the phrase... "petit père" in the scene between Golaud and little Yniold stirred up gales of laughter and exclamations of indignation. To my right in the first tier, a fat woman, indirectly connected with the world of the theater and a frequenter of the public dress rehearsals, where she was noted for her ugliness and malevolence, attracted attention by indignant protests and cries like those of a frightened guinea hen. I can still see her, rolling around in her seat like a ship in a storm, raising her fat, stubby arms and screaming: "Oh! petit père! petit père! It's a scream! Enough! Enough!"[55]

Not only was the oft-repeated "petit père" greeted with laughter, but many in the audience took offense at the entire scene. Critic Camille Bellaigue spoke for this segment when he wrote in his review:

> Several lines seemed truly ridiculous; at least one scene was offensive. When Golaud, unable to reach the window of the chamber in which Mélisande and Pelléas were, put a child, his child, on his shoulders and made him witness and report on what was happening behind the lighted window—that can be read, but it cannot be shown, and it is not viewed without some repugnance.[56]

Two passages in the scene proved particularly offensive: Yniold's disclosure that Pelléas and Mélisande argued because the castle door wouldn't stay open and the exchange between father and son when the latter was propped up to spy on the suspected lovers and was asked if they were near the bed.[57] According to Godet, the audience reaction to the child's reply ("The bed, little father? I don't see the bed") was overwhelming: "... the entire house, united in a league to defend morals, burst into a storm of 'hou!' which made one expect the curtain to fall."[58]

The outbursts continued during the fourth act, again primarily in reaction to the text. Carré recalled:

> Soon, poor Mélisande could no longer utter a word without unleashing hilarity. When, in the second tableau, Golaud brutalizes her and drags her by the hair to obtain her confession, the scene was punctuated by indignant "Oh's!" and "Ah's!", which gave way to an outburst of laughter when she spoke her famous line, "Je ne suis pas heureuse..." ["I am not happy"]. "You're telling me!" someone cried.[59]

According to Busser, Garden's "slight English accent" in her delivery of this line ("Je ne *souis* pas heureuse") also contributed to the laughter.[60] At the same moment Vieuille observed from the stage: "At these words a man in the first row of the orchestra seats stood up and shouted: 'Well, what do you expect?' There was a general outcry and the performance was no longer on stage, but in the hall."[61] Messager recalled that another line from Act IV, scene 2, Golaud's "Simplement parce que c'est l'usage" ("Simply because it is the custom") also evoked derision.[62] Mary Garden was outraged by the audience reaction: "Here was a drama of pure poetry and tragedy, and people were giggling and chuckling as if they were at the Folies Bergère."[63]

Although it was chiefly the text of Maeterlinck rather than its setting by Debussy that gave rise to such incidents, Pasteur Vallery-Radot reported overhearing some criticism directed at the music:

> There was muttering, smiling, protesting. "Why don't they give us some music?" exclaimed an old man, enamoured of the repertory which had delighted him for more than fifty years. "When will they finish tuning?" grumbled another, exasperated.[64]

Debussy, according to Carré, did not react well to this ordeal ("he barricaded himself in my office and didn't want to see anybody"), but Messager maintained his concentraion and presence of mind despite a difficult personal situation:

> ...on the podium, Messager stuck to it, superbly. He had returned to Paris from the country that very morning, after having buried his brother, whom he loved very much. When the act was finished, I looked everywhere for him and finally found him sobbing in a hidden corner of the theater. I spoke a few consoling words regarding the passing of his beloved brother, but he interrupted me, saying simply: "It is not for him that I am crying; it is for *Pelléas!*"[65]

Messager, in turn, praised the composure and professionalism of his orchestra and cast:

> The singers on stage, even though terribly nervous, the orchestra, and all those who participated in this lively matinee, happily kept their composure; the performance, perfect in all details, and also the emotion released by the last part of the work, finally forced themselves on the most malevolent, and the rehearsal ended, at least, in silence.[66]

According to Vieuille, the performers had found it very difficult to concentrate during the final act, but, because of their faith in the opera, they were both willing and able to do so.[67] Carré, like Messager, also noted that the rehearsal ended in relative calm: "Thank God, the final three [actually, two] tableaux...found favor with the public. That is to say, there were some spectators to 'shush' those who were disposed to perservere with uncontrollable laughter."[68]

According to Carré, Debussy was deeply hurt by the audience reaction: "...if Messager and I hadn't held back his hand, the day after the dress rehearsal he would have cut out the most beautiful pages of his score."[69] Carré assured him that the problem was not with his music, but with the text: "What do you expect? One hears every single word of the text, and believe me, it is the text alone which is booed. We must immediately consider some changes and some cuts."[70]

Throughout the rehearsals, Debussy had always insisted on clarity of the text; as Busser recalled:

> Most of the time he wanted a slightly supported *parlante* from the singers and a *pianissimo* from the orchestra in order that no syllable of the text would be lost; in contrast, in the most lyrical passages (for example, the duo at the tower, where Pelléas and Mélisande exchange the first avowals of their love), these must be sung more freely—as Debussy said, "without screaming or bellowing, as they do at the Opéra."[71]

One of his most frequent instructions, according to Busser, was "*Piano, piano, less forte*, I beg of you."[72] Paradoxically, the clarity of text that the composer had worked so hard to achieve proved his undoing at the dress rehearsal.

Two critics commented that some of the same lines that caused trouble at the dress rehearsal had also proved controversial in the original production of the play. Of Yniold's reference to the bed, Paul Souday wrote: "Naturally, disastrous 'booing' occurs, as in the time of Lugné-Poe."[73] And Camille Mauclair, one of the participants in that 1893 production, remarked that Debussy had "assumed responsibility for the play," even

> for those passages which caused laughter in 1893, for example, where Mélisande is beaten unmercifully by Golaud and runs away saying "I am not happy," while Golaud, abruptly pulling himself out of his attack of jealous rage, says, "Besides, all of that is of no importance." These archaic naïvetés are untenable in the theater. M. Debussy nevertheless preserves them.[74]

Changes in the Score following the Dress Rehearsal

But it was not only the audience that was scandalized by the opera—the voice of officialdom also condemned it. Théodore Dubois, director of the National Conservatory of Music, forbade his composition students from attending performances of *Pelléas*,[75] and Henry Roujon, Director of Fine Arts, called the acceptance of *Pelléas* by the Opéra-Comique a "national disgrace."[76] It was the latter who declared the scene between Golaud and Yniold at the end of the third act unacceptable in a state-supported theater,[77] and, the day of the dress rehearsal, told Carré that the scene had to be cut. Debussy explained this turn of events in a letter to a sympathetic critic (possibly Adolphe Jullien), whose review mentioned that cuts had been made following the dress rehearsal.[78] Debussy flatly rejected Roujon's insistence on the excision of the entire scene, a procedure which he considered too "surgical," but he had "to consent to several cuts and to the alteration of certain expressions" and pretended that he would have sought Maeterlinck's approval of these changes if their relationship had not become so strained. The appearance of the manuscript full score suggests that as many as seven cuts, amounting to ninety-nine measures of music, were apparently made in the first and fourth scenes of Act III, and that one line in Act IV, scene 2 was evidently changed. The two most significant cuts, because they became definitive omissions, were the discussion between Golaud and Yniold about whether or not Pelléas and Mélisande were near the bed, and Golaud's final line of the scene: "Nous allons voir ce qui est arrivé!" ("We are going to see what has happened!"). The seven cuts which were evidently made in the aftermath of the dress rehearsal are discussed below in chapter 6.

These adjustments in the score did not go unnoticed, and Adolphe Jullien, whose review may well have been the one which provoked Debussy's letter quoted above, wrote that he regretted that the cuts had been made in the opera between the dress rehearsal and the première, two days later. He expressed surprise that Debussy, a composer of reputed intransigence, had made what he assumed to be concessions to public taste in allowing the suppression of certain lines, especially in Act III, scene 4, just because of audience laughter and protests.[79] Paul Souday was another critic who noticed some cuts, and he observed that, for the actual performances (that is, in contrast to the dress rehearsal), Messager had the orchestra play louder in order to drown out certain offending lines of text.[80] Significantly, neither reviewer (nor any other, for that matter) mentioned Yniold's scene with the little sheep (Act IV, scene 3), which Carré claimed was also cut following the dress rehearsal.[81] Contrary to the recollection of Carré, Godet maintained that the director had insisted on omitting the scene "for reasons of length" early in the rehearsal schedule;[82] on this point Godet is supported by another eyewitness, René Peter.[83] It seems highly unlikely that the suppression of an entire scene could have escaped the notice of every critic, and one must conclude that Carré's recollection was in error. Perhaps the early decision to omit the scene was in part due to the late casting of the role of Yniold and to difficulties that the child may have had with the part. In the second season, the role was assigned to a woman, and the scene was restored.

Peter and Godet have given conflicting accounts of the composer's activities immediately following the dress rehearsal. Peter remembered joining Debussy, Lilly, and a female friend in a ride through the Bois de Boulogne in a hackney coach: "There was hardly a word spoken about *Pelléas!*"[84] The composer's explicit request upon leaving the theater had been: "Let's talk about something else."[85] Godet, who claimed Lilly's corroboration of his story,[86] recalled waiting on the boulevard des Italiens with Erik Satie while Debussy, still in the theater, discussed the cuts and changes to be made in his score. When Debussy finally emerged, they hastened to Fromont's shop where, "with a tired yet steady hand," the composer inscribed a copy of the vocal score of *Pelléas* to Godet, marking in pencil the cut in Act III, scene 4 that removed all mention of the bed. From there they went to Debussy's apartment for tea: "Debussy didn't make a single allusion, not one, to the day's events."[87] On this last point, Peter and Godet were in complete agreement; Debussy did not want to discuss the dress rehearsal. Years later, when Louis Laloy mentioned to the composer that he ordinarily found the public dress rehearsals boring and dismal, Debussy simply replied: "At that of *Pelléas*, I guarantee that you wouldn't have been bored."[88]

The controversial dress rehearsal of *Pelléas* was reported the following day in the pages of *Le Figaro*: "Enthusiastic partisans and obstinate opponents argued with elegance and liveliness.... A humorist, who was asked the fate of the new work, answered: 'The ballots are still being counted' " (DIE, p. 149). In the afternoon of the same day, 29 April, the members of the *Pelléas* cast assembled for a short rehearsal ("raccords")—they were informed of the changes that had been made in the score and went over the affected scenes in their slightly shortened and modified forms. They also may have been given some sort of pep talk in an attempt to offset the anger and disappointment they may have felt after the open rehearsal of the previous afternoon and to ready them for the première the following evening. The cast seemed ready in every sense; in the words of Félix Vieuille, they had faith in *Pelléas*.

The Première (30 April 1902)

On the evening of Wednesday, 30 April, the audience gathered at the Opéra-Comique for the première of *Pelléas*. Among those present were Debussy's parents, André Suarès, Maurice Delage, René Dumesnil, Robert de Montesquiou, Mme and Mlle de Romilly,[89] Pierre Louÿs,[90] Paul Dukas, Charles Koechlin, and Paul Choudens.[91] Also there were "twenty or thirty" young people who attended, not only the première, but all fourteen performances of the opera during the first season; this group included Pasteur Vallery-Radot, Léon-Paul Fargue, Georges Jean-Aubry, Ricardo Viñes, Maurice Ravel, Florent Schmitt, Désiré-Emile Inghelbrecht, Gérard Bauër, André Cain, Robert Kemp, Fernand Gregh, Emile Vuillermoz, Claude-Roger Marx,[92] and Paul Sordes.[93] The meager ticket sales for this nonsubscription première amounted to 1131 francs, suggesting that there must have been many empty seats.[94] The performance began five minutes late, at 8:35,[95] before an audience considerably more appreciative and better behaved than that of the dress rehearsal. Busser recorded his general impression of the evening:

> The première receives a better reception from the public: three or four curtain calls per act. Little Yniold's scene still stirs up some muttering, quickly quieted. Enthusiastic house for the last two acts.... Debussy's name is highly praised at the end of the performance; that of Maeterlinck stirs up some protests. Carré and Messager are restored to serenity and anticipate a lasting success....[96]

Messager acknowledged the marked improvement in the audience response at the première compared to that at the dress rehearsal, but he was still guarded in his appraisal of their appreciation of the work:

> ...the public, rid of the noxious elements which so often corrupt the impression of a first hearing, had an infinitely more seemly attitude. It was not, most certainly, a triumph, but it was already no longer the disaster of the dress rehearsal. It seemed that a certain response occurred. Timid cheering emanated from the upper balconies. Evidently, interest was awakened among some listeners, and one could say that it was from this small nucleus that this capital work slowly gained its success....[97]

René Peter described how the audience was gradually won over:

> The première... is the occasion of new mockery. Then it subsides. The audience assuredly still shows some confusion; but they listen and they applaud, especially in the upper balconies of the theater, where the emotion felt is profound and reaches out: it descends, winning over the spectators in the boxes and in the orchestra seats, silencing their mockery and forcing them to respect the work. (PET, p. 193)

Carré acknowledged his debt to the audience of the fourth balcony: "LET HONOR BE RENDERED TO THE AUDIENCE OF THE FOURTH BALCONY, WHICH WAS THE FIRST TO CORRECT THE ERROR COMMITTED BY THAT OF THE FIRST LOGES AND THE DRESS CIRCLE."[98] Though the initial reception was, in Messager's estimation, essentially unfavorable, Carré stood by the production and refused to shorten or terminate its run.

Subsequent Performances (2, 3, and 8 May)

The first reviews were published the day after the première, and others continued to appear in newspapers and journals in the days and months that followed. *Pelléas* was much discussed in the press, and critical opinion was divided—the opera had its vehement detractors and its equally passionate admirers.[99] The flood of critical commentary, though often negative, seems to have helped the box office, as people went to the Opéra-Comique to see for themselves what the polemics were all about. At the second performance, the evening of Friday, 2 May, ticket sales came to 3938.50 francs, a sizeable increase over those of the première, although the theater was still far from full.[100] More importantly, however, audience reaction seemed to improve along with ticket sales; as Messager observed:

From the second [performance], the audience appeared to be calm and above all, curious to hear this work which was so much talked about. The small group of admirers, pupils of the Conservatoire, mostly young students, grew from day to day, and the future appeared to be more favorable.[101]

Busser also noted that the audience at this performance was "sympathetic and attentive."[102]

The next evening, Saturday, 3 May, was a subscription performance and consequently drew a larger audience, with ticket receipts coming to 5981 francs.[103] Busser again commented on the audience: "Large audience, warmer and more understanding. At the end of the performance, Debussy is cheered, but he refuses to appear on the stage."[104]

After this third performance—"at the moment," recalled Messager, "where victory seemed imminent"—the conductor was forced to leave Paris for London in order to fulfill his responsibilities as artistic director of the Royal Opera at Covent Garden.[105] Messager's departure had been anticipated, and, as early as mid-March, it had been decided that the task of conducting future performances of *Pelléas* would be offered to Henri Busser, who was serving as chorus director for the production. In his memoirs, Busser recalled the moment on 19 March when he was approached by Messager with this proposition:

> ... he says to me brusquely: "Busser, what would you say to Carré if we, along with Debussy, asked you to conduct *Pelléas* when I leave Paris, in the month of May, to return to Covent Garden, in London?" Dumbfounded, I could only answer: "Do you think I am capable of doing it?" "Certainly," he affirms. "We don't want to hear talk of Marty or Luigini, who have already spoken badly of the work. We have all noted your diligence at rehearsals, and I immediately agreed with Carré's suggestion." The same evening, after the Saint-Sulpice act in *Manon,* my director calls me into his office and confirms everything that Messager has said to me. "We have confidence in you," adds Carré. "If you succeed, you will immediately be named conductor."[106]

After a sleepless night, Busser began preparing for this added responsibility, which carried with it the possibility of an important career advancement. Marguerite Long recalled helping Busser study the work by playing the piano reduction while he followed the full score.[107]

On the afternoon of Wednesday, 7 May, Busser was granted a single rehearsal (orchestra and cast) in preparation for the performance the following evening. As a souvenir he kept the "bulletin of notification" of this rehearsal[108] and left an account of the session, which did not even allow him enough time to run through the entire opera:

> I am given barely an hour and a half to work. The musicians grumble a bit: "Why do they make us rehearse? It's absolutely pointless. You will see that everything will go well." I certainly want to believe them, but just the same, I review the difficult spots. Debussy is

behind me and throws out his advice. Albert Carré calls me into his office and has me sign the contract making me a conductor of the Opéra-Comique. He says to me: "You see, I have confidence in you; everything will go well tomorrow."[109]

Debussy's reactions to the rehearsal, revealed in a letter to Messager of 9 May, suggest that there were indeed reasons to worry:

> ...just between us, the management of the Opéra-Comique should have given him a complete rehearsal—Busser, nervous, appearing not to know which end of the score to take. Périer, singing with a voice which seemed to come out of his umbrella! Mademoiselle Garden, absolutely refusing to look at the face of the above-named Busser, on the pretext that she was used to gazing at another, infinitely more agreeable. (This opinion could be successfully defended.) In short, an uncertain and fuliginous impression. Who knows what is going to happen? (MES, pp. 15–16)[110]

Obviously concerned that the fate of his work now rested in the hands of a novice, Debussy and his wife went to see Busser the following day, to warn him about the singers' possible capriciousness. Busser noted that "the two of them seemed very nervous."[111]

The performance, the fourth of the opera, on the evening of Thursday, 8 May, was another subscription program and earned the largest receipts to date—7364 francs.[112] Busser was generally satisfied with his debut and found the cast supportive and complimentary.[113] His claim that he experienced no stage fright was contradicted by Debussy, who sent the following report to Messager:

> ...superb house, including Monsieur Jean de Reszke. Audience respectful. Busser arrives with the look of a man who is about to take a cold bath and who doesn't like it! (The admirable orchestra carries him and prompts him with hints.) He doesn't pay any attention to the singers and throws chords at their legs without the slightest care for their harmonic quality. Finally, it all fell more or less into place and, after the fourth act, three curtain calls rewarded all of those brave souls for their efforts.
>
> To conclude: a fine evening, which lacked only you—and I really mean it! Let me explain: you knew how to awaken the sonic life of *Pelléas* with a tender delicacy that need no longer be looked for to be found again, because it is sure that the interior rhythm of all music depends on him who brings it to life, just as each word depends on the mouth that speaks it. Thus, whatever impression *Pelléas* created was doubled by what your personal emotion sensed in it and gave to it by putting everything marvelously into place. You know as well as I do that this is something that cannot be matched. I know that I am only allowing my regrets to surface, but too bad! You should know it once and for all, and know as well of my loyal friendship. (MES, pp. 16–17)

No doubt a factor contributing to the composer's criticism of Busser was his desire to praise Messager at the expense of his replacement. Whether out of genuine appreciation or as an act of diplomacy, Debussy visited Busser the next day and presented him with a copy of the newly published vocal score of

Pelléas in which he had written: "to Henry Busser, the grateful friendship of Claude Debussy, May 1902."[114] Other participants in the production also received copies of the score with personal inscriptions from the composer: Albert Carré ("to Monsieur A. Carré, and even more to the artist who knew how to create the unforgettable dreamlike atmosphere without which Pelléas and Mélisande would not have been able to live. Claude Debussy, May 1902"),[115] Félix Vieuille ("To Vieuille, who embodied the very tenderness and kindness of Arkel. Claude Debussy"),[116] and Mary Garden ("to Mademoiselle M. Garden. In the future, others will sing Mélisande. You alone will remain forever the woman and the artist that I hardly dared hope for. Your grateful Claude Debussy. May 1902").[117] The score itself carries the printed dedication: "To the memory of Georges Hartmann and in witness of profound affection for André Messager."

The Publication of the Vocal Score

Debussy's distribution of the vocal scores raises the question of when exactly that score was printed. The question has not been definitively settled. It has been mentioned above that the singers used proof sets of the vocal score to learn their parts and that these proofs were still uncorrected in many details. In a letter of 30 March 1902 to Raoul Bardac, Debussy commented that he was soliciting subscribers for the score: "Fromont has been warned and the throng of subscriptions could stampede 40 rue d'Anjou. . . . "[118] The records of Fromont, consulted by Vallas, indicated that the first printing of the score was on 10 May, the day after Busser claimed to have been given a copy of the score by the composer,[119] but the register of copyrights (Archives Nationales, Paris: F[18]* VIII 109, p. 233, no. 2399) records 3 May as the date of the copyright deposit ("dépôt légal"), meaning, presumably, that the score was actually deposited on that date,[120] and it indicates that the initial printing consisted of 250 copies; the register of plate numbers ("livre de cotages") at Durand also confirms the 3 May deposit. As was reported above, Godet insisted on an even earlier date, claiming that the composer gave him a copy of the score when they went to Fromont's shop immediately following the dress rehearsal of 28 April. A letter from Debussy to Fromont, which seems to deal with this very matter, was unfortunately dated simply "Sunday": "If you receive the scores of *Pelléas* tomorrow, don't send them to the Opéra-Comique as I had asked you to. Since everybody is completely exhausted, we're taking the day off!" (Coll. Jobert-Georges). This letter seems to support Godet's story: the Sunday in question could very well have been 27 April, the day before the final dress rehearsal, and Debussy's observation that "everybody is completely exhausted" could easily apply to the eve of this important event. One would assume, however, that Carré and Garden would have been among the very first to receive copies of the score, yet those given them by Debussy were dated "May 1902"; in fact, no score bearing an April dedication has been found. Two critics writing immediately after the première made references in their reviews to the pagination of the vocal score, though they may have consulted the proof sets that were in circulation at the Opéra-Comique rather than copies of the published score; André Corneau wrote in *Le Matin* of 1 May: "You will search in vain through the two hundred and eighty-three pages of the score for any fragment of melody,"[121] and Arthur Pougin, in *Le Ménestrel* of 4 May, pointed out a particular ninth chord on "page 10."[122] Also inconclusive is a letter of 5 May from Dukas to Suarès in which the former stated that Debussy had promised to send a copy of the score to the latter; since the score was apparently never sent, the letter cannot be taken as definitive evidence that the score was already printed.[123] It is difficult to sort out all of these clues: the score was probably printed by 3 May, the date of the copyright deposit, and perhaps as early as 28 April; 10 May, the date offered by Vallas, is surely too late.

At least one substantial excerpt from the opera was generally available before the première: a portion of Act V (76 measures: VS, p. 281, meas. 7–p. 288, meas. 13) was printed as a supplement to *L'Illustration,* No. 3085, of 12 April 1902. Three other excerpts appeared after the première as a supplement to *Le Monde Musicale* of 15 May 1902: two portions of Act III, scene 1 (VS, p. 115, meas. 1–p. 117, meas. 2, and p. 129, meas. 1–p. 131, meas. 11), and the beginning of Act V (VS, p. 268, meas. 1–18).

The Remaining Performances (10 May–26 June)

The fifth, sixth, and seventh presentations of *Pelléas*, all subscription performances, took place on the evenings of 10, 15, and 20 May, and the opera continued to earn impressive ticket revenues—6819.50, 6517.50, and 6221 francs respectively.[124] Debussy, however, was growing more and more displeased with the performances themselves, as he revealed in his letters to Messager. On 14 May he wrote:

> The performance last Sunday [10 May] did not go very well; a lot of ridiculous little things contributed to this, and I cannot be responsible for the ironical means sometimes employed by chance....
>
> Besides, since you left, I have the impression that something is rotten in the kingdom of Allemonde! How true it is that nobody at the Opéra-Comique has the anxious fondness for *Pelléas* that you do. If it goes well, so much the better; if it doesn't, too bad. You know that I am incapable of outward demonstrations and deceptions to revive dejected spirits! (MES, pp. 25–26)[125]

On 21 May he was more specific in his criticism of the performance:

Yesterday was the seventh performance of *Pelléas*. People had to be turned away. (How do you explain that?) To counterbalance that, the performance was weak. [The harpist] Martnenot himself added some unexpected glissandos, which could appear to be excessive! Périer has a cold once and for all, and only Mademoiselle Garden and Dufranne remain unchanged. A very fine evening just the same, it would appear, and a great success. (MES, pp. 19–20)

The enormous success that *Pelléas* was now experiencing was proclaimed in the pages of *Le Figaro,* where the following notice appeared on 21 May: "Yesterday the seventh performance of *Pelléas et Mélisande* confirmed the success of the work by M. Debussy. In the opinion of the public, each evening is a new victory, applauded by the most renowned musicians" (DIE, p. 152). In support of this last remark, Busser noted that a number of prominent conductors were in the audience on that particular evening: Paul Taffanel, Edouard Colonne, and Léon Jehin.[126]

This popular success was Debussy's second revenge on the critics. The first was revenge of a more personal kind, taken in the form of an interview which appeared in *Le Figaro* on 16 May and was entitled "Critique of the critics: 'Pelléas et Mélisande.'" In it he thanked those who had praised his opera[127] and answered those who had attacked it. Debussy, who had relinquished his position as music critic for *La Revue blanche* just a few months before, at the end of December 1901, partially in order to devote his time to the production of *Pelléas*,[128] chided his former colleagues, both individually and collectively:

Critics? They're fine people, very fine! Or so I would like to believe. Certainly they are a contented lot—perhaps I envy them. In their battle, the odds are all on one side: they have the right to pass judgment on the several years' struggles and labors of a work's gestation—all in one hour. (RLS, p. 79; LCr, p. 269)

It was shortly after the publication of this interview that critic Pierre Lalo, who in August 1900 had praised Debussy's *Nocturnes,* wrote a long, penetrating, and highly laudatory article on *Pelléas,* which appeared in the 20 May issue of *Le Temps.* According to Dietschy, the article did not entirely represent the spontaneous and original judgment of a discerning critic, since Lalo's opinion was largely shaped by Dukas, who, together with Gustave Doret and Paul Poujaud, succeeded in winning him over.[129] Nevertheless, Lalo's article, with its statement that *Pelléas* was "the most precious work which has been produced in the last few years,"[130] only enhanced the reputation of a work already growing in popularity. Pierre Louÿs was evidently impressed with this article and wrote to the composer on 22 May:

I hope that you are pleased with Lalo's article! No other musician has received the equal of it during the fifteen years that I have been reading the papers.

I have never seen a journalist cut everybody down, leaving only one man standing and everybody else toppled at his feet. Critics, the public, musicians, he didn't spare anybody. It is very courageous. And awfully well written. (LOU1, p. 171)

The remaining seven performances of *Pelléas* were all nonsubscription, yet there was generally no significant drop in ticket sales—the following sums were realized: Sunday, 25 May (matinee), 6138.50 fr.; Wednesday, 28 May, 5807.50 fr.; Sunday, 1 June (matinee), 3815.50 fr.; Friday, 6 June, 7395 fr.; Wednesday, 11 June, 5322.50 fr.; Friday, 20 June, 7798 fr.; and Thursday, 26 June, 6699.50 fr.[131] Since the première, the only performance to lose money was the matinee of Sunday, 1 June, which attracted the concert-going rather than the opera audience. *Pelléas* was clearly capable of drawing an audience on its own virtues, even without the advantage of guaranteed ticket sales through series subscriptions. This was proof of its triumph.

Beginning with the performance of 1 June, Mlle Delorn[132] replaced Gerville-Réache in the role of Geneviève. This seems to have been an anticipated rather than a last-minute replacement since Delorn had frequent coaching sessions beginning 20 May (and on 21, 26, 27, and 31 May), and on the 29th and 30th she rehearsed the scenes involving Geneviève on stage with the other singers.

In a letter of 9 June Debussy told Messager of the opera's continued financial success and reported an amusing anecdote about Carré:

I forgot to tell you that we took in 7400 francs last Friday! And you cannot imagine how much I am respected! To have written *Pelléas*, that has just an anecdotal significance, but to be good box-office, now that's really something! It's scandalous! In short, all of these people have aesthetics whose principles are expressed in numbers. It's no use bearing them a grudge for it. (MES, pp. 21–22)[133]

You would have a good laugh if you heard Carré talk about *Pelléas*. He puts on a certain artistic and inspired air, as if he had spent his life handling your dreams! He has understood it all, he has figured it all out, and nobody else but him could have come up with the special mise-en-scène which the work required. He said it to my face, without batting an eyelash! I hope, old friend, that your mustache will rise with that fine laugh of yours that I know so well! (TIE, p. 122)

At this stage of the production, Debussy seems to have lost interest in the performances themselves, and their quality had apparently continued to deteriorate. He wrote to Godet on 13 June:

I am finally anxious to see the performances of *Pelléas* come to an end!
Moreover, it is time: they are beginning to treat it like a repertory work! The singers improvise, the orchestra becomes heavy (it is nearly an inconceivable and fantastical tour de force), and soon it will become necessary that one prefer *La Dame blanche*. (GOD, pp. 105–6)

Plans for the 1902-3 Season

While Debussy was longing for an end to the current season, Carré and Messager were already planning the next, and since *Pelléas* had proved such a success, both artistically and financially, they were discussing the possibility of mounting it again in the fall. Having received word that the seventh performance of the opera had sold out, Messager wrote to Carré from London on 26 May:

> As you say, we must therefore think seriously about your next season. And first, since *Pelléas* is making money (and I believe that you could keep it going until the end of June without "squandering" it), we must think about the possibility of presenting it again next year. It has created too big an impression for it to be put aside.[134]

However, there were some complications with the casting, as Messager observed:

> ... there are two grim matters regarding the revival for next season: (1) the child, whose voice will perhaps be completely gone, and (2) Jean Périer, if you don't come to an agreement with him. A child will turn up, but a Pelléas is more difficult to ferret out; the part is too high for a baritone and too low for a tenor. Is Delaquerrière's voice completely gone? Since you did not give him the production that had been requested for him, I suppose that it must have been very bad. But it is possible that in a role which is rather low, he could carry it off, and he is a very good musician, an indispensable quality. What do you think of this? Do you have another idea?

Carré did indeed come up with another idea—making Pelléas a trouser role and giving the part to Jeanne Raunay, a soprano who had been engaged by the Opéra-Comique after appearing in the 1898 Paris première of d'Indy's *Fervaal*. Carré had a precedent for this assignment in the original production of the Maeterlinck play, in which the part of Pelléas was played by a woman, Marie Aubry. Messager wondered how Debussy would react to this proposal and, in a letter of 27 June, asked Carré: "Have you made a definitive decision, then, on the subject of Pelléas? Are you still thinking of Madame Raunay? And what does Debussy think of this?"[135] Debussy had only learned of the plan the day before, as he explained to Messager in a letter of 26 June: "... I saw Carré this afternoon; he spoke to me of having Mme Raunay take over the role of Pelléas. There's some news that merits some development" (MES, p. 29). When he next wrote to Messager, two days later, the assignment seemed nearly definitive, but, having had some time to think it over, the composer had serious doubts and insisted on hearing Raunay:

> Well, my dear friend, Madame Raunay would sing the role of Pelléas next season. This may appear strange, but it is not absolutely idiotic!

According to Carré, this idea came to him following a conversation with Mme Raunay in which she confessed an irregular love for Pelléas, which, in the present case, curiously resembles lyrical onanism, or to be less medical, narcissism.

On the whole, Pelléas has none of the amorous ways of a Hussar, and his sluggish manly decisions are so abruptly mowed down by the sword of Golaud, that perhaps there would be no drawback to this substitution?

I confess, besides, that I really need to see this. Without even speaking of the displacement of sex, there is a sonic displacement which worries me a little; consequently I have more curiosity than real liking for this idea. I await your opinion in order to settle all of this. (MES, pp. 31–32)

After hearing her sing, Debussy decided that the idea was not only "strange" but "idiotic" as well, and he wrote to Messager on 2 July:

I have seen Madame Raunay, and she sang for me some fragments of Pelléas with the voice of an old gentleman who is passionate but a little out of breath. I politely spoke about this to Carré, who naturally assumed that attitude of a hurt noncommissioned officer, which you know so well. Will he ever admit that this scheme is idiotic? It's too much to hope for.

Despite Debussy's veto, Carré evidently decided to keep Mme Raunay in reserve until he found an alternative.

At the end of July, Debussy went with his wife to Bichain for the rest of the summer, leaving Carré and Messager to work out the casting problems themselves. No doubt relieved to have left Paris, Debussy wrote to Durand on 10 August: "Little by little, I forget *Pelléas*, Mr. Albert Carré, and the audience of the Opéra-Comique, and it works like a charm for me."[136] By the end of the month Messager and Carré had agreed that Lucien Rigaux, a young baritone from the Paris Opéra, would succeed Périer as Pelléas. Messager announced his approval in a letter to Carré of 29 August:

I went to the Opéra-Comique yesterday to see Vizentini. Everything is going well.... He seems to be very satisfied with Rigaux. I think therefore that you had better inform Raunay immediately that you have given up the idea of a trouser role.[137]

Although Debussy had never heard Rigaux sing, he was willing to accept this decision. Still in Bichain, he wrote to Messager on 8 September about a report he had received from Busser:

I only hope that the Rigaux solution succeeds! I don't know him at all, but according to a letter from Busser, it appears that he is a "tall, elegant, handsome boy, resonant and penetrating voice ['voix mordante']"—in a word, all you need to be a hero at the Opéra-Comique! (MES, p. 54)

While the search for Pelléas was coming to an end, Carré was also trying to find a singer to replace Blondin as Yniold, and he proposed having a woman, rather than a child, play the part. Again, this was not a completely novel suggestion, but merely followed another role assignment of Lugné-Poe's original production of the Maeterlinck play, which featured Georgette Loyer as Yniold. At least one critic of Debussy's opera remarked, in fact, that Yniold should have been a trouser role; Calvocoressi wrote in *L'Art Moderne* of 4 May 1902:

> The poverty of the company of the Opéra-Comique is such that the role of Yniold, for lack of a woman to play it as a trouser role, which seemed to us entirely indicated, was entrusted to a young boy with a shrill voice; accessorily, one scene belonging to the role was suppressed.[138]

Messager heartily agreed with Carré's proposal regarding Yniold when he wrote to him on 29 August:

> Vizentini also told me your plan to replace the child with a woman. I believe that this will be decidedly better, because I believe that it is especially the *voice* which produced a somewhat ridiculous effect, and then we could restore the scene with the little sheep!! and Debussy will be so happy![139]

Once again Debussy accepted the decision of his directors: the role of Yniold was given to Mlle Suzanne Dumesnil, and, as Messager predicted, the "scene with the little sheep" (Act IV, scene 3) was restored. Dukas praised the casting choice in his review of the revival of *Pelléas* in the fall of 1902:

> ... Mlle Dumesnil has taken the place of the young boy who was, during the first performances, a realistic Yniold, but a too inexperienced singer. One entire part of the work gains infinitely from this substitution; the admirable tower scene [Act III, scene 4] unfolds in all of its tragic beauty, and it was possible to restore the scene in the fourth act where Yniold appears alone. This ravishing page was one of the attractions of the revival.[140]

Although it became traditional at the Opéra-Comique (and elsewhere) to treat Yniold as a trouser role, Debussy never completely abandoned his original conception of casting a child in the part. When a revival of *Pelléas* was being planned at the Opéra-Comique under the direction of Pierre Barthélemy Gheusi and the "Isola brothers" (Vincent and Emile Isola), Debussy wrote to Gheusi, probably in the spring of 1914, to say that he had just heard a twelve-year-old boy who would make a perfect Yniold: "This afternoon I heard a young boy, twelve years old, who has a ravishing voice; I believe that he will make a genuine little Yniold. He must work on the role during the vacation. If you would like to see him, I will send him to you?" [141] Because of World War I, the performances never took place, and *Pelléas* was not performed again at the Opéra-Comique until the spring of 1919, after the composer's death. To cast a child as Yniold thus appears to have been both his first and last wish regarding the role. [142]

The cast for the second season thus included three singers new to their parts: in addition to Rigaux and Dumesnil, Mlle Jeanne Passama assumed the role of Geneviève; the rest of the cast remained the same.

5

Publication of the Full Score and Later Performances at the Opéra-Comique (1902-5)

Plans to Publish the Full Score

Throughout the spring and into the summer of 1902, *Pelléas* dominated the composer's thoughts in other ways as well; the current production and the cast replacements for the following season were not his only concerns. He was also eager to find a way to publish the full score and orchestra parts for his opera. Perhaps such considerations were premature, but if *Pelléas* was to be performed outside of the Opéra-Comique, these performing materials would be a necessity. Aware that his opera had made him famous and no doubt hoping that it would make him rich as well, Debussy wanted to retain the rights to his opera and publish the score and parts at his own expense. Fromont agreed to do the printing and gave the composer an estimate of the cost. Lacking the necessary funds, Debussy formulated the plan of selling the full score by subscription in order to raise the money. In a letter of 9 June he described the situation to Messager:

> Fromont claims that he can only arrive at an exact estimate after he has that of the engraver. As a rough guess, he believes that the complete cost, all inclusive—score, parts, and printing—will be between 5500 and 6000 francs. The price of the score would be 100 francs for subscribers and 125 francs afterwards. All of this appears to me to be a bit American, and it seems to me that it could easily be reduced. Before all else, it appears to me necessary to have our Pothier [trombonist and head copyist at the Opéra-Comique] copy exemplars of the string parts, without which the engraver will flounder. (MES, p. 21)[1]

Debussy seemed confident that this arrangement would work out; just a few days later, on 13 June, he closed a letter to Godet with the following postscript: "I believe I have found a scheme for having the full score of *Pelléas* published" (GOD, p. 106). About a month later, on 2 July, Debussy was able to inform Messager of a new and lower cost estimate:

> For the full score of *Pelléas*, Fromont estimates that the cost will not exceed 3500 francs. The price for subscribers would be 80 francs. The format of the score would be like that of the score of *Hansel and Gretel*. What do you say to all of this? Don't you think it is necessary to have Pothier copy exemplars of the string parts? (MES, p. 36)[2]

Messager's reply included an invitation to visit him in London, an invitation which the composer happily accepted.[3]

Towards the end of the month, shortly after Debussy's return from London, the composer and his wife left Paris for a much-needed vacation at Bichain. Compositionally, the summer was unproductive, as Debussy explained to Messager in a letter written on 8 September, near the end of his vacation:

> I haven't written a note. That is nothing to brag about, but I have for a long while been like a squeezed lemon, and my poor brain no longer wanted to know anything. In order to do what I want, I have to clear out my head. Beginning a new work seems to me a bit like a somersault where one risks breaking one's back. (MES, p. 54)

Even though he found it difficult to compose, he spent some time reviewing the score of *Pelléas*, perhaps hoping for a fall publication, in time for the second season of performances. He wrote to Messager in late July: "I received the fifth act of *Pelléas* here, and I hope that nothing will prevent it from being published on the date that you mention" (MES, p. 49). And on 8 September: "I completely forgot to ask you to give me the manuscript of the 'scene with the little sheep.' If Carré intends to reinstate it, it is perhaps indispensable that it be engraved? (Perhaps it will be necessary to redo some of the music?)" (MES, p. 54). But the enormous task of engraving 409 pages of full score was not accomplished quickly, and, even if begun during the summer months, it is doubtful that it was completed by October 17, the date on which the unique manuscript full score would have been needed back at the Opéra-Comique for the first orchestra rehearsal.

The Second Season of Performances (1902–3)

Almost immediately upon his return to Paris, Debussy once again immersed himself in the production of his opera. Beginning 18 September his presence at the almost daily coaching sessions and rehearsals was recorded in the *livre de bord*.[4] His first activity was to supervise the studies of two of the new cast members, Suzanne Dumesnil as Yniold and Lucien Rigaux as Pelléas, both of whom had already begun to learn their parts with Louis Landry, the former since 1 September, the latter since the 12th. Jeanne Passama, the new Geneviève, began her "lessons" with the composer on 24 September, just five days before the beginning of the ensemble rehearsals. Rehearsals took place nearly every day until the first performance, on 30 October, and Debussy was invariably present. He was not exaggerating when he wrote on 21 October to Paul-Jean Toulet: "I have put off replying to you for so long only because of the numerous rehearsals required for the revival of *Pelléas*. They take up the greatest part of my time and conscientiously benumb the rest of it" (TOU, p. 14).

The "reprise" of *Pelléas*, with Messager once more in the pit, was apparently very successful. In his review of the production, Paul Dukas praised the new cast members and continued to find the singers from the first season (Garden, Dufranne, and Vieuille) "perfect." As noted above, he strongly approved of assigning the role of Yniold to a woman, and he considered the newly restored Act IV, scene 3 (the scene with the little sheep) one of the attractions of the revival. Dukas, a partisan of the opera from the first, concluded his review with the following observation:

> The scandalized shock born of the novelty of such a work, as different from the common lyricism of the fashionable charlatans as from the facile excesses of the neo-Wagnerians, is now pacified. It is in a setting of complete contemplation, or at the very least, of a lively curiosity, that *Pelléas* is now performed. The enthusiastic response is greater and more sincere at each performance. This is because the "connoisseurs" have made room for the public, because the public only asks to be moved and charmed, and because the work of Maurice Maeterlinck and Claude Debussy, all question of "school" aside, is the most irresistibly moving and delightful work that one could hear.[5]

The audiences may have become increasingly more enthusiastic, but the box office receipts did not increase. In fact, ticket sales for the ten performances (30 October 1902–6 January 1903) were, on the average, slightly lower than those of the first season.[6]

Immediately following this string of *Pelléas* performances, Debussy began a second stint as music critic, this time for the daily newspaper *Gil Blas*. His weekly column, which ran fairly regularly from 12 January to 28 June 1903, covered many aspects of the musical life of Paris. His work for the paper even took him to London, where, in late April and early May, he attended the *Ring* cycle at Covent Garden.

The Engraving of the Full Score and the Correction of the Proofs

It was apparently shortly after his return from London (with the *Ring* still resounding in his ears) that Debussy turned once more in earnest to the full score of *Pelléas* and his plan to have it published. Financial considerations were pressing, and Debussy was again planning a subscription drive to finance the project. He explained the situation to Messager in a letter of 6 May:

> I have seen Fromont: he stagnates in a swamp of Negativism! He is afraid that the score cannot be finished. We have begun to draw up the little prospectus, and towards the end of the week it will be distributed. Perhaps one could insinuate to people of good will that they pay for their subscriptions immediately. The paper sellers are terrible people who don't know how to wait; finally, let's be hopeful! (MES, pp. 57–58)

By June, at least, the engraving of the plates must have been very far advanced, perhaps completed, and, though suddenly and unexpectedly occupied with the Saxophone Rhapsody (a year-old commission), Debussy was apparently correcting the first proofs of *Pelléas* at this time; he seemed eager to complete this task before his early July departure for his summer vacation at Bichain. On 25 June he wrote to Raphaël Martenot, first harp in the *Pelléas* orchestra, asking him to send the modifications in the harp parts:

> I would be very grateful if you would be willing to send me as quickly as possible the modifications that you spoke to me about in the harp parts of *Pelléas*. Since I am leaving immediately for the country, I would like to be able to give these corrections [to the engraver] before I leave.[7]

Messager was also helping with the correction of the first proofs, and Debussy thanked him for reading the proofs of the fourth act in a letter of 29 June:

> To orchestrate in 30 degree heat [86 degrees Fahrenheit] is a pleasure which is a bit excessive! Moreover, I can only manage it by wearing nothing but my bare study. For the sake of morals and my personal comfort, I lock my door, but the coolness of the flutes does not help to reduce the temperature. And that is also why I have not yet thanked you for [proofreading] the fourth act of *Pelléas*. One must be truly noble to devote oneself to work such as this. (MES, p. 65)[8]

Debussy's references to orchestration probably pertain to *Pelléas*, so extensive were his modifications of the instrumentation in reviewing the first proofs. It is even possible that the proofs were gone over in two stages, with Messager correcting mistakes and Debussy making changes in the scoring.[9]

At the beginning of July, Debussy and his wife left for Bichain. Having presumably finished correcting the proofs, Debussy now waited for Fromont's engraver, Gulon, to make the changes in the plates and send him the revised proofs in order for the composer to verify the corrections.

Unlike the previous summer, Debussy's 1903 retreat to Bichain was extremely productive compositionally. He seems to have found the strength, the feeling of renewal, that had long eluded him and prevented him from embarking on any new compositional projects. He had finally overcome his fear, expressed in his 8 September 1902 letter to Messager, of the "somersault" into a new work. The summer of 1903 was his first period of compositional productivity since the spring of 1901, when he received the written promise of the Opéra-Comique to perform *Pelléas*. Since then, the opera had dominated his thoughts and consumed his time and energy. With the full score of *Pelléas* about to be published, he finally felt ready to move on to other things.

His first new project, begun in June, was the Saxophone Rhapsody, which had been commissioned in 1901.[10] ("Commissioned, paid for, and consumed more than a year ago," was how Debussy described the piece in a letter of early July to Pierre Louÿs.)[11] Despite his distaste for the project, he seems to have worked hard on it, writing to Messager on 8 June, "I have worked as in the glorious days of *Pelléas*" (MES, p. 62), and to Louÿs a month later, "For the last few days I have been: the-man-who-works-on-a-Fantasy-for-alto-saxophone-in-E-flat (try to say that three times without taking a breath)" (LOU3, p. 35).

Also in July, he composed the three *Estampes* for piano; the proofs were corrected in August and the work was published in October. He wrote the scenario for the projected opera *Le Diable dans le beffroi* (based on Edgar Allan Poe) in August, and he worked on *La Mer* in August and September.

It was thus in the midst of a burst of compositional activity that Debussy received and corrected the second proofs of *Pelléas*. His receipt of the proofs, however, was preceded by a little drama that the composer had not anticipated: Gulon's reaction to the first proofs. Highly skilled and proud, Gulon may have expected to find that he had made a few mistakes—perhaps missing accidentals, too few or too many ledger lines, incorrect clefs, or occasional wrong notes. He was certainly not prepared for what he saw—page after page of extensive "correction." It apparently did not occur to him that Debussy's "corrections" were in large part an extensive revision of the orchestration. His professional pride must have been injured, as he asked to look at the manuscript score in order to see if he had in fact engraved so badly as to necessitate such a superabundance of corrections. He certainly had reason to believe in the accuracy of the score which had, after all, served conductors for two seasons of performances. His error was the assumption that Debussy's work habits were logical!

Fromont reported the "Gulon saga" to Debussy, who replied, probably in early July:

> Your letter this morning recounts a tale in which somebody is crazy! I believe I can guarantee that it is neither you nor I? There remains, then, poor Gulon, who appears to me to be seriously stricken by the "phobia" of "the mistake."
>
> Therefore: (1) It is not a question of mistakes, but a question of *alterations,* which the manuscript score cannot contain because they were made *in the proofs.* (2) Because of the above situation, one can conclude that the manuscript cannot help the aforementioned Gulon in any way at all—quite the contrary. In any case, I don't have it here, It must be at the Opéra-Comique! (3) The alterations are *very clearly indicated.* All of the talent of Gulon

should be applied to engraving them intelligently, without looking for complications which are by no means the province of the engraver. People have a curious mania of never wanting to occupy themselves with what they know. In the present case, this could become dangerous. . . .

Keep me informed of the "Gulon saga." (Coll. Jobert-Georges)[12]

Presumably there was no more to the "saga," and the engraver proceeded to enter Debussy's corrections *and* revisions into the plates. Evidence of Gulon's wounded pride, however, can be found in a handwritten exchange between composer and engraver in the margin of one page of the proofs (Lehmann proofs, p. 329) beside some notes which appear unclear: Debussy objected that "these notes are *badly stamped,*" to which Gulon responded that the problem was not his fault, but the way they were "printed, if you please."

Debussy was very anxious to proceed with his correction of the *Pelléas* score, and a letter of mid-July to Fromont (Coll. Jobert-Georges) included an urgent appeal to send the second proofs. These proofs were quickly forthcoming, and Debussy acknowledged their receipt in a letter to his publisher dated 23 July:

> I have received the proofs and thank you for them, but I am lacking the first proofs of the second act, already corrected, without which I cannot work definitively.
> Let's try to move quickly, old friend; we must absolutely be ready for the reopening, otherwise we will look like damn liars. (Coll. Jobert-Georges)

Debussy had apparently promised that his revised score (and the orchestra parts corrected correspondingly) would be ready for the start of the third season of *Pelléas* performances, which were to begin in the fall.

The correction of the second proofs (together with the new compositions mentioned above) occupied the composer throughout the summer. Debussy seems to have regarded these corrections as final since he directed Fromont to have them forwarded to Pothier, presumably to have the same corrections made in the orchestra parts. Debussy explained this plan to Fromont in a letter of 20 September: "*To save time:* Have Gulon, after he has made the corrections, return the latest proofs of the first act to you, then send them immediately to Pothier. We will do the same for the subsequent acts" (Coll. Jobert-Georges).

In the same letter Debussy asked Fromont to send a vocal score of *Pelléas* to Lucy Foreau (Foreau-Isnardon), who had written him that she was to sing the role of Mélisande at the Théâtre de la Monnaie in Brussels; the young soprano was evidently worried about the difficulty of the work and wanted to meet with the composer. Debussy answered her fears in a letter:

Mélisande thanks you for your interest in her, so delicately expressed. Rest assured that her most cherished wish is to do her best to return this interest. Unfortunately, I will not return [to Paris] until next month, but I hope just the same to have the pleasure of seeing you there?

I am writing to the publisher of the score, and you should thus receive it shortly; but I beg you not to give too much credence to the [supposed] difficulty of my music: it's just talk circulated by people who don't understand music, or who understand it badly—take your pick. (Coll. Gary and Naomi Graffman) [13]

On the last day of September, Debussy announced his imminent departure for Paris: "My dear Fromont, we leave tomorrow for Paris; therefore, don't send me anything her anymore. The joy of living with the fine old trees is dead, and we are obliged to rejoin the hoi polloi" (Coll. Jobert-Georges). A letter written to Jacques Durand on the same day expressed similiar sentiments:

I have put off answering your last letter a bit, wanting to take advantage of my last glorious days of peace. Alas! The joy of living with the fine old trees is over, and we are obliged to rejoin the "upright people of Paris" and listen once again to papier-mâché music. (DUR, p. 15)

The Third Season of Performances (1903–4)

Upon his return to Paris, Debussy began once again to spend his days at the Opéra-Comique rehearsals of *Pelléas,* and once again his activities there detracted from other responsibilities. He was forced to send regrets to Durand, writing him on 25 October: "I have received the 'Estampes'...they are perfect.... I had wanted to thank you in person, but the Opéra-Comique absurdly takes up all of my time. This life of the theater disgusts me as much as it stupefies me" (DUR, pp. 15–16). And to Toulet on 8 November: "...you must excuse me for not having answered your letter; it arrived during the confusion of the revival of *Pelléas,* and I have completely lost the knack of navigating in the troubled waters of the theater" (TOU, pp. 22–23).

For the third season of performances (1903–4), Périer returned in the role of Pelléas and Gustave Huberdeau replaced Vieuille as Arkel for the first six performances; Vieuille returned to his role on 17 January. Again, Messager conducted. Otherwise, the cast was that of the previous season. Twelve performances were given, the first on 30 October, the last on 20 April 1904. For the performance of 19 February there were two substitutions due to illness: Mlle Coulon replaced Passama as Geneviève and Busser returned to the podium to replace Messager. Average ticket sales were slightly higher than those of the previous season, though not quite to the level of the first. [14]

In February 1904, Debussy and Mary Garden recorded for the French Gramophone Company selections from the *Ariettes oubliées* (the 1903 edition of these songs was dedicated "To Miss Mary Garden, unforgettable Mélisande, this music (already a bit old) in affectionate and grateful homage") and the song "Mes longs cheveux" from Act III, scene 1 of *Pelléas*.[15] Debussy's endorsement of the Gramophone was published in the March issue of the monthly bulletin *Gramophone Nouvelles* and reads: "Like all who have heard it, I find the Gramophone a marvelous instrument. Moreover, it guarantees complete and scrupulous immortality to music, and in that, it is indispensable."[16] Mary Garden considered the recordings "dreadful." She commented on their 1937 reissue, saying, "I can think of only one value that the disks made from them [i.e., the reissues] could have. People have a chance to hear Debussy at the piano, and the women who sing Mélisande should listen to those disks over and over again. For they would then understand the tempo to take. Otherwise, those disks are worthless. Debussy didn't enjoy doing them very much."[17] In a letter written on 13 August 1951, she explained to an admirer why she considered recordings (or broadcasts) of *Pelléas* unsatisfactory: "I have not heard the recorded performances of 'Pelléas + Mélisande' + don't want to—that opera is like me, one has to *see* it, not hear it over the air" (Coll. Richard Blackham).

The musical text of Debussy's opera was, for the 1903-4 season, already two layers of revisions different from its state during the previous season. Since, it seems, the corrections of the second proofs had been incorporated into the orchestra parts, the MS full score, which had been the conductor's score during the first two seasons, had become obsolete. Although it would have been possible to enter the same corrections into that manuscript score, it was far simpler to print the newly corrected plates to produce a third set of proofs for the conductor's use. Since the MS full score was never, in fact, brought up to date, the existence of such proofs is a necessary hypothesis. These conjectural third proofs would also provide a link between the second and final proofs. If, as suggested here, a new set of proofs served as the conductor's score during the third season, it is reasonable to think that it might have been in the course of rehearsals and performances that many of the further corrections and refinements in the appearance of the score were made. Messager, who conducted almost all of the *Pelléas* performances that season, was already an experienced proofreader of the score, having assisted in this task in June 1903.[18]

The Final Proofs and the Publication of the Full Score

After the final performance of the season (20 April 1904), these third proofs may then have been sent to the publisher in order for Gulon to enter the changes in the plates. After this task had been completed (no later than June 1904), the third proofs might have been sent along with the fourth for the composer's verification and approval. By now, the third proofs were no longer of use to anybody. Perhaps they remained with or were returned to Fromont, or perhaps Debussy disposed of them or presented them to a friend.

The final proofs (F-Pn, Rés. Vma. 281[19]) were printed like a published score, on both sides of the page and in gatherings. In reviewing these proofs, Debussy found another thirteen mistakes. After making the necessary corrections, he indicated their locations in a note on page 1 and gave his approval for the score to be printed: the instruction "ready for the press" ("bon à tirer") is dated 29 June 1904.

The corrections of the final proofs were duly made in the plates, and within two months time, the score was published. The date of the copyright deposit ("dépôt légal") was 27 August 1904,[20] nearly two years and four months after the première of the opera. The next time that *Pelléas* was performed at the Opéra-Comique (in its fourth season of performances, from 5 April to 22 June 1905), a published score finally rested on the conductor's stand.[21]

Debussy's Divorce and the Sale of the *Pelléas* Copyright

The bound final proofs served another function after accomplishing the final correction of the full score; they were soon to become another in a series of public and private "musical gifts" given by Debussy to Emma Bardac, the woman for whom he left his first wife and who eventually became his second. Her acquaintance with the composer may have dated back to 1901, when her son Raoul began studying composition with Debussy. (They had certainly met by March 1902, when, as was noted, she is mentioned in a letter from Debussy to Raoul.) But the blossoming of their romance did not take place until the spring and summer of 1904. Its progress is indicated in the dedications to her of two of the composer's works: the *Trois chansons de France* were published in May 1904 with a rather formal dedication to "Madame S. Bardac," while the September 1904 dedication of the second series of *Fêtes galantes* consisted of the much more discreet and rather enigmatic "to give thanks to the month of June 1904, A.l.p.M."; the initials stand for "à la petite Mienne," that is, "to my little one."[22] "It's a bit mysterious," admitted the composer in a letter to Durand in which he begged the publisher not to overlook the inscription.[23] (Curiously, the first Mme Debussy, Lilly Texier, was never the dedicatee of any of her husband's works.) When Debussy presented Emma with the final proofs of *Pelléas*, he added the following inscription:

To MadaBardac
These four hundred nine pages of miscellaneous tones which are hardly worth the shadow that your little hand casts on this big book.   July 1904.

As the song dedications indicate, Debussy's affection for Emma grew and flourished through the months of May and June. The joy that this relationship brought him is reflected in his letter of thanks for flowers that she had sent him on 6 June; the extravagance of the composer's language is somewhat reminiscent of Pelléas's tribute to Mélisande in Act III, scene 1: "Forgive me if I have kissed all of these flowers like a living mouth; is this perhaps mad?" (BAR, p. 27). Later that month the two lovers slipped away to Pourville,[24] a tryst which prompted the dedication of the *Fêtes galantes*. On 14 July the two were again together—this time on the island of Jersey. From 7 August until late September they were in Dieppe. Musically these summer months were rather productive: Debussy composed *Masques* and *L'Isle joyeuse* for piano and worked on *La Mer,* which he had begun in August 1903.[25] His troubles began, however, when he arrived in Paris in late September. He did not return to the rue Cardinet apartment which he had shared with his wife, but made a new home at 10, rue Alphand. Lilly's unsuccessful suicide attempt on 13 October was followed by lengthy divorce proceedings, during which Debussy suffered, both emotionally and financially.

Financial difficulties began almost immediately. On 1 October he bought merchandise on credit (perhaps to furnish his new apartment), and he signed an agreement to pay the sum of 861.50 fr. by the end of the year (31 December). Perhaps he got an extension on the loan, since two months after the deadline (28 February 1905) he still owed 860 francs and was unable to pay it. He explained this to Fromont (whose address he gave his creditors as the place where payment would be made) in a letter of 27 February, in which he claimed not to have "the first sou of this sum" that he owed: "Forgive me if you no longer hear talk of me; I am overwhelmed by grief and worries" (Coll. Jobert-Georges).

The composer's distress was not merely monetary, but personal as well, due to the anguish of his divorce and the estrangement of some of his closest friends, Louÿs and Messager among them, as a result of his abandonment of Lilly. He touched on these matters in a letter of 14 April to Laloy, in which he commented on the "desertions" taking place around him and described his state of mind:

> I will not recount here all that I have been through: it's pitiful, tragic, and sometimes, ironically, it resembles a cheap novel. In the end, I have experienced a great deal of moral suffering. Must I pay some forgotten debt to life? I just don't know, but often I have to smile so that nobody will suspect that I am going to cry. (LAL, p. 12)

The obvious solution to his emotional and financial woes was to marry the wealthy Emma Bardac, but this was still impossible since neither of their divorces was yet settled. In order to raise money, Debussy found himself forced to sell the copyright of *Pelléas,* for which he wanted 25,000 francs. This was more than Fromont was willing to pay, but the composer soon found an agreeable buyer in Durand, the firm which had published a number of his works both before and after the beginning of his association with Fromont. In fact, Durand had issued nearly all of the compositions that he had written since 1901 and was soon to publish his latest work, *La Mer* (completed on 5 March 1905), which carried a dedication to Jacques Durand.

Debussy notified Fromont of his negotiations with Durand in a letter of 30 March:

> It is settled with Maison Durand et fils. I thus request that you be willing to do all that is necessary regarding this transfer. And now, once again, please believe that I regret what has happened, but you can say that we have had a bit of happiness with *Pelléas*. Let this console you for the pain of having to relinquish it. (Coll. Jobert-Georges)[26]

The contract of transfer ("contrat de cession"), dated 31 March 1905 (the day after Debussy sent the above letter to Fromont), was signed by Debussy, Maeterlinck, and Jacques Durand.[27] In his memoirs, Durand described his role as a go-between in the negotiations. As a young man, Durand had met Maeterlinck, and their acquaintance had been renewed as a result of discussions pertaining to Dukas's *Ariane et Barbe-Bleue,* which was being published by Durand. Durand recalled that Maeterlinck "was pleased with the idea of our publishing *Pelléas;* it was also Debussy's most cherished wish. I thus negotiated the transaction, serving as an intermediary between the two collaborators."[28]

Debussy soon entered into an exclusive relationship with Durand. (Vallas dated the agreement just prior to Debussy's divorce, which was on 2 August 1905.)[29] According to Seroff, Debussy received a monthly allowance of 1,000 francs, twice what he had received from Hartmann, in exchange for which Debussy promised to offer all future compositions to Durand.[30]

In spite of this guaranteed income and Emma Bardac's divorce settlement (on 4 May 1905), which gave her an annuity of 50,000 francs, the composer's financial woes were not at an end. His own divorce case was decided in his wife's favor, and the settlement required him to pay her a portion of his royalties.[31] Lawsuits involving Lilly continued to plague him for the rest of his life.[32]

Part Two

Studies of the Sources of *Pelléas et Mélisande*

6

The Libretto

Pelléas et Mélisande is Debussy's only completed opera, yet the composer was occupied—even preoccupied—with operatic projects throughout his career. These plans reflect an ever-increasing involvement with the fashioning of his librettos. His first effort (ca. 1887–89) was apparently a setting of *Axël,* a play by Villiers de l'Isle-Adam, but the single scene he is said to have composed has been lost. In *Rodrigue et Chimène* (1890–92), virtually complete in short score (Acts I and III) and piano-vocal reduction (Act II), Debussy set a libretto given him by its author, Catulle Mendès. The text of *Pelléas et Mélisande* (1893–1902) was the composer's adaptation of the play by Maurice Maeterlinck. Four subsequent, aborted projects—*Cendrelune* (1895–98), *Comme il vous plaira* (1902–4), *Orphée-roi* (1907–9) and *L'Histoire de Tristan* (1907–9)—utilized librettos by Pierre Louÿs, Paul-Jean Toulet, Victor Segalen, and Gabriel Mourey, respectively; the texts were written for the composer, either with his collaboration or to his specifications. Finally, Debussy himself wrote the scenario (and a few musical sketches) for *Le Diable dans le beffroi* (1902–12) and the libretto (and an incomplete short score) for *La Chute de le Maison Usher* (1908–17), both of which were based on Charles Baudelaire's translations of stories by Edgar Allan Poe ("The Devil in the Belfry" and "The Fall of the House of Usher").[1]

The disappearance of crucial source materials—Debussy's setting of the scene from *Axël* and Mendès's original libretto for *Rodrigue*—make it impossible to determine Debussy's literary contributions to his first two projects, and it is therefore with *Pelléas* that an examination of the composer's activities as a librettist and literary editor must begin. The transformation of *Pelléas* from play into libretto was far from simple. The process of adaptation continued throughout the nine-year period during which Debussy worked on the opera, and it was further complicated by Maeterlinck's publication of two revised versions of his work before Debussy's opera reached the stage of the Opéra-Comique (30 April 1902).

Maeterlinck's Revisions of Pelléas

Paul Lacomblez of Brussels published the first version of Maeterlinck's *Pelléas et Mélisande* in May 1892,[2] and it appeared in four numbered "editions" (and perhaps in a fifth, unnumbered one) dated 1892.[3] The first revision of the text was made for the "sixth edition" of 1898, while the second was printed in Maeterlinck's *Théâtre* (1901-2), a three-volume collection of his plays. The collected plays were issued in two editions: one illustrated with ten lithographs by Auguste Donnay, published by Edmond Deman of Brussels, and another published jointly by Paul Lacomblez in Brussels and Per Lamm in Paris.[4] The Lacomblez-Lamm edition appeared first. Volumes 1 and 3 were published in October 1901, but volume 2 (which contained *Pelléas*) was evidently issued five months later, since an advertisement in the *Journal général de l'imprimerie et de la librairie* of 8 March 1902 announced that it was scheduled to appear on 20 March. This date was little more than a month before the première of Debussy's opera on 30 April and the almost simultaneous publication of its vocal score. Yet all three versions of the play— the original edition of 1892, the first revision of 1898, and the second of 1902— were used by Debussy during the composition of his opera, and each contributed to the shaping of its libretto.

In the preface to his collected plays, Maeterlinck described his approach to their revision:

> The texts of these short plays, which my publisher now collects together in three volumes, have hardly been changed. It is not at all that they seem perfect to me—far from it. But one does not improve a poem by successive corrections. The best and the worst in it have entwined roots, and often in trying to disentangle them one risks losing the special emotion and the light, almost unforeseen, charm which could only flourish in the shadow of an error as yet uncommitted.
>
> It would, for example, have been easy in *La Princesse Maleine* to suppress many a risky naïveté, a few superfluous scenes, and most of those astonished repetitions which make the characters seem like slightly deaf sleepwalkers constantly roused from painful dreams. I could have thus spared them some smiles, but the atmosphere and the very world in which they live would have seemed changed.[5]

He could have said the same of *Pelléas*: his revisions of the latter play confirm his claim that its text had indeed "hardly been changed."

Nonetheless, the process of revision began even before the première of the play, on 17 May 1893 at the Théâtre des Bouffes-Parisiens in Paris. In a letter of 22 February 1893 to the stage director, Aurélien-François Lugné-Poe, Maeterlinck discussed some of the changes he wished to make in the printed text of 1892:

In the part of Mélisande there is a reply to be suppressed (Act III: page 72, line 11), where she says: "*I look frightful like this.*" It really sounds like the frightful flirtation of a milliner, and I will see to it that the remark is replaced. Likewise, I don't like the song she sings, and I will let Mlle Meuris [the actress performing the role of Mélisande] choose from among about 30 others that I have written the one she thinks will suit her best.[6]

In the 1898 edition of the play, and thus perhaps in the première as well, Mélisande's "frightful" line (in reply to Pelléas's request that she lean forward so that he could see her with unbound hair) "Je suis affreuse ainsi... " was replaced by "Je n'ose pas... " (p. 71). The offending song, "Mes longs cheveux descendent" (sung in Act III), was replaced by "Les trois soeurs aveugles," which was printed in the March 1893 issue of *La Société nouvelle*.[7] This poem, with its images of blindness, lamps, and a tower, was consistent with the symbolism of the play, and it became the definitive substitution. A month after the first performance, its musical setting, composed for the première by Gabriel Fabre, was published under the title "Pelléas et Mélisande (chanson chantée au 3ᵉ acte)."[8] In the 1898 edition of the play the substitute song (with one slight textual change) replaced the original.[9]

Other changes, including cuts, may well have been made for the first performance. Maeterlinck's letter of 22 February 1893 indicated both his faith in Lugné-Poe and his willingness to consider any changes that the trusted man of the theater might recommend: "If anything else displeases you during the rehearsals, please let me know. You have fathomed the work so well that you can no longer be mistaken, and at the moment you see it more clearly than I do."[10] Thus it seems probable that various features of the 1898 revision, and not only the two specified in Maeterlinck's letter to Lugné-Poe, had their origins in the 1893 production.

Maeterlinck's revisions of 1898, although numerous, consist almost entirely of minute changes, cuts, and additions, in each case rarely involving more than three or four words of text. The one major alteration was the replacement of Mélisande's Act III song. The most common revision involves the elimination of some of the immediate repetitions, often of short exclamatory phrases, which are such a common feature of the play. Thus Mélisande's "Ne me touchez pas! ne me touchez pas! ou je me jette à l'eau!... " (1892, p. 17) became in 1898 "Ne me touchez pas! ou je me jette à l'eau!... " (1898, p. 13), and her "Je suis perdue!... perdue!... Oh! oh! perdue ici... " (1892, p. 18) was reduced to "Je suis perdue!... perdue ici... " (1898, p. 15). Some nonadjacent word and phrase repetitions were also eliminated, as in the following exchange (1892, p. 32):

Pelléas: Il aura mauvaise mer cette nuit...

Mélisande: Pourquoi s'en va-t-il cette nuit?...

In the 1898 revision (p. 29), the words "cette nuit" were struck from Mélisande's question.

Elsewhere repetitiousness was reduced by the excision of the short lines in which one character echoes another. For example, in 1892 Golaud tells Mélisande that she must try to find her lost ring (p. 53):

Golaud: Il faut aller la chercher tout de suite.

Mélisande: Je dois aller la chercher tout de suite?

Golaud: Oui.

Mélisande: Maintenant?—tout de suite?—dans l'obscurité?

Golaud: Maintenant, tout de suite, dans l'obscurité. Il faut aller la chercher tout de suite. J'aimerais mieux avoir perdu tout ce que j'ai plutôt que d'avoir perdu cette bague.

In the revision (1898, p. 50), this dialogue was considerably trimmed:

Golaud: Il faut aller la chercher tout de suite.

Mélisande: Maintenant?—tout de suite?—dans l'obscurité?

Golaud: Oui. J'aimerais mieux avoir perdu tout ce que j'ai plutôt que d'avoir perdu cette bague.

Other revisions involved the replacement of a word or phrase with another of identical or similar meaning. More important, however, were the additions which clarified lines that otherwise contained some element of ambiguity. In each of the following examples the italicized words represent the 1898 additions: "Voyez, voyez, j'ai les mains pleines *de fleurs et de feuillages*" (1892, p. 33; 1898, p. 30); "On se trompe toujours lorsqu'on ne ferme pas les yeux *pour pardonner ou pour mieux regarder en soi-même*" (1892, p. 25; 1898, p. 22); and "...les vieillards ont besoin de toucher quelquefois de leurs lèvres, le front d'une femme ou la joue d'un enfant, pour croire encore à la fraîcheur de la vie et éloigner un moment les menaces *de la mort*" (1892, p. 108; 1898, p. 108). In terms of the symbolist aesthetic, this loss of ambiguity does not necessarily represent an artistic gain, and one may well prefer the more suggestive original versions.

The revisions of 1902 were, like those of 1898, mostly minor adjustments of the text, and they fall into the same categories. A striking example, in which Maeterlinck eliminated lines which he evidently felt to be unnecessary or redundant, occurs at the crucial moment in the drama when Pelléas confesses his love for Mélisande (the cut line is bracketed): "Tu ne sais pas pourquoi il faut que je m'éloigne... [Tu ne sais pas que c'est parce que...] *(Il l'embrasse brusquement.)* Je t'aime... " (1892, pp. 119-20; 1902, p. 85). Elsewhere, words or sentences were substituted or added, as in the following exchange between Golaud and Arkel (1892, p. 110; 1902, p. 77). Golaud's added question (italicized) provokes a response from Arkel, whereas the latter's observation was unsolicited in the original version:

> *Golaud:* Voyez-vous ces grands yeux?—On dirait qu'ils sont fiers d'être *purs* [1892: riches]... *Voudriez-vous me dire ce que vous y voyez?...*
>
> *Arkel:* Je n'y vois qu'une grande innocence...

Another addition, like several in the 1898 revision, defined an originally open-ended statement by the physician: "C'est la lutte de la mère contre *la mort...* " (1892, p. 155; 1902, p. 111).

Some passages were rewritten to alter the mood. In Act V, scene 2, Golaud's "Voulez-vous vous éloigner un instant, s'il vous plaît, s'il vous plaît..." (1892, p. 148) became "Voulez-vous vous éloigner un instant, mes pauvres amis... " (1902, p. 104), and his protest "Ce n'est pas ma faute... Ce n'est pas ma faute!" (1892, p. 156) became the observation "Elle ferme les yeux... " (1902, p. 112). The most extensive examples are in the tower scene, where Pelléas's two longest speeches were almost completely rewritten, making him far more ecstatic. For example, his description of Mélisande's hair, "Ils vivent comme des oiseaux dans mes mains... " (1892, p. 75), was changed to "Ils tressaillent, ils s'agitent, ils palpitent dans mes mains comme des oiseaux d'or" (1902, p. 52). In addition, several lines were cut, including the one over which Maeterlinck expressed such concern in his 1893 letter to Lugné-Poe. Not satisfied with the change from "Je suis affreuse ainsi" to "Je n'ose pas," he suppressed the line altogether in 1902.

Debussy's Adaptation of the Play

Debussy completed the first version of his opera in August 1895, when the only available printed text was the original edition of 1892. Although he had attended the first performance of the play (17 May 1893), his setting ignored the changes made for that production: he retained the original song from the tower ("Mes longs cheveux descendent") and kept the original reading of Mélisande's "Je suis affreuse ainsi." This reliance on the printed word accords with his claim, expressed in both an interview and an article, that his desire to compose *Pelléas* came from reading it, not from seeing it in the theater.[11] He owned No. 11 of the twenty-five copies of the first edition printed on Hollande Van Gelder paper.[12] This copy is completely unmarked. It is not known whether he also had a working copy, in which he could have jotted down musical ideas or marked cuts or changes in the text.[13]

Debussy's original intention was apparently to set the play exactly as it was printed. In the earliest surviving complete draft of the first scene he composed (the September–October 1893 draft of Act IV, scene 4), he set every word of the original Maeterlinck text except two: he replaced the word "songe" with its synonym "pense" in Mélisande's line "Je pleure toujours lorsque je songe à toi... ", and he substituted "voyons" for "savons" in Pelléas's "Il restera là tant qu'il croira que nous ne savons pas...."[14] Both changes may have been acidental, the result of Debussy's apparent reliance on knowing the text by heart. In his sketch drafts he typically wrote the vocal parts without their texts. This evident dependence on memory resulted, however, in occasional instances of word (usually synonym) substitution when he later transformed the sketch into a short score, in which the text was completely written out. In such cases the original text was usually restored at some later stage. (This process will be discussed in greater detail below.)

The possibility of making cuts in the play was first raised during Debussy's meeting with Maeterlinck in November 1893, when, as Debussy reported in a letter to Ernest Chausson, Maeterlinck gave him "complete authorization to make cuts, and even indicated some which are very important, *even very useful.*"[15] Maeterlinck evidently did not insist that Debussy adopt the changes which had been made for the Lugné-Poe production. While it is not known what cuts the playwright recommended, they quite possibly included the four scenes that Debussy never set. The absence of musical sketches of these scenes, together with the absence of any mention of them in the composer's correspondence concerning *Pelléas,* suggests that his decision to omit them was made before he began work on the music. The contents of the four scenes can be summarized as follows:

Act I, scene 1: At dawn, the maidservants arrive at the gate of the castle to wash the gate, the threshold, and the steps. "There are going to be great happenings!" they exclaim, then ask the porter to open the gate. With great difficulty he opens it, and the maidservants prepare to do their work.

Act II, scene 4: Arkel explains to Pelléas why the latter must postpone his journey and remain in Allemonde: his father's condition seems to be hopeless, and the famine has caused great discontent among the people. His friend Marcellus is dead and "life has graver duties than the visit to a tomb." Pelléas may be weary of his inactive life, but "activity and duty are not found on the highways." Arkel does not forbid him to undertake his journey. He only asks that Pelléas wait a few weeks, perhaps only days, "until we know what must take place..."

Act III, scene 1: Pelléas and Mélisande are alone in a room in the castle; Mélisande is spinning. Golaud has not yet returned from the chase, Yniold has gone to investigate some noise in the corridor, and everybody else seems to be asleep. Yniold knocks on the door and enters. "That is not the way to knock on doors," says Pelléas. "It is as if misfortune had arrived...." Yniold bursts into tears because he has the feeling that

Mélisande will go away. Pelléas directs his attention to the window, through which he sees swans chasing dogs. Yniold then sees his father and runs to greet him. Golaud and Yniold return with a lamp, and the child notices that his uncle and stepmother have both been weeping. "Do not hold the light under their eyes like that," says Golaud.

Act V, scene 1: The women servants are gathered in a lower hall in the castle, waiting to be called upstairs. They discuss the recent, tragic events. An old servant relates how she discovered Golaud and Mélisande huddled together outside the gate. Mélisande, though hardly wounded, was nearly dead, and Golaud had tried to kill himself with his own sword. Mélisande gave birth three days ago and is now on her deathbed. Pelléas was found dead at the bottom of "Blind Man's Well." There is a sudden silence, and they know it is time to go upstairs.

Each of these is the first or last scene of an act, and its omission therefore does not affect continuity within an act. The two scenes involving servants are, despite their formal, symbolic, and narrative functions, extraneous to the central action of the play, and cutting them could have been justified for that reason alone. The two are structural parallels, since they introduce the events that open and close the drama. Debussy evidently preferred to begin with the action that sets the drama in motion (the chance meeting of Golaud and Mélisande, both lost in the forest) and to proceed directly from the opera's climax (Pelléas and Mélisande's mutual declaration of love and Golaud's slaying of Pelléas in Act IV, scene 4) to its denouement (the death of Mélisande in Act V). The opening scene has symbolic value in its presentation of the image of the castle gate, whose closing (in the middle of Act IV, scene 4) interrupts the love duet of Pelléas and Mélisande and marks a turning point beyond which there can be no return. The first scene of Act V is devoid of action, though it does relate what has happened between the preceding and the following scenes. Yet the knowledge that Golaud had thrown Pelléas's body into the well and then had tried to commit suicide is not essential to an understanding of the play's conclusion, though Golaud's wound may help to explain why he refers to himself in Act V as a dying man. Debussy lost little by cutting this scene; doing so eliminated a lull in the action and made the servants' sudden appearance in the final scene more mysterious. Although probably not a prime motivating factor, the omission of the servant scenes also reduced the number of singers by nine—eight maidservants and a porter.[16] Pierre Boulez has suggested that Debussy's elimination of the servant scenes represents a "rejection of all familiarity" and a desire to present "a world endeavouring to be beyond time . . . and ancillary contingence."[17] Indeed these and other cuts made by Debussy seem calculated to eliminate contact between the inhabitants of the castle (the royal family and their physician) and the "external world." In the opera, outsiders are seen but not heard (the beggars in Act II, scene 3, and the servants in Act V) or are heard but not seen (the sailors in Act I, scene 3, and the shepherd in Act IV, scene 3).[18]

The scene between Pelléas and Arkel, another actionless scene, consists of one long speech and a brief exchange. It announces the death of Marcellus and introduces a new reason for Pelléas's desire to leave home—a general restlessness. In the opera we assume that it is still the wish to visit his dying friend that motivates Pelléas's subsequent announcement (in Act III, scene 1) that he plans to leave the next day. Debussy's cut both simplifies the plot and strengthens a character's motivation.

The remaining scene cut by the composer shows Yniold spending time with Pelléas and Mélisande and thus prepares for the final scene of the act, in which Golaud quizzes his son about the relationship between his wife and brother, then forces the child to spy upon them. Debussy, however, may have found the conclusion of this scene, in which Golaud first witnesses their growing affection, too much like the ending of the next scene, where Golaud's interruption of a meeting between Pelléas and Mélisande results in a more intense confrontation. The inclusion of both scenes would justify Golaud's later remark to Pelléas (Act III, scene 3): "This is not the first time I have noticed there might be something between you."[19] Yet Debussy probably considered the repetition unnecessary.

There is truth in Lockspeiser's observation that Debussy's cuts were made "to relieve the libretto of ideas that were too naïvely symbolical and merely hold up the action." However, one scene that Lockspeiser places in this category, Yniold's scene with the sheep (Debussy's Act IV, scene 3), was always considered by Debussy an integral part of the opera. It was not his wish, as Lockspeiser claims, that the scene should be cut. Rather, he accepted the cut with reluctance during the first season of performances at the Opéra-Comique and was apparently delighted when the scene was reinstated for the second season.[20]

Debussy resumed work on *Pelléas* in December of 1893, shortly after his meeting with Maeterlinck. He began with Act I. Just as with Act IV, scene 4, he composed the first scene (Maeterlinck's scene 2) by setting every word of Maeterlinck's text. In sharp contrast, he reduced the second, which opens with three rather long speeches, by about 40 percent. On the basis of surviving documents, it cannot be determined when the cuts were made. Part of the scene has survived in a sketch-draft, in which Geneviève's opening speech already observes the same three cuts found in the final version.

A scene-by-scene comparison of Debussy's final libretto with Maeterlinck's play shows that only one scene (Act I, scene 1) contains no cuts at all and that only one other (Act III, scene 1) was barely trimmed—by three words. At the other extreme, Act III, scene 3, was pruned to one-third of its original length. A study of the manuscripts reveals that the process of making cuts seems to have been gradual, with further trimming introduced in the course of each successive revision.

Text Revisions in Act IV, Scene 4

Debussy's successive trimmings can best be illustrated by Act IV, scene 4, which exists in more surviving drafts than any other scene. The sources are:[21]

1. Meyer MS (Coll. André Meyer, Paris): short-score sketch of the latter two-thirds of the scene (September–October 1893).
2. Legouix MS (former owner, Robert Legouix: Robert Owen Lehman Collection, on deposit in The Pierpont Morgan Library): short score (September–October 1893); the central pages of this draft were removed and incorporated into the Bréval MS.
3. Bréval MS (former owner, Lucienne Bréval: Paris, Bibliothèque Nationale, Ms. 1206): short score (May 1895); fols. 6–11 taken from Legouix MS.
4. NEC MS (formerly Boston, New England Conservatory of Music: Frederick R. Koch Foundation Collection, on deposit in The Pierpont Morgan Library): short score (January 1900–September 1901).
5. Prudhomme MS (Prudhomme deposit, Bibliothèque Nationale, Ms. 17683): vocal score, used by the engraver (late 1901?).
6. Périer proofs (Prudhomme deposit, Bibliothèque Nationale, Rés. Vma. 237): corrected proofs of vocal score, with additional annotations by Jean Périer, the first Pelléas.
7. Manuscript full score (Bibliothèque Nationale, Mss. 961–65: text written by copyist in Act IV, fols. 55–87 (beginning of scene 4 to fig. 51) and in almost all of Act V (early 1902?).
8. Vocal score (Fromont, Paris, May 1902): first edition.
9. Full score (Fromont, Paris, August 1904): first edition. Several sets of corrected proofs have also survived, but they will not be discussed here.

As noted above, the September–October 1893 score (the earliest layer of the Legouix MS and of the "Legouix" folios of the Bréval MS) was essentially a complete setting of the scene as printed in the first edition of Maeterlinck's play. The first cuts are already evident in the revisions of this draft, notated in the Legouix MS on the blank pages facing the original version, which was written on rectos only. Three cuts were introduced at this stage, affecting the dialogue at a point in the scene shortly after Golaud's presence has been discovered (the cuts are bracketed):

> *Pelléas:* Il ne sait pas que nous l'avons vu... Ne bouge pas; ne tourne pas la tête... Il se précipiterait... [Il restera là tant qu'il croira que nous ne savons pas...] Il nous observe... Il est encore immobile... Va-t'en, va-t'en tout de suite par ici... Je l'attendrai... Je l'arrêterai...
> *Mélisande:* Non, [non,] non!...
> *Pelléas:* Va-t'en! [va-t'en!] Il a tout vu!... Il nous tuera!...

The cut sentence is the longest in the speech and represents Pelléas's rational appraisal of the situation. Without it, his speech becomes a string of short, breathless and spontaneous utterances, a far more dramatic response to the tense circumstance. The two short cuts that follow also contribute to the drama by eliminating repetitions and hastening the pace of the dialogue.

The next stage of composition is represented by the Bréval MS, another short score (dated May 1895); its central folios were taken from the Legouix MS, and the rest was newly written, mostly on the basis of the revisions entered in the earlier manuscript. In writing out the Bréval MS, Debussy introduced further revisions, including two textual cuts. One of them also contributed to the tightening and hastening of the dialogue: Pelléas's exclamation, "Il vient! il vient!... Ta bouche!... Ta bouche!... ", which closely follows the previous example, was shortened by cutting the repetition of "Il vient." The second cut eliminated a substantial portion of the dialogue which, in the play, occurs between Mélisande's "Si, si; je suis heureuse, mais je suis triste... " and Pelléas's "Quel est ce bruit?" The cut lines are:

> *Pelléas:* On est triste, souvent, quand on s'aime...
> *Mélisande:* Je pleure toujours lorsque je pense à toi...
> *Pelléas:* Moi aussi... moi aussi, Mélisande... Je suis tout près de toi; je pleure de joie et cependant... (*Il l'embrasse encore.*) Tu es étrange quand je t'embrasse ainsi... Tu es si belle qu'on dirait que tu vas mourir...
> *Mélisande:* Toi aussi...
> *Pelléas:* Voilà, voilà... Nous ne faisons pas ce que nous voulons... Je ne t'aimais pas la première fois que je t'ai vue...
> *Mélisande:* Moi non plus... moi non plus... J'avais peur...
> *Pelléas:* Je ne pouvais pas admettre tes yeux... Je voulais m'en aller tout de suite... et puis...
> *Mélisande:* Moi, je ne voulais pas venir... Je ne sais pas encore pourquoi, j'avais peur de venir...
> *Pelléas:* Il y a tant de choses qu'on ne saura jamais... Nous attendons toujours; et puis...

Through this cut, Mélisande's expression of emotional turmoil ("I am happy, but I am sad") was left unexplored, as further discussion was forestalled by the sound of the closing gate, which turned the lovers' attention to other matters. The omitted lines explore Mélisande's emotions and cast a troubling doubt on the nature of her feelings towards Pelléas. The latter is all too ready to interpret her weeping as tears of joy, an interpretation she neither confirms nor denies. In fact, her comments show that she lies to Pelléas as readily as she lied to Golaud. When Pelléas says that he did not love her the first time that he saw her, she quickly agrees, "Neither did I... neither did I... ". This directly contradicts her answer earlier in the scene, when he had asked: "Depuis quand m'aimes-tu?", to which she replied, "Depuis toujours... Depuis que je t'ai vu...." This answer had made Pelléas ecstatic, but after expressing his joy he could not help but wonder if she was lying a little, just to make him smile. In fact, he had guessed the truth, though she quickly denied it, saying: "No ... I lie only to your brother." These exchanges make it clear that Mélisande says just what she thinks others want to hear. Her motive is not to deceive but rather to be loved (or, as Virgil Thomson put it, "to avoid not being loved.")[22] Nowhere in the play is this aspect of her personality more apparent, and

Debussy may have wanted to suppress this moment of unintentional self-revelation in order to preserve her qualities of mystery and innocence. Other goals are also served by this cut. It accelerates the action and, by removing discussion of the lovers' past relationship, keeps the focus on the present. It also eliminates some comments made by Pelléas which Debussy may have felt were too obviously fatalistic: "We do not do what we wish... "; "There are so many things one never knows... We are ever waiting... "; and "You are so beautiful that one would think you were about to die... ". The last observation is as ominously prophetic of the opera's tragic outcome as one made earlier by Pelléas's father (reported in Act IV, scene 1): that his son had "the grave and friendly look of those who will not live long."

In revising the Bréval MS, Debussy introduced four further cuts, in each case eliminating the immediate repetition of a word or short phrase. Such eliminations were continued in the NEC MS, chronologically the next surviving draft of the scene. By the time Debussy copied out this manuscript, six more phrases had been trimmed in this fashion. Two further cuts were made in a subsequent revision of the NEC MS. The more significant is the line in Pelléas's opening monolgue—"Mon père est hors de danger; et je n'ai plus de quoi me mentir à moi-même... " ("My father is out of danger; and I have no more reason to lie to myself... ")—which follows "Je vais lui dire que je vais fuir... " ("I am going to tell her that I shall flee... "). The line verbalizes Pelléas's realization that it was really his love for Mélisande and not his concern for his father that had been keeping him in the castle. Debussy may have regarded it as an unnecessary aside and, moreover, an inconsistency in tone, displaying a moment of rationality in the midst of a highly emotional outpouring. Furthermore, the line represents a break from what is otherwise a single-minded preoccupation with his feelings toward Mélisande.[23] The remaining cut removed a single word, the initial exclamation in Pelléas's first statement of "Oh! comme tu dis cela!... " ("Oh! how you say that!... "). Since Pelléas has two consecutive speeches that begin with this line, Debussy may have made the minute change in order to distinguish the two and save the exclamation for the second speech. When copying the manuscript vocal score, he cut the first statement altogether, resulting in an even greater saving.

In addition to the cuts that he progressively introduced at every stage of revision, he also made some changes in the text, usually synonym substitutions. As mentioned above, an evident reliance on his memorization of the text sometimes led to unintentional substitutions. Instances are found at every stage of composition, and usually the mistake was corrected at a later point. Thus, in revising the Bréval MS, he wrote "au bout du jardin" when he meant "au fond du jardin"; he corrected the slip in the NEC MS. The Bréval MS also had "Je n'ai plus de courage!" instead of Maeterlinck's "Je n'ai pas de courage!"; this error too was corrected in the NEC MS. But the NEC MS was also the place where further such errors were introduced. For example, in the line "Tu ne songes pas à moi en ce moment" the word "songes" was changed to the synonymous "penses"; the mistake was carried over into the manuscript vocal score but was corrected at the proof stage. Another word change was introduced in the proofs: while the manuscript vocal score followed Maeterlinck in having Pelléas exclaim "Et maintenant je t'ai trouvée!... Je t'ai trouvée!... ", the proofs were printed "Et maintenant je t'ai trouvée!... je *l'ai* trouvée!... " ("I have found *it*... ", i.e., the beauty he sought). Whether this substitution was accidental or a late effort to eliminate the repetition of a phrase, it was retained in all published scores of the opera.

In scenes other than Act IV, scene 4, some word substitutions can be attributed to confusion with a nearby line. For example, in Act II, scene 1, Pelléas says of Mélisande's lost ring: "nous la retrouverons peut-être. Ou bien nous en trouverons une autre... "; in the NEC MS, Debussy, probably inadvertently, replaced "trouverons" with "retrouverons", repeating that word from the previous line. Even though the substitution does not really make sense, it crept into all of the published scores.

Some changes, though, were obviously intentional, especially in places where Debussy deliberately altered his text to incorporate features of Maeterlinck's 1898 revisions. Two instances occur in the NEC MS draft of Act IV, scene 4. Mélisande's "Nous sommes encore venus ici... " became "Nous sommes venus ici il y a bien longtemps,"[24] and Pelléas's "C'est la dernière fois que je te vois peut-être... " was inverted to become "C'est peut-être la dernière fois que je te vois... ". These examples not only prove that Debussy consulted Maeterlinck's 1898 revisions; they also confirm other evidence that the folios on which these changes appear were written in or after 1898.

Elsewhere in the opera there are other instances of Debussy's adoption of readings from Maeterlinck's 1898 edition. As noted above, at the end of Act I, scene 3, Maeterlinck had added the phrase "de fleurs et de feuillages" to Mélisande's line "Voyez, voyez, j'ai les mains pleines... ". Debussy originally followed Maeterlinck's first edition, but he added the words "de fleurs" in the proofs of the vocal score. He might have included the rest of the phrase had he had more room before Pelléas's reply; while the addition of the entire phrase would have required extensive re-engraving, the partial addition was easily inserted. He also incorporated another 1898 expansion noted above, the addition of the phrase "de la mort" to Arkel's opening speech in Act IV, scene 2, which originally ended "éloigner un instant les menaces... ". He adopted this addition in a revision of the NEC MS, adding the extra notes in the voice part (though neglecting to write in the words).

In Act V Debussy even adjusted his text to incorporate readings from Maeterlinck's second revision, which was not published until 1902, shortly before the opera's première. As noted above, Golaud's line "Voulez-vous vous éloigner un instant, s'il vous plaît, s'il vous plaît... " was changed to "Voulez-vous vous éloigner un instant, mes pauvres amis... ". Also, a synonym substitution was made in Arkel's line "Ne parlez pas trop haut... ", with "haut" changed to "fort". In both cases, the new reading appears in the manuscript vocal score (Bibliothèque Nationale, Ms. 17686). Since the proofs of the vocal score were available for the opera's rehearsals (which began in January 1902), Debussy must have had access to Maeterlinck's second revision in 1901, before its publication. At that time the two were still friendly, since Maeterlinck's mistress, Georgette Leblanc, was being considered for the role of Mélisande; after the part was given to Mary Garden (the announcement was made at the end of December 1901), they were no longer on speaking terms.

Since some of Debussy's textual changes turn out to be adoptions of Maeterlinck's published revisions, the same could be true of those short cuts which eliminated text repetitions—the most common type of cut made by both playwright and composer. However, of the thirteen such cuts made by Debussy in Act IV, scene 4, only two are the same as those made by the playwright. Moreover, the majority were made before the publication in 1898 of Maeterlinck's first revision. This suggests that the composer was acting independently, even though both he and Maeterlinck may have been applying the same principle in trimming the text. (Could this have been one of the subjects of conversation during their November 1893 meeting?) Debussy may also have had a musical motivation for these cuts: a desire to avoid excessive repetition or sequence in the vocal melody.

Although Debussy's treatment of the play consisted almost exclusively of cuts and minor changes, there were a few instances where he made additions to the text. Two minute ones in Act IV, scene 4 were musically motivated. At the end of the scene, Pelléas was given an extra repetition of the word "donne": Debussy wanted Pelléas and Mélisande to sing together (in octaves) at this climactic moment and needed the repetition to balance Mélisande's three statements of the word "toute". This addition first appears as a revision in the Bréval MS. In the same manuscript, Debussy also added an expression of despair, the single syllable "ah," as the final utterance of Mélisande, following her line "Je n'ai pas de courage!... ".

The preceding, detailed description of Debussy's textual modifications in Act IV, scene 4 has relied almost exclusively on speculation along textual lines in its attempt to explain the possible motivations for the changes. Musical considerations must also have been a factor in these decisions, but they are virtually impossible to appraise except in the context of a detailed musical analysis of each draft of the scene. Furthermore, Debussy would probably have been reluctant to admit to musical motivations for his textual changes, that is, beyond the necessity of trimming a full-length play in order to make an opera of it. Music in opera simply takes additional time, no matter how scrupulously a composer may attempt to preserve the literary flow of the text. And, indeed, it was Debussy's intention scrupulously to preserve that flow. In his critical writings he repeatedly protested at the application of symphonic form and development to dramatic action and claimed that he never allowed the music in *Pelléas* "to precipitate or retard the changing feeling or passions of [the] characters for technical convenience. It stands aside as soon as it can, leaving them the freedom of their gestures, their utterances—their joy or their sorrow."[25] Although the preceding discussion has made much of the discreet cuts and minute changes which the composer permitted himself, his essential fidelity to his text source is a confirmation of his adherence to his aesthetic principles.

Text Revisions in Other Scenes

Throughout the opera there are instances of textual modifications similar to those in Act IV, scene 4, namely cuts that reduce repetitiveness, modify characterizations, and alleviate overt fatalism and symbolism, as well as changes that alter the wording without substantially altering the meaning. Selected examples drawn from other scenes will amplify some of these categories and introduce several others. The need to shorten the play to manageable, operatic proportions is reflected not only in the wholesale omission of four scenes, but also in the tendency to trim long, often static, speeches so as to abridge lengthy descriptions or excise irrelevant or redundant information. Thus Pelléas's description of the grotto (Act II, scene 3) and Golaud's of the vaults beneath the castle (Act III, scene 2) were greatly cut, since Debussy was able to use musical evocations rather than extensive verbal imagery to create the proper moods. Geneviève's opening speech in Act I, scene 2, her reading of Golaud's letter, was trimmed by about 30 percent and offers a good example of the informational cut. Debussy removed part of Golaud's account of his discovery of Mélisande (the fact that her gold crown fell into the water and that her torn clothes were like those of a princess, information that is peripheral to his account and already known to the audience), and he also cut Golaud's reasons for fearing Arkel's reaction (that his wedding spoiled a political marriage the king had arranged, information which Arkel will supply in his response to the letter). Later in the scene, however, a small textual addition was required to compensate for information lost as a result of a previous cut: Arkel's statement, "Nous ne savons pas ce que ce retour nous prépare," was made somewhat unclear because Debussy had cut Pelléas's reference to Golaud's return from his preceding speech; therefore, in the interest of clarity, Arkel's line was amended by replacing "ce retour" with "le retour de ton frère." In another instance, a problem with lost information led to slightly more substantial rewriting as Debussy cut, rearranged, and paraphrased a portion of text, though without substantially altering its meaning. The passage, in Act III, scene 3, is part of Golaud's admonition to Pelléas:

> Maeterlinck's text: Mélisande est très jeune et très impressionnable; et il faut qu'on la ménage d'autant plus qu'elle est peut-être enceinte en ce moment... Elle est très délicate; à peine femme; et la moindre émotion pourrait amener un malheur.

> Debussy's text: Elle est très délicate, et il faut qu'on la ménage d'autant plus qu'elle sera peut-être bientôt mère, et la moindre émotion pourrait amener un malheur.

The composer's version evolved in a somewhat roundabout way. He originally cut the entire first sentence of the Maeterlinck text and retained only the second. Later, he must have realized that he needed the reference to Mélisande's pregnancy to prepare the audience for the birth of her daughter in Act V. He then paraphrased the second half of that cut sentence, perhaps to avoid using the word "enceinte" ("pregnant"), and inserted the paraphrase in place of "à peine femme."

In other instances, as at the end of Act IV, scene 1, the elimination of key information altered the sense of a scene. In the play, Pelléas finally identifies the talking he hears behind the door (talking which had made him uneasy and reluctant to speak) as that of strangers who had come to the castle that morning. Debussy's removal of this explanation constitutes another elimination of intruders from the external world and leaves the identity of the talker(s) a mystery, though the musical setting, with its prominent use of the Golaud motive, makes it clear that it is his brother that Pelléas fears.

The expunging of blatantly fatalistic lines and symbolic episodes is also evident throughout the opera. Removed, for example, were such lines as "Il a fait ce qu'il devait probablement faire" (Act I, scene 2), "il faut prendre les choses comme elles sont" (Act II, scene 2), and "Ce matin cependant j'avais le pressentiment que cette journée finirait mal. J'ai depuis quelque temps un bruit de malheur dans les oreilles... " (Act IV, scene 1). A purely symbolic incident was also cut from the end of Act III, scene 3: Pelléas and Golaud observe herds being led to the city, and the latter comments that they cry like lost children, as if they already smelled the butcher. Debussy originally set these lines (NEC MS) but later removed this symbolic intrusion of the external world, probably fearing that the incident resembled too closely Yniold's scene with the sheep (Act IV, scene 3). Similar impulses may also have prompted the suppression of a series of lines in Act III, scene 4, in which Golaud gratuitously directs Yniold's attention to some beggars who are unable to light a fire in the wet forest, then to an old gardener who cannot lift a heavy tree which the wind had blown across the road. Golaud concludes fatalistically: "Il n'y a rien à faire à tout cela... ". Not only did this symbolic digression interrupt the action of the scene; the gardener's dilemma also too obviously anticipated Yniold's own inability (in Act IV, scene 3) to lift a heavy rock under which his ball has rolled. Moreover, Debussy seemed to wish to play down the fact that there was a famine in the kingdom (a concern of the external world); though the beggars figure prominently in Act II, scene 3, and Golaud mentions in Act IV, scene 2 that the body of another peasant who had died of starvation has been found by the sea, reference to the beggars was removed not only here, in Act III, scene 4, but also by the omission of Maeterlinck's Act II, scene 4, and Act V, scene 1.

Debussy also introduced some small changes which altered the pace or character of the language. For example, in Arkel's first speech in Act I, scene 2, the conjunction "et" was twice removed; in the first instance Debussy preferred to run the two phrases together, while in the second he broke the continuity within the speech by replacing the conjunction with a rest. Alterations of Maeterlinck's punctuation sometimes changed the meaning or tone of certain lines, as in two instances where Debussy turned questions into exclamations: Mélisande's "Vous êtes un géant!" in Act I, scene 1, and Pelléas's "Il est tombé!" in Act II, scene 1. In both cases the short score lacks punctuation and the vocal scores provide exclamation marks. (The published full scores also omit punctuation here.) As a rule, Debussy was far from meticulous about preserving Maeterlinck's punctuation and often left it out entirely. Such orthographic details seem not to have interested him; yet he must have been aware of his carelessness in this respect, because in the NEC MS draft of Act III he went systematically through the score, supplying the missing punctuation with a black pencil.

Also affecting the character of the dialogue were a few instances where, contrary to his common practice of curtailing repetitiousness, Debussy introduced text repetitions, perhaps responding to a musical impulse for some element of repetition, sequence, or parallelism in the vocal line. For example, Mélisande's line in Act II, scene 2, "Vous savez... vous savez bien... " was changed to produce an exact text repetition ("Vous savez bien... vous savez bien... ") and a musical parallelism. In Act IV, scene 2, during Golaud's tirade against Mélisande, his lines "Allez-vous-en! Votre chair me dégoûte!... " were made into a symmetrical unit by the repetition of the first exclamation: "Allez-vous-en! Votre chair me dégoûte!... Allez-vous-en!" In Act V a similar change was made in Golaud's response to the entrance of the servants: in his "Pourquoi venez-vous ici?—Personne ne vous a demandées... Que venez-vous faire ici?" the first question was replaced by a repetition of the second. Another instance occurs in Act II, scene 2, where Debussy took two similar (and similar sounding) lines in a character's consecutive speeches and made them the same. While Maeterlinck had Mélisande say "Je suis malade aussi...", then "Je suis malade ici...", Debussy altered the first line to conform with the second. Even if this change was accidental, it was nevertheless retained in the published scores.

A final category of alteration in the libretto concerns the stage settings of the various scenes. Debussy originally adopted those specified by Maeterlinck, but then made some changes, probably in consultation with Albert Carré, the producer of the opera's première at the Opéra-Comique. The setting of Act I, scene 2 was changed from Maeterlinck's "Une salle dans le château" to "Un appartement dans le château," and Act V from "Un appartement dans le château" to "Une chambre dans le château." In the case of Act IV, however, the changes had more than a scenic impact and resulted in both textual and musical differences. In Maeterlinck's play, Act IV requires four different sets, one for each scene: "Un corridor dans le château," "Un appartement dans le château," "Une terrasse du château," and "Une fontaine dans le parc." Debussy's libretto only calls for two sets, the "appartement" for scenes 1–2 and the "fontaine" for scenes 3–4, thus simplifying the set changes considerably. The decision to move scene 1 from a corridor to a room appears to have influenced the ending of that scene. In a preliminary version, scene 1 (still set in the corridor) closed with an additional line, taken from Maeterlinck: Pelléas said "Allons-nous-en", and a stage direction indicated that he and Mélisande were to exit separately. Following the interlude, scene 2 opened in a new setting, with the stage direction "Arkel and Mélisande are discovered." In a subsequent revision, with both scenes sharing the same set, the final line and instruction to exit were removed from scene 1, and scene 2 opened with the direction "Arkel enters," as Debussy evidently intended either having Mélisande remain on stage during the interlude or lowering the curtain after scene 1 and having her appear onstage as it rose for scene 2. In any case, when backstage limitations at the Opéra-Comique forced him to expand the interludes in order to give the scene-shifters more time, the reduction in set changes meant that only one interlude expansion was required in this act.[26]

In addition to the changes Debussy initiated, others were imposed upon him in the aftermath of the riotous public dress rehearsal, two days before the première. Henry Roujon, Director of Fine Arts, declared Act III, scene 4 (the scene in which Golaud interrogates Yniold and forces him to spy on his uncle and stepmother) unacceptable in a state-supported theater.[27] Rather than suppress the scene, Debussy agreed to make certain cuts in it. One of them, which contained the following dialogue, was never restored to the score:

Yniold: Non, petit père.
Golaud: Et... et le lit? Sont-ils près du lit?
Yniold: Le lit, petit père? Je ne vois pas le lit.
Golaud: Plus bas; ils t'entendraient.

The manuscript full score indicates that this cut originally included Golaud's preceding question: "Sont-ils près l'un de l'autre?" The passage was printed in the original edition of the vocal score but was subsequently excised. Although introduced to satisfy prudish objections, this cut was probably retained because it strengthened musical and dramatic values: the passage in question brings the music and action to a halt, while its omission allows momentum to build steadily to the end of the scene. Similar motivations may have prompted the suppression of Golaud's original closing line: "Nous allons voir ce qui est arrivé." This line was likewise never reinstated.

Three other cuts in this scene were at one time indicated in the manuscript full score (which served as the conductor's score until the 1904 publication of the full score); they too were probably made in response to the audience reaction at the public dress rehearsal, but, unlike the preceding two examples, they were subsequently restored:

> *Golaud:* Mais pourquoi ne veulent-ils pas que la porte soit ouverte? Voyons, réponds-moi à la fin! non, non, n'ouvre pas la bouche pour pleurer. Je ne suis pas fâché.
> . . . .
> *Golaud:* Ils s'embrassent quelquefois? Non?...
> *Yniold:* Qu'ils s'embrassent, petit père? Non, non. Ah! si, petit père, si, une fois... une fois qu'il pleuvait...
> *Golaud:* Ils se sont embrassés? Mais comment, comment, se sont-ils embrassés?
> *Yniold:* Comme ça, petit père, comme ça. Ah! ah! votre barbe, petit père!... Elle pique, elle pique! Elle devient toute grise, petit père, et vos cheveux aussi, tout gris, tout gris.
> . . . .
> *Golaud:* Non, non, mon enfant; restons encore un peu dans l'ombre... On ne sait pas, on ne sait pas encore... Je crois que Pelléas est fou...
> *Yniold:* Non, petit père, il n'est pas fou, mais il est très bon.
> *Golaud:* Veux-tu voir petite mère?
> *Yniold:* Oui, oui, je veux la voir!

Two further short cuts were indicated in the first scene of the same act, but they too were restored before the engraving of the full score:

> *Pelléas:* Tes cheveux sont autour des branches... Ils se sont accrochés dans l'obscurité... Attends! attends!... Il fait noir.
> . . . .
> *Golaud:* Quels enfants!... Quels enfants!...

Were these cuts made because the dress rehearsal audience laughed at Mélisande's hair getting caught in the tree and at Golaud's ironic aside at the end of the scene? Audience laughter was evidently the reason for a small but significant text change in Act IV, scene 2, which was entered in the manuscript full score: Mélisande's "je ne suis pas heureuse... " was changed to "je suis si malheureuse... ". Although Mary Garden apparently retained this altered version of the line in her subsequent performances of the role, the substitution was never incorporated into the published scores.[28] Curiously, two of Golaud's lines, which the current Durand vocal score labels as being traditionally cut at the Opéra-Comique—"Evitez-la autant que possible; mais sans affectation, d'ailleurs, sans affectation... ", part of his warning to Pelléas at the end of Act III, scene 3, and "Simplement parce que c'est l'usage; simplement parce que c'est l'usage", his final utterance in Act IV, scene 2— were never marked in the manuscript full score, suggesting that these two cuts were probably not instituted during the first season of performances.

It is difficult to summarize the long and complicated path that led from play to libretto. As his starting point, Debussy used the original 1892 edition of Maeterlinck's play, ignoring the changes the playwright had made for the stage première of 17 May 1893, which the composer attended. Though his decision to omit four scenes seems to have been made before he began work on their music, he was initially very faithful to the published text. His earliest versions of the first two scenes composed (Act IV, scene 4, and Act I, scene 1) set virtually every word of text, but as he proceeded with the composition and subsequent revision of his score, he took greater license with the play, having secured the playwright's authorization to do so. The process of adapting the play was a continuous one, with changes introduced in each new draft. The adaptation consisted chiefly of making cuts; few word changes and very few additions were introduced. The trimming process was almost always progressive; once made, cuts were rarely restored. Debussy tended to pare down long speeches, especially when they contained irrelevant or redundant information or included lengthy descriptions that were better evoked musically. He also seems to have deleted some lines and incidents because they were too obviously fatalistic or symbolic. Dialogue, especially when it tended to hold up the action in the longer scenes (such as Act III, scene 4, or Act IV, scene 4), was also sometimes curtailed. Some of his alterations resemble the changes that Maeterlinck himself made in his revisions of the play, published in 1898 and 1902. The most common of such changes was the small cut eliminating immediate repetitions of words or phrases. Another was the replacement of words or phrases with others that were nearly synonymous. Although some of Debussy's changes were made to conform with Maeterlinck's revisions of the play, most were his own. Some of these word changes appear to have been mere slips of memory on the composer's part; a number of these errors nevertheless remained uncorrected and were incorporated into the published scores.

Although he had authorized Debussy to make cuts in his play, and had even suggested some, Maeterlinck expressed extreme displeasure with the composer's adaptation in a letter to *Le Figaro* written on 13 April 1902 and published the next day. Though the thrust of the letter was his objection to the assignment of the part of Mélisande to Mary Garden rather than his mistress, he took the opportunity to attack the libretto as well, charging that Debussy had treated his play like "conquered territory": he accused him of imposing "arbitrary and absurd cuts" which made the work "incomprehensible" and of retaining material that Maeterlinck intended to suppress or improve, as he had done in his recent revision of the play. Given the special circumstances of this letter, it is hard to regard these criticisms as anything other than a manufactured charge. On the other hand, Maeterlinck may well have had second thoughts about having given Debussy permission to make any cuts he wished. In 1899, when Paul Dukas expressed interest in making an opera of his play *Ariane et Barbe-Bleue,* Maeterlinck let it be known that the play had to be set as it was or not at all (though he eventually accepted the modifications Dukas suggested).[29]

In an interview with Charles Henry Meltzer in 1908, Debussy commented on the subject of musical length and spoke of *Pelléas*:

> I am not quite sure that people want any more long works. I am not greatly in sympathy with the huge in music. In view of modern intellectual processes, operas in five acts are tedious. I don't mind owning that I think my own 'Pelléas et Mélisande' far too long. In which act? Oh, it is too diffuse generally. But that is the fault of the story.[30]

A desire to reduce the play's diffuseness may indeed have been the chief motivation behind his progressive trimming of the text, but other factors unexpectedly complicated the shaping of the libretto, most notably the playwright's concurrent revisions of his play, the exigencies of the opera house and Debussy's own occasional carelessness. All of these factors contributed to the complex, and at times "impressionistic," process through which Maeterlinck's symbolist play became Debussy's only completed opera.

7

Manuscripts, Proofs, and Editions

Preliminary or Sketch Draft (Meyer MS)

The Meyer MS is unique among the extant manuscripts of *Pelléas* in representing the earliest surviving stage of composition—the rough, hastily written preliminary or sketch draft of the music, in which Debussy fixed his ideas using the minimum of notational symbols that would later permit him to copy out a short score in full detail.[1] The notation is therefore very incomplete. With few exceptions, the vocal lines are not identified by either the name of the character singing or the words sung.[2] Only in a few spots has Debussy given, as a reminder to himself, the first initial of the character singing or a few words of text (or abbreviations of those words). At times the vocal parts themselves have been left out and in places the accompaniment is lacking. Clefs, key signatures, and time signatures are typically omitted, accidentals not consistently indicated, and the pitches so carelessly positioned on the staves that it is usually difficult and often impossible to tell with certainty which notes were intended.

Included in the Meyer MS are drafts of Acts II and V complete, the latter two-thirds of Act IV, scene 4, the beginning of Act I, scene 1, and two portions of Act I, scene 2. This manuscript (along with the short score Bréval MS) has been reproduced in facsimile in *Esquisses de "Pelléas et Mélisande" (1893–1895),* ed. François Lesure (Geneva: Minkoff, 1977), abbreviated hereinafter as LPm.

Debussy presented the manuscript to Henry Lerolle, and the signed dedication, which appears on the final folio of Act V, was dated June–July 1895. Although the dates are clearly part of the dedication, they are meaningless as a date of presentation. In all probability, Debussy would not have been willing to part with the manuscript until 17 August, when he finished copying out the short score, and he probably did not present it to Lerolle before late September; a letter of 23 September from Debussy to Lerolle makes it clear that the latter had not yet heard the most recently composed scenes, which are contained in the Meyer MS, so the June–July dates in the dedication must refer to the months in which Debussy wrote or worked from these pages. According to the composition schedule that has been established, we know that Debussy worked on Act IV, scene 4 in May 1895, completed Act V in June 1895, and worked on Act II between June and 17 August 1895, the date on which he completed the opera. The June–July 1895 dates therefore represent the principal block of time during which at least most of these pages were written. The Act IV portion of the manuscript cannot be explained this way since these pages predate the September–October 1893 draft of the scene (the Legouix MS); possibly Debussy might have wanted this earliest draft on hand while he was writing the May 1895 draft of the scene (Bréval MS). The presence of Act I sketches in the Meyer MS also suggests that Debussy may have reworked portions of that act during the same summer months.

Perhaps it is misguided to try to pin each page to June and July 1895. Debussy surely had a great many pages of drafts, and perhaps Lerolle was even allowed to choose what portions he wanted, in which case he selected the most recent pages, which he had not as yet heard (Acts II and V), something from the beginning of the opera, including the prelude to Act I, and something from the climax of the opera, the scene which Debussy had composed first and with which he had entertained his friends, Lerolle included, as early as October 1893. We do know from other sources that additional pages of *Pelléas* manuscripts probably survived. In her memoirs, Mary Garden expressed the belief that manuscripts of *Pelléas* had been in the possession of Debussy's first wife, Rosalie Texier, and Misia Sert described purchasing "the manuscript of *Pelléas*" from her around 1920: "Alas! there were only a few stained pages of it. Of course, I bought them from her, all the same, for the modest sum she asked...."[3]

The Meyer MS is written on three types of paper, all in upright format: 28- and 30-stave paper, approximately 400 mm. x 300 mm., and 20-stave paper, 345 mm. x 265 mm. (Act II, scene 3 only). The blind stamp of the paper maker is visible (though not legible) on every page (see fig. 1). The paper was apparently prepared in nested gatherings and stamped in the upper left corner, next to the fold. The stamp consequently emerges with varying degrees of clarity depending on the position of the particular folio during the embossing process.

The manuscript was written in black, blue, orange, and green pencil and black ink. These colors often provide invaluable assistance in sorting out the compositional layers, and it is unfortunate that economic considerations prevented the facsimile from being reproduced in color. The editor has attempted to compensate for the lack of color differentiation by providing a list of the pencil and ink types uses on each page (LPm, p. 9), but obviously this list is only of limited value since it cannot specify the particular use or even the frequency of the particular colors. Thus, for example, pages 34 and 38 of

Figure 1. Paper Maker's Blind Stamp: Meyer Manuscript.

the facsimile (Act II, fols. 8 and 11) are both identified as "blue pencil and black ink," yet the former was written primarily in blue pencil with a few corrections of the voice parts in black ink, while the latter is almost entirely in black ink, with a few blue pencil additions and corrections. Since Debussy typically sketched in pencil, copied in ink, and corrected with a contrasting color (pencil or pen), this additional information helps to conclude that page 34 probably represents an earlier sketch, and page 38, an ink copy of a pencil sketch which had probably been extensively revised. Debussy also sometimes used different colors to differentiate the instrumental strands in the accompaniment.

Another shortcoming of the facsimile is that it does not preserve the foliation of the manuscript—the relationship of rectos to versos; this is immediately apparent from pages 29–30 of the facsimile, where a 28-stave page has a verso with 30 staves! This aspect of the manuscript is crucial since (except for fair copies made to serve as *Stichvorlagen*) Debussy usually wrote on rectos only. In the case of preliminary drafts, when both sides of the page contain music, it is usually because one side contains the latest draft and the other, part of an earlier, rejected draft: rather than discard these pages of rejected draft, Debussy sometimes reused the pages, writing on the blank versos. In most cases (the Meyer MS Act IV, scene 4 is the chief exception) one "reads" the scene by arranging the rectos in the proper sequence, ignoring the versos. Another, related shortcoming of the facsimile is that it does not reproduce the folio numbers in the upper right corners of the pages, most of which (in Acts II and V) appear to have been written by the composer. On some pages in Act II, scenes 2 and 3, two or three different page numbers are visible, as Debussy apparently changed the pagination of the manuscript. This can be a clue to the order in which the pages were actually written; a page with a single page number surrounded by pages with two or three layers of them is likely to be a replacement page, written later.

With the exception of the Act IV pages, the manuscript is entirely in separate folios. The three unnumbered Act I folios correspond to the facsimile as follows: fol. 1^r = p. 21, 1^v = 22, 2^r = 23, 2^v = 24, 3^r = 25, and 3^v = 26 (blank). The twenty-two folios of Act II are numbered 1–22; all are written on rectos only, with the following exceptions: fol. 10^v (numbered p. 9) = LPm, p. 37; 12^v (p. 11) = LPm, p. 40; and 22^v (unnumbered) = LPm, p. 51. The nineteen folios of Act V, numbered 1–19, are also mostly written on rectos only; the exceptions are: fol. 6^v = LPm, p. 69; 9^v = LPm, p. 73; and 12^v (upside down with respect to fol. 12^r) = LPm, p. 77. The facsimile reverses the order of fols. 17^r (LPm, p. 83) and 18^r (LPm, p. 82).

The Act IV, scene 4 pages are nearly all in bifolios. Loose and unnumbered by the composer, they have evidently been shuffled around over the years. The folio structure shown in figure 2 has rearranged them and assigned folio numbers to reflect the proper sequence of the pages. (The page numbers of the facsimile follow in parentheses; unlabeled sides are blank.) These pages of the Meyer MS are the earliest surviving sketches of *Pelléas* and (except for the concluding bars, which are not included) represent the latter two-thirds of the scene—from the point where Pelleas sings, "On dirait que ta voix a passé sur la mer au printemps!..." (VS, p. 245, meas. 8; this point is determined on the basis of the accompaniment alone since both the voice part and the text were entirely omitted in the first system of fol. 1^r). Most of these sketches can be easily identified by matching the untexted notes of the vocal lines, syllable for syllable, with the text of the original 1892 edition of Maeterlinck's play. The task is sometimes facilitated by Debussy's inclusion of a few words or syllables or initial letters of words of text and also by the resemblance of some sections to the corresponding passages in later short score developed drafts and even in the published vocal score. It is thus possible to reconstruct the proper sequence, which does not correspond to the order in the facsimile and may not reflect the order in which pages were written: 1^r (LPm, p. 53)—2^v (61)—3^v (60)—4^r (58)—5^v (54; systems 5–7 precede 1–4 and system 8 is an insert in system 2)—6^r (55)—7^r (57). Fol. 6^v (56) was written as a replacement for part of fol. 5^v (systems 5–7 and continuing through most of system 1), and fol. 4^v (59) contains three measures of unidentified music. The only lapse in perfect continuity from one page to the next is between fols. 5^v and 6^r, where one measure seems to be lacking.

The folio structure shows Debussy initially writing on either both outside pages of a bifolio, or both inside pages. The advantage of this procedure (over, say, rectos only) is that the composer, if he wished, could open up the bifolios and lay out his entire draft face up (see fig. 3). In the initial bifolio, the pages read right to left when laid out this way; in the remaining two, they read left to right. The reverse sides of these pages were used in one case (4^v) to notate other ideas, and in another (6^v), to revise a previously written page. The latter procedure had the disadvantage that Debussy was unable to look at his original page (5^v) while writing its replacement. This situation is absolutely contrary to the composer's usual habit in his developed drafts of writing on rectos only and using the facing versos for corrections.

Figure 2.   The Folio Structure of the Meyer Manuscript, Act IV, Scene 4.

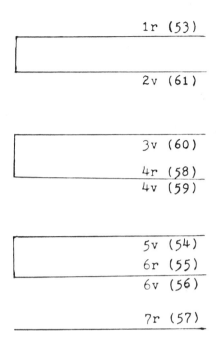

Figure 3.   The Folios of the Meyer Manuscript, Act IV, Scene 4 Arranged Face Up.

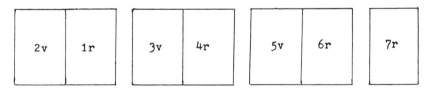

The blank bottom third of fol. 6ᵛ (LPm, p. 56) helps to identify it as a replacement page, as Debussy generally started each page from the top and proceeded to fill it to the bottom. As already mentioned, the striking exception to this is fol. 5ᵛ, in which the two halves of the page appear in reverse order. Fol. 4ʳ also has enough empty staves at the bottom of the page to accommodate another system, suggesting the possibility that this too could have been the replacement of a page from an earlier draft, or that Debussy only needed to write to this point in order to join up with a previously written page. The question of compositional order, in this scene and in Act V, is discussed in detail by Carolyn Abbate in her article "*Tristan* in the

Composition of *Pelleas*," in which she concludes that Debussy conceived the scene in separate subsections and in some cases worked backwards in a process of "retrograde accretion," in which "a block of material existed at hand, and the section anterior to it was written down at some later time and spliced onto it."[4] Her argument depends to a degree on the unstated assumption that the surviving pages were the very first written and were not preceded by an earlier draft.

At this stage of composition, Debussy apparently laid out the page as he composed, usually using systems of four or five, but sometimes three, staves. He typically left one blank stave between systems. The vocal parts were most often allotted two staves, although in Act IV, scene 4, the parts of both Pelléas and Mélisande were sometimes written on the same stave; this procedure posed little difficulty for the composer since the opera contains almost no simultaneous singing—none in this draft of the scene. Nevertheless, the allotment of two staves for the voices guaranteed space either directly above or below for the revision of the vocal parts. Directly beneath them, Debussy used two or three staves for the orchestra reduction.

The conspicuous exception to these practices is, once again, fol. 5ᵛ (LPm, p. 54). Not only are the two halves of the page written in reverse order, but there is more music squeezed onto this than any other page. The top half especially has more the appearance of a rough sketch than any other part of the manuscript. Here Debussy's prime intent seems to have been to draft the continuity of the orchestra; its primacy is already evident from the fact that it occupies the two topmost staves on the page, and in none of these top four systems did Debussy allow any staves for the voices—he only left single blank staves to separate the systems. The vocal lines appear to have been added afterwards, sometimes above and sometimes below the orchestra, and sometimes even superimposed on the same staves. In spots they were entirely omitted.[5] In the second system of the page (meas. 3–6), Debussy miscalculated in sketching the accompaniment and allowed only four measures to accommodate approximately thirty words of text. Since this was obviously insufficient, he added four measures at the bottom of the page, signalling the addition with plus signs that marked both the measures to be inserted (sys. 8) and the point of insertion (sys. 2, meas. 6).[6] Even this proved insufficient, and the Legouix draft included an additional five measures at this point, making a total of nine measures which had to be added to the original four.

At two other points on this page, Debussy compensated for other such apparent miscalculations by directing that pairs of measures be repeated: in both places (sys. 1 and 4) he bracketed the measures and wrote the instruction "2 fois" ("two times") above them. In the first instance he directed that the voice enter on the repeat, writing "la 2 f" (i.e., "la deuxième fois," or "the second time") in the margin. In the second instance, where the voice was to sing throughout the four measures, he simply left it out.

In these passages, where the orchestra seems to have been sketched first and where the voice parts are often absent, Debussy evidently considered the music to be controlled by the orchestral development rather than by the voice, and the vocal lines that were later added were thus dependent upon and determined by the melodic and harmonic content of the accompaniment. This phenomenon was not limited to situations where the omission of the voice part was due to space limitations or notational peculiarities. A conspicuous example, already noted, occurs in the very first system of fol. 1^r (LPm, p. 53), where the orchestra develops one of the scene's love themes (called "ecstasy" by Gilman and "love declared" by Emmanuel),[7] but the vocal part has been omitted, its allotted stave left empty. The text at this point is Pelléas's "aria," which begins with: "On dirait que ta voix a passé sur la mer au printemps!... Je ne l'ai jamais entendue jusqu'ici. On dirait qu'il a plu sur mon coeur!..." ("One would say that your voice had blown across the sea in spring!... I have not heard it until now. One would say it had rained on my heart!... "). A similar situation occurs in the last measure of the same page, where Pelléas sings another very important line: "Je n'avais jamais rien vu d'aussi beau avant toi..." ("I had never seen anything so beautiful before you..."); here too the voice part was left out, as a new motive, notated in some detail, is introduced in the orchestra. For the continuation of this section on fol. 2^v (LPm, p. 61), Debussy sketched the orchestral development of yet another new theme for six measures (a full harmonization is provided only in the first measure; for the rest, only the melody and some hints of the harmony are given), but he supplied the vocal part for just the beginning and the ending of the passage ("J'étais inquiet, je cherchais partout dans la maison... Je cherchais partout dans la campagne, et je ne trouvais pas la beauté... Et maintenant je t'ai trouvée!... Je t'ai trouvée!..."; "I was restless; I looked throughout the house... I looked throughout the countryside, and I found no beauty... And now I have found you!... I have found you!... "). Yet another example occurs in the fifth system of the same page, where a three-measure sequential pattern was written out for the orchestra, but without the voice part ("Viens, dans la lumière. Nous ne pouvons pas voir combien nous sommes heureux. Viens, viens... "; "Come, into the light. We cannot see how happy we are. Come, come... "). In each of these instances, new thematic material was being introduced in the orchestra, and Debussy's first concern was to work out the symphonic development of that material, no doubt bearing in mind the number of measures he would need for the delivery of the text. Only later did he add the vocal parts, and in doing so, sometimes discovered that his estimates had been in error.

Debussy's occasional notation of the voice parts as stems without noteheads may appear to be an extension of this practice, with the composer employing a purely rhythmic notation, without regard for the pitches, while he worked out the accompaniment in detail. But in almost every case, the notation is simply a shorthand for representing repetitions of the same pitch—that of the first note, whose pitch is usually given. This occurs, for example, on fol. 4^r, sys. 2, meas. 2 (LPm, p. 58), where the four headless stems at the end of the measure represent repetitions of the note immediately preceding, which is the first note of the phrase (f^1). However, an exception to the rule is found in the Act I folios, in Geneviève's opening speech of Act I, scene 2 (fol. 1^v; LPm, p. 22). In sys. 2, meas. 1, the shorthand is clearly intended, but no initial note is given to indicate the pitch of the stems. True, Debussy may have intended them to continue the vocal pitch of the preceding measure (d^1), but more likely his concern in the measure was primarily with the accompaniment, which contains a statement of the Mélisande motive, and the vocal melody was of secondary importance. This conclusion is supported by two pieces of evidence—the final version of the measure (VS, p. 28, meas. 9), which does not have a monotone vocal line, and the fact that, five measures later on the same Meyer folio, when the Mélisande motive returns, Debussy omitted the vocal line altogether. In this case, the appearance of a character leitmotif in the accompaniment took precedence over the pitches and even the rhythms of the text declamation.

Another indication that Debussy sometimes regarded the orchestra as the dominant force is provided by certain revisions. In the phrase shown in Ex. 1a, from the Meyer draft of Act IV, scene 4, for example, the vocal line doubles the accompaniment. In a later revision of these measures (represented in Ex. 1b by the published vocal score), Debussy altered the pace and rhythm of the text declamation, essentially moving it back one beat with respect to the bar lines, but the accompaniment was left in place and so was the parallel melodic shape of the voice part, although different syllables were assigned to each note. It was the orchestra, not the vocal melody, which was fixed—the orchestra which was the determining factor. The revised voice part, with its new relationship between text and melodic contour, gives different emphasis to the text.

The orchestra was not always primary (though in this draft of the scene that is usually the case), as there are points in the draft where Debussy evidently followed the opposite procedure, first fixing the voice parts and leaving the accompaniment to be filled in at some later stage. One example appears in the final two measures of fol. 3^v (LPm, p. 60), where the vocal part is given in full (Pelléas: "Je ne pouvais pas admettre tes yeux... Je voulais aller tout de suite..."; "I could not acknowledge your eyes... I wanted to go away at once... "), but the only accompaniment is a single whole note in the first measure, perhaps intended to represent a trill on the note A♭ throughout the two measures. When the accompaniment for this passage was written out in full in the short score draft (Legouix MS, fol. 6^r), Debussy added two statements of the Pelléas theme above the A♭ trill. Despite the fact that he may

Ex. 1. (a) Meyer MS, IV, fol. 6ʳ, sys. 2, meas. 3–5 (LPm, p. 55).
(Downward stems in the voice part are from the Brèval
MS, fol. 15ʳ, meas. 7–8; LPm, p. 117.)

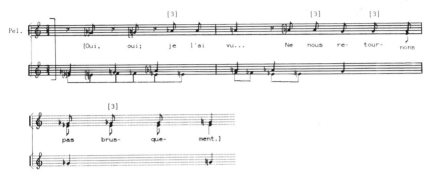

(b) VS, p. 261, meas. 12–p. 262, meas. 3.

already have envisioned using an important character motive in the accompaniment, the Meyer MS sketch suggests that Debussy's primary focus here was on the vocal melody and that the orchestra was secondary.

Another example is in meas. 7–10 of fol. 2ᵛ (LPm, p. 61). Again the vocal melody is given (Pelléas: "Je ne crois pas qu'il y ait sur la terre une femme plus belle!..."; "I do not think there could be on the earth a woman more beautiful!..."), but no accompaniment is provided. The nature of this expressive melody is such that Debussy could not have intended it to be unaccompanied, but whatever orchestra part he imagined, he left no hint of it here. Later drafts provide no real clue since their vocal melodies differ from what is written here, though it is possible that, as in subsequent drafts of the passage, Debussy might have planned here some use of the theme of "ecstasy."

Further light is shed on this question of vocal-orchestral priority by the Act II folios of the Meyer MS. In contrast to the Act IV folios, which were written entirely in black pencil (the only exception being some jottings that are not part of the draft: the black ink sixteenth-note figuration at the extreme right of fol. 3ʳ, sys. 1 and 5; LPm, p. 58), Act II was written using a variety of colors—blue, black, orange, and green pencil and black ink—and these colors are used in a functional way. Relevant to the present issue is Debussy's practice of using blue pencil for the voice parts and black pencil for the accompaniment throughout most of scene 1 and on isolated pages in scenes 2 (fol. 10^v; LPm, p. 37) and 3 (fol. 19^r; LPm, p. 47). This color differentiation was probably useful to the composer since the voice parts here as elsewhere in the Meyer draft are almost never identified by their texts or by the name of the character singing. This two-color system, however, provides some indication of which part—voice or orchestra—was written first. The indicator of priority is the color of the bar lines, since Debussy was likely to draw the bar lines with whichever color pencil he used for the part he wrote first. Thus blue bar lines would suggest that the voice was the earlier layer, while black would indicate the primacy of the orchestra.

Fol. 1^r (LPm, p. 27) shows as well as any how the process worked. The orchestral opening (meas. 1–13) was written entirely in black pencil. In meas. 14, with Pelléas's first lines, the black pencil of the accompanying chords is joined by the blue pencil of the vocal melody, and for the next three measures (15–17), the bar lines are in blue, as Debussy concentrated on the voice; it is not necessarily that the orchestra is subordinate here, but rather that it consists of repetitions of material which has already been heard: meas. 15 repeats the music of meas. 14 (and is so marked) and meas. 16–17, though left blank, were most likely conceived as a virtual repetition of meas. 12–13, the fountain motive (this is the reading in all later versions). In meas. 18–19 the accompaniment contains a new continuation of the fountain motive, and the orchestra appears to have been written first: the bar line between meas. 18 and 19 is black. Debussy then wrote the vocal parts, with blue bar lines on either side of meas. 20. In this bar, the accompaniment assumes the grace note motive of meas. 9, a figure also associated with the fountain. This pattern of alternating groups of blue and black bar lines continues throughout much of the scene, suggesting that Debussy wrote a few bars at a time, first accompaniment then voice, or vice versa. He evidently did not proceed bar by bar, writing both. When the orchestra has independent material of thematic importance, it is generally notated first, especially when that material is new; when the orchestra merely provides supportive harmonies or repeats material it has already presented, it is usually written after the voice parts.

In comparison with the Act IV, scene 4 sketches, the more flexible compositional procedure evident in the manuscript of Act II, written nearly two years later, is perhaps indicative of some evolution in Debussy's methods: an increased sophistication or subtlety in the handling and balancing of the vocal and orchestral components. The question of course remains whether the phenomenon observed in the Act II sketches reflects *compositional* order or merely *copying* order, since there is no way of being sure that this manuscript represents the very first draft of any given passage. Perhaps stronger evidence is found in the rejected pages which have survived as versos of the scene 2 folios. Fol. 10^v (LPm, p. 37) contains fifteen measures of music, from Mélisande's "Voulez-vous boire un peu d'eau?" through the first three syllables of her "Fermez les yeux et tâchez de dormir" (corresponding to VS, p. 79, meas. 4–p. 81, meas. 1). This page was the original continuation from fol. 8^r (LPm, p. 34), but the setting here is completely different from that found in its replacement, fol. 9^r, and in the published score, not only in the vocal rhythms and melodies, but in the accompaniment as well. That of the rejected draft is based entirely on the theme associated with Mélisande's wedding ring (itself derived from the Golaud motive), which is prominent in Act II, scene 1 (see various forms of the motive in VS, p. 66, meas. 3 and 6, and VS, p. 68, meas. 7–8). The use of colors on this page corroborates the conclusion already reached, as the orchestra part seems to have been written first whenever the "ring" theme constitutes the accompaniment: whenever that theme is present, the bar lines are black, and when the bar lines are blue the accompaniment is omitted, suggesting, perhaps, simple chordal accompaniment or repetitions of some preceding measures.

Further evidence is found in fol. 12^v (LPm, p. 40), another discarded page from scene 2, which contains only seven-and-a-half measures and represents part of Golaud's interrogation of Mélisande, from his "Est-ce le roi?" almost to the end of her reply, "C'est quelque chose [qui est plus fort que moi...]" (VS, p. 85, meas. 1–p. 86, meas. 1). Here Debussy has sketched the vocal parts completely, but indicated the accompaniment in only the final full measure (meas. 7). Priority here was clearly given to the vocal lines, as Debussy apparently conceived the passage as recitativelike, with the accompaniment serving a secondary, supporting role. In the final version, most of this passage is in precisely this style. In fact, parts of this draft are quite similar to the final version; in meas. 3–7 the vocal pitches appear to be identical, although the rhythms are sometimes different. Debussy seems to have decided on the melodic contour appropriate to the text and then changed his mind about the pace of the speech; the revision, although altering the rhythm, preserved the original pitches (see Ex. 2). The nature of this revision supports the conclusion that here the vocal line was the dominant element.

The scene 2 recto folios also provide insights into this question. A striking example of the omission of accompaniment occurs at the end of Golaud's opening narrative, in which he recounts how his horse bolted at the stroke of twelve. For nine measures, only the voice part is given (fol. 8^r, sys. 5–6; LPm, p. 34; the text is: "Je suis tombé, et lui doit être tombé sur moi; je croyais avoir toute la fôret sur la poitrine. Je croyais que mon coeur était écrasé [later changed to 'déchiré']. Mais mon coeur est solide. Il paraît que ce n'est rien... "; "I fell, and he must have fallen on me. I thought I had the whole forest on my

Ex. 2. (a) Meyer MS, II, fol. 12ᵛ, meas. 4–7 (LPm, p. 40).

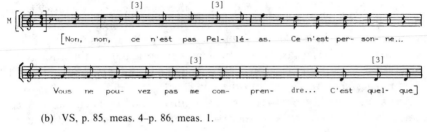

(b) VS, p. 85, meas. 4–p. 86, meas. 1.

breast. I thought my heart was crushed. But my heart is sound. It appears that it was nothing... "). In the final version (VS, p. 78, meas. 4–p. 79, meas. 3) the accompaniment here is mostly a series of chords over a pedal.

In an essay on *Pelléas,* Pierre Boulez discussed Debussy's very special solution to the nineteenth-century operatic problem of integrating action or information (which in earlier opera would have been set as recitative) and reflection or commentary (arias or ensembles). He described the music of *Pelléas* as "an extremely closely woven fabric of action and reflection": "... often subtle, the passing from *information* to *reflection,* from the *fact* to the *symbol,* is seen nevertheless clearly expressed. The vocal line frees itself from diction to gain its autonomy: the texture of the orchestra changes its meaning: from *support* it is transformed into *sharing.*"[8] To the extent that it can be determined from the Meyer draft, Debussy's compositional sequence, the relative priority of voice and orchestra, seems to be a reflection of this stylistic division. In passages chiefly conveying factual information, Debussy employed a recitativelike style, with a vocal line that is speechlike in character and an accompaniment which supports and punctuates its inflections and cadence. For such passages, Debussy seems likely to have sketched the voice part first, concentrating on the rhythm and melodic contour of the text delivery. But for those moments that are more reflective, where characters give free expression to their feelings, the orchestra becomes more independent and prominent. In such cases, it seems, Debussy first worked out the purely musical development of the orchestra part and then superimposed the voice parts over it.

Turning to other features of Debussy's notational habits, some of his musical abbreviations should be mentioned. In view of the speed with which he evidently worked at this compositional stage, abbreviated notation was employed quite frequently. His use of the instruction "2 fois" ("two times") to signal the repetition of a group of measures has already been noted. Another way of directing the same result while allotting staff space to the repetition (and thereby allowing room for the voice parts to be written), was by numbering the measures to be repeated and then simply using the numbers to stand for those measures. In Act IV this notation is used on fols. 5^v, 6^r, and 7^r (LPm, pp. 54, 55, and 57). In Act II, scene 3, Debussy used even more "informal" signs to achieve the same result: for example, on fol. 19^r (LPm, p. 47) he indicated that the accompaniment of the two measures of the second system was to be repeated in the third by means of the symbol))======((written in orange pencil (for contrast) across the two measures of that latter system. Similar improvised symbols appear elsewhere. Where Debussy needed to indicate the repetition of a single measure or of part of a measure, he often used the symbols ⅔ and ⅀ . Octave doublings could be designated by a wavy line under a melody (Act II, fol. 9^r, meas. 2; LPm, p. 35) or by vertical strokes under each note (Act II, fol. 14^r, sys. 3, meas. 1; LPm, p. 42).

Although key signatures are generally lacking, Debussy included them at three points in Act IV, scene 4, not in the conventional manner, but by naming the tonality: "Fa+" (fol. 5^v; LPm, p. 54) and "Fa♯" (fol. 2^v; LPm, p. 61) for F-sharp major, and "Re" (fol. 5^v; LPm, p. 54) for D major. On one of the Act I pages (fol. 1^r; LPm, p. 21), Debussy used figured bass notation as a harmonic shorthand. Only one stage direction is included in the manuscript: the moment when the servants fall to their knees, signalling the death of Mélisande (Act V, fol. 17^r; LPm, p. 83).

In the discussion of Debussy's compositional schedule it was noted that his first idea for Act V was orchestrational: before he had written a note of music he had the thought of employing an orchestra on stage. And even in the relatively early stage of composition represented by the Meyer MS, there are indications that he was thinking orchestrally. While much of the accompaniment resembles a piano reduction, there are places where Debussy deliberately used additional staves, probably to separate the instrumental strands. On one page (Act IV, fol. 7^r, system 2; LPm, p. 57) he even specified particular instruments, noting in the right margin that statements of the Pelléas theme were first to be played by the cellos and then by violins (?) doubling either French horns or the English horn ("Vi et Cors." or "Cang." for Cor anglais). Other instrumental indications are found in Act II: flute ("Fl") on fol. 13^r (LPm, p. 41), and in Act V: harp ("Harpe") on fol. 3^r (LPm, p. 65), three first violins ("3 1° V°"), flute ("Fl."), harp harmonics ("Harpe s[ons] harmoniques"), second harp ("2^e H") on fol. 17^r (LPm, p. 83), and first violins

("1° V°") on fol. 18ʳ (LPm, p. 82). The heavy concentration of these indications in the last pages of Act V suggests that Debussy may have been thinking more orchestrally or was more motivated to jot down his instrumental thoughts as he neared the end of the scene and was about to copy out the short score.

The three Act I folios of the Meyer MS contain portions of the first two scenes. The scene 1 fragment consists of the opening, from the beginning of the prelude through the first few lines of Golaud's opening speech (through "et voici des traces de sang"), and it occupies the recto sides of the first two folios (LPm, pp. 21 and 23). The second of these contains just the last four measures of this opening, followed by two crossed-out measures of accompaniment only: a statement of the Forest/Antiquity theme[9] (which opens the prelude) in a form very close to the accompaniment later used in VS, p. 21, meas. 4–5. These measures may have been the original continuation of the bars that precede it, but since the voice part was omitted, one cannot be sure. The scene 1 music was written entirely in black pencil; in the middle of the second folio Debussy wrote another five measures of unidentified music in black ink. The scene 2 portions, written in black ink, consist of two fragments: Geneviève's opening speech from "Je ne sais ni son âge..." to the end (written on the versos of the scene 1 folios, but in reverse order, beginning on fol. 2ᵛ and concluding on fol. 1ᵛ; LPm, pp. 24 and 22) and part of Arkel's response, from "...et ce mariage allait mettre fin..." through "Il ne l'a pas voulu ainsi" (fol. 3ʳ; LPm, p. 25).

In spite of the incompleteness of the notation, it seems that, with the exception of the prelude to the act, this draft is very close to Debussy's final version. Even the cuts he made in Geneviève's speech (cuts with respect to the play) are already observed. One finds only slight differences in the vocal rhythms and pitches. In view of the frequent omission of accidentals, it is perhaps surprising to find dynamic markings (a crescendo sign and "pp") in one place (fol. 1ᵛ, sys. 2). On another page (fol. 2ᵛ) meter changes are indicated by time signatures: 3/4 (sys. 3, meas. 3) and "C" (sys. 4, meas. 3). The more "finished" appearance of the scene 2 pages—the use of dynamic markings, the relative completeness of the notation, and the fact that they were written in ink instead of pencil—suggests a late phase in this stage of composition, and these pages were probably copied or revised from an earlier draft. This could explain why Debussy left eight blank staves at the top of fol. 2ᵛ: it may be that this page represents the corrected version of a corresponding page whose topmost system was not in need of revision. There is also evidence that the scene 1 pages too were copied from earlier drafts or sketches: the crossing out and confusion in the first three measures of the last system of fol. 1ʳ are most easily explained as a result of copying errors.

The most fascinating portion of the Act I folios is the prelude to the act.

The differences between this draft and Debussy's final version provide a valuable glimpse into the composer's creative process and deserve a separate study. A few comments will have to suffice. The two versions follow the same general structural plan and are based on the same principal themes: the Forest/Antiquity theme (VS, p. 1, meas. 1–4), one of the Golaud themes (VS, p. 1, meas. 5–6), and the Mélisande theme (VS, p. 1, meas. 14) with its continuation (VS, p. 2, meas. 1–2). In addition, the Meyer draft uses a motive derived from the Golaud theme which, in the published version, appears later in the scene, at Golaud's "et voici des traces de sang" (VS, p. 4, meas. 1–2; note especially the lower stave of meas. 2). The themes are not quite identical in the two versions, and they are also used differently. In general, the Meyer MS prelude tends to proceed through simple repetitions of two- or four-measure blocks, while the final version introduces variation in its repetitions.

The Meyer MS prelude opens with a nine-measure string of themes: the first two measures of the Forest/Antiquity theme (harmonized almost identically to meas. 8–9 of the published score), these two measures repeated, the first measure of the Mélisande theme, this measure repeated, a one-measure series of four chords (which may be related to a progression found in VS, p. 36, meas. 4 and elsewhere, and which Calvocoressi called the "Threat-motive"),[10] this measure repeated, one measure of a held chord (bringing the rhythmic motion to a halt), and an entire measure of rest. This opening could be represented as: a a b b c c d (rest). In contrast, the first phrase in the final version uses fewer (and some different) themes, and it displays greater variation and sense of organic growth. It too opens with the Forest/Antiquity theme, but in a starker harmonization and lower register. Debussy also introduces an element of rhythmic variation on the repetition, one which serves to emphasize the theme's major second, the intervallic link to the theme which follows—the Golaud theme. The following repetition of this one-measure motive is also subjected to rhythmic variation and is in turn followed by a measure-long timpani roll, which continues from the previous two measures. The opening of the final version can thus be represented as a a′ b b′ c, with motivic and orchestrational links connecting the three elements. The rhythmic changes in both themes accentuate their common interval—the major second—and also make the increase in motion throughout the phrase more continuous, with new and smaller rhythmic subdivisions introduced in each unit: half note, quarter note, eighth note and eighth-note triplet, sixteenth note, and finally, indeterminately short values (timpani roll). This rhythmic progression is matched by a harmonic one—incomplete triads (no third) in meas. 1 and 3, complete triads in meas. 2 and 4, and whole tone chords in meas. 5–6. In comparison with the final version, the Meyer MS prelude is more repetitious and blocklike, the progression of materials less organic.

In both versions, the opening statement is followed by a varied repeat of that statement, leading to an extensive development of the Mélisande theme. The Meyer counterstatement opens with an exact repetition of its opening four bars, followed by the Mélisande theme (with a new accompanimental figure), then this measure repeated with a new ending to connect with the Golaud theme (nearly identical to VS, p. 1, meas. 12), which is also repeated with variation; these eight measures then lead to a thirteen-measure expansion of the Mélisande theme.

In the final version, the counterstatement shows at once a stronger relationship with its original statement (it uses the same themes in the same sequence) and also greater variation with respect to that statement. Here the Forest/Antiquity theme is moved to a higher register, the Golaud theme is transposed to a different pitch level (now using the same pitches [G–A] as the Forest theme's major second), and both themes are completely reharmonized. When the Mélisande theme then enters in meas. 13, it is an entirely fresh theme, not having been heard before. This moment in the Meyer draft was "spoiled" since it was already the third time that the theme had been presented. The very elaborate arpeggio accompaniment that Debussy entered in the Meyer draft at this point shows that he viewed this as a moment of important contrast, but its effect was somewhat undermined by the previous "overexposure" of the theme. The final version helped to emphasize that contrast by making the change thematic as well as textural. It also gave more equal weight to the two character themes; in the Meyer version, the Golaud theme is heard in explicit form in only two measures.[11]

In the Act II sketches, the variety of paper types, the pencil and ink colors, and the layers of folio numbers help to establish the chronology of the drafts. Three different types of paper were used: 30-stave (scene 1: fols. 1–3; scene 2: fols. 8–9, 11, 13–16), 28-stave (scene 1: fols. 4–7; scene 2: fols. 10 and 12), and 20-stave (scene 3). The 28-stave folios of scene 2 are those whose versos contain earlier discarded drafts of parts of the scene, suggesting that the entire scene (and possibly scene 1 as well) may first have been written in a complete draft on 28-stave paper. This hypothesis is supported by the fact that this type of paper was used in the Meyer MS draft of Act V, completed just before the composition of Act II. Continuing this conjectural chronology, the scene 2 pages (and possibly the first three pages of scene 1) were replaced by revisions written on 30-stave paper. Finally, three pages of this latest draft (fols. 9–11) were replaced by pages written in ink. (The anomalous carry-over of 28-stave paper resulted from the recycling of pages whose rectos were discarded but whose versos were blank.) These three folios have a more complete and "finished" appearance than the other pages in the draft: they are laid out in an absolutely regular fashion in systems of two vocal and three instrumental staves, separated by single blank staves, the singers' parts are consistently written on separate staves and are identified by the characters' initials, and the notation is more complete, even including one time signature and one clef. As previously mentioned, Debussy generally used ink when making copies he felt would be final. On fol. 11, Debussy had to squeeze the final measures onto the page, to the point of requiring a brief insert (notated between the second and third systems) to join up with fol. 12. Even these three ink folios were probably not written in order, as the revision at the top of fol. 11 suggests that it was written before fols. 9 and 10, and had to be modified to link up with them. The more compressed writing on these ink folios allowed Debussy to consolidate pages, resulting in a renumbering of the pages that follow. It was this process of revision through replacement that produced the layers of page numbers on most of the folios in the latter half of the act. Thus, on the evidence of this scene, at least, it would appear that the music went through several sketch drafts before Debussy copied it out as a developed, fair-copy short score.

Despite a number of differences, especially in vocal pitches and rhythms, the Meyer MS drafts of scenes 1 and 2 are very close to the published version. (One measure of the first interlude and the first four measures of the second scene are not included in the manuscript.) A comparison of some of the Meyer MS readings with the final version shows Debussy revising the vocal lines to achieve greater independence from the accompaniment. In the Meyer MS version, Mélisande's line, "Avec l'anneau qu'il m'a donné" ("With the ring he gave me"), nearly doubled the accompaniment, which is a statement of the ring motive. The revision altered the voice part to produce a more independent contour (see Ex. 3). In another case, the Meyer MS setting of Pelléas's line, "Il ne faut pas s'inquiéter ainsi pour une bague" ("You need not be so troubled over a ring"), was also a statement of the ring theme and the accompaniment was omitted (fol. 6^r, meas. 10–11: LPm, p. 32). In the final version, the ring theme became the principal material of the accompaniment and Pelléas was given a new vocal line, though one which is nearly parallel to its accompaniment (VS, p. 69, meas. 8–9).

The Meyer second interlude and third scene are very different from their counterparts in the final version although there are sections of the scene which are quite similar, notably VS, p. 108, meas. 1–7, and VS, p. 111, meas. 2–p. 114, m. 1. The very end of the scene was much revised: there are two different versions in the Meyer draft (fols. 22^r and 22^v: LPm, pp. 50 and 51) and a further three in the NEC MS (II, fol. 19^r), the last finally reaching the state of the published version.[12] The Meyer setting of Pelléas's first speech is quite different from the publication (Debussy had not yet arrived at the triplet ostinato patterns that were later to dominate its accompaniment), and it makes frequent use of a theme which had been heard towards the end of scene 2, at Golaud's "La mer sera très haute cette nuit" ("The sea will be very high

Ex. 3. (a) Meyer MS, II, fol. 5ʳ, meas. 2 (LPm, p. 31).

(b) Vocal part as in VS, p. 66, meas. 3.

tonight"; VS, p. 100, meas. 4). In the Meyer MS version of Pelléas's scene 3 speech, the theme underscores three of his lines: "Il n'y a pas d'étoiles de ce côté" ("There are no stars on this side"), "elle [la lune] éclairera toute la grotte et alors nous pourrons entrer sans danger" ("the moon will light up the whole grotto, and then we can enter without danger"), and "Mais je pense que la clarté du ciel nous suffira" ("But I think the light of the sky will be enough for us"). This theme, which seems to be associated with the darkness of the grotto (the theme appears whenever Pelléas mentions the natural forces that could provide them with light: the stars, the moon, and the sky), was also one of the principal themes of the second interlude, and its subsequent removal from scene 3 resulted in its concomitant excision from the preceding interlude. The Meyer draft lacks the particular variant of the Golaud motive which represents the sound of the sea and which became the principal "organizing theme" of the final version: there it dominates the second interlude (VS, p. 104, meas. 3, 5, and 13–14), it appears near the middle of the scene (when Pelléas asks Mélisande if she hears the sea behind them, VS, p. 110, meas. 2–5), and it returns in the closing bars (VS, p. 114, meas. 9–11). The appearance of the NEC short score draft of scene 3 (particularly the type of paper used) suggests that the extensive revisions which brought the scene to its final state were made after 1898.

As in the Act II draft, the Meyer Act V gives evidence of Debussy's compositional procedures, particularly his habit of revision through rewriting and replacing pages. Act V is nearly complete: Debussy left out just one measure, although he left space for it in the manuscript (fol. 8^r, sys. 5; LPm, p. 71); the measure requires just a single note corresponding to Mélisande's unaccompanied "Oui" (VS, p. 287, meas. 5). The ten measures corresponding to VS, p. 281, meas. 2–11 are missing between fols. 6^r and 7^r (LPm, pp. 68 and 70), but are contained, though in a preliminary form, on two of the verso pages: the first of these measures (with Golaud's text, "Je suis un malheureux"; "I am an unfortunate man") is the last measure of fol. 6^v (LPm, p. 69), and the remaining measures follow the crossed-out portion of fol. 12^v (LPm, p. 77), upside down with respect to fol. 12^r. These two versos otherwise represent rejected pages, and it appears that fol. 6^v was written to join up with the previously written fol. 12^v, after the latter's first two systems had been crossed out. Fol. 6^v was the original continuation from fol. 5^r (LPm, p. 67), but when the last seven measures of fol. 5^r were crossed out, fol. 6^r was written to replace both those measures and all but the last of fol. 6^v.

The third of the verso pages, fol. 9^v, contains little more than two measures and is one of three Meyer MS attempts to set Mélisande's line "Y-a-t'il longtemps que nous nous sommes vus?" ("Is it a long while since we saw each other?"; VS, p. 279, meas. 7–8); the others are found on fols. 6^r and 6^v. All three have the Forest/Antiquity theme from Act I, scene 1 in the accompaniment, signifying Mélisande's recollection of her first meeting with Golaud.

The Short Score (NEC, Legouix, and Bréval MSS)

The short score (or developed draft) stage is represented by three manuscripts: the complete draft (NEC MS) and two manuscripts containing folios that were at one time part of this draft but were, as a result of subsequent revisions, removed from it (Legouix and Bréval MSS).

After completing his preliminary draft of a scene or act, Debussy's next step was to write out a clean short score. He evidently did this right away, while the music was still fresh in his mind, as it was only incompletely and rather roughly sketched in the preliminary draft. For Debussy, it seems, it was the writing out of the short score and not the preliminary draft that marked the "completion" of an act or scene. This can be inferred from the express letter ("pneumatique") which Debussy sent to Henry Lerolle on 20 June 1895 to announce his completion of Act V and in which he wrote out the final bars of that act, not as they appear in the Meyer draft, but in the form they were to take in the short score. Furthermore, the music in the express letter is completely orchestrated—written on two staves but with the instrumentation indicated.

The writing of the short score was therefore not just an act of copying for Debussy, but involved a certain amount of revision and refinement as well as the continuation of his process of indicating the orchestration. There are thus places in the score where a passage will be written (copied), crossed out, and immediately rewritten, and a comparison with the preliminary drafts shows that Debussy sometimes introduced revisions or retouchings in the course of copying.

In contrast to the Meyer MS preliminary drafts, the short score was always written in ink (though corrections and annotations were often made with colored pencils); the orchestral reduction, the vocal parts, and the text were written out in full; stage directions were given; and there were many indications of the instrumentation. Dynamics and articulation marks were generally omitted, though. In contrast to the separate folios of the preliminary drafts, the short score was usually written on bifolios, rectos only, with the versos reserved for revisions. The short score was laid out fairly consistently in systems of five staves, two for the voices and three for the orchestra (the chorus in Act I, scene 3 occupies an additional two or three staves when it participates), and Debussy generally left a blank stave between systems. This allowed, in most cases, five systems per page on 30-stave paper and four per page on 26-stave paper.

Despite its neat appearance and relatively complete notation, the short score was still a private document. Key and time signatures were notated, but clefs were often omitted and accidentals sometimes left out. It was from this manuscript that Debussy prepared the two scores that were destined for the performers and the public: the vocal and full scores.

Until recently, the complete short score (NEC MS) was owned by the New England Conservatory of Music, Boston. According to the recollections of Wallace Goodrich, the *Pelléas* short score was the gift of Eben D. Jordan, President of the Boston Opera House as well as President of the Conservatory's Board of Trustees, and it was obtained for him in Paris by Henry Russell, General Director of the Boston Opera Company, probably around 1910–11.[13] The absence of a signed inscription in the manuscript suggests that it was sold to Jordan and not offered as a gift. Before he parted with the manuscript, Debussy removed one page (fol. 17 of Act II), inscribed it to a Dr. René Vaucaire, and presumably presented it to him as a gift.

Jordan may well have seen *Pelléas* when it was first performed in Boston, on 1 April 1909, by Oscar Hammerstein's Manhattan Opera Company, or three years later, on 10 January 1912, presented by the Boston Opera Company, with Georgette Leblanc as Mélisande and André Caplet conducting. During the summer of 1911, Russell had taken a model of the Boston Opera House stage to Paris in order to show the scenery and mise-en-scène to Debussy and Maeterlinck. Both seem to have been impressed, but neither crossed the Atlantic to attend the performances.[14]

The NEC MS was sold by Christie's, New York, on 21 May 1982 for a record $350,000. It was purchased by Frederick R. Koch and deposited in The Pierpont Morgan Library, New York. Less than three weeks later, on 9 June, the folio that had been removed from the manuscript in 1910 was sold by Stargardt, Marburg; it too was purchased by Koch and was restored to its original place in the complete manuscript.

The short score was assembled by Debussy as he progressed with the composition of the opera, with each scene or act inserted as it was written. In the course of later revisions (some made even before the opera was finished), it sometimes became necessary to remove and replace certain folios. This is known from the survival of some of these rejected pages (viz., the Legouix and Bréval MSS), from information contained in the composer's correspondence, and from the physical appearance of the NEC MS, especially the types of paper used.

In writing the short score, Debussy used three types of paper, all in upright format, approximately 400 mm. x 300 mm.: 26- and 30-stave paper bearing the same blind stamp as the pages of the Meyer MS ("LARD-ESNAULT/Paris/25, RUE FEYDEAU"), and 30-stave paper with the watermark "LATUNE ET CIE BLACONS" and a different blind stamp (see fig. 4). This embossment appears in a Debussy manuscript for the first time (as far as I know) in the *Stichvorlage* of the first two *Chansons de Bilitis* (F-Pn, Ms. 1007), a manuscript which was written in 1898 (before September, when the corrected proofs were given to Pierre Louÿs), the year in which Edmond Bellamy's name was apparently added to the blind stamp of the firm H. Lard-Esnault. [15] Therefore, any page of the short score that bears the Bellamy blind stamp must date from 1898 or later, while pages with the Lard-Esnault stamp most likely predate 1898 and were probably part of the draft completed in 1895.

Figure 4.   Paper Maker's Blind Stamp: NEC Manuscript (Folios Dating from 1898 or Later).

The breakdown of the NEC MS according to paper type is given below. Each act has its own title page and its folios are numbered separately:

Act I   The original pages seem to be those on 26-stave paper with the Lard-Esnault stamp: fols. 2–15, which contain scene 1 from Golaud's entrance on, and scene 2, almost to the end of Arkel's long speech (VS, p. 3, meas. 1–p. 32, meas. 2). Here as elsewhere in the manuscript, the interludes are those of the first edition, before they were expanded. Fol. 1 is on 30-stave paper with the same stamp and is probably a replacement for the original prelude; the blank space in the last system suggests this. Also on this type of 30-stave paper are fols. 18–19, the very end of scene 2, the interlude, and the beginning of scene 3, almost to the point of Pelléas's entrance (VS, p. 37, meas. 5–p. 42, meas. 3). The remaining pages carry the later embossment and were inserted in or after 1898: fols. 16–17 (including three measures on fol. 17^v), which constitute approximately the last third of scene 2 (VS, p. 32, meas. 3–p. 37, meas. 4), and fols. 20–23, the latter two-thirds of scene 3 (VS, p. 42, meas. 4–p. 54). Altogether, about one-quarter of the act (6 out of 23 fols.) was to some extent rewritten in or after 1898. Interestingly enough, the last folio, which contains the dates of composition (December 1893, January and February 1894), is one of these later pages, and Debussy must have copied these dates from the original concluding page. The same is true of the final folios of Acts II and IV, demonstrating that the composer had some interest in preserving the chronology of his composition, despite his later dismissal of such concern for dates as "perfectly useless."[16]

Act II   Fols. 1–14 are on 30-stave paper with the Lard-Esnault stamp and contain scene 1 and almost all of scene 2 (through VS, p. 102, meas. 4); the balance of the act, fols. 15–19, is on the later paper, demonstrating that scene 3, which is so different from the Meyer version, was probably rewritten in or after 1898.[17] Fol. 19 bears the two dates, June and 17 August 1895.

Act III   The third act is entirely on 30-stave paper bearing the earlier stamp, with the single exception of the final page (fol. 33), which has the later stamp. The music on this folio corresponds roughly to the ending found in the original Fromont edition of the vocal score, p. 168, meas. 15–p. 169, which contains music cut from both the full score and the 1907 Durand vocal score. Despite the nearly complete uniformity of paper type, there is evidence that the first 32 folios were not written in sequence and that replacements were made. Bifolio 5–6 appears to have been written after fol. 7, as Debussy, after writing to the bottom of fol. 6^r, needed to write three measures on fol. 6^v (revised and compressed into two bars on the staves beneath) in order to join up with the previously written fol. 7^r.

Act IV   More than half of this act was written on replacement pages. The original pages, on 30-stave paper with the earlier embossment, are fols. 5–14, all but the last page of scene 2 (through VS, p. 218, meas. 4), and fols. 17–19, the major and central portion of scene 3 (VS, p. 224, meas. 5–p. 230, meas. 10). The remaining pages are all written on the later paper: fols. 1–4 (scene 1), fols.

15–16 (the end of scene 2 and the beginning of scene 3), and fols. 20–33 (the end of scene 3 and all of scene 4). The final folio of this act is the only *Pelléas* manuscript to contain a date after 1895; four dates are listed: September–October 1893 (the date of the Legouix MS Act IV, scene 4), March 1895) (the date of the Bréval MS), January 1900, and September 1901. In addition, Debussy mentioned in a letter to Laloy (LAL, p. 26) that scene 4 was done over in May 1901. It is probable, then, that scenes 1 and 4 date from 1900–1901.[18]

Act V About half of Act V was also rewritten after the opera was first completed. Fols. 3–10 are on the earlier 30-stave paper, while fols. 1–2 (VS, p. 268, meas. 1–p. 272, meas. 4) and fols. 11–18 (VS, p. 293, meas. 7–p. 310) are on the later paper.

Differences in certain features of Debussy's handwriting also differentiate the pre- and post-1898 pages. One of the best indicators, since they appear on every page, are the short horizontal strokes with which Debussy bracketed the vocal and instrumental staves of each system; in the earlier pages he used single strokes, while in the later pages he tended to use double strokes. There are also differences in the way Debussy identified the characters singing—the way he abbreviated their names or wrote their initials in the left margin beside their parts. For example, in Act IV, scene 3, "Yniold" was abbreviated "Yn." in the earlier pages and "Y^d" in the later ones. He also tended to write the letter G (for Golaud or Geneviève) in two different ways: in the earlier pages, he usually wrote it with two separate strokes and an open loop at the bottom ($\mathcal{G}$), and in the later pages, generally with a single, continuous line and a closed loop ($\mathcal{f}$).

The scrutiny of handwriting and paper types thus shows that a considerable portion of the opera was reworked in the short score stage between 1898 and 1901: essentially, the latter portions of scenes 2 and 3 of Act I, scene 3 of Act II, scenes 1 and 4 of Act IV, and the beginning and latter half of Act V. These revisions were accomplished during the period when Debussy had reason to expect that a production of *Pelléas* was forthcoming. It was in May 1898 that the opera was accepted "in principle" by the Opéra-Comique and in May 1901 that he received Carré's written promise that it would be presented during the coming season.

Debussy's manner of revising his short score can be better understood through a study of the Legouix and Bréval MSS (which consist of pages which were once a part of and then removed from the "complete" short score) and through a comparison of these manuscripts with the NEC score.

The Legouix MS is named for its former owner, the Paris dealer Robert Legouix; the manuscript was purchased at a Paris auction in December 1979 by Robert O. Lehman and deposited in The Pierpont Morgan Library, New York. The final folio is dated "September–October–93" and signed by Debussy with the three-initial monogram C.A.D. (🎼·), which is also found in the 1891 manuscript of "Fantouches" from the first set of *Fêtes galantes* (Coll. Jobert-Georges) and on the title page of *Rodrigue et Chimène*, dated 1892 (Lehman deposit, Pierpont Morgan Library). The Legouix MS is written on six bifolios of the same type of paper used in parts of the Meyer MS and in the earlier sections of the NEC MS: 30-stave paper with the Lard-Esnault blind stamp. The Legouix MS is the earliest surviving (and probably the first) short score that Debussy made of Act IV, scene 4, and it was evidently written shortly after the completion of the preliminary draft of the scene, a portion of which is included in the Meyer MS. Originally, the Legouix draft contained the entire scene on nine bifolios, three of which were later removed, and was written on rectos only. A handwriting characteristic unique to this draft is the use of pairs of heavy diagonal strokes as system separation marks, written as part of the system bracket, just above the topmost stave in each system.

The manuscript is written in black ink with indications of the instrumentation in green pencil. Debussy entered his revisions of the draft in two different manners. Where it could be easily done, he superimposed his revision directly over the original version using a contrasting color (green pencil), or else he used empty stave space directly above or below the material to be replaced. Where the revision was so extensive that it could not be easily entered in this manner, Debussy sketched it on the empty facing verso page: fols. 7^v, 8^v, 9^v, and 10^v were so used. In the Legouix MS these revisions have the appearance of the writing in the preliminary drafts: the notation is rough and incomplete, it appears to have been written rapidly, and the voice parts are lacking their texts. In sketching these revisions, Debussy probably had the intention of writing them out neatly and completely soon afterwards in another draft of the short score, just as the preliminary drafts, it seems, were copied in short score soon after they were completed. In other words, most of the revisions of the Legouix MS were probably made just before Debussy wrote out the second short score draft of the scene, contained in the Bréval MS, in May 1895. Legouix MS fol. 12^v contains the sketch of a single measure, which corresponds to meas. 9–10 of the Act IV prelude in its earliest surviving version (Basel MS, p. 104; similar to VS, p. 189, meas. 5). This suggests that Debussy may have been working on scene 1, either revising or perhaps even composing it, at the time that he was revising scene 4.

The Bréval MS (F-Pn, Ms. 1206) is named for the singer Lucienne Bréval, who left this manuscript to the library of the Paris Conservatoire, from which it went to the Bibliothèque Nationale.[19] This manuscript, written on the same type of paper as the Legouix MS, is in two parts: fols. 2–17, eight bifolios, are a draft of Act IV, scene 4, complete, and fols. 18–19, a single bifolio, contain the latter half of Act IV, scene 1 (from the measure corresponding to VS, p. 192, meas. 6).[20] Fol. 17, the final page of scene 4, is dated September–October 1893 and May 1895: Debussy evidently recorded the dates of both the first version of the scene and of the revision. Bréval MS fols. 5–17 were numbered 24–36 by Debussy, indicating that they were indeed once part of a draft of the entire act. (The NEC MS Act IV occupies 33 folios; in successive revisions scene 4 occupied fewer and fewer pages: 18 in Legouix, 16 in Bréval, and 14 in NEC; the differences are the result of both successive cuts in the scene and, in the case of the NEC MS, more compact handwriting.) The Act IV, scene 1 bifolio of the Bréval MS was also once part of the complete draft, one in which these folios continued directly to the current NEC MS, IV, fol. 5. Bréval MS fol. 19ᵛ contains a rewriting of the interlude between the first two scenes, replacing the top two-and-a-half systems of NEC MS, IV, fol. 5.

In writing the Bréval MS Act IV, scene 4, Debussy not only copied from the Legouix MS, incorporating its revisions, but actually removed three bifolios from it and made them part of the new draft (Bréval MS, fols. 6–11 [LPm, pp. 99–110], which originally followed Legouix MS, fol. 4). The peculiar system separation marks of the Legouix MS are visible on these pages and other physical features confirm the insertion.[21] The juncture is also apparent since the preceding Bréval MS fol. 5 duplicates the first twelve measures of the initial page of the Legouix insert; these measures were simply crossed out in the latter.

The creation of the Bréval MS draft was not simply an act of copying, although much copying was clearly involved. At many points the two drafts are identical, and in one spot on fol. 5, Debussy, evidently in a lapse of concentration, started to write out one bar a second time and had to cross out the duplicated measure. In general, the composer incorporated into the Bréval draft the revisions he had entered in the Legouix MS on both its recto and verso pages. However, sometimes, in an apparent change of heart, he chose to disregard a Legouix revision and perpetuated the original reading, as in the passage where Mélisande sings "Comme nos ombres sont grandes ce soir," copied directly from Legouix fol. 9ʳ to Bréval fol. 14ʳ, ignoring the Legouix revisions on both fols. 8ᵛ and 9ʳ. Very often Debussy seems to be recomposing while copying, as parts of the Bréval draft are completely different from the setting in Legouix and no sketched revision is present. A striking example is the passage beginning with Pelléas's "Quel est ce bruit?" (Legouix MS, fols. 6ʳ–7ʳ; Bréval MS, fol. 12ʳ), which follows a twenty-four-measure section present in Legouix but cut from Bréval: six measures of music in Legouix (through Pelléas's "Ecoute! écoute!...") became ten measures in Bréval, entirely different in both voice and orchestra parts.

Just as the Legouix pages were revised and replaced by those in Bréval, so the latter too were removed from the complete draft and replaced with revised substitutes. By the time they were replaced (in January 1900, May 1901, or September 1901, three dates given by Debussy for revisions of Act IV), these pages themselves were much revised—in black, red, blue, purple, and two shades of green pencil and in black, red, and blue ink. As in the Legouix MS, the revisions are entered on both rectos and versos. The verso revisions in Bréval tend to be neater than those in Legouix, and most are written in ink. On fols. 10^v and 13^v and at isolated points on fols. 4^v and 15^v, the vocal parts are even supplied with texts. (It was in this revision on fol. 15^v that Debussy first introduced the simultaneous singing of the two lovers, an effect he had not exploited in the earlier drafts.) In the former two cases, the revision is as neat as the original, suggesting that at least some of these revisions were written with the intention of having them stand in the manuscript; they were not roughly sketched simply as preparation for a newly copied draft.

The NEC MS contains very few revisions on its verso folios, and one of them is of the type just discussed—neatly and completely notated, with the text written in full (Act IV, fol. 19^v). Another (Act III, fol. 17^v), which involved a revision of text, was rather more hastily notated, but its text was also given. Other versos contain revisions of the interludes and on others Debussy sketched some of the orchestration. These last were probably entered during the process of writing out the full score.

Although few revisions were made on the verso pages, the NEC MS contains many changes, additions, and annotations on the rectos—in black, blue, and two types of red ink and in black, red, purple, two shades of blue, and two shades of green pencil. The principal reason for all of these colors was contrast: to differentiate the various layers of revision. The great variety of colors no doubt arises from the fact that this manuscript was written and revised over a period of many years: some of its pages may date from as early as 1893 while others are from 1901. Some of the infrequent colors at least, such as purple or yellow-green pencil, were probably used in specific limited time periods, perhaps even in a single sitting. Sometimes certain colors were used for specific purposes: blue ink was often used for scene titles and set descriptions, stage directions, and tempo markings, and red ink and green pencil were often used to indicate the instrumentation of the orchestra reduction.

Debussy signalled some revisions in Act I, scenes 1 and 2 (usually of the voice parts) with proofreaders' marks in the right margin, evidently as a reminder to add these corrections to a score that had already been copied before the changes were made. Since both the vocal and full scores were written on the basis of the short score (and in that sequence), the marks generally signal changes that were made during the orchestration process and needed to be transferred to the previously written vocal score, either in the proof stage or in a subsequent edition of that score.

The NEC MS contains many more instrumental indications than either the Bréval or Legouix MSS, and they are sometimes extremely precise in specifying particular orchestrational effects, such as muted strings playing sul tasto ("Cordes sourdines s. la touche") and stopped trumpets ("Trompettes sons bouchés") (Act II, fol. 15), four solo double basses divisi ("CB divisées en 4 soli") (Act III, fol. 13), two solo violins without mutes ("2 s.v.s./ sd") (Act V, fol. 16), and violas divisi in 2 and cellos divisi in 3 ("Alt en 2/ V^c d en 3") (Act I, fol. 1). In the interlude between scenes 1 and 2 of Act III (fol. 12), the orchestration is meticulously annotated; Debussy even indicated the polyphonic strands in his chord progressions, drawing red ink lines to show the voice leading he wished to employ in his orchestration.

Manuscript Piano-Vocal Reduction (Basel MS; F-Pn, MSS 17683 and 17686)

As mentioned above, the manuscript short score provided the basis for both the manuscript piano-vocal reduction and the manuscript full score. The former served as the *Stichvorlage* for the published vocal score, which the singers needed in order to learn their parts. The latter served as the conductor's score for the early performances, was the source for the orchestra parts, and then became the *Stichvorlage* for the published full score. Therefore, these two manuscript scores had to be carefully and completely notated, as any imprecision, inaccuracy, or ambiguity could adversely affect the performances of the work.

The vocal score is not so much a reduction of the short score (it was evidently made before the complete orchestration of the opera), as it is a recreation of the (imagined) orchestral accompaniment for piano. Throughout the composition of *Pelléas* and during the years preceding the première, Debussy often gave private performances of portions of the opera, singing the voice parts and accompanying himself at the piano. Since he had often played from the short score in this manner, it was probably a relatively simple task for him to make the piano reduction. The experience of piano rehearsals of *Pelléas* has shown that, when played by a skilled and sensitive pianist, the reduction is really quite beautiful in and of itself, and not merely as a reminder of the way the orchestra sounds.

Debussy evidently did not write out the piano reduction until he had to, that is, not until there was a serious prospect for the performance and possible publication of the work. Only Acts IV and V of the vocal score *Stichvorlage* have come to light: Act IV, scenes 1 and 2 and Act V (F-Pn, Ms. 17686, gift of Mme Jobert-Georges, 1981) evidently remained with Fromont after the publication of the score and became the property of Jean Jobert, Fromont's successor; Act IV, scenes 3–4 (F-Pn, Ms. 17683, on deposit from the collection of Mlle Françoise Prudhomme, 1978) formerly belonged to Jean Périer, the creator of the role of Pelléas. Annotations in the score by A. Gulon,

Fromont's engraver, verify that these manuscripts were the *Stichvorlage* of the first edition of the vocal score: Gulon marked the system and page ends of the engraved score into the manuscript by indicating the number of staves each system required (counting from the top of the page) and for page ends, adding the number of the page.

The two halves of the Act IV manuscript appear to have been separated during the publication process. The manuscripts of both acts are written mostly on bifolios: 24-stave pages, approximately 345 mm. x 270 mm., with the Bellamy blind stamp. Acts IV and V were written as separate units, each ending with a complete bifolio even though only the first recto was needed, and each enclosed in a bifolio of the same type of music paper, with the outer recto serving as a title page, and further enclosed in an orange folder bearing the name of the opera and the number of the act. (The Act IV bifolio folder remained with the manuscript of the first two scenes.) Debussy wrote these manuscripts almost entirely in black ink and on both sides of the page. Since the score was destined for the engraver, it was not necessary to leave blank versos for revisions. Some scene headings and tempo indications are in blue ink, and in the interlude between scenes 1 and 2 of Act IV, two omitted notes were inserted in red ink. Other changes were made through erasure and rewriting in black ink. The music of Act IV occupies 41 pages, numbered 103–43, but Debussy only put page numbers on the outside pages of each bifolio—only what was necessary to keep the pages in order. Pages 107/108 and 109/110 are single sheets and are the only folios where both sides are numbered. The latter is evidently a replacement for the original 109/110, which probably formed a bifolio with 107/108 (the last measure of p. 110 is a slightly revised copy of the first measure of p. 111, and the latter is crossed out in blue pencil). Even at this stage, it seems that Debussy sometimes revised through page replacement. Pages 131/[132] and [133]/134 are also single sheets, but appear to be a bifolio which has simply separated. The break in the manuscript occurs between the single sheets 119/[120] and [121]/122, which probably once formed a bifolio; neither p. 120 nor 121 was given a page number by Debussy. At the top of p. 121 the engraver first stamped (by mistake) "CORRIGÉ/ A. GULON" and then over it, "GRAVÉ/ A. GULON," to indicate that he had engraved the music on these pages. Usually he would place such a stamp only on the first page or title page of a work he was engraving, and its appearance here would seem to suggest that he may have received the music of this act in two installments. The break occurs close to a musical division (just before the interlude joining scenes 2 and 3; VS, p. 219, meas. 12 is the first measure of p. 121), but it does not coincide with the end of a page in the first edition.

The twenty-one pages of Act V are numbered 144–64, also almost all bifolios with the page numbers written on the outside pages only. The sole exceptions are pages 156/[157] and [158]/159, which are single sheets that appear to be a separated bifolio.

If Act IV was last revised in September 1901, then the manuscript vocal score of this act was probably written soon after. Act V was probably written afterwards, as its page numbers follow precisely from where Act IV leaves off. Also pointing to its late origin is the fact that its text contains two changes of wording adopted from Maeterlinck's second published revision of his play, which did not appear in print until 1902 but which the playwright probably shared with the composer at a meeting in Paris, perhaps in June 1901.

Was the piano reduction of the first three acts also written in the summer of 1901 or was there an earlier draft of the entire vocal score? In April 1900 Hartmann, believing that *Pelléas* might be scheduled at the Opéra-Comique in the coming season, urged the composer to give him "before April 30th, latest delay, the completed reduction of *Pelléas*" so that it could be printed by 1 September. These plans were aborted due to Hartmann's death on 22 April, and it remains uncertain whether or not Debussy actually made the requested reduction. It is also possible, of course, that such a manuscript existed even prior to this but that the composer's Act IV revisions of January 1900 had made it necessary to redo at least those pages. Debussy might have made a piano reduction as early as 1898, when *Pelléas* was accepted "in principle" by the Opéra-Comique, or perhaps even earlier.

While this is all speculative, some light is shed on the question by the survival of several pages of a manuscript vocal score which represents a preliminary version of the opera. This manuscript (in a private collection in Basel) consists of seven folios: twelve pages of music written on both sides of six folios preceded by a title page on which Debussy has written "Pelléas et Mélisande./4eme Acte."[22] The manuscript contains Act IV, scene 1 and the beginning of scene 2, through Golaud's "Pelléas part ce soir" (VS, p. 205, meas. 11). The first page of music is page 104, but not every page is numbered—only pages 104, 108, 112, and 115—a pagination which suggests that the six music folios are actually three bifolios and that Debussy only numbered the first page of each as well as the last page of the manuscript; the fragility of the current binding makes it impossible to verify this structure without endangering the binding. The paper is the same type found in the other vocal score manuscripts (24-stave paper with the Bellamy embossment), and as in all other *Pelléas* manuscripts written on paper with this stamp, Debussy used the double stroke bracketing convention. This means that the Basel manuscript could not have been written before 1898. Like the other vocal score manuscripts, it was written in black ink, and while evidently intended as a *Stichvorlage,* it never reached the engraver. (There are no engraver's marks on it.)

The Basel MS seems to be based on the short score, but at a time when the

Bréval MS pages of scene 1 were part of the complete draft, i.e., before the current NEC MS, IV, fols. 1–4 were written. It captures the Bréval MS at an intermediate stage, after some changes had been made, but before its final revisions. For example, the Basel MS scene 1 does not observe a seven-measure cut indicate on Bréval MS, fol. 19^r, nor does it adopt the interlude revision found on Bréval MS, fol. 19^v; these major changes and other less dramatic ones were obviously made in the Bréval MS after the Basel MS had been written. The Basel draft stands in a similar relationship to NEC MS, IV, fols. 5–9, where again some of the latter's revisions have been adopted but other changes were yet to be made. Although evidently based on these specific short score pages, Debussy seems to have made spontaneous revisions in writing out the vocal score, and the Basel MS contains several independent readings.

This manuscript is thus valuable for several reasons. It represents the only surviving pages from a preliminary version of the piano reduction, and it fixes an intermediate stage where Debussy obviously considered his opera a finished work and no longer a work in progress. Furthermore, it is the only surviving source of a preliminary version of the first half of Act IV, scene 1. It preserves the earlier, longer act prelude, and a comparison with the definitive draft provides good examples of the types of refinements that Debussy made in revising passages which were primarily recitativelike in character. Compared with this earlier version, the later drafts tended to eliminate some rests between sentences, removing pauses within speeches. They also shortened some of the sustained chords, producing more "silence" in the accompaniment. Several important thematic changes were also made in the orchestra part subsequent to the Basel draft, all textually or dramatically motivated; these thematic revisions (the addition of leitmotifs) will be discussed in chapter 9.

The Basel MS is bound with the *Stichvorlage* of *Pour le piano,* inscribed to Nico Coronio (dedicatee of the third movement, Toccata) with the dates January–April 1901. Just as in the Meyer MS, these are the dates of composition and not of the inscription. A letter from Debussy to Fromont of 28 August 1901 discusses the proofs of *Pour le piano* and the manuscript of this work was probably returned to the composer in order for him to correct the proofs. In all probability, the Basel *Pelléas* pages were removed from a complete piano reduction at around the same time and were also presented to Coronio, perhaps in September 1901 when Debussy returned to Paris from his vacation in Bichain. Since Debussy evidently revised Act IV in September 1901, the Basel pages, whenever they were written, certainly became obsolete by this date and had to be replaced.

It appears that the Basel MS was once part of a complete draft of the piano reduction. Its page numbers indicate that the first three acts had already been written, and since its last page is written to the very bottom, there is no sign that this draft was aborted in midstream. Furthermore, it does not appear that Debussy merely replaced the three bifolios of the Basel MS and otherwise retained the existent draft of Act IV. Rather, it seems that all of Acts IV and V were written around September 1901, for reasons given above. Again, one wonders if Debussy also rewrote the piano reduction of the first three acts during the summer of 1901 or if he merely retained those acts from the earlier complete draft of which the Basel MS pages were once a part. The fact that the Basel MS Act IV begins with page 104 while the *Stichvorlage* Act IV begins with page 103 might indeed suggest that they belong to entirely different drafts of the complete opera. On the other hand, Debussy may merely have made a mistake in numbering the pages of the new Act IV.

Proofs and Publication of the Vocal Score (Fromont, 1902)

Two incomplete sets of proofs for the first edition of the vocal score (Fromont, 1902), formerly in the collection of Jean Périer, are now in the Bibliothèque Nationale (Rés. Vma. 237, on deposit from the collection of Mlle Françoise Prudhomme, 1978). Each set contains three acts: one includes Acts I–III, and the other, Acts II–IV; Périer may have had little interest in keeping Act V (or he may not have been given it) since the character of Pelléas (which he sang) dies at the end of Act IV. The singer gave both sets of proofs to a woman named Henriette, along with the following note, written on his calling card and dated 1933: "Here are the proofs of *Pelléas*, corrected by Debussy. It was from these proofs that I learned my role. Keep them in remembrance of me."

For the first set of proofs, each act is enclosed in a heavy orange paper folder on which Debussy has written the name of the opera and the number of the act. The proofs are on separate sheets of relatively thin paper, printed on one side only. The first page of each act is stamped "CORRIGÉ/ A. GULON," which is the engraver's way of indicating that the corrections marked in the proofs have been transferred to the plates. The corrections are entered in a variety of colors, in pencil and in pen, and their presence is signalled by proofreaders' marks in the margins. Most of the changes are indeed corrections of mistakes or omissions and involve notes (pitches and rhythms), accidentals, clefs, ties, slurs, scene titles and headings, and the spelling and punctuation of the text. Many dynamic markings were added in the proofs and Debussy also introduced a number of revisions, mostly in the rhythm, but sometimes in the pitches, of the voice parts. Some changes in the part of Pelléas in Act III, scene 1 appear to have been made specifically for (or perhaps even by) Périer, as they invariably lower the tessitura (sometimes moving a passage down an octave), adapting it to his "baryton Martin" range. These changes were not intended to become a definitive part of the score, and they were not incorporated into the first or any other edition of the opera.

Such changes are much more frequent in the second set of proofs (Acts II–IV), which bears other signs of having been printed expressly for the singer's use. These proofs look more like a published score, printed on both sides of the page, on heavier paper, and with the pages of each act arranged in nested bifolios. Périer's signature is on the cover of each act, perhaps to mark it as his property when he brought it to rehearsals at the Opéra-Comique. These proofs were pulled after the corrections of the previous proofs had been made in the plates, though they still do not bring the score to the state of the first edition. In all likelihood, Périer started to learn his part from the earlier proofs but then replaced them with the new proofs once they became available. Though primarily used by the singer, these second proofs also contain a number of corrections not related to his role, which are signalled by proofreaders' marks in the margins and which were to become part of the published score.

As one would expect, the part of Pelléas is heavily annotated: the beats are numbered in practically every measure in which that character sings and there are frequent warnings regarding the rhythmic execution, such as "Watch the rhythm," "Pay attention to the triplets," and "Be careful to observe the rhythmic values." Sometimes words are underlined, either for emphasis on those words or to warn of a particular difficulty. At many points in Act IV, scene 4 (as in Act III, scene 1 in the earlier set of proofs), the part of Pelléas was altered to lower the tessitura for Périer. Towards the end of the scene, a change was also made in the text: "Ta bouche! Ta bouche!" ("Your mouth! Your mouth!") was changed to "Ta bouche! donne!" ("Your mouth! give it!") (VS, p. 264, meas. 9–p. 265, meas. 2). It is not known whether, or to what extent, Debussy sanctioned such changes, but it appears that Périer's rewriting of his part may have been an ongoing process. On 18 June 1908, Debussy wrote to Jacques Durand, complaining about Périer's performance at the Opéra-Comique: "One rather comic detail is that people find Périer more and more admirable. This is undoubtedly due to the fact that he no longer sings my music at all" (LL, p. 171). The evidence of these proofs shows that Debussy's remark had a basis in fact and was a commentary, not merely on the execution, but on the intent as well.

The issue of adapting the part of Pelléas was raised in 1906, when it was proposed that the tenor Edmond Clément sing the role in Brussels, and the singer submitted to Debussy the modifications he wished to make in the part to adapt it to his voice. Debussy was horrified by the proposed changes and wrote to Durand on 14 August 1906 that he found them unacceptable:

> I don't know if you have looked at the score of *Pelléas* annotated by Clément, which I received today. It's scandalous! This man is even less of a musician than has become usual in the world of tenors. He certainly marked it—for destruction ["Ce n'est pas du 'pointage' mais du carnage"]; not a single phrase has been left intact. It would be necessary practically to rewrite the entire score.

> Ultimately, it is extraordinarily impudent! I am writing to Kufferath [codirector of the Théâtre de la Monnaie] to explain this to him and to beg him to be truly willing to seek another solution.
>
> Rest assured that to accept such conditions would represent a lack of respect for what I believed to have written. (Coll. Durand)

Despite the tone of this letter, Debussy was apparently willing to negotiate and told Clément what changes he would approve. Five days later, on 19 August, he wrote, presumably to Kufferath, indicating that he had reached an agreement with the tenor:

> I received this morning a letter from Clément, in which he agrees, very cordially, to what I believe acceptable to modify in the role of Pelléas.
>
> Unnecessary to declare my satisfaction with this resolution.[23]

As it turned out, the part was sung, not by Clément, but by a young baritone, Georges Petit. Nevertheless the letter reveals that the composer was not completely averse to modifying the role to suit the voice of a particular singer; he seems to have been as agreeable to adapt the part to Clément's tenor range as to Périer's baritone.

The publication history of the vocal score first edition (Fromont, 1902; plate no. E. 1416. F) has already been recounted in detail. The score went through at least three different printings, the first of which included a deluxe edition of fifty numbered copies on "papier Japon" and another fifty on "papier Hollande." This first printing contained an embarrassing error on the cast page, giving the first name of "chef du chant" Landry as Albert instead of Louis. This mistake was corrected in a second printing, and in a third, at least one change was made in the score (a wrong note in the vocal part was fixed);[24] other mistakes, however, were not rectified at this time.

Manuscript Full Score (F-Pn, Mss. 961–65; US-AUS, 4 pp.)

The manuscript full score of *Pelléas,* bound in five volumes (one for each act), is in the Bibliothèque Nationale: Mss. 961–65. This score was used by Messager and Busser to conduct the first performances of the opera, and it was also the *Stichvorlage* of the published full score (Fromont, 1904).

The manuscript is entirely written on recto sides of single sheets, approximately 400 mm. x 300 mm., with the Bellamy blind stamp and the watermark "LATUNE ET CIE BLACONS." Act I contains 65 folios: a title page, 63 pages of music (numbered 1–20, 20A–20G, 22–37, 37bis, 37ter, 38–55), and a blank final folio. Act II contains 104 folios: a title page, 102 pages of music (numbered 1–30, 31^1–35^5, 32–74, 75^0–75^3, 76–95), and a blank final folio. Act III contains 88 folios: a title page, 86 pages of music (numbered 1–86), and a blank final folio. Act IV contains 109 folios: 109 pages of music (numbered 1–16, 18–40, 41bis, 42, 42bis, 43–53, 54A–54I, 55–101). Act V contains 47 folios: 47 pages of music numbered 1–47. Folio 17 of Act IV is not missing; rather, Debussy omitted that number by mistake. Otherwise, the anomalies in the page numbering of Acts I, II and IV are the result of interlude expansions inserted in the score during the rehearsals for the first performance; in Act IV they are also the result of the physical removal and later restoration of scene 3. In Act III, scene 4, two cuts were made in the scene by fastening pages together (fols. 77–78 and 82–83): the first of these is the discussion of "the bed," which proved so controversial at the public dress rehearsal of 28 April 1902. At other points in the scene there are indications that cuts had once been made (pages were fastened together and measures were covered with blank paper), but these were subsequently opened up. (These cuts were discussed in chapter 6.)

Debussy started writing the score on 30-stave paper, then switched to 32-stave paper towards the end of Act II. The break is not a clean one, however, with fols. 70–89, 91, and 94–95 on 32-stave paper and fols. 90 and 92–93 on 30-stave paper. (Fol. 32 is the only page in the manuscript on 28-stave paper; it is pasted over the original 30-stave fol. 32.) A similar alternation between paper types occurs at the start of Act III, with fols. 1–2, 4–5, and 7 on 30-stave paper and fols. 3, 6, and 8 onwards on 32-stave paper. Acts IV and V are entirely on 32-stave paper, as are all of the folios added for the interlude expansions.

The score is written in black ink with a contrasting color (blue or red ink) often used for tempo markings, scene changes, stage directions, time signatures, etc. Corrections and additions were also sometimes made using a contrasting color or medium, usually red ink or blue or black pencil.

Numerous annotations in the NEC MS short score show that it was the source of the MS full score. As mentioned above in connection with that manuscript, Debussy indicated the instrumentation of many passages, and on some verso pages he even made sketches for the orchestration. On fol. 1^v of Act IV, for example, he began to lay out the page as if for the full score, writing, in pencil, brackets for the instruments and instrumental groups along the left side of the page, together with the abbreviated names of some of the instruments. This may have been done for a sketch of the orchestration, or perhaps simply to count the number of staves that would be required for a particular page of the full score. Such an arithmetic operation can be seen on fol. 2^r of Act III, where columns of numbers in the right margin represent precisely such calculations. As he wrote out the full score, Debussy marked his progress by annotating the NEC MS, either to project the layout of the full score as he orchestrated or to mark that layout once it had been accomplished. He used several systems, the simplest being to write an "x" in the short score to mark page endings of the full score. Sometimes the number of the full score page is written beside the "x." This system was used throughout much of Act I and sporadically in Act II: at a single point in the latter act (fol. 8), the beginning of page 43 of the full score is indicated by that number. In Act III and in Act IV (through the middle of scene 3), Debussy marked full score page beginnings by writing and circling their page numbers. These circled numbers are sometimes followed by the number of measures that fit on the page; where two systems fit, Debussy sometimes marked the point of the system break with an "x" or else wrote the number of measures in each system as a fraction, immediately after the circled page number. Thus, ⑥⑤5/4 on fol. 26 of Act III marks the point at which page 65 of the full score begins and indicates that the page has two systems, the upper with five measures, the lower, four. In places it is apparent from these markings that Debussy sometimes rewrote pages of the full score; in so doing, he redistributed the music on the new pages, crossed out the original page end or beginning markings, and wrote in new ones. This evidence of reorchestration is especially apparent at the beginnings of Acts III and IV.

The absence of page end markings in Act IV, scene 4 and Act V may be due to the fact that a copyist, and not Debussy, wrote the vocal parts and texts and may also have laid out most of these pages (Act IV, fols. 55–87 and Act V, fols. 3–18 and 20–45; at one point on Act V, fol. 41, where the NEC draft was ambiguous, the copyist tentatively sketched the voice part and text in pencil, and Debussy went over them in ink). Pressed for time, Debussy had this task done for him and afterwards filled in the orchestra parts himself. The procedure used is clarified by a rejected page whose blank verso was subsequently used as fol. 45^r of Act V. Here the copyist first drew in the bar lines (in blue pencil) in the upper system of the page and then wrote the voice part in black ink; he would next have filled in the text and then proceeded with the second system, except that an error in the vocal line forced him to reject the page and redo it (fol. 13 of Act V). The blank verso of the rejected page was then used for fol. 45. Since the copyist used the short score as his source, he did not incorporate certain changes in the voice parts that Debussy had introduced in writing out the vocal score. The resultant inconsistencies in the voice parts will be discussed in detail in chapter 8.

It was also Debussy's practice to use blue pencil to draw bar lines in the full score, and only later did he reinforce them in black ink. The reinforcement was never done on the folios of Act IV, scene 3 (fols. 51–54l), apparently since the scene was removed from the score before the première and was not restored until the second season of performances. The same blue pencil bar lines are found in three rejected pages of full score housed in the Humanities Research Center of the University of Texas at Austin. All three pages belong to Act I and are written on 30-stave paper with the Bellamy stamp, as are most of the pages in that act. One page, bearing the folio number 40, corresponds to that folio of Act I and is laid out the same way. Debussy had filled in the voice and string parts in black ink and was in the process of writing out the winds when he realized that he had misaligned the flutes with the other parts, so he rejected and rewrote the page. Two other pages, though unnumbered, were written as fols. 20–21 of the score and contain the original interlude between scenes 1 and 2. Debussy marked numerous blue pencil revisions of the orchestration (redistributing string parts and altering wind doublings) on the former page and recopied it as the correct fol. 20. The latter page is incomplete (the last two measures were never filled in), and it was probably rewritten as fol. 21, only to be replaced by fols. 20A–20G when the interlude expansions were added.

The Humanities Research Center also owns a half-page of 30-stave paper containing 16 measures of music, written in black ink in short score (three staves). The music does not correspond precisely to any part of *Pelléas* but is probably a sketch (never used) for one of the interlude expansions that Debussy had to add during the rehearsals. The use of the Pelléas motive in meas. 5–6 and 13–14 makes the connection of this sketch with the opera fairly certain.[25]

The pattern of revising, removing, rewriting, and replacing pages, found at every compositional stage, was also, as has been shown, a feature of the manuscript full score. Since this was a performing score, changes could not be made on facing verso pages, nor could they be added on adjacent staves, as either method would doubtless cause confusion on the podium. When changes were not made by removing and replacing pages, they were accomplished by pasting the new version over the old (Act II, fol. 32 and Act III, fol. 27, top system) or, more usually, by erasing the original version and writing the revision in its place. This was done either by Debussy himself or sometimes by another hand, though surely at the composer's direction. Though written essentially by Debussy (with the aid of a copyist as described), the manuscript contains some writing and annotations in hands other than the composer's. Debussy's correspondence with the harpist Martenot reveals his occasional uncertainty when it came to writing for the harp, and indeed the parts for that instrument on fols. 2, 8, 18, and 29–30 of Act II were written by somebody other than Debussy. Otherwise, the writing not by the composer generally consists of performance indications, written in blue and black pencil, probably by Messager and Busser, both of whom conducted from this score. Messager is also evidently responsible for most of the curtain signals ("Rideau") and for the orchestra rehearsal numbers, all of which became part of the published score.

As mentioned, this score was used by Gulon in engraving the plates for the first edition of the full score, and the pencil markings he made in laying out the pages are visible throughout, even though an attempt was made to erase them in places. The title page of the first act, written by Debussy in red ink, was modified in pencil in order to produce a cover design for the binding of these volumes.

Proofs of the Full Score

Portions of the first and second proofs of the *Pelléas* full score are currently housed in two collections: the first proofs of Act I and the second of Act III are in the Bibliothèque Nationale, Ms. 1029, and the second proofs of Acts I–II and the first of Acts III–V, all five bound together in a single volume, are in The Pierpont Morgan Library, Robert Owen Lehman deposit. In only three cases was the sequence of the proofs specified by Debussy: he labeled the Lehman Act V, "first proof" ("1ere Epreuve"), and the Lehman Act II and Bibliothèque Nationale Act III, "second proofs" ("2eme épreuve"). Otherwise, the order must be determined through a comparison of the proofs with one another as well as with the manuscript full score, on the one hand, and the first edition, on the other. The final proofs, marked "ready for the press" ("bon à tirer") and dated 29 June 1904 by Debussy, are also in the Bibliothèque Nationale, Rés. Vma. 281 (gift of Mme de Tinan, 1980). The present location of four additional pages of proofs for the end of Act I, scene 3 (pp. 65–68) is unknown. Listed in a 1972 sale catalogue (Librairie C. Coulet & A. Faure, *Spectacles,* p. 175, no. 1045), these pages may fill the gap between the Lehman second proofs and the final ones.

Of the first proofs, Act I was printed in bifolios on both sides of the page; Acts III–V were printed on rectos only, Acts III and IV in single folios, Act V mostly in bifolios. Acts I and III were corrected (by Debussy) principally in red ink. Act I has additional corrections in black ink and in blue and black pencil; Act III, in black ink and blue pencil. The black ink notations in Act III, which deal purely with printing errors, were made by a proofreader and not by Debussy. The contrasting appearance of the first proofs of Acts IV and V (printed on different and heavier paper and corrected primarily in black crayon) suggests that they may have been printed and corrected around the same time. In addition to the black crayon, there are some additional corrections made by a proofreader in black lead pencil; Act IV also has some in red ink, and Act V, in red ink and brown pencil. One proofreader of the first proofs was Messager, whose assistance with the proofs of Act IV was acknowledged by Debussy in a letter of 29 June 1903.

Three pages from the first proofs of Act III are missing from the bound volume (pp. 169, 170, and 236), and all three are to be found together with the second proofs of that act in Ms. 1029. In the case of page 236, Gulon had simply neglected to engrave the corrections that Debussy had made in the first proofs, so the second proofs were printed exactly like the first. Debussy noticed this and first started transferring the corrections, but then decided that it was simpler to resubmit the original page to Gulon. He wrote across the top of it: "Also correct this proof, which hasn't been done." There seems to be no particular reason that pages 169–70 should also have ended up with the second proofs. The pages were probably displaced while Debussy was correcting the second proofs and comparing them with the first.

The first proofs contained the kinds of printing errors that one would expect to find—wrong and missing notes, accidentals, clefs, dynamics, text, and even scene titles. More in Acts I and III (especially the latter) than in Acts IV and V, Debussy not only corrected printing errors but also made revisions in the proofs that amounted at times to extensive reorchestration of extended passages. The types of orchestrational changes made most often include altering the doublings, reassigning parts to different instruments, and lengthening or shortening held notes or chords to alter the degree to which they overlap with other parts. In some cases new instrumental parts were introduced, and in one instance (just before fig. 69 in Act III, p. 249) an entire measure was added. Examples of Debussy's orchestrational revisions will be given below in a more general discussion of his orchestration and the problems of establishing a critical edition of *Pelléas*.

The correction of the second proofs was accomplished during the summer of 1903, as can be ascertained from Debussy's letters to Fromont. Internal evidence confirms this dating, as the verso of the patch which Debussy attached to page 93 (Act II) contains the opening measure of "Pagodes," the first of the three *Estampes*, which Debussy composed in July 1903. It appears that this was to have been a fair copy for the publisher—it was written in blue ink on the third and fourth staves from the top of the page and was indented from the left edge. Debussy discarded it after writing the first bar as he was still unsure of how to notate the rhythm. After writing it one way, he corrected it to correspond with the published version, but the correction made his intention unclear. He subsequently recopied the music (F-Pn, Ms. 988, also in blue ink) and sent the score to Durand. The proofs were corrected in August and the work published in October. The rejected first page of the manuscript was salvaged and was used as a patch for the second *Pelléas* proofs.

The second proofs were printed almost entirely in bifolios, on both sides of the page. Acts I and II were printed continuously: page 69, the last page of Act I, is the first of a new bifolio which is completed by the first three pages of Act II. The extant second proofs (Acts I–III) were corrected primarily in black pencil, Act III exclusively so. Acts I and II have additional corrections in brown pencil and black crayon. In Act II, the patch on page 93 was written in blue ink and black pencil, and page 139 alone has corrections in red and black ink as well as black pencil. In fact, page 139 is somewhat of an anomaly and is probably a page from the first proofs: it is the only page containing red ink corrections, which is characteristic of the first proofs of Acts I and III; it is printed on a thinner type of paper, like the Act III first proofs; and, also like them, it is a single folio printed on one side of the page only, creating a break in the regular sequence of bifolios. The explanation for the appearance of this odd page can only be conjectured. Two pages of the second proofs were not printed: page 96 of Act II (Debussy petulantly wrote across this blank page: "There are some measures missing. They are in the manuscript and will easily fit on this page") and page 174 of Act III. The reason for the latter omission may be found in the first proofs, where, on this page, Gulon had neglected to provide a stave for the violas (upper system) and mistakenly gave their part to the cellos, who should have had three measures of rest. Because of this mistake, Gulon had to re-engrave the entire page, and perhaps he decided to save time by doing the less time-consuming corrections first and saving this large task for later.

The corrections of the second proofs do not bring the score to the state of the final proofs. More correction and revision were still to be done before the publication of the score in the summer of 1904.

As a proofreader, Debussy was apparently very conscientious, though there were inevitably some things that escaped his attention. Part of the problem was that proofreading was for him a dual process. The correction of the first proofs involved both the verification that the score had been accurately copied from the manuscript, and the introduction of modifications in the score. It sometimes seems that the latter activity interested him more than the former. Thus, there are several instances where Gulon omitted something in engraving the plates and Debussy failed to restore it in correcting the proofs. (Of course it is possible that the composer was aware of the omissions and approved of them.) One example is on page 271, meas. 3, where the manuscript (Ms. 964, fol. 21) indicates a part for the double bass which does not appear in the first proofs. In fact, this missing part supplies the bass of the harmony, which is otherwise absent. (The part is present in the vocal score, VS, p. 202, meas. 7.)

Other instances of this phenomenon (material present in the manuscript but missing from the first proofs) may have been the result of changes or additions made in the manuscript after the plates had been engraved. This might have occurred, for example, if Gulon had done some of the engraving before the second season of *Pelléas* performances (30 October 1902–6 January 1903), and if Debussy then made changes in the score during or after these performances. Several examples, especially in the Act II interludes, involve retouchings of the orchestration (generally, the addition of doublings to reinforce a particular line or to give it a different coloring) or the addition of dynamic and articulation marks. Some of these changes and additions are quite conspicuous in the manuscript (they are written in red ink) and it is hardly conceivable that Gulon failed to notice them. It is far more likely that they were simply not there when the plates were engraved, and that Debussy, in correcting the proofs, either failed to notice the omissions or perhaps noticed them and either changed his mind about their merits or decided that they did not justify the extensive re-engraving that their addition would sometimes have required.

An editor of a critical edition may give serious thought to restoring some of these omitted or altered readings to the score of the opera. However, since Debussy supervised every stage of publication and since some of the proofs are missing, it is surely risky to propose such restorations, even when there is some evidence that their failure to appear in the published score may have been the result of careless proofreading. Such evidence is provided in instances where the composer emended his personal copy of the published score (Bibliothèque François Lang) with certain manuscript readings that had been mistakenly altered or simply omitted during the process of publishing the score. For example, on page 316, he repeated the triangle part of meas. 3–4 in meas. 7–8,[26] and on page 331, meas. 7, he corrected the final cello note to c, in both cases altering his personal score to conform with the manuscript.

Other errors crept into the score between proof stages, as a result of an emendation being either overlooked by Gulon or incorrectly engraved by him. Again, Debussy failed to notice the error in reading the proofs.

Like the published score (and unlike the first and second proofs), the final proofs were printed on both sides of the page and in gatherings. In spite of their "finished" appearance, Debussy found thirteen small corrections which still needed to be made. These corrections, which seem to have been done in two sittings (the first four are in black pencil, the remaining nine in brown pencil), are all minor ones, involving the addition of missing ties, accidentals, rests, and dynamic and expression marks and indications. After making these corrections in the proofs, Debussy listed their locations at the top of p. 1, along with his approval to proceed with the printing of the score ("bon à tirer"), dated 29 June 1904.

After the corrections were transferred to the plates, these final proofs were returned to the composer, and he had them bound. Since the preliminary pages of the full score (title page, index, cast list, and instrumentation) had apparently not yet been printed, those of the vocal score were used in their place. Debussy modified the title page, changing "Score for Voice and Piano" ("Partition pour Chant et Piano") to "Orchestra Score" ("Partition d'Orchestre") and "raising" the price from 20 to 150 francs. He did not bother to change the erroneous page references of the index to correspond with the pagination of the full score. In July, Debussy presented these bound proofs, with an inscription, to Emma Bardac, who was to become his second wife. The full score (plate no. E. 1418. F.) was not published until the following month, in August 1904: the copyright deposit was on 27 August and the initial printing included 300 copies (Archives Nationales, Paris: F[18]* VIII 116, p. 15, no. 4775). Surprisingly, Debussy's oversight with regard to the index was perpetuated in the printed full score, whose index gave the page references of the vocal score.

Since the second proofs did not bring the score to the state of the final proofs, the existence of interjacent proofs must be hypothesized. As has already been discussed in reconstructing the history of the score, the correction of the second proofs was apparently accomplished during the summer of 1903, in time for the performances of the 1903–4 season, but the score was not actually published until afterwards. The four additional pages of proofs from the end of Act I (pp. 65–68 of the score; present location unknown) may be part of a set of proofs which accomplished this penultimate layer of corrections. There may also have been a set of proofs which doubled as a conductor's score during the 1903–4 season.

A study of the *Pelléas* proofs is valuable for at least two reasons: the proofs document Debussy's improvements and refinements in the orchestration and also give evidence important towards the establishment of a critical edition of the opera.

Full Score (Fromont, 1904)

Debussy's extensive revisions in the instrumentation of his opera are in part responsible for the fact that the orchestration was not fixed and the full score not published until more than two years after the première and the publication of the piano reduction. This unusual chronology explains some of the differences between the full and vocal scores, only some of which were eliminated through the publication of subsequent editions of both scores.

One difference which had no effect on the "sound" of the opera concerned the key signatures. Three examples from Act III, scene 1 will illustrate this point: at fig. 6 in the full score (p. 156), Debussy cancelled the sharp in the key signature, while the vocal score made that change three bars later; at 6 bars before fig. 12 in the full score (p. 168), there is no change of key signature, while the vocal score changes from zero to four sharps; and at fig. 15 (OS, p. 175) the key signature changes to five flats, while the vocal score changes to six. Debussy was also sometimes inconsistent in his use of accidentals: a vocal part may be notated in sharps in one score and in flats in another.

There are also places where the two scores have different time signatures: one score may be written in simple meter (say, 4/4) and the other in compound meter (in this case, 12/8). This difference is particularly noticeable in Act I, scene 3, and it occasionally caused the composer some confusion, as he seems at times to have forgotten which meter he was in. At 3 bars before fig. 37 (p. 48), the full score retains the original meter of 12/8 while the vocal score switches to common time for three measures. At 1 bar before fig. 38 (p. 49), the full score still retains 12/8 while the vocal score keeps that meter for the voice, but notates the accompaniment in common time. The result of this difference is that the vocal score (even in the revised form of its 1907 edition) does not exactly correspond to the full score in the rhythm of the accompaniment. At 6 bars after fig. 40 (p. 53), Debussy shifts the voice parts from 12/8 to common time in both scores, but in the full score he inadvertently anticipated the meter change by one bar; the preceding measure, though still under the 12/8 time signature, is notated as if in 4/4. At fig. 43 (p. 61), the full score has the solo voices in 4/4, the vocal score, in 12/8. In several places following this point, Debussy, in writing out the full score, seems to have forgotten that he had shifted to simple meter: at fig. 44, the last beat of Mélisande's measure is mistakenly written as a dotted quarter; at fig. 45, Geneviève's first beat has an extra eighth rest; and at 3 bars before fig. 46, her entire measure is written as if in 12/8. At 3 bars before fig. 45, the full score introduces a slight change in Pelléas's rhythm, perhaps a deliberate revision or perhaps a mistake resulting from confusion over the meter. Meter changes also took the form of rebarring—a type of revision that Debussy introduced in the full score in three passages; these will be discussed below in conjunction with the French-English vocal score (1907).

A discussion of the numerous differences in the substance, rather than merely the notation, of the scores will be postponed until all of the scores have been described. One important difference will be noted here: the full score contains two measures of interlude between scenes 2 and 3 of Act III that were mistakenly omitted from the vocal score (the two bars before fig. 34, pp. 197–98; these measures were contained in the short score and were not affected by the interlude expansions of 1902).

In preparing the full score, Debussy took the opportunity to make several small changes in the text,[27] but in correcting the proofs, he seems to have been so intent on revising the orchestration that he neglected to notice some glaring errors in the vocal parts; even aside from wrong notes and rhythms, there are instances of missing lines, words, and syllables, and of some erroneous word substitutions.[28] Most of these errors were corrected in the revised edition of the full score.

Vocal score (Durand, 1905)

Having purchased the rights to *Pelléas* in 1905, Durand proceeded to bring out its own editions of the vocal and full scores and to print a set of parts for the opera. The orchestra material would be a necessity if the opera was to be performed outside of Paris, since up to this point, the only parts in existence were the manuscript set in use at the Opéra-Comique.

The first Durand edition of the vocal score (plate no. D. & F. 6576) was printed from the same plates as the Fromont edition. Naturally the Fromont plate number was eliminated from the bottom of each page, and the Durand plate number was added to the score's final page (p. 283). Also, the preliminary pages and the first page of music (p. 2) were altered to display the name of the new publisher. The initial printing of 500 copies was recorded in the Durand archives (Book of Plate Numbers ["Livre de cotages"], No. 3) as having taken place on 10 February 1905, seven weeks before the signing of the contract of transfer (31 March); this printing date therefore seems unlikely.[29]

Along with the rights to the opera, Durand apparently acquired the unsold copies of the deluxe vocal score. One copy, on Holland paper ("Van Gelder zonen"), formerly belonging to Maurice Ravel (F-Pn, Rés. Vma. 227), is the original Fromont edition, adapted by Durand by removing the prefatory pages and the first page of music (p. 2) and substituting replacements bearing their own name and the plate number D. & F. 6576. Inadvertently, the index of the full score was used here, a curious counterpoise to Fromont's mistaken use of the vocal score index in its full score.

By 1905, however, the vocal score was badly in need of revision. After all, the original Fromont vocal score of 1902 was in certain respects obsolete from the very moment that it rolled off the presses. This obsoleteness was the result of the numerous changes that Debussy had introduced into the score, first, while preparing the orchestration, then in the course of rehearsals and performances, and finally, while correcting the proofs of the full score. Some of the differences were rather conspicuous. For example, the Fromont vocal score did not contain the expanded interludes that had been added for the first performances, nor did it reflect two cuts (of fifteen and thirteen measures) that had since been made in Act III, scene 4 (FVS, pp. 164–65 and 168–69). In addition, there were numerous, less obvious revisions, including slight changes in the rhythms and pitches of the vocal parts, some alterations in the substance of the accompaniment, the rebarring of certain passages, and adjustments in dynamics, articulation, and tempo.

Therefore, when copies of their original printing were exhausted, Durand undertook a revision of the plates in order to bring the vocal score into closer agreement with the full score; this second printing, of 1000 copies, was accomplished in January 1907. A number of mistakes (missing or wrong accidentals, wrong rhythms) were corrected and a number of modifications were introduced to incorporate some of the readings of the full score, which had been published in 1904. The principal changes were in the vocal parts and mostly involved the rhythm of declamation; a few pitches were also altered. (Some of the specific changes will be discussed below in chapter 8, where the vocal parts of all of the editions will be compared.) There were relatively few changes in the piano accompaniment, even though the orchestration process had resulted in some striking differences; those changes that were made in the vocal score involved mostly details of articulation or dynamics, changes easily made in the plates with a minimum of re-engraving. Although the extended interludes had been an integral part of the opera since 1902, they were not added to this edition. Such an insertion would obviously have required a great deal of re-engraving, and besides, Durand had already issued the interlude expansions as a separate volume in 1905 (see below). Other changes in the accompaniment, however, could have been made relatively easily, but for some reason were not. Of the many that might have been made, only four small changes were introduced, each involving the addition or deletion of only one or two notes. Clearly, priority was given to the correction of the vocal parts, understandable considering that an important use of the score was for singers to learn and study their parts. From this point of view, changes in the accompaniment were less crucial and the presence of the expanded interludes was almost completely unimportant. Curiously, changes in tempo indications, which would obviously be of great importance to performers, were not transferred from the full score. The two cuts that had been made in Act III, scene 4 were indicated in the score by written instructions, not by removing or striking the measures involved. The score does not indicate that Act IV, scene 3 was to be cut.

Interludes (Durand, 1905)

The omission of the revised interludes from the 1905 vocal score was quickly remedied by Durand's publication of the interlude expansions as a separate score with the title "Interludes pour *Pelléas et Mélisande*," in piano reduction by Gustave Samazeuilh (plate no. D. & F. 6590).[30] The appearance of this volume should not suggest that the interludes were to be considered as independent pieces.[31] Rather, the new publication, first printed in June 1905,[32] was designed to be used in conjunction with the vocal score. The interludes were not printed in their entirety (however that may be defined); only those portions needed to augment what already appeared in the vocal score were given, with written instructions indicating where and how they were to be inserted.

The interludes continued to be printed as a separate score until 1939, long after they had been incorporated into the completely re-engraved French-English vocal score of 1907. The purchasers of the volume must have been owners of the earlier French-only vocal scores or of the Italian or German vocal scores, none of which included the expanded interludes.

Full Score and Parts (Durand, 1905)

There was really no immediate need for Durand to issue its own edition of the full score, because it was apparently not the publisher's intention to offer the score for general sale. Instead, the score was to be rented along with a set of parts whenever *Pelléas* was to be performed, and there were apparently enough unsold copies of the Fromont edition to fill this need. Rather than go to expense of reprinting the large, 409-page volume, Durand simply modified the existing Fromont scores, printing new preliminary pages (title page, cast list, index, and instrumentation) to replace those of the original (dedication, title page, cast list, and index), and reprinting pages 1 and 2 of the score in order to remove the Fromont plate number (E. 1418. F.) and substitute its own (D. & F. 6577) at the bottom of page 1; pages 3–409 retained the original Fromont plate number.[33] The title page and the page listing the cast, directors, and designers of the original production were essentially the same in the two scores, except, of course, that the name and address of the publisher differed. Also, as the Durand score was basically for rental use, there was no price given on the title page.[34] The index of the Durand score was correct, unlike the Fromont score, which mistakenly used that of the vocal score. While Durand omitted the score's dedication to Hartmann and Messager, it added a page listing the instrumental resources of the opera and giving a summary of the rights and restrictions on performance and copying.

As the *Pelléas* orchestra and chorus parts had never been published by Fromont, Durand had to undertake their engraving and printing.[35] The chorus parts for male and female singers ("Choeurs Hommes," plate no. D. & F. 6579, and "Choeurs Femmes," D. & F. 6579bis) were first printed in May 1905. The printed parts used at the Opéra-Comique (along with a manuscript copy for the choral conductor, labeled "Répétiteur des choeurs") are in the Bibliothèque de l'Opéra (Mat. F. 230). The orchestra parts (D. & F. 6578) required a total of 552 engraved plates and were printed in July 1905. The job of engraving these parts was entrusted to Ch. Douin, who had also engraved the edition of the interludes. The manuscript parts from the Opéra-Comique were recently (1984) found in the Bibliothèque de l'Opéra; an examination of them may reveal many details about the early performances of the opera and about the history of the publication of the parts.

It seems as if Debussy's impulse to revise a work was often stimulated by its publication (or in the case of a manuscript, its binding). The printed parts were no exception. Before they were to see use in the orchestra pit, they were to fall victim to yet another of Debussy's changes of heart with regard to the instrumentation of his opera. Annotations in a copy of the full score (Durand, 1905) in the Durand archives partially chronicle the history of this latest revision. The score's cover bears the inscription, "Copy corrected [by] J[?]LR, 25 August 1905," and on page 1 is written, "Copy from which the orchestra parts were corrected, J[?]LR, August 1905."[36] The body of the score contains about 550 autograph corrections, revisions, and additions entered by several hands, including Debussy's. It thus seems that the score was corrected by the Durand copyist (and others) on (or by) 25 August 1905 and that, in the same month, the corrections were transferred to the published parts—parts which had just been printed the previous month! Even though only a small percentage of the changes are in the composer's hand, it must be assumed that they were all made with his knowledge, indeed, at his insistence. One cannot imagine Durand undertaking this elaborate correction process for any other reason.

This reconstruction of events, however logical on the basis of existing evidence, is difficult to verify because the original published parts are not available for consultation. It seems to have been the publisher's policy to discard parts once they had become worn and to replace them with fresh copies from the existing supplies. When the supplies ran out, the parts were reprinted. Since the reserves of parts for different instruments were evidently depleted at different times, the parts were reprinted on an irregular and staggered basis. Each part had four printings between July 1905 and September–November 1966.[37] With the exception of copies of the Violin I part, sent to the Bibliothèque Nationale (Vm[15]. 1546) and to the Library of Congress in order to establish copyright, the only accessible parts are those printed in 1966. These most recent parts do contain the corrections of the above-mentioned score, but they do not help to answer the question of when the corrections were made in the plates from which the parts were printed.

The changes in the Durand score can be divided into three categories: corrections of mistakes, regularization of the notation and layout, and revisions of or additions to the vocal and instrumental parts. Simple mistakes would likely have come to light during the rehearsals and performances of the 1905 spring season, the first season in which the full score was used. These could very well have been copied from the conductor's score. (Alexandre Luigini conducted the six performances that spring.) Changes of the second category could have been made at any time by anybody with musical training and a knowledge of editorial conventions. But the additions and revisions of content could have come only from Debussy himself, and they could have been made at any time following the 1904 publication of the score.

The implication of the copyist's inscription is that the changes in the score postdate the printing of the orchestra parts. This is not entirely true. The 1905 Violin I part, for example, contains the *pizzicato* g[1] at fig. 13 (p. 12), missing from the published score but added in the corrected Durand copy. Obviously, this change in the distribution of the string parts was made before the July printing of the part. Other orchestral revisions, however (such as the violin doubling of the flutes in meas. 8–9 after fig. 25, on p. 33, and the added violin tremolos at 4 meas. after fig. 40, on p. 53), were not in the 1905 part but were added in a later printing; they are found in the current 1966 part. Of course, it should be noted that the full score may well have contained mistakes where parts were correct (and vice versa); the printed parts may have been prepared from MS parts and not from the printed score. Therefore, a correction in the score may not necessarily imply that a corresponding mistake existed in the parts. It does seem, though, that whatever their previous state had been, the August 1905 correction process brought the parts in line with the corrected score.

Once the parts had been corrected, first by a copyist's hand in the already printed parts and later by correcting and reprinting the plates, the published scores became outdated and needed to be corrected to correspond with the parts. Rather than go to the expense of correcting the plates and reprinting the scores (an expense that Durand had avoided just a few months before in modifying the scores acquired from Fromont), a copyist simply transferred the corrections of the Durand score into the volumes that were to be rented for performances. Just such hand-corrected volumes are to be found in the Durand archives.

Further inscriptions in the same corrected Durand score ("Corrected, D" on the cover, and the stamp "CORRIGÉ" with the signature and date "L. Dérumaux—April 1949" on page 1) apparently indicate the month in which the score's corrections were transferred to the plates of the full score. These plates, however, were not printed until July 1966 (100 copies), which was, rather surprisingly, only the second printing of the full score.[38]

Study Score (in 16) (Durand, 1908)

Although the corrections of the score would have been known to every conductor of the opera, they only reached the general public, and even then, almost inadvertently and completely unidentified, with the fifth printing of the study score, in January 1950.[39] The study score of *Pelléas* (D. & F. 7018) was first issued by Durand in January 1908 (the month in which Debussy married Emma Bardac), and it was made by photographically reducing the full score ("électrogravure" by Dogilbert & Cie.). As it was made from the original 1904/1905 edition, it did not contain the manuscript changes of August 1905. The first printing comprised 500 copies, and successive printings occurred in July 1912 (200 copies), June 1920 (300), January 1947 (500), January 1950 (1000), April 1964 (1000), July 1971 (1000), and November 1976 (1000). In preparing the printing of January 1950, Durand must have had new zinc plates made, and they were made from the recently (April 1949) corrected plates of the full score. Thus, this and subsequent printings of the study score do contain the corrections and revisions of August 1905, even though the scores are advertised on the cover as "Edition originale."[40] These scores carry the plate number of the full score (D. & F. 6577) rather than that of the study score. (In a 1950 copy the plate number appears on p. 409; in the 1976 issue it is visible on pp. 1, 199, 282, and 297.)

Annotated Full Scores

The process of emending the score of *Pelléas* did not stop in 1905, as Debussy continued to make adjustments in his opera (chiefly in its orchestration and tempos), entering the changes in his own copy of the full score (Fromont, 1904). This score remained in the composer's possession until his death in 1918, and it was sold at auction by his widow in 1933. (She died the following year.) This famous auction, organized by Georges Andrieux, also included many important "souvenirs" of the composer: sketchbooks, manuscripts of published and unpublished works (musical and literary), corrected proofs, annotated scores, letters sent by the composer to Chausson and Toulet, letters sent to the composer (by, among others, Maeterlinck and Georgette Leblanc), and books and scores inscribed to him. The *Pelléas* score was among the items purchased by the pianist François Lang, and it is now part of the Bibliothèque François Lang in Royaumont.

According to the auction catalogue, this full score of *Pelléas* "was used constantly by the master for performances." Since Debussy never conducted the opera, the score would have been used by him during his supervision of the rehearsals for various productions, including those at the Opéra-Comique (nearly every year from 1905 to 1914), the Théâtre de la Monnaie in Brussels (January 1907), and Covent Garden in London (May 1909).

The relationship between the emendations in Debussy's own score and those in the corrected score in the Durand archives is rather complex. Many of the changes are identical, some are similar but differ in detail (even those which appear in both scores in the composer's own hand), some are different (the same passage modified in different ways), and many are independent (changed in one and not in the other). In general, the changes in the composer's personal score go beyond the 1905 emendations. This is especially apparent in the tempo modifications which appear in the former but not in the latter. Since many of these tempo indications figured in the 1907 revision of the vocal score, it would seem that at least some of the changes in Debussy's score are post-1905. Thus, while some of its annotations and corrections are probably earlier than those of the Durand corrected score, the composer's personal score seems to represent his final thoughts concerning the orchestration (and pacing) of his opera.

Some of the same types of changes are found in both scores. Speaking only of revisions (and not of corrections), most involved the addition of doublings—the reinforcement of a line (usually at the unison, sometimes at the octave), most often by an instrument of a contrasting family. Changes of sonority were also achieved in other ways, such as changing string parts from *arco* to *pizzicato* or redistributing the string parts to get a different quality of sound.[41] In other places, Debussy added a pedal, making explicit a pedal tone which exists in the harmony but is not sustained in a single voice.[42] Other additions were of more independent material: in some cases, figuration of a coloristic nature (such as string tremolos), and in a few instances, the principal themes ("leitmotifs") of the opera.[43] The harmony was also enriched in some places,[44] and in a few spots, words or phrases of dialogue were dramatized by the addition of well-placed rhythmic impulses (*pizzicato* string chords).[45]

While we can be confident that Debussy intended the autograph corrections of 1905 (in the Durand score) to become a permanent part of the score, the status of the changes entered into his own score is less certain. Some of the revisions, especially those involving very subtle orchestrational effects (such as the addition of four solo violins, marked "p très doux," to double the flutes at the beginning of Act II), may have been provisional experiments which the composer did not regard as definitive improvements. Perhaps they were never tested in performance or perhaps they were tested and ultimately not adopted. (The latter possibility is probably unlikely if Debussy let the revision remain in his personal score.) The appearance of proofreaders' marks in the margins beside most of the changes certainly suggests that Debussy intended the emendations of this score to be copied into the orchestra parts, into other copies of the score, and presumably even into the plates of the full score, in order to be incorporated into future editions. Debussy's score also indicates two cuts which serve to shorten the interludes between the first two scenes of Act II and between the second and third scenes of Act IV.[46] Again, one wonders if these should be regarded as definitive or provisional.

One conductor who was aware of these changes was Pierre Monteux, who gained access to Debussy's annotated score through his professional association and personal friendship with François Lang. Monteux incorporated most of the score's readings into his performances of *Pelléas* and even, according to Mme Henry Goüin, sister of François Lang, borrowed the score and conducted from it for his performances in Amsterdam in February 1935. The *New York Times* discussed the production under the headline: "Debussy Work's Première. Revised Version of 'Pelléas' Called Superior to Original." The article commented: "The general opinion here is that this version is superior to that usually performed, especially as regards orchestration."[47] Monteux's use of the score in performance would explain the occasional conductor's markings in the score—brass, timpani, English horn, and second violin cues, certain tempo modifications, and cautionary dynamic markings, all in blue pencil and not in Debussy's hand.

Monteux also planned to use the score for a revival of *Pelléas* at the Opéra-Comique which was scheduled for 8 April 1959. (Postponed several times, the performances finally took place in May, but with a different conductor.) An article in the April 1959 issue of *Musica-Disques* not only drew attention to the fact that Debussy's own score was to be used, but solicited the following remarks from Monteux himself:

The interest of this revival in Paris rests in the fact that, having in hand Debussy's personal score, kept up to date until the Master's death, the performances will conform with the last wishes and desires of the inspired composer.

In fact, this orchestra score contains an extraordinary number of modifications, written in Debussy's own hand: corrections in black pencil, blue pencil, red ink, etc.

All of these modifications could, moreover, be considered improvements of the orchestration.[48]

Since Monteux had used (and intended to reuse) this score in performance, it was necessary for a set of parts to be corrected to conform with it; Durand assigned rental parts and score No. 40 for this purpose. The Durand files note of this set: "Parts corrected according to M. Monteux's score." The score (and presumably the parts, which were not available for consultation) had already been modified to incorporate the revisions of August 1905; these were entered in black ink. The modifications of Debussy's personal score were then superimposed in pencil by at least two hands. Finally, certain mistakes that remained, even after these two operations, were corrected. Since the score has been used by a number of conductors for more than a dozen productions between 1925 and 1964, other markings and other hands are also in evidence.

Obviously convinced of their authority and merit, Monteux copied (or had someone else copy) both sets of changes—those presumably ordered by Debussy in August 1905 and those contained in the composer's personal score—into his own study score of the opera. An inscription in that score indicates that it had been corrected according to the full score that corresponds to the set of parts, No. 40. This study score miraculously survived a fire in the Monteux home in Hancock, Maine (the cover was burned but the contents were spared), and it remains in the possession of the conductor's widow.[49]

In addition to his personal score of *Pelléas,* Debussy is also said to have kept the score at the Opéra-Comique up to date of his latest corrections and revisions in the orchestration. As Felix Aprahamian noted: "Even in the last years of his life, Debussy would go to the Opéra-Comique and make alterations in the full score there. These corrections and amendments [were] listed by Roger Désormière . . . "[50] D.-E. Inghelbrecht was another conductor who was aware of the emendations in the conductor's score (and parts) at the Opéra-Comique. He copied the changes into his own score and into the parts belonging to "Radio française."[51]

The conductor's score of *Pelléas* which belonged to the Opéra-Comique is now in the Service de la Copie of the Paris Opéra, where it was taken when the Opéra-Comique was closed. The score is a first edition, published by Fromont, which suggests that it had been at the Opéra-Comique since 1904, or at least before the title page was modified by Durand in the spring of 1905. The score's first page is stamped: "Théâtre National de L'Opéra-Comique, Propriété de L'État, Direction Albert Carré." The abundant applications of adhesive tape and the myriad notations in numerous hands are testimony to the heavy use that the score has withstood over the years.

One hand not in evidence is that of Debussy. If there was a score at the Opéra-Comique that was personally annotated by the composer it is not to be found either at the Opéra-Comique or at the Paris Opéra. There may have been such a score. The Durand records note that a full score of *Pelléas* (which they recorded as score No. 7) was sent to the Opéra-Comique on 20 March 1906. This score, which would surely have had a Durand title page, has not been located. Whether it was annotated by Debussy is a question that cannot be answered.

The emendations in the Opéra-Comique conductor's score were entered principally in green ink, but also in black, red, and blue ink and black pencil. In addition, numerous conductors' markings were made in black, red, and green pencil. Marginal proofreaders' marks are almost completely absent, suggesting that this was a score *into* which, rather than *out of* which, changes were copied. That the score's corrections were connected with performance rather than publication, is demonstrated by the fact that only those changes which affect the content, rather than the appearance, of the score were made. For example, the correction of the English horn key signature on pages 10–18 was ignored here while it figured in the corrected score at Durand which served as the basis for the revised edition of the opera.

Insofar as its revisions are concerned, the Opéra-Comique score is not directly or exclusively dependent on either the Durand corrected score or Debussy's personal score, even though it shares many features with each. Indeed, many revisions are identical, or nearly so, in all three. Others are not. In instances where the Durand corrections differ from those in Debussy's score, the Opéra-Comique revision tends to follow the former in preference to the latter; and in cases where a revision is contained only in Debussy's score, that change is sometimes adopted by the Opéra-Comique score and sometimes ignored.

The Opéra-Comique score also has versions of certain changes which differ from those in either of the other two annotated scores. One particular class of revision involves pedals or harmonic progressions which change orchestration as they proceed. While the additions in the other scores sometimes call for abrupt shifts from one instrument to another (usually changing on the first beat of a measure), the Opéra-Comique revisions extend the first instrument to overlap slightly with its successor, producing a more gradual and less obvious shift of instrumental color.[52] This technique serves to minimize the accent of an entrance, and is consistent with Inghelbrecht's view of correct Debussy style: "The most common interpretive error in the music of

Debussy consists of having the instruments *enter* as in a symphony by Saint-Saëns or Beethoven, when rather, they should *slip in* ['s'insinuer'] most of the time."[53] A few revisions are unique to the Opéra-Comique score,[54] and there are also some corrections of wrong notes overlooked by the other annotated scores.[55]

Another score containing autograph corrections is a copy of the study score (Bibliothèque Nationale, Rés. 2729) which Debussy presented to his wife Emma in April 1908. The score was No. 162 of the first printing of the score, issued in January 1908. This was probably the score whose binding was mentioned in a series of letters written by the composer to his friend Georges Jean-Aubry in the spring of 1908: "Would it be possible for your binder to give me information about what he thinks he can do with the score of *Pelléas*." (6 March); "Thank you for the score of *Pelléas*, which, except for the title, is entirely successful." (10 April); and finally, and all too characteristically, "Forgive me for having forgotten to ask how much I owe you for the binding of *Pelléas*." (24 April) (GOD, pp. 112, 113, and 115). Bound in at the beginning of the score are a pressed, dried flower (visible through cellophane windows in the pages that contain it) and a page of autograph music manuscript containing three measures of music: OS, p. 197, meas. 2–p. 198, meas. 2.[56] At the top of the page Debussy identified the passage as the beginning of Act III, scene 3. The previous scene found Pelléas and Golaud in the menacing, foul-smelling, and stifling vaults beneath the castle, and the passage copied here corresponds to the moment when the curtain rises at the start of scene 3, which finds the two relieved to emerge into the fresh air on a terrace at the entrance to the vaults. Pelléas's first words will be, "Ah! je respire enfin!..." ("I can finally breathe"). The significance of the passage is suggested by the dedication on this page: "to my dear little wife, this music which waited for her. Claude Debussy. April 1908." Debussy and Emma were finally married on 20 January 1908, more than two years after the birth of their daughter Chouchou on 30 October 1905 and following difficult divorce proceedings. Debussy was evidently comparing his present happiness with the relief that Pelléas experienced upon leaving the stifling vaults. Like Pelléas, he too could "finally breathe."

The score itself contains corrections on pages 1–2, 4–5, and 10–18 written in blue (and possibly black) ink. There is also an additional correction of a vocal part on page 391, made in pencil. It seems as if Debussy began to correct the score but gave up after going only about two-thirds of the way through the first scene. The corrections correspond essentially to those in Debussy's annotated full score, although they are not so extensive. This may have been due to a somewhat less than fastidious job in copying the corrections, or it may indicate that some of the emendations of the full score were made later.[57]

A critical edition of *Pelléas* would have to take a variety of published and manuscript materials into account. The special problem of the vocal parts will be dealt with in chapter 8, but as far as the orchestration is concerned, the Durand revised edition (the 1966 full score, readily available as a study score since 1950, though prepared under Debussy's supervision in August 1905) would serve as a basis. One would also, though, have to look back to the manuscript full score and to the corrected proofs and first edition to consider some readings which, perhaps inadvertently, failed to be perpetuated, or which were inaccurately transmitted in the process of correcting the proofs and transferring those corrections to the plates. One would also have to look at a number of annotated scores for revisions made either independently from or later than the 1905 corrections found in the score at Durand. The most important such score is, of course, Debussy's own, now in the Bibliothèque François Lang, but others should also be consulted, especially the study score in which Debussy began to enter his revisions and the conductor's score from the Opéra-Comique. One would also probably profit from examining scores (if they exist) corrected and annotated by various musicians who conducted *Pelléas* under Debussy's supervision or who had personal contact with the composer—conductors such as Messager, Caplet, Inghelbrecht, Ansermet, Toscanini, and Monteux. The *Pelléas* recordings of Ansermet, Inghelbrecht, and Désormière differ in details from the published scores, and the modifications they introduced were probably based on an authority that had its source in the composer. Finally, there remain errors in the published score which need to be corrected.

The question of the authority of the various annotated scores raises a thorny editorial problem, one which is further complicated by an anecdote that Ansermet related in a 1968 interview. The young conductor once asked Debussy a question concerning the *Nocturnes,* and in answer, the composer produced his own heavily corrected and annotated score (now, like his *Pelléas* score, in the Bibl. F. Lang). When Ansermet asked him, "What is right?" Debussy allegedly replied: "I don't know. Take the score with you and bring it back in a few days and say what seems good to you." Ansermet used this story to justify his own edition of the work.[58]

A rather different account of this meeting was given fifty years earlier, in a letter of 23 January 1918 from Godet to Debussy:

> ... Ansermet very carefully copied the red ink corrections written in the score which you were good enough to lend him on Sunday in Paris. But there were others (he tells me) in green ink at the end of "Sirènes" (whose seaweed hair obviously must have affected this coloring). Ansermet had thought that these green corrections were only conjectural and that they represented for you merely a kind of provisional memento; in returning the volume to you, he had the impression that he had been mistaken and that you had made your decision regarding them and that consequently, far from committing an indiscretion in taking note of these modifications as well, he would have been well advised to do so.[59]

The letter then goes on, posing specific questions concerning details of the orchestration, questions which suggest that Ansermet wished to make some independent changes in the score, based on his own speculation concerning the composer's intent.

From Godet's account it seems that Debussy regarded the corrections in the *Nocturnes* score as definitive. This is certainly the impression given by the composer's letter of 30 January 1914 to Gustave Doret:

> I do not have the parts for the *Nocturnes* and am sending you the corrected score. It is quite long and delicate, especially in "Sirènes." Could you perhaps entrust this tedious job to an elegant copyist? In addition to errors, there are numerous changes!!![60]

If Debussy did regard his corrections as definitive, one wonders why he never had them incorporated into the published score (they did not become part of the score until 1930, more than a decade after his death). He gave an explanation in a letter to Stravinsky of 24 October 1915, again concerning Ansermet's interest in the work. Debussy explained that, not only was the work published by a firm with which he no longer had dealings (Fromont), but he did not know any copyist capable of such a delicate task (LL, p. 266). This reasoning is not very convincing, and one suspects that perhaps Debussy (subconsciously?) resisted the publication of his revisions in order to keep open the possibility of even further revisions.

Certainly the excuse of being out of touch with the publisher obviously did not apply to Debussy's relationship with Durand, and the composer did indeed provide that publisher with his corrections of the *Pelléas* score as of August 1905. Are we then to regard the corrections made, presumably, subsequent to that date as provisional (and optional) or as definitive? And what happens when two independent corrections are in disagreement? These decisions must be made by each individual conductor, but we are now sufficiently removed from Debussy's time that the options are scarcely known today—much less, certainly, than when the opera was conducted by men who had a direct link with the composer. The tendency nowadays is to perform the work as it is printed in the rental score and parts obtained from the publisher, that is, following Debussy's version of August 1905. A much-needed critical edition of the opera would make other options available, as well as help to settle the somewhat complicated question of the most authoritative source for the vocal parts, a question which will be addressed in chapter 8.

German Vocal Score (Durand, 1906)

Foreign performances of *Pelléas* prompted the publication of vocal scores with foreign texts. While the first production of the opera outside of Paris, at the Théâtre de la Monnaie in Brussels on 9 January 1907, was naturally in

French, the second, in Frankfurt on 19 April 1907, was sung in German. In anticipation of the latter production, a German language vocal score was issued.[61]

On 8 August 1906 Debussy sent Durand the corrected proofs of this edition, along with the following letter:

> You will receive in the same mail delivery the proofs of *Pelléas* in German; the translation is perfect, almost all of the accents are in place, and that is truly a tour de force. Besides, the German text is more poetic than the French. This really goes beyond our expectations![62]

The vocal score of *Pelleas und Melisande* (plate no. D. & F. 6774) was printed in October 1906 (500 copies) and the copyright deposit was on 17 November 1906. Additional printings were in October 1908 (500 copies), February 1927 (500), and February 1928 (500). The German adaptation was done by Otto Neitzel, based on the translation of the Maeterlinck play by Friedrich von Oppeln-Bronikowski, which was published in 1902 as part of his translation of Maeterlinck's collected works.[63] In this vocal score, not only the text, but also the tempo and stage directions, were translated. The preliminary pages too were in German.

While Debussy had high praise for the way the German text fit his music, the translator attached a note to the score, cautioning singers not to overemphasize text accents, especially when they did not coincide with the musical accents. The conductor Ernest Ansermet strongly approved of performing *Pelléas* in translation for non-French audiences and with non-French singers, but he was willing to make greater sacrifices in the accuracy of the translation for the sake of the musical accentuation. As he explained to an interviewer in 1962:

> In Hamburg not long ago we did it in German, and for the German singers and audience, I preferred it that way. This opera is very much concerned with speech, with words, and the important thing is to find not just the right words but the right accentuation to fit the music. For example, to translate the words "la vérité, la vérité" into German, we rejected the existing version, which reads "die Wahrheit nur, die Wahrheit nur" and chose instead "das sag' ich dir, das sag' ich dir." The words of the official translation were more correct literally, but the other has the same accents as the French, and that is more important.[64]

The score was based essentially on the original Fromont edition of 1902. It does not include the expanded interludes, which had been published the year before, though certain details in the accompaniment were corrected.

Durand's representative for performances in Germany and Austria-Hungary was the publishing house Albert Ahn in Cologne. Following the Frankfurt performance, other German (or German language) productions of *Pelléas* were soon given in Cologne (15 September 1908), Prague (28 September 1908), Munich (9 October 1908), Berlin (6 November 1908), and Vienna (23 May 1911).

French-English Vocal Score (Durand, 1907)

After Frankfurt, the next foreign production of *Pelléas* (and the first in the English-speaking world) was given by Oscar Hammerstein's Manhattan Opera Company in New York on 19 February 1908. The negotiations that preceded the production began early in 1907, and Gustave Schirmer, partner with his brother Rudolph in the family publishing firm, G. Schirmer, Inc., made the initial contact on behalf of Hammerstein. Hammerstein wanted to bring French opera to New York, and he wanted to engage Mary Garden to sing it, so Schirmer, who had served an apprenticeship to Durand and had maintained a friendly personal and professional relationship with the firm, cabled Jacques Durand to begin discussions with Garden over the possibility of her appearing with the Manhattan Opera Company during its 1907–8 season. A contract was finally signed in May 1907, but only after Hammerstein traveled to Paris to negotiate directly with Garden and after he accepted her conditions, which included a production of *Pelléas* with the cast of the Opéra-Comique. Thus, much of the cast of the Paris première participated in the first American performance of *Pelléas*: Mary Garden as Mélisande, Jean Périer as Pelléas, Hector Dufranne as Golaud, and Jeanne Gerville-Réache as Geneviève. Other cast members were Vittorio Arimondi (Arkel), Ludmilla Sigrist (Yniold), and Armand Crabbé (the doctor). Cleofonte Campanini, principal conductor of the company, conducted the seven performances of the opera that were given in the course of the season, performances which introduced Périer and Dufranne to American audiences. In the following season, 1908–9, the production was repeated four times, with some substitutions in the cast: tenor Charles Dalmorès sang Pelléas, Félix Vieuille of the original Opéra-Comique production was Arkel, and Emma Trentini appeared as Yniold. At the end of the New York season, Hammerstein took his company on tour, which included a performance of *Pelléas* in Boston on 1 April 1909.[65]

Although the New York performances were sung in French, it may have been the anticipation of success in the English-speaking world that prompted the decision to publish in 1907 a vocal score of *Pelléas* with English translation. Unlike the German score, this one was bilingual, retaining the original French text and placing English beneath it. The translation, by Henry Grafton Chapman, was singable rather than literal; nevertheless, for the first English-language performance of *Pelléas*, in Birmingham, England on 19 September 1913, a translation by Edwin Evans was used instead.

Writing to Durand on 3 September 1907, Debussy expressed a willingness to review the proofs of the new score, which he referred to as "*Pelléas* in English" (DUR, p. 55). This was soon accomplished and 1000 copies were printed in October 1907, well in advance of the New York première. The score was assigned the plate number D. & F. 6953 and the copyright deposit was on 23 November 1907. By December 1976, the score had gone through twenty-two printings, with 24,500 copies issued.[66]

Unlike the 1905 Durand vocal score, which had been printed (after corrections) from the same plates as the original Fromont edition of 1902, the 1907 score was newly engraved, providing an opportunity to undertake a more extensive correction of its contents, including the addition of the interlude expansions: the transcriptions of the interludes made by Samazeuilh were inserted in their proper places.[67] Debussy also removed the measures which constituted the two permanent cuts that had been made in Act III, scene 4. The voice parts were taken directly from the 1905 vocal score (which had been corrected in January 1907); the few differences were due either to the correction of mistakes in the earlier score or to errors that inadvertently crept into the new one.

However, extensive changes affecting the accompaniment were made on nearly every page of the score. Tempo indications were added, deleted, or altered, and while some of these changes corresponded to the full score, others did not. In fact, numerous discrepancies exist between the two scores in this regard, and it is the vocal score which generally seems to contain the more complete and meticulous tempo instructions. In some places, however, the scores present absolutely contradictory directions: for example, where the 1907 vocal score has "Même mouv^t" (i.e., "Lent") (p. 104, meas. 1), the full score has "poco mosso" (p. 130, meas. 1), and where the vocal score indicates a return to a fast tempo, "au Mouv^t (animé)," after two bars of holding back ("retenu") (p. 127, meas. 5), the full score (in the revised printing) directs the opposite, "Plus lent" (p. 166, meas. 7). The resolution of such discrepancies might be found in Edgard Varèse's copy of the *Pelléas* score. In a letter to Varèse of 12 July 1910, Debussy expressed his willingness to supply him with metronome markings for *Pelléas*, even though he had no confidence in such indications (LL, p. 193). If this was actually done, the Varèse score would be extremely valuable as a documentation of Debussy's preferred tempos.

In addition to its changes in tempo markings, the 1907 vocal score also contained adjustments in articulation, dynamic, and expression markings. The majority of the dynamic changes (most taken from the full score) served to reduce the dynamic level of the accompaniment and improve the audibility of the voices. These changes involved shifts to softer dynamic levels, added diminuendos, and such instructions as "très doux," "aussi doux que possible," "doux et pénétrant," "en dehors," "très en dehors," "expressif et en dehors," and "doux et expressif." Other performance instructions that were added did not necessarily suggest a softer accompaniment ("expressif et soutenu," for example), and there was even the occasional added "marqué" and "très marqué."

The 1907 vocal score also incorporated one change in meter that appeared in the full score: on page 212, meas. 4, the meter was changed from common to cut time. There were also eight small modifications in the substance of the accompaniment, all bringing it closer to that of the full score.

The vocal score of *Pelléas* currently available from Durand is a revised edition of the original 1907 score.[68] In addition to correcting some misprints (though others were overlooked), the new edition continued the process of bringing the vocal score into closer agreement with the full score. The most conspicuous such changes involved the rebarring of three passages. In one case (p. 118, meas. 4), a bar of 9/4 was subdivided into two bars, of 3/4 and 6/4 respectively, which simplified the cue for the singer. In the other two instances, however, the new bar lines, by changing the positions of the downbeats, altered the accentuation of the text. On page 66, the metric emphasis in the line "Ne jouez pas ainsi audessus d'une eau si profonde" was shifted from the word "au-des-*sus*" to its natural climax, the second syllable of "pro-*fon*-de," which contains the longest durational value. The third such change (pp. 121–22), the most extensive of the three, involves six measures rebarred into seven. The new metric layout moved the bar lines (and potential downbeat accents) from the middles of two sentences, thus eliminating downbeats during these lines which might have caused the singers to make accents where Debussy evidently did not want them. Other metric changes in this passage affected the accentuation of the text by creating different downbeat accents: in Pelléas's lines, "donne-moi du moins ta main ce soir avant que je m'en aille... Je pars demain," the metric stresses were shifted from *"moi"* and *"ail*-le" to *"soir"* and *"de-main,"* the two words which refer to the passing of time and which are the subsidiary and final melodic goals of the passage.

Another metric revision to conform with the full score was accomplished by removing a beat from the second measure on page 8, changing it from 4/4 to 3/4. (The effect of this change will be discussed in chapter 8.) One correction that was neglected involved the time signature on page 153, meas. 4, which should have been corrected from 3/4 to 3/2.

The revised vocal score also contains nine new changes in the accompaniment, again corresponding to the full score. The most striking change was the addition of two-and-one-half measures of accompaniment to a passage that was unaccompanied in previous editions of the vocal score (p. 154, meas. 6–8). Another "gap" in the accompaniment was filled in the third interlude of Act IV (p. 231, meas. 17). Three changes affected the rhythmic and melodic figuration of the accompaniment (p. 22, meas. 7; p. 41, meas. 6; and p. 188, meas. 1–2), and two involved shifting punctuating chords from one beat to another (p. 90, meas. 3 and p. 101, meas. 5). Two final changes were optional additions (printed in small notes), which added short thematic materials that had not previously been included in the piano reduction (p. 52, meas. 2–3 and p. 138, meas. 2); the first of these additions was the Mélisande motive.

Finally, the revised score marks three cuts which had, according to the score, become traditional at the Opéra-Comique. The first, at the end of Act III, scene 3, suppressed Golaud's line, "Evitez-la autant que possible; mais sans affectation, d'ailleurs, sans affectation..." ("Avoid her as much as possible, but without affectation, however"; pp. 156–57), the second eliminates his "Simplement parce que c'est l'usage; simplement parce que c'est l'usage" ("Simply because it is the custom"; pp. 218–19) at the end of Act IV, scene 2, and the third removes an entire scene, Yniold's scene with the little sheep, Act IV, scene 3 (pp. 222–31).

The Opéra-Comique has a copy of the 1907 vocal score (in its original version), marked "Répétiteur 1" on the cover, which is apparently the only score of *Pelléas* still owned by the theater. This score contains numerous annotations, most notably some changes in the part of Pelléas to adapt it to the range of Fernand Francell, who sang the role in the Opéra-Comique revival of 1919, a year after the composer's death.[69] Other pitch changes were made in the part of Yniold, again, perhaps, for a particular singer. (Was it that singer's weight, the director's staging, or Golaud's bad back that caused the latter's line on page 180 to be changed from "I am going to lift you up to the window" to "you are going to lift yourself up to the window"?) Some metronome markings were also added to the score.

More relevant to the present study, the score also contains some adjustments and additions to the accompaniment. Some of these are identical to changes made in the published revision of the 1907 score, but others go beyond that score, making the accompaniment an even more accurate representation of the opera's scoring. For example, this score deletes the bass figures occupying the first beats of measures 6 and 13 on page 1, and it adds the horn figure (the rhythm of the Golaud motive on repeated d-flats) in measure 4 of page 3.

Debussy never intended his piano score to be a black and white schematic of his orchestration. As someone who had at various times earned money by giving public and private performances of excerpts from Wagner operas, he understood the need to find keyboard equivalents for his orchestral effects, not always achieved through literal transcription of the entire orchestral fabric onto two staves. Anyone who has heard a piano rehearsal of *Pelléas* with a first-rate pianist in the pit knows how well Debussy succeeded in this task. The piano reduction is a marvelous composition in its own right. There are, however, ways of improving its accuracy (with respect to the full score) without sacrificing its own special qualities, and the annotations in the Opéra-Comique score show some ways that this can be done.

Italian Vocal Score (Durand, 1908)

In an interview printed in the *New York Times* on 15 March 1925, shortly before the first performance of *Pelléas* at the Metropolitan Opera in New York, Giulio Gatti-Casazza, the Met's general manager, described the circumstances surrounding the opera's Italian première, which took place at La Scala in Milan on 2 April 1908, while he was its director.[70] In the spring of 1905, Cleofonte Campanini, conductor at La Scala, was in Paris directing a season of Italian opera at the Théâtre Sarah Bernhardt. He heard *Pelléas* at the Opéra-Comique and recommended the work to Gatti-Casazza. However, in later conversations in Milan, they decided "that the time was not yet ripe and that the experiment might be dangerous." After all, during the previous season (his first at La Scala), Campanini had conducted the world première of Puccini's *Madama Butterfly* (17 February 1904), and it had been a fiasco. Gatti feared a similar fate for *Pelléas*. In the autumn of 1906, following Campanini's resignation, Arturo Toscanini returned as La Scala's chief conductor and artistic director, a post he had held from 1898 until 1903. Encouraged by the success of Strauss's *Salome* during the 1906–7 season, Toscanini and Gatti decided to present *Pelléas* in 1907–8, in place of Luigi Mancinelli's *Paolo e Francesca,* which had originally been scheduled. Toscanini's own interest in *Pelléas* dated back several years. Shortly after reading through the score he wrote to a friend of his admiration for the work:

> I hardly even knew the name of [a] composer who has won all my sympathy: the Frenchman Debussy, with his *Pelléas et Mélisande.* . . . His art overturns everything that has been done until now. He doesn't have Strauss's technique, but he is a greater genius, more elegant and undoubtedly more daring. On first venturing upon him, you are completely disoriented; but once you have begun to converse a little more familiarly in his language—and that of his inspirer, Maeterlinck—you end by being fascinated. Thinking of the theatre, of Maeterlinck's characters, I can confirm my opinion that Debussy's music is the fulfillment of that art. However, our public today, in all countries, is not yet mature [enough] to sense this, let alone to accept it.[71]

Even before the Italian public had a chance to judge the work, there was difficulty with the publisher Edoardo Sonzogno, Durand's representative in Italy, who, according to Gatti, "had too little faith in 'Pelléas' to meet the expenses of translation and preparation of the material." As Gatti recounted: "When I went to him with my offer he said: 'Very good! But with so many operas that I have ready here, and the success of which they are certain, why do you insist on the opera of a futurist?'" Durand apparently had a hand in persuading Sonzogno of the merits of Debussy's opera. In a letter of 3 September 1907 to Durand, Debussy commented on the Italian's attitude with a combination of amusement and irritation:

> You can certainly see that this M. Sonzogno hides, beneath the exterior of a recently discovered mummy, the soul of a crafty dilettante.... Have you asked yourself what the word "éclat" could possibly mean in relation to *Pelléas*? Does he intend to insert some vocalises in it?
>
> In the end, I am satisfied and congratulate you for having reached such a good result. (DUR, p. 54)

The cast of the Italian première consisted of Cesira Ferrani (Mélisande), Fiorello Giraud (Pelléas), Pasquale Amato (Golaud), Giulio Cirino (Arkel), Tina Schinetti (Yniold), Nerina Lollina (Geneviève), and Constantino Thos (the Doctor). Toscanini conducted; the décors were by Angelo Parravincini, Vittorio Rota, Mario Sala, and Carlo Songa; and costumes were by the theatrical costumers Chiappa.[72]

Although Debussy had been invited to attend the rehearsals and the première, he regretted being unable to accept, as he explained in a letter to Durand of 18 December 1907, because of conflicts with conducting engagements in Italy (in Rome on 6 April and in Milan on 21 April). He ultimately cancelled those appearances, however, explaining in a letter of 14 March 1908 to Toulet:

> I am not going to Italy; first of all, its climate is overrated, and then, I've done enough conducting, having also realized that I no longer have any time to compose music. Perhaps that is not very expedient, but it is surely the most agreeable solution that I have found so far! (TOU, p. 45)

The composer sent his regrets to Toscanini:

> I put *Pelléas*' fate in your hands, sure as I am that I could not wish for more loyal or capable ones. For this reason as well, I would have liked to have worked on it with you; it is a joy which one does not often find along the path of our art.[73]

At the première, certain scenes created an uproar, especially Act III, scene 2, but Toscanini continued calmly, and the final scene of the act was rewarded with a huge ovation. The performance ended in triumph. The grateful composer sent the conductor his photograph, with the signed inscription (dated July 1908): "to Maestro Toscanini, whom I could never thank enough!" On the reverse he copied the first bar of Act III, scene 2 (VS, p. 142, meas. 1) with the commentary: "from where Toscanini emerged victorious after all."[74]

Toscanini later regretted having performed *Pelléas* in Italian translation, and when he revived the opera at La Scala on 17 May 1925, it was done in French, with a predominantly French cast.[75] The first performance in Rome, on 28 March 1909, was conducted by Giorgio Polacco with an Italian cast and was sung in Italian.

The Italian vocal score was prepared during 1907 in order to be ready for the Milan performances in April 1908. With plans underway at this time for the new French-English vocal score, the 1905 French vocal score, which had just gone through its second and final printing in January 1907, was about to be replaced. Rather than discard the old plates (which had been engraved by Gulon for the original Fromont edition of 1902 and were subsequently corrected by Durand), it seemed economical to modify them to serve as the Italian vocal score. In essentially retaining the same plates, Durand even kept the same plate number, D. & F. 6576. This reuse of the earlier plates meant that the Italian score did not include the corrections that had been made for the French-English score. Most notably, it lacked the expanded interludes, guaranteeing a market for Durand's separate publication of the interlude expansions. Purchasers of both the Italian and German vocal scores would need to buy the additional volume to acquire the complete opera.

Except for the dedication page, which remained in French, the preliminary pages of the score (title page, cast list, and index) were replaced with their Italian equivalents. And in the score itself, Italian text and performance directions were also substituted for the French originals. The translation ("versione ritmica," i.e., a translation designed to match the vocal rhythms) was by Carlo Zangarini. So far, there had been no Italian translation of the Maeterlinck play; the first, by Carmine Gallo, was not published until 1914. The Italian vocal score, *Pelleas e Melisanda,* was first printed in December 1907 (500 copies) and subsequently went through two more printings, in September 1908 (500 copies) and April 1952 (500). The copyright deposit was on 21 January 1908.

Other Editions and Arrangements (Durand)

Another score of *Pelléas* transcended all language barriers—an arrangement of the opera for solo piano by Léon Roques (1907, D. & F. 6868). Roques also fashioned a 215-measure *Fantaisie* for piano, which consists of a collage of passages drawn from Acts I–IV of the opera; the *Fantaisie* was issued in two versions—for solo piano and for piano duet (1911, D. & F. 8215 and 8227, respectively).

Durand also published four extracts from the opera in two bilingual piano-vocal editions, French-English and German-Italian:[76]

1.   Récit de Geneviève, *La lettre.* "Voici ce qu'il écrit à son frère Pelléas" (Act I, scene 2).
     French-English (1905, D. & F. 6652)
     German-Italian (1908, D. & F. 7067)
2.   *Duo à la fontaine* (Pelléas et Mélisande). "Vous ne savez pas où je vous ai menée" (Act II, scene 1).
     French-English (1906, D. & F. 6680)
     German-Italian (1908, D. & F. 7094)

3. Récit de Pelléas, *Les cheveux.* "Oh! oh! Qu'est-ce que c'est?" (Act III, scene 1).
    French-English (1905, D. & F. 6653)
    German-Italian (1908, D. & F. 7068)
4. *Récit d'Arkel à Mélisande.* "Maintenant que le père de Pelléas est sauvé" (Act IV, scene 2).
    French-English (1905, D. & F. 6654)
    German-Italian (1908, D. & F. 7083)

Three excerpts were issued in solo piano and piano duet arrangements by Roques: *Duo à la fontaine,* Act II (1906, D. & F. 6691 and 6788); *Les cheveux,* Act III (1906, D. & F. 6731 and 6793); and *La mort de Pelléas,* Act IV (1906, D. & F. 6744 and 6794). The same three excerpts were also published as melodramas, for recitation with piano accompaniment.

The popularity of the opera is further suggested by the publication of instrumental arrangements of portions of it. Henri Mouton arranged *Pelléas* ("with cuts," fortunately!) for performance "en trio": for piano, violin, and cello; piano, flute, and violin; and piano, flute, and cello (with clarinet and double bass *ad libitum*). Roger Branga arranged eight excerpts for "small orchestra with piano-conductor and with interchangeable instruments in case some are lacking" (*Les cheveux, récit de Pelléas; Prélude;* four *Interludes; Récit d'Arkel;* and *La lettre, récit de Geneviève*). Finally, J. Bouchel transcribed a *Pelléas Fantaisie* for wind band. Knowing how fussy Debussy was about the manner in which his opera was presented, one can only imagine what he would have thought of these "popular" arrangements.

8

Revisions of the Vocal Parts

In a 1907 article on *Pelléas*, Romain Rolland pointed to Debussy's reform of the recitative as one of his chief contributions to the history of opera.[1] Rolland viewed this accomplishment as the fulfillment of the ideal described by Jean-Jacques Rousseau in his *Lettre sur la musique française* (1753): Rousseau, observing that "the shrill and noisy intonations" of French opera recitative were completely unrelated to the "harmonious and simple" accents of spoken French, described an ideal style of French recitative, which should

> wander between little intervals, and neither raise nor lower the voice very much; and should have little sustained sound, no noise, and no cries of any description—nothing, indeed, that resembled singing, and little inequality in the duration or value of the notes, or in their intervals.

Rolland also considered Debussy's creation of a speechlike recitative the logical musical response to the more natural declamation current in the contemporary theatrical presentations of Antoine, Gémier, and Guitry.

Debussy himself, in a note of 1902 entitled "Why I Wrote *Pelléas*," commented on his eschewal of conventional melodic formulas in his effort to create a more natural vocal style:

> The characters of this opera try to sing like real people, and not in an arbitrary language made up of worn-out clichés. That is why the reproach has been made concerning my so-called taste for monotonous declamation, where nothing seems melodic. First of all, that's not true. In addition, a character cannot always express himself melodically: the *dramatic* melody has to be quite different from what is generally called melody. (RLS, p. 75)

Although commentators have frequently discussed Debussy's vocal writing in terms of recitative or even as recitative, the composer apparently did not use that term with reference to his opera. A dozen years later he wrote in a letter to an unnamed journalist that "recitative, as conceived by our ancient masters, has almost completely disappeared, or at least it has changed character so much that it should no longer be called by that name." He commented that "it is very tricky to establish what is and is not recitative," but nevertheless defined it as "part of the musical thread, woven into the harmonic background, which binds the various episodes of the musical drama."[2]

Recitative or not, Debussy's style of vocal writing in *Pelléas* has been the subject of much commentary. Joseph Kerman stressed the aspect of natural declamation when he wrote that "Debussy tried to catch literally the accents of French day-by-day speech,"[3] but, as Virgil Thomson has pointed out, Debussy's vocal style is not exclusively speechlike; sometimes it is rather more stylized, like psalmody, or, in the words of Paul Landormy, a special "manner of speech, quite strange, but very striking"—"not as it is spoken in everyday speech, but as we hear it within ourselves."[4] Pierre Boulez found an even greater range of vocal style in *Pelléas* and charged that, "by dint of only seeing in *Pelléas* a continuous recitative, in reaction against Wagner's endless melody, its true novelty has been filched."[5] As was mentioned in the preceding chapter, Boulez saw in *Pelléas* a special solution to the age-old operatic problem of integrating action and reflection; in contrast to the traditional division into polarized styles of recitative and aria, Debussy has created "an extremely closely woven fabric of action and reflection," with frequent and subtle shifts between the two modes. The voice is not just "a transcription which seeks to be solely faithful and exclusively literal," but in moments of reflection, "frees itself from diction to gain its autonomy." Boulez's discerning analysis amplified the view of one of the earliest and most perceptive commentators, Louis Laloy, who wrote in 1905 that Debussy's declamation was very simple, without melodic conventions, but that "each emotion... is expressed in the vocal line itself, with miraculous precision, accuracy, and intensity, modeled on speech, yet at the same time profoundly musical."[6]

The vocal lines thus strive to satisfy both requirements, achieving purely melodic expression while accurately preserving the inflections of the spoken language. These two qualities are combined in different proportions according to the context of any given passage (that is, whether the text constitutes "reflection" or "action"), and any analysis of the voice parts must take both into account. For example, in his discussion of Debussy's successive revisions of a passage near the beginning of Act IV, scene 4, Robert Orledge illustrated the composer's meticulous care with the pace and accentuation of his text setting, precisely the sorts of concerns one would expect in a speechlike section, yet Orledge wisely did not neglect melodic considerations (ORL, pp. 83–87). In a contrasting example, he pointed to the revision of an adjacent passage which merely altered the relationship of the text to a fixed melody.[7] While such an example might, on the surface, suggest that Debussy was more concerned here with the purely melodic expression than with the relationship of particular syllables to particular notes, such a conclusion, while containing an element of truth, would be too limited, as it fails to consider the positive results of the text adjustment, such as its shift of the melodic climax from the word "douleur" (woe) to "joie" (joy). (The line is "I am going to flee, crying out for joy and woe, like a blind man fleeing from his burning house.") Thus, regardless of the perceived or intended function of the vocal lines, they must be analyzed simultaneously in terms of both declamatory and melodic values.

This chapter will focus on Debussy's postpublication, rather than his manuscript revisions of the vocal parts. This approach serves two purposes: by concentrating on the final stages of the process, it shows the composer's continual preoccupation with refining his work in order to arrive at the most convincing setting of the text, and by examining the manner in which these revisions were introduced, it raises questions crucial to the establishment of a critical edition of the opera.

The opera's complex publication history has considerably complicated the task of determining which score is the most authoritative source for the vocal parts. Quite independent of the need to establish textual authority, the question is crucial here in order simply to determine for any given passage which of two divergent readings represents the original and which, the revision. The issue cannot just be settled by the chronology of publication dates. The confusion has its origins in the manner in which the manuscript vocal and full scores were written: although both were based on the same source (the manuscript short score), their vocal parts are not always in agreement since the two scores were written at different times (the vocal score first). In some cases, the differences resulted from changes made in the short score after the manuscript vocal score had been prepared.[8] In such cases, the full score, which was written afterwards, reflects the later reading and may be regarded as the revision; this is confirmed by the fact that these revised readings were often incorporated into later editions of the vocal score. In contrast, there are instances where a change in the vocal parts was made in the manuscript vocal score (or later in the proofs of that score) and was not transferred back to the short score. Thus, when the full score was written, it failed to incorporate the revision. A clear example of this is in Act V, where the rhythm of Golaud's "En ce moment?" is identical in the short score (NEC MS, V, fol. 14, meas. 9) and the full score, p. 399, meas. 7, but different in the 1902 vocal score, p. 276, meas. 1, which follows the manuscript vocal score (Ms 17686, p. 160, meas. 8). The result represents a reversal of our chronological expectation: the 1904 published full score (engraved from the manuscript full score) contains the earlier reading, while the 1902 published vocal score contains the revision.

These two examples illustrate the point that every disagreement among the scores must be treated as a separate case, and preference cannot automatically be given to the latest score. The situation is further complicated by the fact that every new score inevitably contained some engraving errors, and in some cases these may easily be mistaken for revisions. Additional confusion sometimes resulted when an obvious error in a particular edition was corrected differently in two later scores. For example, the incorrect rhythm shown in Ex. la appeared in the 1902 vocal score and was "corrected" one way in the 1904 full score (Ex. lb), and another in the 1907 vocal score (Ex. lc). In this instance, the full score contains the reading found in the manuscript short score, so it apparently reflects the composer's original intent; one may thus regard the 1907 reading as either a revision or an inaccurately entered correction. It need hardly be added that the difference is so slight as to go unnoticed in performance, but the matter was evidently of some importance to the composer.

Ex. 1. (a) VS (1902), p. 118.

(b) OS (1904), p. 174.

(c) VS (1907), p. 132.

Where a discrepancy between scores involves pitches rather than rhythms, the judgement as to whether the difference represents a revision or a publishing error is sometimes more difficult to make; an incorrectly notated rhythm is often demonstrably wrong, but, given Debussy's harmonic style, a "wrong" note in the voice may often fit into the harmonic context. However, in cases where a pitch change was introduced in the full score (1904) and adopted by later editions of the vocal score (1905 rev. and 1907), these may safely be regarded as revisions of the score. Such examples enable one to analyze the principles which Debussy applied in revising the vocal parts.

Pitch changes generally affected the degree of emphasis on particular words of text. In Ex. 2, the revision, in addition to being easier to sing, produces a line of simpler shape and also reduces somewhat the emphasis on the word "mort" (death) by approaching it through a smaller interval, a minor third rather than a minor sixth.[9] Another revision also serves to de-emphasize a particular word, this time by eliminating a change of pitch on the word "bruit" (noise). The revised reading of the line, all on a single pitch, is "quieter," more in keeping with the meaning of the sentence, "They no longer make any noise" (see Ex. 3). Other changes were made to produce, rather than reduce, emphasis, as in Ex. 4, where a change of pitch is introduced to stress "la bouche" (mouth) in the line, "Do not put your hand like that in your mouth." Similarly, the revisions shown in Ex. 5a, b and Ex. 5c, d, emphasize the word "père" (father).

Ex. 2. (a) VS (1902), p. 4.

(b) OS (1904), p. 6; VS (1905 rev.), p. 4; VS (1907), p. 3.

Ex. 3. (a) VS (1902), p. 207.

(b) OS (1904), p. 317; VS (1905 rev.), p. 207; VS (1907), p. 230.

Other changes of pitch affect only the full score, since the later vocal scores retain the readings of the original edition of the vocal score. Some of these differences may be dismissed as errors, either on purely musical grounds or because they were corrected by Debussy in the revised edition of the full score or in a personal copy of the score. But other cases cannot be so easily dismissed and may be regarded as alternatives. The merits of each difference must be evaluated separately. In Ex. 6, the vocal score versions seem preferable.

Ex. 4. (a) VS (1902), p. 145.

Ne mets pas ain - si la main dans la bou - che...

(b) OS (1904), p.223; VS (1905 rev.), p. 145; VS (1907), p. 163.

Ne mets pas ain - si la main dans la bou - che...

Ex. 5. (a) VS (1902), p. 147.

(b) OS (1904), p. 225; VS (1905 rev.), p. 147; VS (1907), p. 165.

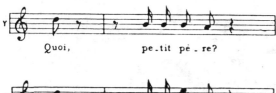

Quoi,   pe-tit pè - re?

Quoi,   pe-tit pè - re?

(c) VS (1902), p. 154.

(d) OS (1904), p. 232; VS (1905 rev.), p. 154; VS (1907), p.173.

Quoi,   pe-tit pè - re?

Quoi,   pe-tit pè - re?

In the first example (Exx. 6a and b), having the pitch change occur between the words "qu'il" and "était" seems better than having it in the middle of the latter word. The same argument could be used in support of the full score reading in the second example (Exx. 6c and d); however, the vocal score's change of pitch, which splits the syllables of "aimé" (love), appropriately draws attention to that key word in a way which would have been

Ex. 6. (a) VS (1902), pp. 171–72; VS (1907), p. 191.

  (b) OS (1904), p. 255.

  (c) VS (1902), p. 261; VS (1907), p. 287.

  (d) OS (1904), p. 384.[9]

inappropriate for "était." Also, the triadic outlining in the third bar of the full score version, while yielding a more perfectly sequential relationship with Golaud's preceding phrase, produces a somewhat sing-song effect, which is avoided in the vocal score. In the two examples shown in Ex. 7, both readings have merit. In the second example (Ex. 7c and d), the major third on "chose" sounds more "natural," the diminished fifth more menacing and disturbed. (Both harmonize with the accompaniment.) The latter seems more appropriate in this scene (Act IV, scene 2), in which Golaud threatens and abuses Mélisande. In Exx. 8 and 9, the versions in the full score seem better. In the first (Ex. 8), the e^1 on the final syllable of "encore" allows the arrival on f^1 to coincide with the corresponding harmonic change in the accompaniment and eliminates the unnatural accent on that syllable that the change of pitch produces. In Ex. 9, the full score version gives more emphasis to the word "père," and the more angular line seems a better reflection of Yniold's agitated state.

  One change in pitch was initiated in the revision of the 1905 vocal score and did not figure in the full score (see Ex. 10). The motivation for the change is not clear, as the original fit better harmonically with the accompaniment. While the shortening of the word "de" in the revisions (1904, 1905 rev., and

Ex. 7. (a) VS (1902), p. 178; VS (1907), p. 198.

(b) OS (1904), p. 264.

Maintenant que le pè.re de Pellé _ as est sau.vé

A.

Main.te.nant que le pè.re de Pel.lé _ as est sau.vé

(c) VS (1902), p. 189; VS (1907), p. 209.

(d) OS (1904), p. 280.

Cro.yez.vous que je sache quelque cho.se?

Go.

Croy.ez.vous que je sa.che quelque cho.se?

Ex. 8. (a) VS (1902), p. 37; VS (1907), p. 42.

Il semble en.co.re fa.ti.gué de vous a.voir at.tendue si longtemps...

(b) OS (1904), pp. 50–51.

Ge.

Il semble encore fa.ti.gué de vous a._ voir attendu si longtemps

Ex. 9. (a) VS (1902), p. 146; VS (1907), p. 164.

(b) OS (1904), p. 224.

Ex. 10. (a) VS (1902), p. 149.

(b) OS (1904), p. 227.

(c) VS (1905 rev.), p. 149; VS (1907), pp. 167–68.

1907 editions) places a slightly greater emphasis on the word "quoi," the elimination of the change of pitch at this point tends to lessen that stress (1905 rev. and 1907).

There are also two instances of pitch changes in the vocal parts that appear only in the 1907 vocal score. In both cases, the original version seems preferable, suggesting that the later versions may be engraving errors rather than revisions. In the first of these examples (Ex. 11a and b), the d^2 of the revision (on "rappelle") harmonizes better with the accompaniment, but the $c\#^2$ of the original is melodically superior; the half step drop for the final unaccented syllable also seems appropriate. In the second example (Ex. 11c and d), the original reading is somewhat more poignant by virtue of the fact that only the final two words, "de moi" (to me), are set off by the pitch change. In both of the examples, however, a preference for the original readings may also be based on the grounds of stylistic consistency in the vocal melody: in the vast majority of cases where Debussy introduces a single pitch change in a triplet figure, the change occurs on the third note. One could almost regard this as a mannerism of his vocal writing.

The rhythmic differences among the various editions are far more numerous than the pitch differences. Debussy's alterations in the text declamation have a subtle, yet telling effect. One category of change affects the pace of dialogue exchange, the speed with which one character replies to another. Ex. 12 gives three different versions of the same passage from Act I, scene 1. The revision in the full score shortens the first syllable of Golaud's "belle," producing a more natural declamation, and makes Mélisande's reaction more urgent by moving it one beat closer so that it follows Golaud's comment after a sixteenth rest, rather than the longer pause of the original edition. The revised 1907 vocal score, by retaining the original rhythm of "belle," eliminates the rest altogether, making Mélisande's exclamation almost an interruption of Golaud's thought.

Towards the end of the same scene (Act I, scene 1), Golaud asks Mélisande to give him her hand, and again she replies, "Oh! don't touch me!" In revising this exchange, Debussy delayed Mélisande's "Oh!" one beat (Ex. 13). This change, by eliminating much of the pause between the two parts of Mélisande's reply, made that reply a more convincing utterance. The added delay in her response may indicate that she has become less afraid of Golaud, or perhaps the extra time was intended to allow some stage action, Golaud moving or reaching toward her. Other examples illustrate the same kind of adjustment. In the two contained in Ex. 14, the changes appear only in the full score. The first change produces an accelerated reply, the second, a delayed one. In the latter, the elimination of the rest between Yniold's two "oui's" and the other rhythmic alterations in his exclamation make his reply a more compact and unified rhythmic unit, producing an effect of more unrestrained

Ex. 11. (a) VS (1902), p. 210; OS (1904), p. 322.

(b) VS (1907), p. 234.

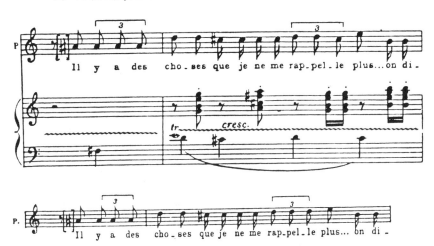

(c) VS (1902), p. 253; OS (1904), p. 375.

(d) VS (1907), p. 278.

Ex. 12. (a) VS (1902), p. 7; VS (1907), p. 7.

Ex. 12. (cont.)

(b) OS (1904), p. 9.

(c) VS (1907 rev.), p. 7.

Ex. 13. (a) VS (1902), p. 20; VS (1905), p. 20; VS (1907), pp.
20–21.

(b) OS (1904), p. 23; VS (1907 rev.), pp. 20–21.

Ex. 14. (a)   VS (1902), p. 36; VS (1905), p. 36; VS (1907), pp. 41–42.

   (b)   OS (1904), pp. 49–50.

   (c)   VS (1902), p. 160; VS (1905), p. 160; VS (1907), p. 180.

   (d)   OS (1904), p. 239.

enthusiasm. In his 1905 revision of the full score, however, Debussy restored the rest (though he kept the four sixteenths for "oui, je veux la").

Other changes in the pace of speech were accomplished through the placement of rests. In Ex. 15, the insertion of a rest serves to set off the final phrase of the statement, giving it additional emphasis. In Ex. 16, two parts of a compound sentence are separated by the addition of a rest. In another revision (Ex. 17), the change in the placement of a rest affects the grouping of sentences (and the accentuation of the question, whose position with respect to the barline has been altered). In the revision, the question, "Haven't you noticed it yourself?" becomes associated more with the statement that follows ("The entire house seems to have revived") rather than the one that precedes it ("My mother listened to him and wept with joy"). The result is a far more logical

Ex. 15. (a) VS (1902), p. 30; VS (1905), p. 30; VS (1907), p. 33.

(b) OS (1904), p. 39.

Ex. 16. (a) VS (1902), p. 116; VS (1905), p. 116; VS (1907), pp.
           130–31.

(b) OS (1904), pp. 171–72.

"reading" of the text. In another case, a meter change was eliminated in order to reduce the length of a pause between two sentences. The new version is more urgent, in keeping with the sense of the text ("Let me go, let me go... Somebody may come... ") (see Ex. 18).

Other rhythmic revisions altered the very rate at which the singers delivered their lines. In the first example (Ex. 19a and b), the speech is slowed down, in the second (Ex. 19c and d), speeded up. The latter example also illustrates another type of change—the elimination of a rhythmic emphasis on a particular word or syllable in order to achieve a more natural style of speech, with more even and regular durational values. Some other examples are shown in Exx. 20-22.

Ex. 17. (a) VS (1902), p. 173.

Ma   mère l'écoutait et pleurait de   joie.   Tu ne t'en es pas aper _ cue?   Tou_te la mai_

(b) OS (1904), p. 257; VS (1905 rev.), p. 173; VS (1907), p.
192.

Ma   mère l'écoutait et pleurait de   joie.   Tu ne t'en es   pas aper_cue?   Tou_te la mai_

Ex. 18. (a) VS (1902), p. 117.

Laisse moi,   laisse   moi...   Quelqu'un pourrait ve   _   nir...

(b) OS (1904), pp. 173–74; VS (1905 rev.), p. 117; VS
(1907), pp. 131–32.

Laisse moi,   laisse   moi...   Quelqu'un pourrait ve _ nir...

Ex. 19. (a) VS (1902), p. 107.

(b) OS (1904), p. 157; VS (1905 rev.), p. 107; VS (1907), p.
120.

MÉLISANDE

Je suis affreuse ainsi...

MÉLISANDE

Je suis af _ freu_se ain   si...

(c) VS (1902), pp. 234–35.

(d) OS (1904), p. 353; VS (1905 rev.), pp. 234–35; VS
(1907), p. 259.

Je ne vois   per _   son_ne...

Ex. 19. (cont.)

(d)

Je ne vois per_   son_ne...

Ex. 20. (a) VS (1902), p. 24; VS (1905), p. 24; VS (1907), p. 27.

(b) OS (1904), p. 31.

el _ le   pleu_re tout à coup comme un enfant, et san_glo _ te

Ge.

el _ le   pleu_re tout a coup comme une en_fant   et san_glot _te,

(c) VS (1902), p. 24; VS (1905), p. 24; VS (1907), p. 27.

(d) OS (1904), p. 32.

_sée   et je n'en sais pas plus que le jour de no_tre ren   _   con _ tre.

Ge.

et je n'en sais pas plus que le jour de no_tre ren_   _con   tre

(e) VS (1902), p. 142.

(f) OS (1904), p. 219; VS (1905 rev.), p. 142; VS (1907), p.
     159.

nous sommes tout juste assis sous les fe_   _nê_tres de pe_ti_te me _   _ re.

nous sommes tout juste assis sous les fe_   _nê_tres de pe_ti_te mè _   _ re.

(g)   OS (1904), p. 367.[10]

(h)   VS (1902), p. 244; VS (1905), p. 244; VS (1907), p. 269.

mort   ce n'est donc pas   vous qui l'a_vez tu_ée,

mort...   ce n'est donc pas   vous   qui   l'a _ vez   tu _ ée.

In Ex. 21, the original version's dotted eighth-sixteenth pattern separates the words "sans doute" from the rest of the sentence, as if that phrase were set off by a comma. Debussy may have felt that the even values of the revision produced a more deadpan, dispassionate delivery, appropriate to the physician. In Ex. 22, greater continuity within a sentence was produced by eliminating a rest in the middle of it.

Ex. 21.   (a)   OS (1904), p. 399.[11]

le M.

C'est vers l'enfant sans doute.

(b)   VS (1902), p. 275; VS (1905), p. 275; VS (1907), p. 302.

LE MÉDECIN

C'est   vers l'en_fant sans doute.

Ex. 22.   (a)   VS (1902), p. 8.

doux et calme

yez,   je reste_rai i _ ci,   contre l'ar _ bre.

(b)   OS (1904), p. 9; VS (1905 rev.), p. 8; VS (1907), p. 7.

doux et calme

yez,   je reste_rai i _ ci,   con.tre   l'ar _ bre.

In contrast to those cases in which Debussy sought to reduce the emphasis on a particular word through a more even distribution of durational values, there were other revisions which accomplished the opposite effect, highlighting key words by introducing unequal durations. In Ex. 23, the revised versions place emphasis on the words "fille" (girl), "rien" (nothing) and "tu" (you), respectively, by lengthening their durations. In contrast, isolated exclamations were given a more excited, and therefore more emphatic quality, by being shortened, as shown in Ex. 24.

Ex. 23.   (a)   VS (1902), p. 6.

(b)   OS (1904), p. 8; VS (1905 rev.), p. 6; VS (1907), p. 5.

(c)   VS (1902), p. 45.

(d)   OS (1904), p. 66; VS (1905 rev.), p. 45; VS (1907), p. 52.

(e)   OS (1904), p. 109.[12]

(f)   VS (1902), p. 76; VS (1905), p. 76; VS (1907), p. 86.

Ex. 24. (a) VS (1902), p. 59.

(b) OS (1904), p. 86; VS (1905 rev.), p. 59; VS (1907), p. 67.

(c) VS (1902), p. 115.

(d) OS (1904), p. 169; VS (1905 rev.), p. 115; VS (1907), p. 129.

(e) VS (1902), p. 152; VS (1905), p. 152; VS (1907), p. 170.

(f) OS (1904), p. 230.

Maeterlinck's text is full of repeated words or phrases, and Debussy often set such repetitions in a sequential pattern, with longer durational values the second time. The effect was to give greater stress to the repetition.[14] In revising the score, Debussy utilized the technique with greater frequency and greater force, sometimes shortening the durations of the first statement to allow the second to stand in greater relief. Three examples of this are shown in Ex. 25.

A further category of revision pertains to sentence beginnings; Debussy was concerned that the first word in a sentence receive the proper degree of

Ex. 25. (a) VS (1902), p. 60.

(b) OS (1904), p. 87; VS (1905 rev.), p. 60; VS (1907), pp. 67–68.

(c) VS (1902), p. 112.

(d) OS (1904), p. 164; VS (1905 rev.), p.112; VS (1907), p. 125.

(e) VS (1902), p. 281; VS (1905), p. 281; VS (1907), p. 308.

(f) OS (1904), p. 407.

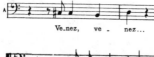

stress and would sometimes alter the rhythm to shift the first note from off the beat to on the beat, thus giving added stress to the opening. Conversely, he would sometimes weaken the stress on the first word by doing the opposite, moving it from on to off the beat. Many of the changes of the first type affected sentences beginning with "il" or "ils" while those of the latter type often began with "je"; Debussy was giving greater stress to "he," "it," and "they," and less to "I." Examples of the first type are shown in Ex. 26. Similar changes affect the following sentences: "Ils m'inondent encore jusqu'aux genoux!... "—off the beat in VS (1902), p. 115, VS (1905), p. 115, and VS (1907), p. 130, and on

Ex. 26. (a) VS (1902), p. 37; VS (1905), p. 37; VS (1907), p. 42.

(b) OS (1904), p. 51.

(c) VS (1902), p. 7.

(d) OS (1904), p. 9; VS (1905 rev.), p. 7; VS (1907), p. 6.

the beat in OS (1904), p. 169; "Il est près de minuit"—off the beat in VS (1902), p. 123, and on the beat in OS (1904), p. 182, VS (1905 rev.), p. 123, and VS (1907), p. 139; and "Ils ne s'approchent pas l'un de l'autre?"—off the beat in VS (1902), p. 166, VS (1905), p. 166, and VS (1907), p. 185, and on the beat in OS (1904), p. 246. In this last instance, the revision of the full score not only moved the initial word to a beat, but doubled its length. Another shift from off to on the beat enhanced the effect of retard at the end of Mélisande's song at the start of Act III (see Ex. 27). Most of these changes, it will be noted, figure only in the full score and were not transferred to later editions of the vocal score.

Ex. 27. (a) VS (1902), p. 104; VS (1905), p. 104; VS (1907), pp. 116–17.

Ex. 27.   (cont.)

    (b)   OS (1904), p. 154.

The changes from on to off the beat, however, were more consistently adopted by later vocal scores after first appearing in the 1904 full score. Examples illustrating this are shown in Ex. 28. Other sentences were revised in a similar fashion: "Mais je le vois, je le vois si clairement aujourd'hui... "—on the beat in VS (1902), p. 257, and off the beat in OS (1904), p. 380, VS (1905 rev.), p. 257, and VS (1907), p. 283; and "Ses yeux sont pleins de larmes"—on the beat in VS (1902), p. 275, and off the beat in OS (1904), p. 398, VS (1905 rev.), p. 275, and VS (1907), p. 301. In another instance where a sentence began on the beat, Debussy lengthened the first note, moving it back one beat in order to give further emphasis to the first word, which now coincided with an attack in the accompaniment (see Ex. 29). Debussy must have changed his mind about this revision; the revised 1905 and the 1907 vocal scores and the revised edition of the full score restored the original version of this passage.

Ex. 28.   (a)   VS (1902), p. 37; VS (1905), p. 37; VS (1907 orig.), p. 42.

    (b)   OS (1904), p. 51; VS (1907 rev.), p. 42.

    (c)   VS (1902), p. 109.

    (d)   OS (1904), p. 161; VS (1905 rev.), p. 109; VS (1907), p. 123.

Ex. 29. (a) VS (1902), p. 194; VS (1905), p. 194; VS (1907), pp.
214–15.

(b) OS (1904), p. 288.

In cases where sentences began on unaccented upbeats, Debussy sometimes changed the length of that first note. Lengthening it tended to place greater stress on the initial word or syllable while shortening it tended to put more emphasis on the downbeat that followed. Representative examples of lengthened upbeats are shown in Ex. 30. Though the opera contains a number of changes of this type, examples of shortened upbeats are less numerous; some have already been cited above in the context of Debussy's technique of using longer durational values to give added emphasis to the repetitions of words or short phrases. The opposite technique (shorter values on the repetition) was also sometimes used to achieve a different effect, as in Ex. 31, in which Geneviève recalls, with some sadness, how long she has been living in Allemonde. The revision, by shortening the upbeat in the first phrase, produces a string of notes of equal length, reflecting some of the monotony that Geneviève has come to feel. Debussy's changes were not always consistent. In Ex. 32, he lengthened the initial note in the full score but shortened it in his revisions of the vocal score.

A final category of rhythmic revision concerns the lengths that final notes of sentences are held. The full score contains more than fifty instances of shortened or lengthened phrase endings. One example of each is shown in Ex. 33. Most changes of this type affect only the full score; the vocal scores are

Ex. 30. (a) VS (1902), p. 12.

    (b) OS (1904), p. 13; VS (1905 rev.), p. 12; VS (1907), p. 12.

Je vais essayer de la prendre...

Je vais essayer de la prendre...

    (c) VS (1902), p. 21.

    (d) OS (1904), p. 23;[14] VS (1905 rev.), p. 21; VS 1907, p. 21.

Mais venez avec moi.__

Mais venez avec moi.__

Ex. 31. (a) VS (1902), p. 36.

vi_te...   Il y a long_temps, il y a longtemps...

    (b) OS (1904), p. 48; VS (1905 rev.), p. 36; VS (1907), p. 41.

vi_te...   Il y a long_temps, il y a longtemps...

Ex. 32. (a) VS (1902), p. 10.

(b) OS (1904), p. 11.

(c) VS (1905 rev.), p. 10; VS (1907), p. 9.

Ex. 33. (a) VS (1902), p. 136; VS (1905), p. 136; VS (1907), p. 153.

(b) OS (1904), pp. 208–9.

(c) VS (1902), pp. 204–5; VS (1905), pp. 204–5; VS (1907), p. 228.

(d) OS (1904), p. 314.

generally in agreement. Many of the shortened notes correspond to mute syllables, as in Ex. 34. The full score version, with less weight on the mute syllable, more closely matches the declamation of natural speech. Again, Debussy was not always consistent in his revisions, as comparison with the previous example shows; there the mute final syllable of "terre" was considerably lengthened in the full score.

Ex. 34. (a) VS (1902), p. 38; VS (1905), p. 38; VS (1907), p. 44.

et ce-pen-dant la mer est som - bre.

(b) OS (1904), p. 53.

et cependant la mer est som - bre

The full and vocal scores often differ in the notation they use for setting words ending with a mute "e." In the vocal scores, Debussy generally assigned a note to the final, mute syllable, often the same pitch as the preceding syllable. In such cases where the two pitches were identical, the full score sometimes combined the two durational values into a single note, as in Ex. 35, in which the word "dire" is set with two notes in the vocal scores, but only one in the full score. In one instance, the opposite relationship can be observed, with the simplified notation for the word "silence" found in the vocal scores (see Ex. 36).

Ex. 35. (a) VS (1902), p. 9; VS (1905), p. 9; VS (1907), p. 8.

Je ne   veux   pas   le   di - re!

(b) OS (1904), p. 10.

Je ne veux pas le dire!

Ex. 36.   (a)   VS (1902), p. 281; VS (1905), p. 281; VS (1907), p. 308.

Il lui faut le si-lence,   main-te-nant...

(b)   OS (1904), p. 407.

Il lui faut le si-len-ce maintenant...

As can be seen from the examples described above, some of the changes that appeared in the 1904 full score were adopted in the revision of the 1905 vocal score and were perpetuated in the vocal scores published subsequently. Others were not. In general, the vocal parts were prepared with greater care in the vocal scores; after all, these, and not the full score, were intended for use by singers of the opera. Consequently, they often have dynamic markings absent from the full score. On the other hand, the full score sometimes includes accents that the vocal scores do not contain, as shown in Ex. 37. Some of these accents may have been added to the manuscript full score by conductor André Messager, but they were nonetheless copied by the engraver and accepted by Debussy as part of the full score.

Ex. 37.   (a)   VS (1902), p. 16; VS (1905), p. 16; VS (1907), p. 16.

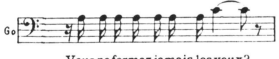

Vous ne fermez jamais les yeux?

(b)   OS (1904), p. 18.

Vous ne fermez jamais les yeux

In general, the revised 1907 vocal score is, aside from a few misprints, the best single source for the voice parts. However, there are numerous variant readings in the full score which may be preferable or more definitive. An editor preparing a critical edition of *Pelléas* would have to judge each discrepancy individually, guided by knowledge of the complicated publishing history of the work and the relationship between the manuscript and printed sources, and, of course, taking into account the musical merits of each reading. In many instances, however, Debussy's independent revisions sometimes produced divergent readings, and these would have to be offered as variants in the score and alternatives to performers.

While Debussy may have avoided preexistent conventions of musical declamation, he invented new ones to create his own kind of stylized recitative. The preceding survey of some of his revisions of the vocal parts touched on some of the features of this style and represents a small contribution towards a more precise and comprehensive definition of the principles upon which that style was based.

Pelléas and the "Wagnerian Formula" in the Light of Source Evidence

Debussy's Opinions Relative to Wagner and Wagnerism

Much has been written about Debussy's relationship with and attitudes toward Wagner and Wagnerism. The subject is extensively discussed in the two principal modern biographies of the composer (Dietschy, *La Passion de Claude Debussy*, pp. 62–77 and passim, and Lockspeiser, *Debussy: His Life and Mind*, I: 89–102), and a recent monograph is devoted to the topic (Holloway, *Debussy and Wagner*).[1] Each, Dietschy most completely, chronicles Debussy's early contact with the works of the German master. He first became acquainted with the music in 1876 at the Conservatoire. In addition to his studies of the scores, he also had opportunities to hear the music in concert and in the theater: Act I of *Lohengrin* at the Concerts Pasdeloup on 20 April 1879, *Tristan* in Vienna during the fall of 1880, *Lohengrin* in Rome and again at the Eden-Théâtre, Paris, on 3 May 1887, *Parsifal, Meistersinger,* and *Tristan* at Bayreuth during the summers of 1888 and 1889, *Lohengrin* at the Paris Opéra on 22 March 1893, *Rheingold* (excerpts performed in concert with Debussy and Raoul Pugno playing a two-piano reduction) at the Paris Opéra on 6 May 1893, and *Walküre*, staged at the Paris Opéra a week later, on 12 May 1893. On 3 February 1894 Debussy began a series of "Ten Wagnerian Sessions," planned as weekly two-hour afternoon gatherings (4 to 6 p.m.) in which he was scheduled to play and sing *Parsifal, Tristan,* and *Meistersinger* (one act per session), and excerpts from *Siegfried*. The readings were given at the home of Mme Escudier, Chausson's mother-in-law, but the series was apparently interrupted in mid-March after the fifth session (Act II of *Tristan*), when Debussy broke off his engagement to Thérèse Roger.[2] There were also many other opportunities to hear Wagner's music in Paris; between 1880 and the fall of 1893 (when Debussy began composing *Pelléas*) music of Wagner was played in nearly 350 concerts given by the Concerts Pasdeloup, Colonne, and Lamoureux, and the Concerts du Conservatoire.[3]

The young Debussy was an ardent Wagnerian. He described himself during his years at the Villa Medici (1885–87) as "Wagnerian to the point of forgetting the most fundamental good manners."[4] Indeed, for the young composer, the issue of Wagner could stand in the way of a friendship; in early 1887 he wrote to the Paris bookseller Emile Baron: "The day you discover that Wagner is not a worthless skunk you will become, for me, the most complete of friends" (DIE, p. 63). This passion for Wagner reached its peak in the two visits to Bayreuth. He later wrote of these experiences and his vivid memories of them: "1889! a delightful time when I was madly Wagnerian. Why am I no longer? Forgive me, but that is another story."[5]

Erik Satie took credit for this transformation, claiming to have explained to Debussy in 1891 that the "Wagnerian adventure" did not correspond with the natural aspirations of French composers, who should have a music of their own ("without sauerkraut, if possible"), based on the representational methods of Monet, Cézanne, and Toulouse-Lautrec.[6] But the advice of Satie was merely the reinforcement of an opinion that Debussy had long held, at least in part. Even during his years of ardent Wagnerism, he realized that his future as a composer did not lie in following the Wagnerian model. In a letter to Eugène-Henry Vasnier of 19 October 1886, two years before his first trip to Bayreuth, he wrote from the Villa Medici of his compositional projects and aspirations: "I have, moreover, undertaken a task which is perhaps beyond my strength, one having no precedent, I find myself compelled to invent new forms. Wagner could be useful to me, but I don't need to tell you how ridiculous it would be to try that. I could take up just his particular method in the linking of scenes, but besides that, I would like to reach the point where the vocal expression ("l'accent") remains lyrical without being absorbed by the orchestra."[7]

In the aftermath of the Bayreuth visits, such personal doubts were joined by some disenchantment both with Wagner's music and with his compositional techniques. Upon his return from the second Bayreuth trip, he reported in September 1889 to Ernest Guiraud: "I envy you for having stayed in Paris and for not having had the desire to travel. How tedious, these leitmotifs! How they are perpetually hurled at one!... The *Nibelungen*, where there are pages which astound me, are a bundle of tricks ("machine à trucs"). They even taint my beloved *Tristan*, and it grieves me to feel myself detached from it."[8]

Years later, Debussy described how his aesthetic principles in composing *Pelléas* developed from a rejection of the Wagnerian model. In a note written in April 1902 and entitled "Why I Wrote *Pelléas*" he included the following paragraph on Wagner:

> After some years of passionate pilgrimages to Bayreuth, I began to have doubts about the Wagnerian formula ("la formule wagnérienne"), or, rather, it seemed to me that it was of use only in the particular case of Wagner's own genius. He was a great collector of formulae,

and these he assembled within a framework that appears uniquely his own only because one is not well enough acquainted with music. And without denying his genius, one could say that he had put the final period after the music of his time, rather as Victor Hugo summed up all the poetry that had gone before. One should therefore try to be "post-Wagner" rather than "after Wagner."[9]

Despite Debussy's conscious rejection of Wagnerism, the specter of Wagner haunted the composition of *Pelléas*, and Debussy was acutely aware of it. In a letter to Chausson of 7 May 1893 he had described Wagner as "one of those strongholds that the public likes to put in opposition to every new aesthetic" (LL, p. 43), but it was not just the public that was preoccupied with Wagnerian comparisons; Debussy himself rejected his first draft of Act IV, scene 4 of *Pelléas* when he detected a Wagnerian influence in it, and he tried to exorcise the "ghost of old Klingsor," as he called it, by announcing a forthcoming (and apparently unwritten) article entitled "On the Uselessness of Wagnerism."

One can thus trace the development of Debussy's growing anti-Wagnerism, from a reluctance to use Wagner as a compositional model in October 1886, to criticism of both the music and the method in September 1889, and finally to a total repudiation of Wagnerism by September 1893. Though his position with respect to the "Wagnerian formula" was surely fully formed by this last date, it was not expressed in print until the spring of 1901, when he began his journalistic career. His articles in *La Revue Blanche,* and later in *Gil Blas* and elsewhere, consistently expressed the view that composers, especially French composers, should not attempt to imitate Wagner or adopt Wagnerian techniques. "Wagner, if one may be permitted a little of the grandiloquence that suits the man, was a beautiful sunset that has been mistaken for a sunrise," he wrote.[10] "Wagner was not a good teacher of French."[11]

Debussy's specific objection to the "Wagnerian formula" was twofold— its application of symphonic form and development to dramatic action and its use of a system of leitmotifs—and he gave journalistic expression to this opinion at what seems to have been the earliest possible opportunity: a review of Alfred Bruneau's *L'Ouragan,* which was part of Debussy's fourth article for *La Revue Blanche,* printed in the issue of 15 May 1901. The review is prefaced by an attack on the Wagnerian "formulas" for composing theater music. "One day," wrote Debussy, "we shall see how useless they all are." He explained in some detail his objection to symphonic developments in opera:

Music has a rhythm whose secret force shapes the development. The rhythm of the soul, however, is quite different—more instinctive, more general, and controlled by many events. From the incompatibility of these two rhythms a perpetual conflict arises, for the two do not move at the same speed. Either the music stifles itself by chasing after a character, or the character has to sit on a note to allow the music to catch up with him. Nonetheless, there are miraculous moments where the two are in harmony, and Wagner has the honor of being responsible for some of these. But they are for the most part due to chance, and more often than not awkward and deceptive. All in all, the application of symphonic form to dramatic

action succeeds in killing dramatic music rather than saving it, as was proclaimed when
Wagner was crowned king of opera. (RLS, p. 36)

This view was one the composer evidently held for more than a decade prior to
this published statement. In conversations with Ernest Guiraud recorded in
October 1889 by Maurice Emmanuel, Debussy discussed the role of the
orchestra and the use of symphonic themes in opera. Again, he praised
Wagner in this regard: "In *Tristan* the themes heard in the orchestra are
themes of the action. They do no violence to the action." Yet in discussing his
own operatic aspirations he recognized the problem of coordinating
symphonic developments with the drama: "Music in opera is far too
predominant.... [There should be] no developments merely for the sake of
developments. A prolonged development does not fit, cannot fit, the words"
(LOC, I: 205–6).

Debussy's second objection to the "Wagnerian formula," its use of
leitmotifs, likewise dated back to the period immediately following the
Bayreuth visits, but what he found tedious in 1889, he found ridiculous in
1901. In the review of *L'Ouragan* he spoke of the "Leitmotif Guide" as an aid
to "those who cannot read a score" and, speaking specifically of Bruneau's
opera, commented: "As you would expect, each symbol takes the form of a
leitmotiv; once again music is weighed down by these obstinate little phrases,
which insist on having their say no matter what else is going on" (RLS, pp.
35–36). Debussy loved to make fun of leitmotifs and was at his wittiest on the
subject, as in his review of a London *Ring* cycle, published in *Gil Blas* on 1
June 1903:

> My lord! How intolerable these men in helmets and animal skins become by the fourth
> evening.... Remember they never appear unless accompanied by their damnable leitmotiv,
> and there are even those who sing it! It's rather like those silly people who hand you their
> visiting cards and then lyrically recite key information they contain. Most annoying to hear
> everything twice! (RLS, p. 203)

This last comment hints at the common denominator of Debussy's two
objections to Wagnerism and in turn helps to define a crucial aspect of his
operatic ideals. What Debussy took exception to was a quality of redundancy,
or worse, incongruity, between corresponding musical and dramatic (or
textual) elements, whether between the purely musical development and the
rhythm of the dramatic action, or between the musical symbol (the leitmotif)
and the dramatic fact. The same attitude seems to have influenced his choice
of a prose rather than a verse libretto: the former avoided potential conflict
between the musical expression of his text setting and the inherent musicality
of a poetic text.[12] In creating an operatic fusion of each of these pairs of
corresponding elements (the musical and the textual-dramatic), Debussy was
conscious of maintaining a flexible balance between the two, careful to
prevent either element from rendering its complement incongruous or

redundant. In order for such a scheme to work, he needed a very special kind of libretto—one written in prose, with relatively few characters (requiring few leitmotifs), and with relatively little action. His search for such a text, which culminated in the discovery of *Pelléas*, began as early as October 1889; in his conversation with Guiraud he raised some of these very issues and prophetically described the ideal librettist: "One who only hints at what is to be said (celui des choses *dites à demi* [more literally, 'one who says things by halves']). The ideal would be two associated dreams" (LOC, I: 205).

The Wagnerian Influence on *Pelléas*: The Opinions of the Critics and the Composer

Debussy's anti-Wagnerism, fully developed and articulated a full year before the première of *Pelléas*, thus evidently had its roots in his reaction to the Bayreuth performances of 1889 and was likely formulated by 1893, the year in which he began composing his opera and in which he announced his article "On the Uselessness of Wagnerism." The anti-Wagnerian attitude, then, seems to have been one consistently held throughout the composition of *Pelléas*. With the beginning of Debussy's journalistic career, opinions formerly shared with friends in private became public knowledge, and his anti-Wagnerian stance was surely known to the critics who reviewed the première of *Pelléas* in 1902. Did this inhibit them or encourage them to seek out Wagnerian traces in Debussy's opera? Whether or not this factor influenced their judgments or perceptions, most of the critics did raise the issue of Wagner, specifically of leitmotifs, in reviewing *Pelléas*. Debussy's 1893 observation still seemed to hold true: Wagner was still, in certain respects, the stronghold against which the public (and critics) measured new aesthetics.

Though far from unanimous on the subject, the majority of the critics detected no leitmotifs in Debussy's opera. Pierre Lalo, writing in *Le Temps*, bluntly declared, "There is nothing, or almost nothing of Wagner in *Pelléas* . . . no display of those leitmotifs."[13] Others echoed this opinion— "there is no trace of leitmotif" (*Bibliothèque Universelle*),[14] "no apparent leitmotif" (Raymond Bouyer, *Nouvelle Revue*)[15]—and still others phrased the observation in a most unflattering way, as in Camille Bellaigue's remark in *Revue des Deux Mondes* that "there are no leitmotifs for the simple reason that there are no motifs at all. . . ."[16] In the minority were some critics who were aware of something like leitmotifs in *Pelléas*. Most often their descriptions of them seem deliberately vague, as in Gaston Carraud's comment in *La Liberté*, "The short, arresting, suggestive *motifs* are no sooner formulated, than they vanish to make way for others, and then flash back for an instant,"[17] or Adolphe Jullien's in *Le Journal des Débats*, "There are not, strictly speaking, leitmotifs or characteristic phrases, but there are (how shall I say?) the beginnings or embryos of phrases immediately cut off, which reappear; sighs and inflections in the orchestra which can in a strict sense serve as points of reference."[18] Jullien seemed to have discovered leitmotifs in *Pelléas*, but balked at using the Wagnerian term to describe them.

Jean Marnold, writing in *Mercure de France*, showed no such qualms. His review of *Pelléas* included almost an entire page (out of eight) on the subject of leitmotifs, and he even identified two of them. Marnold was perceptive in recognizing Debussy's dependence on recurring symphonic motives throughout the opera.

> In *Pelléas et Mélisande*, the composer has used all of the resources of the *leitmotiv*, but in his own manner, which is the most delicate, fine, and subtle. His inspiration, unforeseen and new, like his harmony, consists of short themes, profoundly expressive and connected with the feeling or character in question. They accompany the action of the drama step by step.... All of the movements of the soul are underlined or divulged by the metamorphoses and the intertwining of the leading motives.... It would be necessary to cite everything—nearly every measure of every system of every page—to show with what inexhaustible ingenuity, with what art, completely personal and unprecedented, the composer has integrated and developed the thematic material.[19]

As an example he cited the polyphonic combination of the Pelléas and Mélisande themes in the interlude following Act III, scene 1. Marnold's insight is impressive, even if he had an advantage over his colleagues working for the "dailies"; his review followed the première by about a month, giving him extra time to study the vocal score and the possibility of hearing the opera several times.

In his "Reply to the Critics," printed in the 16 May 1902 issue of *Le Figaro*, Debussy responded to the charges of a Wagnerian influence. When, according to a subhead in the article, "The Interviewer Imprudently Mentions the Name of Richard Wagner," the composer replied: "Certainly my method of composing—which consists above all of dispensing with 'methods of composing'—owes nothing to Wagner." He then proceeded to reiterate his twofold objection to the Wagnerian model:

> In his [Wagner's] work each character has, one might say, his own "calling card," his image—his leitmotiv—which must always precede him. I must confess that I find this procedure somewhat gross. Also, the symphonic development that he introduced into opera appears to me to conflict continually with the moral argument in which the characters are involved and with the play of passions, which alone is important. (RLS, pp. 80–81)

Debussy thus publicly denied his use of leitmotifs in *Pelléas*, though he was apparently willing to discuss it in private, as in a letter to an English friend, Edwin Evans, Jr. It seems that Evans, in preparation for a lecture on *Pelléas* that he was to give on 25 May 1909 at London's Royal Academy of Music, wrote to the composer with certain queries. Debussy's response reiterated some of the points he had made in his 1902 "Reply to the Critics," but, even while continuing to deny any dependence on leitmotifs, he acknowledged that there was a theme which accompanied Mélisande throughout the opera. The letter, published by the *New York Times* in its obituary of the composer on 5 May 1918, was apparently first printed in *The Daily Telegraph* of London. It is so little known that it is worth quoting in full:

> The composer wrote that, on reflection, he found it rather difficult to speak of "Pelléas" and to underline its characteristic portions, so he begged his correspondent to excuse what follows:
>
> "Before all, you will do well to eliminate from discussion whether there is, or is not, melody in 'Pelléas.' It must be decisively understood that melody—or song (Lied)—is one thing, and that lyrical expression is another. It is illogical to think that one can make a fixed melodic line hold the innumerable nuances through which a character passes. That is not only a mistake of taste, but a mistake of 'quantity.'
>
> "If in 'Pelléas' the symphonic development has, on the whole, small importance, it is to react against the pernicious neo-Wagnerian aesthetic which presumes to render, at the same time, the sentiment expressed by the character and the inner thoughts which impel its actions. In my opinion, these are two contradictory operations, from a lyrical point of view, and, when united, can only weaken each other. Perhaps it is better that music should by simple means—a chord? a curve?—endeavor to render the successive impulses and moods as they are produced, without making laborious efforts to follow a symphonic development, foreseen, and always arbitrary, to which one will necessarily be tempted to sacrifice the emotional development. That is why there is no 'guiding thread' in 'Pelléas,' and its characters are not subjected to the slavery of 'Leit-motive.' Take note that the motive which accompanies 'Mélisande' is never altered. It returns in the fifth act unchanged at any point, because, in reality, Mélisande is always unchanged in herself, and dies without any one—or, perhaps, only old Arkel—ever having understood her.
>
> "The simplicity of 'Pelléas' must be insisted upon. I spent twelve years in removing from it everything of a parasitic nature that might have crept into it. Never did I seek in it to revolutionize anything whatever. But the habit has grown of dragging music into places of ill-repute, or of making of it a game of skill that none can understand without hard training. I have endeavored to prove that people who sing can yet remain human and natural, without ever needing to resemble madmen or puzzles. That at first disturbed the professionals, and also the simple public, who, accustomed to being moved by means as false as they were grandiloquent, did not at first understand that all that was being asked of it was a little good-will. That is all I can find to tell you. The rest belongs to anecdote, on which I am badly 'documented,' " was the composer's conclusion.[20]

It was also in a letter to Evans that Debussy professed an "inability to understand why a character should be a slave of his *Leitmotiv,* as a blind man is a slave of his dog or his clarinet."[21]

Debussy also identified the Mélisande motive around the time of the *Pelléas* première, when he wrote out musical excerpts to accompany photographs of the production for the journal *Le Théâtre.* The excerpt reproduced beneath a photo of the scenery for the third tableau (Act I, scene 3—"Before the castle") consisted of the first four measures of the scene. Significantly, they were labeled, in Debussy's hand, "initial theme of Mélisande" ("Thème initial de Mélisande"), obviously in reference to the oboe melody which opens the scene and precedes Mélisande's entrance (with Geneviève).[22]

Despite Debussy's statement in his "Reply to the Critics" that he "owes nothing to Wagner," some critics and analysts continued to find a Wagnerian influence in *Pelléas.* Friedrich Spigl, in an article entitled "Wagner et Debussy," which appeared in *La Revue Blanche* of December 1902, declared that he considered Debussy "a true disciple of Wagner," and that there were a number of melodic figures, rhythms, and harmonic progressions scattered throughout the score of *Pelléas* which could be given labels defining their precise meanings and assembled into a "guide," much like the "horrible treatment" that had been applied to Wagner's scores.[23]

Louis Laloy, in a 1905 article on *Pelléas,* came to the composer's defense and took pains to contrast Debussy's style with the Wagnerian manner. On the subject of leitmotifs, he spoke of a number of motives which recur at different points, but which he claimed were associated with feelings (*sentiments*) rather than with objects, actions, or characters. He substantiated his claim with several illustrations. For example, he showed that the motive which seems to belong to Golaud (meas. 5–6 of the Act I prelude—see Ex. 1c) is also used to depict the threatening sound of the sea (in the interlude before Act II, scene 3) and therefore seems to express anxiety (*l'inquiétude*) rather than represent Golaud. Similarly, the motive which accompanies Pelléas's entrance in Act I, scene 2 is used to open Act II, scene 1, where it expresses melancholy tenderness, and not the character of Pelléas. Laloy concluded that the role of the motives was "to manifest the hidden feelings, to render the soul transparent, to allow one to understand it to its depths, to sketch around vague speeches, as embellishments of the revealed Unconscious."[24] These motives, in contrast with those of Wagner, are very short, and their continuous modification successfully mirrors the instability of human feelings, which are in a state of constant flux. Debussy, declared Laloy, "has renewed all at once music and drama," and any new work "will only be viable if it draws its inspiration from his principles, just as in former times there was no escape from the Wagnerian reform."[25] The composer appreciated this article and wrote a letter of thanks to its author, his friend of three years: "It seems to me difficult to go further in the understanding of a work" (LAL, p. 15).

Despite Laloy's arguments, some subsequent commentators ventured thematic analyses of *Pelléas* which did associate particular motives with characters and objects. In her 1908 monograph on Debussy, Mrs. Franz (Louise) Liebich, an English friend of the composer, identified three character motives, those of Pelléas, Mélisande, and Golaud.[26] And Lawrence Gilman, whose book *Debussy's "Pelléas et Mélisande." A Guide to the Opera* appeared in the previous year, provided an extensive thematic study of the opera; his analysis identified nineteen themes, which he called "sound wraiths" rather than leitmotifs. Gilman's "sound wraiths" were associated, not only with characters, but with places and settings (the forest, the fountain, night), feelings (awakening desire, vengeance, ardor, pity, sorrow), character attributes (Mélisande's naïveté, Mélisande's gentleness), and forces (fate).[27] Other such studies followed, the most important being Maurice Emmanuel's *Pelléas et Mélisande de Claude Debussy. Etude historique et critique. Analyse musicale* of 1926. This book contains a table of thirteen themes which the author took great pains *not* to call leitmotifs and which he labeled, often with the greatest reluctance and tentativeness. Emmanuel's labels are not always in agreement with those of Gilman; he sometimes gave a different name to the same motive or the same name to a different one. In addition, Emmanuel found one motive which represented an object (the ring) and another which signified a state of being (death).[28]

Gilman was aware of Debussy's inconsistency with respect to the leitmotif, the apparent paradox of his exploiting a technique which he repudiated. He attempted to justify the composer's stance (Debussy's statement that he found the Wagnerian leitmotif system "somewhat gross") by pointing out that Debussy used his themes in a far more subtle and sparing way than did his predecessors.[29] For Gilman, Debussy was more consistent with regard to his other objection to the Wagnerian method. In fact, he considered Debussy's handling of the orchestra and his eschewal of Wagnerian symphonic developments as the composer's great contribution to opera. In a 1908 article in *The Musical Standard* entitled "Wagner and Debussy," Gilman attempted to demonstrate that *Pelléas* was the first opera "to carry the principles of the 'Camerata,' of Gluck and Wagner to their ultimate and effective conclusion." In the course of his argument, he tried to clarify the differences between Debussy and Wagner in the ways they used the orchestra: "Debussy's orchestra is unrivalled in musico-dramatic art for the exquisite justness with which it enforces the moods and action of the play. It never seduces the attention of the auditor from the essential concerns of the drama itself; never, unlike the music of Wagner, tyrannically absorbs the mind.... His use of the orchestra differs from Wagner's in degree rather than in kind. As he employs it, it is a veracious and pointed commentary on the text and the action of the play, underlining the significance of the former and colouring and intensifying the latter; but its comments are infinitely less copious and voluble than are Wagner's—indeed, their reticence and discretion are, as it has been said, extreme." Gilman concluded: "By releasing the orchestra from its thraldom to the methods of the symphonic poem, to which Wagner committed it: by making it a background, a support, rather than a thing of procrustean dominance, Debussy has restored freedom and clarity of dramatic utterance to the singing-actors. That is his notable achievement."[30]

The purpose of this lengthy introduction was to explore in some of its detail and complexity the development of Debussy's attitudes toward Wagner and Wagnerism, and to show how *Pelléas* was perceived in terms of Wagner by both the composer and his contemporaries. This examination will serve as a background for a study of Debussy's sketches and drafts of *Pelléas*, one which will focus on his use of leitmotifs and which will attempt to discover if that use was consistent throughout the compositional process or if it evolved, and if so, in which direction it evolved.

The Role of the Leitmotif in the Thematic Revisions of Act IV, Scene 4

According to Robert Godet, Debussy's first musical sketches for *Pelléas* were the theme in Act IV, scene 4 accompanying Pelléas's words, "On dirait que ta voix a passé sur la mer au printemps!..." (VS, p. 245), and the two most fundamental motives of the opera—the five-note "arabesque" associated with Mélisande and the rhythm which represents the ponderous walk of Golaud.[31] The themes are reproduced in Ex. 1 with the labels assigned to them by Gilman and Emmanuel.

Ex. 1. (a) Ecstasy (Gilman), Love Declared (Emmanuel).

(b) Mélisande (Gilman, Emmanuel).

(c) Golaud (Emmanuel), [Fate (Gilman)].

The earliest surviving sketch, the draft of the latter part of Act IV, scene 4 in the Meyer MS, does indeed begin with the passage described by Godet (Ex. 1a), in a form rather close to the final version, but since the page (LPm, p. 53) begins in the middle of the theme, it would probably be a mistake to conclude that this was the first page written. This observation, of course, in no way contradicts Godet, but rather demonstrates that the "ecstasy" theme was in fact included in the earliest surviving sketches. The same cannot be said of the Mélisande and Golaud motives, which are nowhere to be found in the Meyer draft of this scene. In this case, the absence of these motives in a scene where their presence would certainly have been appropriate (they appear in the final version of the scene) does cast suspicion on Godet's testimony, especially since the motives are also absent from the Legouix draft. On the basis of manuscript evidence, then, it would seem that these two character motives were probably not invented before December 1893, when Debussy began the composition of Act I.

Perhaps, though, there is another kind of significance to Godet's recollections; that is, that Debussy's first ideas for his musical setting of the Maeterlinck play were not settings of vocal lines, but orchestral themes associated with characters or emotions. This priority is often encountered in the early drafts, as there are places where Debussy, in his haste to fix his musical ideas, supplied the accompaniment, but omitted the vocal lines. A case in point is the very passage signalled by Godet, Pelléas's "song" in Act IV, scene 4. In the Meyer draft of this section, the accompaniment was sketched in considerable detail, but the vocal melody, which carries very important words ("On dirait que ta voix a passé sur la mer au printemps!... Je ne l'ai jamais entendue jusqu'ici. On dirait qu'il a plu sur mon coeur!..."), was completely omitted. Evidently Debussy's first priority here was the working out of the "ecstasy" theme. When, in a subsequent draft, he supplied the voice part, he found that he had to insert two measures in order to accommodate the text. (Compare the Meyer and Bréval MSS; LPm, pp. 53 and 103.)

In addition to the "ecstasy" theme of Ex. 1a, the Meyer and Legouix MSS share three other motives which have come to be identified as principal themes (or leitmotifs) of the opera (see Ex. 2). Gilman's identification of Ex. 2b as the Golaud theme is one with which most analysts disagree. The theme generally associated with Golaud is the one given in Ex. 1c, which Gilman labeled "Fate." In fact, both themes are associated with the character at different points in the opera, and a study of the manuscripts suggests that Gilman's theme was Debussy's original Golaud motive. As his work on the opera progressed, however, Debussy invented a second Golaud motive (perhaps while composing Act I), and in subsequent composition and revision, he began to use the new theme more and more consistently in relation to that character. The original Golaud theme was not entirely removed from the opera, although many appearances of it were eliminated or replaced by the new motive. It remained in many crucial places, for example, marking Golaud's threatening entrance at the end of Act III, scene 1 (VS, pp. 138–40), at his declaration in Act II, scene 2 that he would rather lose everything he owned than the ring he gave to Mélisande (VS, pp. 99–100; in diminution, labeled "Vengeance" by Gilman), or to signal his impending arrival at the end of Act IV, scene 4 (VS, pp. 259 and 261; also in diminution, labeled "Death" by Emmanuel) (see Ex. 3).

Both diminuted forms are clearly derived from the original Golaud motive, whose first appearance (in the opera as performed, not as composed) accompanies Golaud's first mention of his name in Act I, scene 1, as he introduces himself to Mélisande: "I am Prince Golaud, the grandson of Arkel,

Ex. 2. (a) Pelléas[32] (Gilman, Emmanuel).

(b) Golaud (Gilman).

(c) Rapture (Gilman), Desperate Love (Emmanuel).

Ex. 3. (a) Vengeance (Gilman).

(b) Death (Emmanuel).

the old king of Allemonde" (see Ex. 4). The second measure of this example, with its mention of Arkel, contains the motive associated with that character throughout the opera.[33]

The following study of Debussy's thematic handling will begin with an examination of the earliest surviving *Pelléas* manuscripts: the Meyer preliminary draft of the latter two-thirds of Act IV, scene 4, and the Legouix developed draft of the entire scene, six folios of which are contained in the Bréval MS. A comparison of the two will illustrate Debussy's use of the leitmotif in the early stages of composition (September-October 1893).

As already mentioned, the theme of "ecstasy" is the first one encountered in the Meyer MS (when its pages are arranged in order), where it accompanies Pelléas's "On dirait que ta voix a passé sur la mer au printemps!..." (fol. 1ʳ; LPm, p. 53). But it is the original Golaud motive (Ex. 2b) that is the predominant thematic material in the portion of the scene preserved in the Meyer MS. It too appears on the very first page (LPm, p. 53, meas. 14–16), appropriately at the point where Mélisande refers to her husband, telling Pelléas: "Non, je ne mens jamais; je ne mens qu'à ton frère..." ("No, I never lie; I lie only to your brother... "—see Ex. 7a). The next appearance of the motive,

Ex. 4. VS, pp. 14–15.

Je suis le prin_ce Go_laud le pe _ tit fils d'Arkel le vieux roi d'Allemon _ de...

several pages later (fol. 4ʳ; LPm, p. 58, sys. 2, meas. 4), coincides with the moment where Pelléas and Mélisande hear the sound of the closing castle door, just before Pelléas's line, "Quel est ce bruit?" ("What is that noise?"). The logic of its use here is that Golaud is the one who has closed the door, preventing them from turning back, and that he is now moving towards them. The Golaud motive is extensively developed here through sequence and repetition, first in its original rhythm and then in diminution. This development originally continued for more than twenty measures (fols. 4ʳ and 5ᵛ; LPm, pp. 58 and 54, sys. 5–7), up to the point where Pelléas sings, "Viens! viens... mon coeur bat comme un fou jusqu'au fond de ma gorge..." ("Come, come... My heart beats like a madman, up to my very throat... "). Then (fol. 5ᵛ; LPm, p. 54, sys. 1), the "rapture" theme enters to accompany the embrace of the two lovers; that theme is repeated, immediately followed by the "ecstasy" theme in augmentation, while Pelléas exclaims: "Ecoute! écoute! mon coeur est sur le point de m'étrangler..." ("Listen! listen! my heart is nearly strangling me..."). When Debussy rewrote the latter portion of this passage on another page of the Meyer MS (fol. 6ᵛ; LPm, p. 56), he curtailed the extensive development of the Golaud motive, replacing it with a triadic theme and motives derived from the "rapture" theme. (This revision is similar to the final version: VS, pp. 257–58.)

The Golaud theme next enters in diminution, at the moment where Mélisande becomes aware of Golaud's presence and sings, "Il y a quelqu'un derrière nous..." ("There is somebody behind us... ") (fol. 5ᵛ; LPm, p. 54, sys. 2, meas. 3–4). The "rapture" theme returns as Pelléas tries to turn their thoughts back to love, dismissing her fear with the explanation that she only heard the crackling of dead leaves because the wind had died down while they were kissing. Then Mélisande spots Golaud ("Ah! Il est derrière un arbre!"—"He is behind a tree!") and his motive returns in diminution to accompany the discovery (fol. 6ʳ; LPm, p. 55, sys. 1). Again the motive is developed extensively by repetition and sequence, dominating the accompaniment until the end of the scene (or as far as the draft goes; compared with the Legouix MS, the Meyer version is lacking the final seven measures that conclude the scene). Other themes are heard during these final pages, though. At the moment where, according to the play, Pelléas and Mélisande "kiss desperately" (just before he sings, "Oh! oh! toutes les étoiles tombent!"—"All the stars are falling!"), the Pelléas theme is combined contrapuntally with the Golaud theme (fol. 7^r; LPm, p. 57, sys. 2), as the desires of the two brothers come into open conflict, Pelléas boldly expressing his ardor in the face of Golaud's impending attack. This thematic combination continues for ten measures, until the lovers' final moment of shared passion (he sings, "Donne! donne!" ["Give!"] and she responds, "Toute! toute! toute!" ["All!"]). At this point, the Golaud theme momentarily vanishes (practically the only time it does so during these final two pages), and the themes of "rapture" and "ecstasy" burst forth for the last time. As Golaud pursues Mélisande with his sword, his motive once again returns.

In addition to the measures in which it is superimposed upon the Golaud motive, the Pelléas theme makes only one other appearance in the Meyer draft, when, in reply to Pelléas's observation that she does not look happy, Mélisande sings, "Si, si, je suis heureuse, mais je suis triste..." ("Yes, yes, I am happy, but I am sad...") (fol. 3^v; LPm, p. 60, sys. 1-2; see Ex. 6a). The appropriateness of this use of the theme is better understood by looking at the first part of the scene in its earliest surviving draft, the Legouix MS.

In the Legouix MS, the Pelléas theme dominates the opening of the scene, providing the principal material for its prelude (see Ex. 5). It is also persistent throughout the first part of Pelléas's opening speech (fol. 1^r) and returns shortly after Mélisande's entrance, when Pelléas beckons her, singing, "Viens ici, ne reste pas au bord du clair de lune" ("Come here; do not stay at the edge of the moonlight") (fol. 3^r). To Mélisande's reply that she wishes to stay in the light, Pelléas explains that they might be seen from the windows of the tower, and the orchestra underscores this explanation with two ominous statements of the Golaud motive, naming the danger, or perhaps simply the fear, that consciously or subconsciously prompts Pelléas's caution (fols. 3^r-4^r). A few bars later, Pelléas asks Mélisande if she had been able to leave the castle without being seen, and she replies affirmatively, explaining that Golaud was asleep. On her last syllable, the orchestra again introduces the Golaud theme, which continues, accompanying Pelléas's response as he anxiously observes, "Il est tard; dans une heure on fermera les portes. Il faut prendre garde" ("It is late; in an hour they will close the gates. We must be careful") (fol. 4^r). Pelléas wants to know why she is so late and she explains that her husband had had a bad dream. This reference to Golaud elicits another two-measure statement of his theme in the orchestra, as Mélisande relates how (rather symbolically) she tore her gown on the nails of the gate (fol. 4^r). Pelléas comments that she is "still out of breath, like a hunted bird," and the orchestra has another two-bar statement of the Golaud theme, naming Mélisande's "hunter," and thus anticipating the tragic outcome of their meeting (Bréval MS, fol. 6^r [originally

Ex. 5. Legouix MS, fol. 1ʳ.

part of the Legouix MS]; LPm, p. 99). At this point in the scene, the two lovers turn their thoughts from Golaud and the potential danger he poses. When Mélisande recalls their previous meeting at the well, "Nous sommes venus ici il y a bien longtemps... Je me rappelle..." ("We came here long ago... I recall... "), her remark is underscored with a single statement of the Pelléas theme (Bréval MS, fol. 6ʳ), and that theme returns a few bars later for Pelléas's "C'est la dernière fois que je te vois peut-être..." ("It is the last time that I shall see you perhaps... "—Bréval MS, fol. 7ʳ; LPm, p. 101). On the following folio we reach the point corresponding to the beginning of the Meyer MS.

With this overview of the entire scene in its earliest surviving draft, it is possible to summarize Debussy's thematic usage at this early compositional stage. The scene opens with Pelléas's entrance and soliloquy, musically reflected by appearances of his theme in the prelude and during the first part of his opening speech. After Mélisande's entrance, the conversation turns persistently to Golaud, and that character's motive is heard in the orchestra whenever there is a reference to him. Eventually they are able to put these thoughts aside and the Pelléas theme returns as they begin to acknowledge their growing love. As Pelléas rhapsodizes over their mutual declaration of love, the first of the love themes (the theme of ecstasy) makes its first appearance. Throughout the balance of the scene one continues to note a functional use of the four principal themes: the two love themes for the expression of love, the Pelléas theme to reflect his troubled mood, and the

Golaud theme to signal, first references to him, and then his actual presence. As the scene unfolds, the Golaud theme becomes all pervasive. Thus, the action of the scene is reflected by the thematic usage, with the Pelléas theme gradually dominated and finally defeated by the Golaud motive; at a climactic moment shortly before the end, the two themes come into direct combat and are superimposed, and of course it is the latter that survives the confrontation and brings the scene to its close.

While it is clear that the Golaud theme represents that character in a very basic sense—it is heard when he is directly or indirectly referred to, when he is approaching, when he is *heard* approaching, and when he is actually present— it is not clear that the other themes function in quite the same manner. The love themes do not so much represent love as express it, and the Pelléas theme too seems more to express his feelings than to represent his persona. As it is used here, the Pelléas theme is far more expressive than symbolical, while the Golaud theme seems to be both in equal measure. (The difference is perhaps comparable to Dahlhaus's distinction between emotive and allegorical motives in Wagner, though, as Dahlhaus points out, the distinction between the two types is not always clear cut.)[34] Our perception of the Pelléas theme is further obfuscated by two appearances of it which are not directly connected to that character: when Mélisande recalls their having come to the well before, and when she expresses her emotional confusion, saying that she is both happy and sad (Ex. 6a).

Although it differs from the Meyer MS at many points, the Legouix draft is, in general, very similar in its dependence on the same principal themes. In a few instances, however, the use of those themes has been altered. A case in point is the example just mentioned; the Legouix revision (Ex. 6), by eliminating the second statement of the Pelléas theme, removes the apparent contradiction or ambiguity, and allows the theme to be unambiguously understood as the expression of Pelléas's, rather than Mélisande's, feelings, that is *his* worry over her apparent unhappiness. Two other Legouix revisions add the Pelléas theme to express that character's sensitivity: when he confesses, "Je ne pouvais pas admettre tes yeux... Je voulais m'en aller tout de suite..." ("I could not acknowledge your eyes... I wanted to go away at once...") (see Legouix MS, fol. 6ʳ and Meyer MS, fol. 3ᵛ [LPm, p. 60]; the Meyer MS omitted the accompaniment at this point), and when he asks her, "Pourquoi me regardes-tu si gravement?" ("Why do you look so gravely on me?") (Bréval MS, fol. 11ʳ; LPm, p. 109).

On the other hand, the use of the Golaud motive was considerably curtailed in the Legouix draft, as in Ex. 7, where Debussy removed it from the accompaniment to Mélisande's remark, "I lie only to your brother." Though the essential harmonies have been retained (transposed up a major second), the motive itself is obscured .

Even more striking changes occur towards the end of the scene, where

Ex. 6. (a) Meyer MS, fol. 3ᵛ (LPm, p. 60).

Debussy eliminated a lengthy thematic expansion of the two character
motives: the ten-measure superimposition of the Pelléas and Golaud themes
was removed, and in its place (Legouix MS, fol. 11ʳ) he used the "rapture"
theme to mark the lovers' defiant embrace and accompanied their subsequent
exchange with the descending triadic figure that had underscored their
previous embrace (see Legouix MS, fols. 7ʳ-8ʳ and Meyer MS, fol. 6ᵛ [LPm, p.
56]; this parallel use of the triadic figure remains in the final version of the
passage [compare VS, pp. 257–58 and 265–66], making this motive a third
love theme). He also made an adjustment in his use of the original love themes
at the end of the scene, just before Golaud's attack: while the Meyer draft used
both themes in succession, the Legouix used only the "ecstasy" theme.

Bearing in mind that these revisions were made in September-October
1893, at the time of Debussy's announced article "On the Uselessness of
Wagnerism," and recalling that he confessed in early October to have rejected
a draft of the scene because he detected a Wagnerian influence in it, it is
tempting to view these changes as manifestations of anti-Wagnerism. But if
such an impulse did motivate these revisions, it was obviously not simply to

Ex. 6 (b). Legouix MS, fol. 5ʳ.

eliminate leitmotifs; after all, in the Legouix MS the Pelléas theme finds increased and more consistent use. Rather, any anti-Wagnerism must be found in Debussy's curtailment of his excessive dependence on the Golaud theme, which, when spun out through repetition and sequence, may have seemed to him dangerously like a Wagnerian symphonic development. The tendency to eliminate such passages was already noted in a revision which took place within the Meyer MS; the Legouix MS simply continued the practice.

In tracing Act IV, scene 4 from the Legouix MS draft to the Bréval MS version of May 1895, one observes a continuation of this same process of eliminating musical developments of the Golaud theme, but there is also evident an apparent desire simply to reduce the frequency of leitmotif appearances. Most of these changes affect the final third of the scene, and two consecutive passages will illustrate the point. Ex. 8 is the Bréval MS version of the section discussed above in Ex. 6; here the Pelléas motive is completely eliminated and a wrenching dissonance is introduced for Mélisande's acknowledgement of her sadness.

Ex. 7. (a) Meyer MS, fol. 1ʳ (LPm, p. 53).

(b) Bréval MS, fol. 9ʳ (LPm, p. 105).

Immediately following, the Golaud theme too was replaced by other materials; instead of using that motive as the sound which prompts Pelléas's startled "What is that noise?" Debussy substituted crescendo repetitions of a grace note figure and added a reference to the Golaud theme *following* Pelléas's question, as if providing the answer to it, or rather, the answer that Pelléas fears (Bréval MS, fol. 12ʳ; LPm, p. 111). For the exchange which follows, in which Pelléas and Mélisande discuss the closing of the gate, Debussy replaced a development of the Golaud motive with a succession of nonthematic chords (see Ex. 9).

This example also suggests a subtle, yet crucial way in which Debussy's concept of the leitmotif seems to have shifted. Having Golaud's theme *be* the sound of the closing gate (as in Ex. 9a), reflects a point of view external to the characters on stage; it is rather the point of view of the composer, who, by telling his audience the identity of the gate-closer, comments on the action from outside of it. In the revision (Ex. 9b), the orchestra reflects the feelings of the characters on stage, here specifically, Pelléas and his fear that Golaud may have trapped them. (A subsequent revision of the MS eliminated even this statement of the Golaud theme, apparently in order to delay the musical "warning" of his approach.)

Ex. 8. Bréval MS, fol. 12^r (LPm, p. 111).

Ex. 9. (a) Legouix MS, fol. 6^r.

Ex. 9.   (cont.)

(b)   Bréval MS, fol. 12^r (LPm, p. 111).

Another revealing example concerns two parallel dramatic moments—first, where Mélisande becomes aware of Golaud's presence and exclaims, "There is someone behind us!" and a little later, when she actually sees him, "Ah! He is behind a tree!" In the Meyer and Legouix MS versions, the accompaniment is nearly identical in the two passages (see Ex. 10). The Bréval version, however, differentiates the two passages without effacing their relationship, and it does so by removing or obscuring some repetitions of the Golaud theme. The second passage, where Golaud is actually spotted, is appropriately given the greater motivic clarity. The revision also compresses the dialogue, eliminating some of the four-plus-four bar squareness of the original (see Ex. 11). In another instance, towards the end of the scene, at Mélisande's "So much the better!" ("Tant mieux! tant mieux!..."), the Bréval version eliminated a ten-measure development of the Golaud theme (compare Legouix MS, fols. 10^r-11^r with Bréval MS, fol. 16^r [LPm, p. 119]).

Thus, while the thematic revisions of September-October 1893 achieved greater consistency in the use of the Pelléas theme and reveal an apparent desire to reduce the scene's dependence on the Golaud theme (especially on musical developments based on that theme), the revisions of May 1895 seem to reflect a more explicitly anti-Wagnerian motivation (in Debussy's sense of the word): they both reduced the number of leitmotif appearances and further eliminated symphonic developments of the Golaud theme.

It was only in his later revisions of the Bréval MS, made between 1895 and September 1901, that Debussy introduced into Act IV, scene 4 both the Mélisande motive and the new Golaud motive (Exx. 1b and 1c), even though both had evidently been invented years before. His progressive addition of these leitmotifs would seem to suggest, if anything, a *pro*-Wagnerian thrust to these later revisions. The sole explicit reference to the Mélisande theme in what appears to be the original layer of the Bréval MS is, appropriately, at the climax of the scene, where it is combined with the "ecstasy" theme to accompany the lovers' final embrace (see Ex. 12).

In post-1895 revisions, however, the Mélisande motive was added at many points in the scene, as in the latter half of Pelléas's opening soliloquy (beginning with "Je ferais mieux de m'en aller sans la revoir..."—"It would be better if I left without seeing her again... "), where his thoughts shift from an analysis of his own feelings to a preoccupation with Mélisande and his intentions regarding their imminent meeting. In this section, the Bréval MS draft already contained a four-note melodic figure intervallically related to the Mélisande motive. Like that motive, it begins with successive rises of a major second and minor third, and Debussy used it both to open and close this section (Bréval MS, fols. 3^r-4^r; LPm, pp. 93–95; see VS, pp. 234–36). This use of the motive, already present in the Legouix MS, fols. 2^r-3^r, was probably not intended by Debussy as a deliberate reference to the Mélisande theme, which appears not to have been invented when the Legouix draft was written; had that been his intent, the reference would surely have been more explicit. The figure seems to have another significance, however, as it recurs later in the scene, in the measures immediately preceding the mutual declaration of love (Bréval MS, fol. 7ʳ; LPm, p. 101; see VS, p. 243, meas. 6–p. 244, meas. 2).[35] In both instances, Pelléas is mustering his courage: first, to resolve to tell Mélisande "all that [he had] never told her," and second, actually to tell her that he loves her. The motive seems to express the love that Pelléas feels towards Mélisande, which allows him to overcome his natural reticence in order to take action.[36] In revising the Bréval version, Debussy seems to have recognized the motivic and symbolic relationship between this motive and the Mélisande theme, and he revised the accompaniment to reinforce that relationship. At Pelléas's "Et je n'ai pas encor regardé son regard..." ("And I have not yet beheld her glance... "), Debussy's Bréval MS revision (fols. 2ᵛ-3ʳ; LPm, pp. 92–93) added an explicit statement of the Mélisande motive and altered the accompaniment in the measures that follow to contain references to that motive (see Ex. 13). Earlier in the same speech, at another point where Pelléas makes a direct reference to Mélisande's appearance ("Il faut que je la regarde bien cette fois-ci..."—"I must look well at her this time... "), another Bréval MS revision added the Mélisande motive (fol. 2ᵛ; LPm, p. 92), but this change was not retained in future drafts (compare Ex. 14 with VS, p. 234, meas. 4). However, in orchestrating the score, Debussy did add a sequential statement of the Mélisande motive in the two measures following this example (OS, p. 322, meas. 4–5; the addition does not appear in the published vocal score: VS, p. 234, meas. 5–6). The notes of the Mélisande theme were already present in the harmonies of the accompaniment and it was relatively simple to express them melodically (see Ex. 15).

The result of these revisions is that the second half of Pelléas's opening speech, in which his thoughts turn to Mélisande, has undergone a dramatic change in thematic content. The original version contained a melodic figure which could be perceived in retrospect as related to the Mélisande motive (at most, a proto-Mélisande motive), but in the revised version, the Mélisande motive dominates the entire passage and its explicit statements serve to reinforce the motivic link to the proto-Mélisande motive while providing an unequivocal musical complement to the shift in Pelléas's thoughts.

The Bréval MS revisions also added the Mélisande motive in two other passages where an orchestral statement of that character's motive was appropriate: where Pelléas sings, "Je n'avais jamais rien vu d'aussi beau avant toi..." ("I had never seen anything so beautiful before you... ") (Bréval MS, fol. 10ʳ; LPm, p. 107; VS, pp. 249–50), and towards the end of the scene, where he sings, "Oh! oh! toutes les étoiles tombent!" ("All the stars are falling!") and she responds, "Sur moi aussi!" ("Upon me too!") (Bréval MS, fol. 16ʳ; LPm, p. 119; though absent from VS, pp. 265–66, the motive is found in the short score, NEC MS, IV, fol. 32ʳ, and in OS, pp. 360–61). Two further additions of

Ex. 10. (a) Legouix MS, fol. 8ʳ.

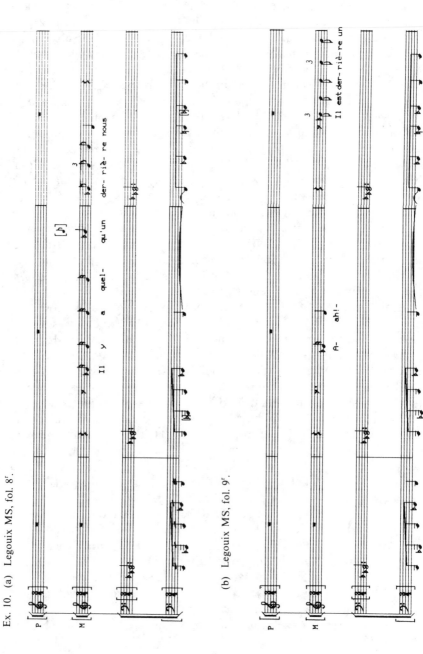

Il y a quel- qu'un der- riè- re nous

[♭]

(b) Legouix MS, fol. 9ʳ.

A- ah!- Il est der- riè- re un

Ex. 10 (a). (cont.)

Je ne vois per- son- ne...

J'ai en- ten- du du bruit...

Ex. 10 (b). (cont.)

Qui [?]

Go- laud? - où donc? - je ne vois rien

ar- bre!

Go- laud[!]

Ex. 11. (a) Bréval MS, fol. 14^r (LPm, p. 115).

(b) Bréval MS, fols. 14^r–15^r (LPm, pp. 115 and 117).

Ex. 12. Bréval MS, fol. 16ʳ (LPm, p. 119).

the Mélisande motive appear for the first time in the short score (NEC MS) and probably date from 1900–1901; in both instances it is the sadness of Mélisande which is expressed through the motive. These examples illustrate the relative ease with which the motive could be added to practically any context. In the first instance, Ex. 16, the pitches of the motive were already present in the harmony. The second instance affects a passage that has already been discussed and illustrated above in Exx. 6 and 8. The successive changes reflect a growing consistency in the use of the character motives, from two sta.   ˙nts of the Pelléas motive (Meyer MS: Ex. 6a), to one (Legouix MS: Ex. 6b˙ to a pattern of nonthematic chords (Bréval MS: Ex. 8), to a single statement of the Mélisande motive just as she acknowledges her sadness (NEC MS: Ex. 17). In the NEC MS, the Mélisande theme was added while retaining

Ex. 13. (a) Bréval MS, fol. 3^r (LPm, p. 93).

the harmonic progression of the Bréval revision; the extra "silence" in the revision only added to the eloquence of the thematic statement.

    The capacity to fit into a variety of harmonic contexts is an even more striking feature of the new Golaud motive, which is identified more by its rhythm (especially by its dotted figure) than by its pitches, an oscillation between two notes a major second apart. This fact made it especially easy for Debussy to work the new theme into any accompaniment. The theme could even be expressed as a repeating-tone figure, as in the following example, where it was added as an octave pedal at the point where Pelléas asks Mélisande if she had been able to leave the castle without being seen, and she answers affirmatively, explaining that Golaud was asleep. Even without the pitch oscillation, the characteristic rhythm makes the reference unmistakable (see Ex. 18). This statement of the second Golaud motive is, in the final version

Ex. 13. (b)   Bréval MS, fols. 2ᵛ–3ʳ (LPm, pp. 92–93).

[Et je n'ai pas en- cor re- gar- dé son re-   gard...

Il   ne me res- te rien si je m'en vais ain- si...]

Ex. 14.   Bréval MS, fol. 2ᵛ (LPm, p. 92).

[Il   faut   que   je   la   re- gar – de]

Ex. 15.   VS, p. 234, meas. 5–6 with added English horn and oboe parts.

bien cette fois-ci...   Il y a des cho_ses que je ne me rap_pel_le plus... on di_

Ex. 16. (a) Bréval MS, fol. 11ʳ (LPm, p. 109).

(b) NEC MS, IV, fol. 27ʳ (see VS, p. 251, meas. 3).

Ex. 17. VS, pp. 254–55 (as in NEC MS, IV, fol. 28ʳ).

of the scene, the first musical reference to him, appropriately coinciding with the first time in the scene that he is directly discussed by the characters on stage. The particular use of the motive is also dramatically apt, with the dotted figure returning to punctuate the gap in Mélisande's reply. This addition was made very late in the compositional process, during Debussy's

Ex. 18. VS, p. 238, meas. 1–2 with added horn parts, as in OS, p. 326, meas. 3–4.

Ex. 19. (a) Bréval MS, fol. 15ᵛ (third Bréval version) (LPm, p. 118). (The starred stave is a revision of the measure below it)

(b) NEC MS, IV, fol. 32ʳ (with margin addition); see VS, p. 266, meas. 11–15.

postpublication refinements of the orchestration; it probably dates from 1905, three years after the première and one year after the publication of the full score. For this reason, the motive is absent from the vocal scores and from the first edition of the full score.[37]

Other additions of the second Golaud motive were made earlier, in the course of Debussy's revision of the Bréval draft, and invariably these additions were consistent with the dramatic action, as at the terrifying moment at the end of the scene where Golaud strikes Pelléas with his sword. In the third Bréval MS version of this much-revised passage (fol. 15^v, sys. 2; LPm, p. 118), Debussy seems to depict the sword strokes with three jabbed B's, but he then transformed them into a brutal intrusion of the second Golaud motive, a use which was made even more emphatic in a revision of the final short score draft (NEC MS, IV, fol. 32^r) (see Ex. 19).[38]

In two cases, the new Golaud motive was added to passages whose accompaniments had originally contained the first Golaud motive, but whose subsequent revision had removed it. The first occurs where Mélisande confesses lying only to Golaud (Ex. 20; compare Ex. 7). The use of the Golaud motive is obviously logical here, as Mélisande's words and thoughts turn to her husband. Perhaps Debussy found the musical reference to Golaud too blatant in the Meyer draft. After all, Pelléas, in his excitement, does not seem to have heard the second half of her answer; at least, the remark about his brother and Mélisande's confession that she does indeed lie do not seem to register with him, and Debussy probably initially preferred no reference at all to one that was so heavy-handed. The use of the second Golaud motive (especially as refined in the final version, VS, p. 247) seems the perfect compromise; the point is made, but with more subtlety.

A second instance of what essentially amounts to motive substitution occurs later in the scene, shortly before Golaud's attack, where Pelléas sings, "He watches us... He is still motionless.... " In the Meyer and Legouix drafts, this passage occurs in the midst of a lengthy development of the original Golaud theme, while in the Bréval draft, this thematic use was largely eliminated. In revising Bréval, however, Debussy adjusted his new accompaniment to include unambiguous statements of the new Golaud motive (cf. Exx. 21 a and b).

Elsewhere in the scene, Debussy made other substitutions of the new Golaud motive for the original one. A most striking instance is in the ten-measure passage beginning with Pelléas's "Il est tard..." ("It is late... "). This section has already been discussed in the context of the Legouix draft, where it was noted that statements of the original Golaud theme permeated the accompaniment. In revising the Bréval draft (fol. 4^v; LPm, p. 96), Debussy rewrote the passage, removing all references to that theme and providing a new accompaniment in which the new motive was all-pervasive. A further revision of the two measures starting with the text, "Pourquoi es-tu venue si tard?" ("Why have you come so late?") (Bréval MS, fol. 4^v, staves 6–8 in center of page; LPm, p. 96), curtailed the effect of a lengthy development of the new motive and brought the passage closer to its final version (VS, pp. 238–40).

Ex. 20. Bréval MS, fol. 9ʳ (final layer) (LPm, p. 105); see VS, p.
     247, meas. 3–4.

In other places, Debussy did not remove the original Golaud theme, but
either altered its rhythm to resemble the new motive or superimposed the new
theme on it. A change of the former type is found in the NEC MS, at Pelléas's
exclamation, "The great chains!" (see Ex. 22). The superimposition of Golaud
motives is illustrated by Debussy's addition of the characteristic dotted figure
of the new motive at the moment where Mélisande first sights her husband, a
passage already underscored by statements of the original Golaud theme.
Even the pitches with which the two lovers say Golaud's name were altered to
resemble his motive, with its rise of a major second (compare Ex. 23 with Exx.

Ex. 21. (a) Legouix MS, fol. 10ʳ.

Ex. 21.   (cont.)

(b) Bréval MS, fol. 15^r (LPm, p. 117) (starred stave is a
revision of the stave below it); see VS, p. 263, meas.
3–7.

Ex. 22. (a) Bréval MS, fol. 12^r (LPm, p. 111).

(b) Accompaniment as in NEC MS, IV, fol. 29^r (see VS, p.
256, meas. 4–7).

10b and 11b; the addition was made in a revision of the Bréval MS, fol. 14ʳ; LPm, p. 115) (see Ex. 23).

The Pelléas theme was also affected by Debussy's later revisions of the scene, and it was more often removed than added. The result is that its use in the final version, while more sparing, is all the more telling, since full appearances of the theme (that is, ignoring fleeting references to fragments of it) are restricted to Pelléas's passionate outbursts in moments of emotional turmoil, musically emphasized through dynamic climax. Debussy eliminated the Pelléas theme from the prelude to the scene (which was completely rewritten) and deleted several statements of it at the beginning of his opening speech, leaving it only at the expressive (and dynamic) peak, when he sings, "Je vais fuir en criant de joie et de douleur comme un aveugle qui fuirait l'incendie de sa maison" ("I will flee, crying out for joy and woe like a blind man fleeing from his burning house") (VS, p. 233, meas. 4–5). In the course of the subsequent dialogue, the theme returns at another high point, Pelléas's "Il y aurait plutôt de quoi pleurer..." ("There is rather cause to weep... ") (VS, p. 241, meas. 5–6), and eight measures later, after sequential hints of the motive, for his impassioned "Il faut que je m'en aille pour toujours!" ("I must go away forever!") (VS, p. 242, meas. 5).

Ex. 23. VS, p. 261, meas. 3–8.

The desire for greater precision and dramatic consistency of thematic usage also influenced the choice of material used to replace the Pelléas motive wherever it was removed. For example, Debussy recognized a dramatic link between two passages in which the Pelléas theme had figured prominently and, in removing that motive, substituted the same new theme in both places. In the first passage (VS, p. 236), Pelléas, fearing that they will be seen from the windows of the tower, asks Mélisande to come out of the moonlight and into the shadow of the linden. In the second (VS, p. 252), he makes the opposite request and asks her to come into the light so they can see how happy they are; he explains, "We are already in the shadow. It is too dark under this tree." By inserting the same new theme for these two spots, Debussy's revision provides a musical parallel to match the dramatic correspondence and so underscores the change that has taken place in Pelléas's attitude, first wanting to hide in the shadows and later wanting to leave them for the light. Recognizing this connection, Gilman (p. 76) labeled this new theme "The Shadows." The new theme provides a precise thematic cross-reference and in that sense is an improvement over the prior use of the Pelléas theme.

Thematic cross-references were also possible between scenes. At another point in the scene (VS, p. 241), Mélisande suddenly (and conveniently) changes the subject of conversation, observing, "We came here long ago... I recall..." "Yes," replies Pelléas, "long months ago." They are obviously recalling their previous meeting at the well in the opera's other "Scène de la fontaine," Act II, scene 1, and to underscore the recollection, Debussy changed the accompaniment from a statement of the Pelléas theme to a motive from the earlier scene associated with the clarity and coolness of the well water (see VS, p. 57, meas. 1–4), thus linking their daytime meeting at the well (Act II, scene 1) with their nighttime meeting at the same spot (Act IV, scene 4). The original use of the Pelléas theme was obviously not inappropriate, especially since that is the theme which opens the second act (VS, p. 55), but the use of the "Fountain" theme (as Gilman, p. 64, labeled it) produces a more precise and evocative musical reminiscence. Because Act II was composed after Act IV, scene 4, the Fountain theme had not yet been created when the latter scene was first drafted; the "reminiscence" therefore had to be introduced as a revision.

The net result of all of these changes is that the final version of the scene is more dependent on a system of leitmotifs than the preliminary versions. While the earliest draft had only two character motives, the final version has four, two of them associated with Golaud. The addition of the Mélisande and the new Golaud motives not only benefited the scene itself, but contributed to the musical unity of the opera as a whole by making the scene thematically consistent with the rest of the opera, where these motives play a crucial role. Other thematic improvements made in the revisions include the more selective and more specific use of the Pelléas theme, the introduction of a thematic reminiscence of a previous scene (the "Fountain" theme), and the creation of a new theme of internal recollection (the "Shadows" theme).[39]

Thus, while the revisions that Debussy made in Act IV, scene 4 between September 1893 and May 1895 seem deliberately anti-Wagnerian (again, in Debussy's sense of the word) due to their reduction in the frequency of leitmotif appearances and, even more dramatically, their elimination of musical developments based on the original Golaud motive, the subsequent revisions reversed this tendency, though only in the area of leitmotif frequency. In fact, it seems that Debussy's invention of the new Golaud motive and his decision to introduce it into Act IV, scene 4 (sometimes in place of the original motive) greatly facilitated the curtailment of some of the symphonic developments of the original motive. The new motive, essentially rhythmic rather than melodic, could be reduced to and represented by a distinctive two-beat dotted figure and had the advantage of being able to fit easily into any accompanimental context. In contrast, the triadic shape of the original motive *determined* the content of the accompaniment whenever it was present. In other words, the very nature of the original motive seems to have invited a developmental treatment, while the new one could be introduced, when desired, with great subtlety. A further advantage was that, while the original theme could not be represented by its rhythm alone (which was identical to that of the Pelléas motive), the new Golaud motive, in addition to being more succinct and flexible, provided clear rhythmic differentiation among the character motives.

The Character Leitmotifs

Both the use and the very nature of Debussy's leitmotifs indicate that flexibility and adaptability were prime concerns. Pierre Boulez, in his article "*Pelléas* Reflected," commented on this feature of the character motives when he described them as "arabesques . . . with no variation other than decorative, which are integrated into the general context without effort, are sometimes superimposed with ease, but do not totally irrigate the texture." The main character motives (the Pelléas, Mélisande, and new Golaud motives) are all melodically simple and based on returning tone patterns. All three start with a rise of a second. Debussy capitalized on this simplicity and achieved even greater flexibility by allowing interval sizes to be altered to suit the situation. Thus, the Mélisande theme, whose characteristic four-note opening typically includes a major second and minor third, also appears with a minor second and minor third, a minor second and major third, and a major second and major third. Sometimes, as in the prelude to Act I, the minor third is even notated as an augmented second (VS, p. 1, meas. 14–15).[40] Despite these intervallic changes, and even with altered rhythms, the identity of the motive is never in doubt, as the examples in Ex. 24 demonstrate.

The Pelléas motive, though less varied rhythmically, appears with even greater interval modification. At that character's first entrance (Act I, scene 2), the motive appears as in Ex. 2a, and contains a major second, major third, and perfect fourths. In other appearances the second and third are minor, and elsewhere the theme consists of only three different pitches instead of four, with different sized seconds and fourths (see Ex. 25). Even the Golaud motive, though almost always consisting of an oscillation of a major second, becomes a minor second in the interlude between scenes 2 and 3 of Act I (VS, p. 38, meas. 2–5 and 12–13) and a repeating tone in Act IV, scene 4 (see Ex. 18).

Ex. 24. (a) VS, p. 268, meas. 1–2.

(b) VS, p. 103, meas. 10–11.

(c) VS, p. 197, meas. 14–15.

The theme associated with Yniold is, in contrast, invariant in terms of rhythm and melody, but the comparison is perhaps misleading, since the motive appears in only one of that character's two scenes (Act III, scene 4). Still, it is similar in design to the character themes discussed above, as its essential figure is a returning tone pattern, consisting of four notes and two intervals, a perfect fourth and a major second (see Ex. 26).

The Arkel motive, like the original Golaud theme but unlike the others, is based on thirds: its first four notes outline a seventh chord. Again, like the original Golaud theme, its first appearance in the opera coincides with the first mention of his name, in Act I, scene 1 (VS, p. 15, meas. 1; see Ex. 4). The particular type of seventh chord varies according to the harmony that

Ex. 25. (a) VS, p. 179, meas. 3–4.

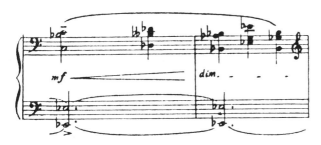

(b) VS, p. 41, meas. 7.

(c) VS, p. 86, meas. 2.

(d) VS, p. 242, meas. 5.

Ex. 26. VS, p. 158, meas. 4–5.

p doux et expressif

Debussy wished to use. In its first appearance and when it marks Arkel's entrance in Act IV, scene 2 (VS, p. 197, meas. 6–7) it is a dominant seventh chord; in that interlude before Act I, scene 2 (VS, p. 25, meas. 5–7), within the scene just before Arkel's first words (VS, p. 29, meas. 9–11), and in Act V at his line, "Vous ne savez pas ce que c'est que l'âme..." ("You do not know what the soul is...") (VS, p. 303, meas. 9–10), it is a minor seventh chord; [41] and elsewhere in the opera, when the motive appears in diminution, it is a half-diminished seventh (VS, pp. 25, 37, and 200–202).

The intervallic flexibility of the character motives allows them to fit into any accompanimental context, even over a stationary harmony.

Leitmotif Functions and Further Thematic Revisions

The process of thematic revision, though most dramatically revealed through the many surviving sources of Act IV, scene 4, was not restricted to that scene. Telling examples are found throughout the opera and at every compositional stage, from preliminary sketches to postpublication refinements of the orchestration. Debussy's skill in integrating and manipulating thematic elements seems to have grown as his work on *Pelléas* progressed, not only in successive revisions, but in the course of the composition itself, as he wrote scene after scene. The first two scenes of Act II, the last act to be written, are perhaps the most masterful in motivic handling, with a sophisticated network of thematic cross-references underpinning the action and linking these dramatically connected scenes. In general, the constant and consistent use of motives accomplished at least two things on the structural level: the constancy created a musical continuity with the scene, serving to counterbalance the composer's shunning of set forms and his heavy dependence on a recitativelike style, while the consistent use of certain motives throughout the opera created an overall unity in a work whose many short scenes could potentially produce an effect of excessive fragmentation. And, as has been pointed out by many commentators, the recurrent themes provided an appropriate musical analogue to Maeterlinck's literary symbolism, with its recurrent poetic images (blindness, hair, water, etc.). [42] In fact, Debussy seems to have designed certain leitmotifs precisely to elucidate certain symbolic relationships. Thus, the theme of Mélisande's wedding ring, the symbol of her bond (and bondage) to Golaud, is a clear derivative of his theme (see VS, p. 66, meas. 3; the relationship is even clearer in the recurrence of the theme three bars later). Similarly, the grotto by the sea, where Golaud sends Mélisande, along with Pelléas, on a futile search for her lost ring, is a symbol of the unconscious, of yet unknown desires, with undertones of a mysterious menace threatening death,[43] and its theme too is derived from the Golaud motive, symbolizing his responsibility for the unfolding of the tragedy (see VS, p. 110, meas. 2–5).

In his essay on *Pelléas* in *Opera as Drama,* Joseph Kerman made a useful distinction between "organizing themes" which provide the "musical mortar" of a scene and leitmotifs which recur throughout the opera.[44] The two categories are not, of course, mutually exclusive, and the distinction is one of primary function and not of musical attributes. As the following examples reveal, Debussy's apparent consciousness of these functions seems to have been a motivating factor in some of his thematic revisions.

At one point in writing out the NEC MS short score of Act I, scene 1, Debussy seems to have recognized the advantage, in terms of motivic unity, of using a direct, rather than an oblique reference to the scene's "organizing theme," the Forest/Antiquity theme (VS, p. 1, meas. 1–4). Immediately after copying the two-and-one-quarter bars reproduced in Ex. 27a below, he crossed them out and replaced them with the definitive reading of this passage, an unambiguous derivative of the Forest/Antiquity theme (Ex. 27b). The revision not only altered the harmony and enhanced the expressive value of these measures, but it eliminated the hints of the Golaud motive which the theme's rhythm suggested, while helping to secure the motivic unity of the scene and to reinforce the identification of this theme with the first meeting of Mélisande and Golaud, thus supporting the associative value of its recollection later in Act V, when Mélisande thinks back to that first meeting (VS, p. 279, meas. 7–8).

A similar sort of revision was made in Act IV, scene 1, where Pelléas reports to Mélisande a remark that his father had made to him: "Why, I had not noticed it before, but you have the grave and friendly look of those who will not live long...You must travel." In an early version of the scene, contained in the Basel MS vocal score, the accompaniment consists of a series of nonthematic chords over a pedal point (the same note on which Pelléas recites his father's words) (see Ex. 28). In revising the passage, Debussy retained the pedal and the original voice part, but replaced the nonthematic chords with a variant of the Pelléas motive, perhaps to reflect Pelléas's recollection of his feelings upon hearing his father's words (see VS, p. 191, meas. 11–p. 192, meas. 2). As in the previous example, a motive with

Ex. 27. (a)   NEC MS, I, fol. 3ʳ.

(b)   VS, p. 6, meas. 1–2.

associative and structural significance replaced one without associations, though here the addition was a character motive used throughout the opera, rather than an "organizing theme" of the particular scene.

Later in the same scene, Debussy replaced one motive with another—where Pelléas asks Mélisande if she would meet him in the park near "Blind Man's Spring" (VS, p. 193, meas. 8–9). In the Basel MS and in the earliest layer of the Bréval MS, the accompaniment contains the Pelléas theme (Ex. 29), but in revising the Bréval draft, Debussy replaced that motive with the Fountain theme which frames Act II, scene 1 and functions as its "organizing theme" (see VS, p. 56, meas. 1–2).[45] The substitution introduces a musical reminiscence, a device which Debussy used rather sparingly, and the appearance of the Fountain theme at Pelléas's mention of that location serves to recall Act II, scene 1 and prepare for Act IV, scene 4, which takes place in the same setting.

In other revisions, Debussy introduced character themes to represent and express one character's thoughts about another, the themes almost

Ex. 28. Basel MS, p. 106.

Ex. 29. Basel MS, p. 107.

functioning as reminiscence motives. In Act V, for example, during Golaud's first speech, his line, "They had kissed like little children," was originally accompanied by a series of chords (Meyer MS, V, fol. 2^r; LPm, p. 64—copied with some changes in NEC MS, V, fol. 2^r); but in revising the short score copy of this passage, Debussy added the Mélisande motive, choosing its pitches essentially from the notes of the chords. The revision gives thematic expression to Golaud's thoughts about his wife (see Ex. 30). Similarly, in Act III, scene 4 the Mélisande motive was added to the accompaniment of

Ex. 30. NEC MS, V, fol. 2ʳ:
  (a) first version.

  (b) revision of accompaniment (see VS, p. 271, meas. 1).

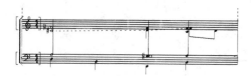

Golaud's anguished "Ah! misère de ma vie!" ("Oh! plague of my life!"), indicating thematically that it is his suspicion of his wife's infidelity that is the source of his agony. This addition was made during the orchestration of the scene and appears in the full score (OS, p. 228, meas. 3–4: winds), but not the vocal score (VS, p. 168, meas. 5–6).

In one thematic revision of Act I, scene 3, Debussy added the Mélisande motive at Geneviève's exit, where it serves the dual functions of thematic unity and character allusion. For one thing, this motive acts as the "organizing theme" of the scene, not only framing it, but recurring throughout; in that sense this revision is similar to the addition of the Forest/Antiquity theme in Act I, scene 1.[46] However, the use of the theme here also pertains to the character of Mélisande, as it coincides with the moment when Pelléas turns from looking out to sea, and presumably his thoughts (and perhaps his glance) focus on Mélisande ("Nothing can be seen any longer on the sea," he says). The motive seems to indicate the thoughts behind his words. This addition was made during the orchestration process, appearing in the full score (OS, p. 66, meas. 3–4: violins), but in neither the manuscript short score (NEC MS, I, fol. 23ʳ) nor the early editions of the vocal score (see VS, p. 52, meas. 2–3). The motive was added in the published revision of the 1907 Durand French-English vocal score.

Despite Debussy's comment, quoted above, that a character should "not be a slave of his *Leitmotiv,* as a blind man is a slave of his dog or his clarinet," another category of thematic revision pertains to the use of a character's motive to mark his entrance or first (or even last) utterance in a scene. For example, Golaud's entrance in Act I, scene 1 was originally accompanied by the Forest/Antiquity theme (VS, p. 2, meas. 9–12), but in orchestrating the passage, Debussy added the rhythm of the second Golaud theme in the timpani (OS, p. 5, meas. 2–5; this appears in neither the NEC MS nor VS). It was also during the orchestration that Debussy added statements of the same motive, this time in the horns, to the accompaniment of Golaud's opening lines (OS, p. 6, meas. 1–3); again, these additions are not present in the NEC MS short score or in the vocal score (VS, p. 3, meas. 4–6).

Another example occurs at Golaud's first words in Act V. In the Meyer MS, Golaud's speech follows Arkel's remarks almost directly, and its first measure is accompanied by a single sustained chord. In the NEC MS version, Debussy set off Golaud's speech with two measures of orchestral music, conveying Golaud's feelings and containing a discreet reference to his theme. In revising the NEC MS, Debussy replaced the discreet reference with a more obvious one, reducing the two measures to one with no loss of expressive value (see Ex. 31). (Golaud's repetition of his opening sentence was also cut.) Debussy also used Golaud's motive to underscore his final utterance in the opera (his textless sobs at VS, p. 307, meas. 10–11), but in the process of sketching the Meyer MS, he changed his mind as to which of the two motives to use: at the bottom of fol. 17ʳ (LPm, p. 83) he used the original Golaud theme for the accompaniment, but this was crossed out, and the revision at the top of fol. 18ʳ (LPm, p. 82) utilized the second Golaud motive in its place, almost as in the published score.

Thematic Revisions of Preludes and Interludes

The use of character motives in conjunction with entrances and first or last words also figures in some of Debussy's revisions of the act preludes and the interludes between scenes. For example, Act IV, scene 2 opens with Arkel and Mélisande, and the interlude preceding the scene originally contained a very prominent statement of the Arkel motive: he is the character being introduced (Mélisande having appeared in the previous scene), and the scene begins with a lengthy speech by him (Bréval MS, fol. 19ʳ-NEC MS, IV, fol. 5ʳ, originally continuous; copied after corrections in Basel MS, pp. 109–10). When Debussy revised the interlude (Bréval MS, fol. 19ʳ-19ᵛ; LPm, pp. 89–90; copied in NEC MS, IV, fol. 4ʳ), he used the motives of both characters, with three statements of each; Arkel's entrance coincides with the second statement of his theme (VS, p. 197, meas. 6–7). The new version is thus a better representation of the characters involved in the beginning of the scene: the Mélisande theme is heard while she remains on stage during the interlude and the Arkel motive marks his precise entrance.

Similarly, the presence of the Yniold theme in the interlude preceding Act III, scene 4 was a second thought; the theme does not appear in the original

Ex. 31. (a) Meyer MS, V, fol. 2ʳ (LPm, p. 64).

(b) NEC MS, V, fol. 2ʳ: original layer.

(c) Idem: revision (see VS, p. 270, meas. 4–6).

interlude (NEC MS, III, fol. 19ᵛ), but was added in a revision (NEC MS, III, fol. 20ʳ; see VS, p. 158, meas. 4–12). The use of the theme here has several functions. The opening of this scene is Yniold's first appearance in the opera, and Debussy probably wanted to identify his theme with him at the outset. Also the theme sets a mood of tender innocence, one which will change dramatically in the course of the scene; part of the scene's power is the way its climax builds from such an apparently innocent beginning. Also, the theme recurs during the early part of the scene for many of Yniold's lines, and its appearance in the preceding interlude provides a motivic continuity between interlude and scene.

The desire to create such a motivic connection seems to have motivated other prelude and interlude revisions. For example, the original interlude before Act IV, scene 4 (Legouix MS; see Ex. 5) was largely based on the

Pelléas motive, a theme which was prominent in the accompaniment at the beginning of the scene; in fact, meas. 5–7 of the interlude are melodically nearly identical to the three measures which accompany Pelléas's line ten measures later, "Je vais fuir en criant de joie et de douleur comme un aveugle qui fuirait l'incendie de sa maison." Debussy's later revisions of the scene, however, made the Pelléas theme a less ubiquitous feature of the opening, and he introduced a new triplet figure in its place (Bréval MS, fol. 2^r; LPm, p. 91). Correspondingly, the interlude was rewritten, and Debussy again adopted the procedure of linking the interlude to the accompaniment of the opening: he expanded three measures of the new accompaniment figure (VS, p. 232, meas. 13–p. 233, meas. 1) into fifteen measures of interlude (VS, p. 231, meas. 13–p. 232, meas. 10).

The revision of the prelude to Act III seems to have been based on a similar motivation, though here he did not so much replace the thematic content as alter it to achieve a more precise and compelling connection with the following scene. The revision expanded the original prelude of six measures (Ex. 32) into seventeen (VS, p. 115, meas. 1–17). Motivically, the most important feature of this prelude is the three-note figure heard twice in meas. 3, which, repeated in steady eighth-note motion, is the chief "organizing theme" of the scene. Its early appearances in the scene are notable for the chromatic alteration of the first note, as at Pelléas's entrance (VS, p. 117, meas. 1–2); this motive was labeled "Night" by Gilman and the "combing" motive by Richard Langham Smith.[47] The revised prelude makes this important motive its most prominent feature. In conjunction with this revision, Debussy also rewrote correspondingly the two-measure orchestral interruption of Mélisande's song (in its original version it is roughly equivalent to meas. 2–3 of the original prelude; compare Ex. 32 and VS, p. 116, meas. 7–8).

The thematic alteration of another act prelude had quite a different effect. The prelude to Act IV, in all of its surviving versions, is based on a continuous sixteenth-note motion, which seems to represent the sound of talking behind the door. Over this activity, the Pelléas motive is heard (VS, p. 189, meas. 7–10),[48] but in orchestrating the prelude, Debussy added the

Ex. 32. NEC MS, III, fol. 1^{r}.

Golaud theme, two octaves below it in the second violins and violas (see Ex. 33). The Golaud motive was also added just before Pelléas and Mélisande enter (OS, p. 254, meas. 4–5), and again when the sixteenth-note figuration returns at the end of the scene (OS, p. 260, meas. 10–p. 261, meas. 1 and p. 261, meas. 5–8). None of these additions is included in the vocal score. Their significance is suggested by a line delivered by Pelléas twice during the scene: "I hear talking behind this door." The added motive suggests that Golaud is the potential eavesdropper that Pelléas fears. That fear is certainly justified by the events of the previous act: Golaud interrupted Pelléas's meeting with Mélisande in scene 1, he threatened Pelléas and warned him to avoid Mélisande in scenes 2 and 3, and he forced Yniold to spy on them in scene 4 (though presumably without their knowledge). The parallel thematic additions to the prelude and to the interlude following the scene not only introduce a strong element of dramatic tension, but reflect Debussy's desire to promote unity within the scene by using a consistent framing motive.

Ex. 33. VS, p. 189, meas. 7–10 modified to reflect OS, p. 253, meas. 3–6.

The preceding examples have demonstrated that Debussy's thematic revisions of the preludes and interludes achieved some of the same ends as his revisions within the scenes: they strengthened motivic unity both within the scenes and in the opera as a whole, and they introduced motives of reminiscence and foreshadowing. As was true of the rest of the opera, the revisions of the purely orchestral passages tended to make them more dependent on a system of recurring motives than were the originals.

A comparison of the early drafts of Act IV, scene 4 may indeed have revealed evidence of Debussy's anti-Wagnerism in practice, but subsequent revisions of the scene and of the rest of the opera show that, despite the composer's staunch anti-Wagnerian stance, the compositional process was marked by a progressively more extensive and more consistent use of leitmotifs—the same leitmotifs that he loved to hate in the music of others. Thus, Debussy altered his score in a way which, in his own terms, would not only be considered Wagnerian, but Wagnerian in a way which he found objectionable and even ridiculed in both public and private statements. As an added irony, Debussy was forced to graft interlude expansions onto his opera during the rehearsals for the première; of necessity written very quickly, these "symphonic developments" of the opera's principal motives probably constitute the most "Wagnerian" feature of the score. In fact, Carolyn Abbate and Robin Holloway have found these interludes to be a rich source of Wagnerian quotations.[49]

It is important, though, to understand the special and personal way in which Debussy used his leitmotifs, a way which was entirely consistent with his operatic principles. The relative reticence, subtlety, and economy of the motives have often been noted,[50] and a study of the sources has shown that the compositional process promoted these qualities. Though the composition of certain passages may have begun with the sketching of leitmotifs in the orchestra, many of these appearances were later removed from the accompaniment, and it was only in subsequent revisions that Debussy discreetly worked his leitmotifs, those simple melodic "arabesques," back into the orchestra, making it, in Gilman's words, "a support, rather than a thing of procrustean dominance." Virgil Thomson made an additional important observation when he wrote: "It is the special quality of this work that though the orchestra comments constantly, and even individual instruments comment on the progress of the play, the pit never becomes a Greek chorus speaking for the author; it remains an extension of the stage."[51] The development of this point of view has also been traced in the manuscripts, as has been shown in Debussy's initial use and subsequent rejection of the Golaud theme as the sound of the closing castle doors in Act IV, scene 4. The appearances of the motive following the closing of the doors thus came to be understood, not as Debussy's signals to the audience that Golaud was on his way, but rather as a reflection and representation of the fear that the characters on stage had of his approach. This procedure is a clear demonstration of Debussy's expressed intention, reported in his May 1902 "Reply to the Critics," to merge the musical expression with the emotions of the characters. "Above all," he said, "I respected the characters themselves— their ways. I wanted them to have their own expression, independent of me. I let them sing within me. And, hearing them, I tried to present them faithfully" (RLS, p. 79). As he explained in the letter to Edwin Evans quoted above, he deliberately sought to challenge "the pernicious neo-Wagnerian aesthetic which presumes to render, at the same time, the sentiment expressed by the character and the inner thoughts which impel its actions." He believed instead that "music should by simple means...endeavor to render the successive impulses and moods as they are produced." In striving towards this goal, Debussy never denied the importance of the orchestra in expressing these emotions; in a letter of congratulations to the conductor Cleofonte Campanini following the New York première of the opera, he wrote: "The orchestration of 'Pelléas' is a frail piece of architecture, which supports the work and expresses its feeling."[52] Debussy's system of leitmotifs, a web of flexible and intervallically related themes, was crucial to these structural and expressive goals.

The repeated attempts throughout this chapter to give simple, rational explanations for Debussy's use of his leitmotifs only suggest part, and perhaps not even the most important part, of the effect these themes were intended to convey. Much more important than the mere presence of the motives are the particular shape they are given and the musical context in which they appear—their harmonization, accompaniment, orchestration, etc.—all that creates the musical emotion, which is our key to the feelings of the characters. Laloy's belief that the motives are associated, not with objects, characters, or actions, but with feelings, presents this other side of the issue and is a useful corrective to the thoughtless detection and identification of the motives. Even beyond this, some appearances of the motives seem not always to aim for unambiguous clarity, but often attempt to express the ambivalence, confusion, or indecision that the characters on stage are feeling at the moment. For Debussy, capturing this feeling was part of portraying the humanity of his characters, of being true to them. There also seems to be some element of deliberate obscurity—one which Laloy unintentionally made apparent—with motives being used to establish symbolic and intuitive connections, not just rational ones. Perhaps it was the desire to preserve these elements of humanity and of mystery in the work that moved Debussy to discourage the identification of leitmotifs in *Pelléas*. That he used leitmotifs is undeniable, but in adopting this Wagnerian technique, he adapted it to his own personal style.

Appendix

Catalogue of the Sources of *Pelléas et Mélisande*

Text Source/Libretto

Maurice Maeterlinck, *Pélléas et Mélisande*, 1st ed. (Brussels: Paul Lacomblez, 1892)
F-Ptinan: Copy printed on Holland Van Gelder paper and bound in vellum, belonged to Debussy (OCexp, p. 40, no. 130).

Maurice Maeterlinck, *Pélléas et Mélisande*, 6th ed. (Brussels: Paul Lacomblez, 1898).

Maurice Maeterlinck, *Pelléas et Mélisande*, in *Théâtre*, II:1–113 (Brussels: Paul Lacomblez; Paris: Per Lamm, 1902).

Pelléas et Mélisande, drame lyrique en cinq actes, tiré du théâtre de Maurice Maeterlinck, musique de Claude Debussy, nouvelle édition, modifiée conformément aux représentations de l'Opéra-Comique (Brussels: Paul Lacomblez, 1902).

Preliminary Draft (Sketches)

F-Pmeyer ("Meyer MS"): 55 ff (61 pp. music). Act I, sc. 1–2 (frags.), 5 pp.; Act II, 25 pp.; Act IV, sc. 4 (inc.), 9 pp.; Act V, 22 pp.
Dated: June–July 1895.
Dedication: "pour H. Lerolle. Claude Debussy. Juin–Juillet 95."
Catalogue: LCat no. 88, A1; Lesure and Bridgman, *Collection Musicale André Meyer*, I:12; BNexp, p. 43, no. 132.
Facsimile: LPm, pp. 19–84 (complete); Lesure and Bridgman, *Collection Musicale André Meyer*, I: pl. 9 (Act V, fol. 17^r); Goléa, *Claude Debussy*, opp. p. 65 (Act V, fol. 17^r).

US-AUS: 1 f. (1 p. music). Sketch of an interlude? Catalogue: Lake, Catalogue: Lake, *Baudelaire to Beckett*, p. 66, no. 161.

Developed Draft (Short Score)

US-NYpm, Robert Owen Lehman Coll., on deposit ("Legouix MS," former
  Coll. Robert Legouix): 12 ff. (17 pp. music). Act IV, sc. 4 (orig. 18 ff.: 6 ff.
  removed by Debussy, became part of Bréval MS).
Dated: September–October 1893.
Catalogue: LCat no. 88, A2; OCexp, p. 54, no. 228; Thierry Bodin sale cat. (14
  December 1979), no. 31; Turner, "Nineteenth-Century Autograph Music
  Manuscripts," p. 64; Turner, *Nineteenth-Century Autograph Music
  Manuscripts*, p. 22.
Facsimile: ORL, p. 53 (fol. 1^r); Thierry Bodin sale cat. (14 December 1979),
  cover (fol. 12^r) and no. 31 (fol. 9^r); Turner, *Nineteenth-Century Autograph
  Music Manuscripts*, pl. 6 (fol. 9^r).

F-Pn, Ms. 1206 ("Bréval MS," former Coll. Lucienne Bréval): 20 ff. (29 pp.
  music). Act IV, sc. 1 (inc.), 3 pp.; Act IV, sc. 4, 26 pp.
Dated: September–October 1893, May 1895.
Catalogue: LCat no. 88, A3; OCexp, p. 54, no. 229; BNexp, p. 43, no. 133;
  Cogeval and Lesure, *Debussy e il Simbolismo*, p. 200, no. 134.
Facsimile: LPm, pp. 87–120 (complete); TIE, opp. p. 9 (fol. 2^r); Lockspeiser,
  Debussy, 5th ed., pp. 46–47 (fol. 2^r); BNexp, pl. IV (fol. 11^r); Gauthier,
  Debussy. Documents iconographiques, pl. 48 (fol. 17^r).

US-NYpm, Frederick R. Koch Foundation Coll., on deposit ("NEC MS,"
  former Coll. New England Conservatory of Music, Boston): 131 ff. (137 pp.
  music). Act I, 25 pp.; Act II, 20 pp.; Act III, 37 pp.; Act IV, 37 pp.; Act V, 18
  pp.
Dated: Act I, December 1893, January–February 1894; Act II, June, 17
  August 1895; Act IV, September–October 1893, May 1895, January 1900,
  September 1901.
Dedication (Act II, fol. 17 only): "pour le Docteur René Vaucaire. Claude
  Debussy."
Catalogue: LCat no. 88, B6; Albrecht, *Census*, p. 99, no. 640; Barksdale,
  Composer Portraits and Autograph Scores, pp. 33–35, no. 41; Winternitz,
  Musical Autographs, I:135; Christie's sale cat., no. 5145 (21 May 1982);
  Stargardt sale cat. (9 June 1982) (Act II, fol. 17^r); Turner, Kendall, and
  Parsons, *Four Centuries of Opera*, pp. 92–93.
Facsimile: Barksdale, *Composer Portraits*, p. 34 (Act II, fol. 1^r); Turner,
  Kendall, and Parsons, *Four Centuries of Opera*, p. 91 (Act II, fol. 17^r);
  Winternitz, *Musical Autographs*, II: pl. 173–74 (Act III, fol. 12^r; Act IV, fol.
  19^r).

Piano-Vocal Score

Manuscripts

CH-B, private collection ("Basel MS"): 7 ff (12 pp. music numbered 104–15). Act IV, sc. 1–2 (inc.).
Catalogue: Seebass, *Musikhandschriften in Basel,* p. 78, no. 136.
Facsimile: Seebass, p. 79 (p. 105).

F-Pn, Ms. 17686 ("Jobert MS," gift of Mme Jobert-Georges): 25 ff. (39 pp. music). Act IV, sc. 1–2, 18 pp. music numbered 103–20; Act V, 21 pp. music numbered 144–64.
Catalogue: LCat no. 88, B6; OCexp, p. 54.

F-Pn, Ms. 17683, Françoise Prudhomme Coll., on deposit ("Prudhomme MS"): 13 ff. (23 pp. music numbered 121–43). Act IV, sc. 3–4.

Corrected Proofs of First Edition (Fromont, 1902)

F-Pn, Rés. Vma. 237, Françoise Prudhomme Coll., on deposit ("Périer proofs," former Coll. Jean Périer): Acts I–III (pp. 2–169); Acts II–IV (pp. 48–242).

Editions

French vocal score, Fromont, 1902 (E. 1416. F.), 283 pp. Later printings contain corrections.

French vocal score, Durand, 1905 (D. & F. 6576), 283 pp. Later printing [1907] with extensive revisions.

Interludes, arr. for piano by Gustave Samazeuilh, Durand, 1905 (D. & F. 6590), 10 pp.

German vocal score (German trans. by F. von Oppeln-Bronikowski adapted by Otto Neitzel), Durand, 1906 (D. & F. 6774), 254 pp.

French-English vocal score (English trans. by Henry Grafton Chapman), Durand, 1907 (D. & F. 6953), 310 pp. Later printings with extensive changes and corrections.

Italian vocal score (Italian trans. by Carlo Zangarini), Durand, 1908 (D. & F. 6576), 283 pp.

Other Publications

Supplément musical à *L'Illustration,* no. 3085, année 1902, no. 7 (12 April 1902), pp. 49–53. Excerpt from Act V.

Supplément musical au *Monde Musical* (15 May 1902), 6 pp. Excerpts from Act III, sc. 1 and Act V.

Annotated Scores

US-A US: First edition (Fromont, 1902) with annotations by André Messager and autograph dedication to Albert Carré by Debussy.
Dedication: "à Monsieur A. Carré, et plus encore à l'artiste qui sût créer l'atmosphère de rêve inoubliable sans laquelle Pelléas et Mélisande n'auraient pu vivre. Claude Debussy. Mai/1902."
Catalogue: OCexp, p. 56, no. 249; BNexp, p. 45, no. 144; Lake, *Baudelaire to Beckett,* pp. 65–66, no. 159.

F-Po, Rés. 2156: first edition (Fromont, 1902) with annotations by Henry Busser and autograph dedication to him by Debussy.
Dedication: "à Henry Busser, l'amitié reconnaissante de Claude Debussy. Mai/1902."
Catalogue: OCexp, p. 56, no. 253.

Full Score

Manuscripts

F-Pn, Mss. 961–65: Act I (Ms. 961), 65 ff. (63 pp. music); Act II (Ms. 962), 104 ff. (102 pp. music); Act III (Ms. 963), 88 ff. (86 pp. music); Act IV (Ms. 964), 109 ff. (109 pp. music); Act V (Ms. 965), 47 ff. (47 pp. music).
Catalogue: LCat no. 88, B1; OCexp, pp. 53–54, nos. 223–27; BNexp, p. 44, no. 140 (Mss. 962–63).
Facsimile: Debussy, *Pelléas et Mélisande* (study score) (New York: International, 1962), opp. p. 1 (Ms. 961, fol. 1); booklets accompanying recordings of *Pelléas* conducted by André Cluytens (Angel 3561 C/L) and Roger Désormière (EMI C 153-12513/15) (Ms. 961, fol. 1); Gerstenberg and Hürlimann, *Composers' Autographs,* II: pl. 107 (Ms. 962, fol. 20); *Zodiaque,* no. 53 (July 1962), pl. 6 (Ms. 964, fol. 26).

US-A US: 3 ff. (3 pp. music) rejected from Ms. 961 above. Act I, sc. 1 (2 ff. corresponding to fols. 20–21 of Ms. 961); Act I, sc. 3 (1 f. numbered 40, corresponding to fol. 40 of Ms. 961).

Catalogue: LCat no. 88, B4; Lake, *Baudelaire to Beckett*, p. 66, no. 161.

Corrected Proofs of First Edition (Fromont, 1904)

F-Pn, Ms. 1029: Act I (first proofs), pp. 1–69; Act III (second proofs), pp. 151–251 (extra pp. 169, 170, and 236 from first proofs; p. 174 not printed).
Catalogue: LCat no. 88, B3; Cogeval and Lesure, *Debussy e il Simbolismo*, p. 201, no. 135 (pp. 62–63).

US-NYpm, Robert Owen Lehman Coll., on deposit: Act I (second proofs), pp. 1–69; Act II (second proofs), pp. 70–150 (p. 96 not printed); Act III (first proofs), pp. 151–251 (pp. 169, 170, and 236 missing, part of Ms. 1029 above); Act IV (first proofs?), pp. 252–364; Act V (first proofs), pp. 365–409.
Catalogue: LCat no. 88, B2; Coulet & Faure sale cat., *Spectacles* (1972), pp. 169–75, no. 1044; Turner, "Nineteenth-Century Autograph Music Manuscripts," p. 64; Turner, *Nineteenth-Century Autograph Music Manuscripts,* p. 22.
Facsimile; Coulet & Faure sale cat., *Spectacles* (1972), pp. 169–74 (portions of pp. 93, 160, 165, 172, and 173 of proofs).

Location Unknown: Act I (third proofs?), pp. 65–68.
Catalogue: Coulet & Faure sale cat., *Spectacles* (1972), p. 175, no. 1045.

F-Pn, Rés. Vma. 281: Acts I–V (final proofs, marked "bon à tirer"), pp. 1–409.
Dated: 29 June 1904.
Dedication: "A MadaBardac... Ces quatre cent neuf pages de timbres variés qui valent à peine l'ombre que fait ta petite main sur ce gros livre...juillet 1904."
Catalogue: LCat no. 88, B5.

Editions

Conductors' score

Fromont, 1904 (E. 1418. F.), 409 pp.

Durand, [1905] (D. & F. 6577 on p. 1; E. 1418. F. thereafter), 409 pp.

Durand, revised ed., 1966 (D. & F. 6577), 409 pp.

Study score

Durand, [1908] (D. & F. 7018), 409 pp.

Durand, revised ed., [1950] (D. & F. 6577), 409 pp.

Annotated Scores

Conductors' score

> *F-ASO:* Fromont, 1904. Debussy's own score with many revisions and annotations by him. Also, performance markings, probably by Pierre Monteux (?).
> Catalogue: Andrieux sale cat. (30 November–8 December 1933), p. 37, no. 194; BNexp, p. 45, no. 145.

> *F-Pdurand:* Durand, [1905]. Corrections and revisions by Debussy and copyist: basis for correction of parts (August 1905) and full score (April 1949).
> Dated: 25 August 1905 by copyist.

> *F-Po* (Service de la Copie): Fromont, 1904. Corrections, revisions, and annotations in many hands. Used by conductors at the Opéra-Comique, perhaps since 1904–5 season.

Study score

> *F-Pn,* Rés. 2729: Durand, [1908]. Revisions and corrections entered by Debussy, pp. 1–2, 4–5, 10–18, and 391. Includes 1 p. music manuscript (full score) with dedication to Emma Bardac dated April 1908 (see "Dedication and Other Autograph Fragments" below).

Parts

Orchestra Parts

F-Po, uncatalogued: manuscript parts from Opéra-Comique.

Durand, 1905 (D. & F. 6578). Violin I part in *US-Wc*: deposited for copyright, 10 November 1905. Another copy in *F-Pn,* Vm^{15} 1546. All parts later reprinted with revisions (to correspond with revised score).

Chorus Parts

Durand, 1905 (men: D. & F. 6579; women: D. & F. 6579bis).

F-Po, Mat. F. 230: 13 copies of D. & F. 6579 and 8 copies of D. & F. 6579bis, with MS annotations, from Opéra-Comique; also MS part for contraltos and MS choral score for choral director.

Dedication and Other Autograph Fragments

Former Coll. Mme Jean de Polignac: Japanese fan decorated with birds and flowers with musical autograph and dedication by Debussy to Yvonne Lerolle. Act I, sc. 3, meas. 1–5 in short score, labeled: "Pélléas et Mélisande (Acte I: scène III). Devant le Château (Entrent Geneniève et Mélisande; Mélisande les bras chargés de fleurs)."
Dedication: "à Mademoiselle Yvonne Lerolle, en souvenir de sa petite soeur Mélisande. Claude Debussy. Fev. 94."
Catalogue: OCexp, p. 55, no. 233; Thierry Bodin sale cat. (14 December 1979), no. 32.
Facsimile: Thierry Bodin sale cat. (14 December 1979), frontispiece and no. 32; Cogeval and Lesure, *Debussy e il Simbolismo*, pp. 32–33.

Former Coll. Henri Lerolle: pneumatic sent 20 June 1895 to Henri Lerolle to announce the completion of Act V. Last five meas. of Act V (short score, preliminary version) marked "Fin" at end.
Dedication: "(pour H. Lerolle) Voici, pour le voyage de l'âme de Mélisande. Votre, Claude Debussy. Juin 95."
Facsimile: Denis, *Henry Lerolle et ses amis*, p. 31; Thompson, *Debussy: Man and Artist*, p. 126; Gauthier, *Debussy. Documents iconographiques*, pl. 46.

Location unknown: six autograph extracts to accompany photographs of the décors and of scenes from the première production of the opera, which appeared in a special issue of *Le Théâtre*, no. 84 (June 1902).
Facsimile: *Le Théâtre*, no. 84 (June 1902), p. 6, "1ʳ. Acte = Prélude" (Act I prelude: meas. 1–27; short score); p. 11, "Scène III. Devant le château. Thème initial de Mélisande." (Act I, sc. 3: meas. 1–4; short score); p. 12, "Acte II. Scène I. Prélude. Une fontaine dans le parc." (Act II prelude: meas. 1–13; short score); p. 16, "Acte III. Scène III. Une terrasse au sortir des souterrains." (Act III, sc. 3: VS, p. 153, meas. 4–p. 154, meas. 2; piano-vocal reduction); p. 18, "Acte IV. Scène II." (Act IV, sc. 2: VS, p. 215, meas. 6–9; piano-vocal reduction); p. 22, "Acte V. (la mort de Mélisande)" (Act V: VS, p. 308, meas. 6–p. 309, meas. 1; piano-vocal reduction). Some of these

have been reproduced elsewhere: Act I prelude in Inghelbrecht, *Comment on ne dois pas interpréter Carmen, Faust, Pelléas*, opp. p. 58; Act I prelude and Act V excerpt in booklet accompanying *Pelléas* recording conducted by André Cluytens (Angel 3561 C/L); Act I, sc. 3 excerpt in Chennevière, *Claude Debussy et son oeuvre*, opp. p. 16; Act IV, sc. 2 excerpt in booklets accompanying *Pelléas* recordings conducted by Roger Désormière (EMI C 153–12513/15) and Herbert von Karajan (Angel SZCX—3885).

Location unknown: autograph extract written for Camille Mauclair (?); illustration in his review of *Pelléas* in *Revue Universelle*, no. 65 (1 July 1902). "Pelléas et Mélisande. 1^r. Acte. (fragment du prélude). Claude Debussy. Juin/1902." (Act I prelude, meas. 1–14; short score).
Facsimile: Camille Mauclair, "*Pelléas et Mélisande*," *Revue Universelle*, no. 65 (1 July 1902), p. 332; Koechlin, *Debussy*, p. 41.

Location unknown: autograph extract to accompany a photograph of a scene from the première production of the opera in *L'Art du Théâtre* (August 1902). "(3eme acte—1er Scène: Pélléas et Mélisande)" (Act III, sc. 1: VS, p. 132, meas. 10–p. 133, meas. 4; piano-vocal reduction).
Facsimile: *L'Art du Théâtre*, no. 20 (August 1902), p. 158; Rohozinski, *Cinquante ans de musique française*, I: 153.

F-Pn, Rés. 2729 (pasted in): 1 f. (1 p. music). "'*Pelléas et Mélisande* (3eme acte)' Scène III. Une terrasse au sortir des souterrains." Interlude between sc. 2 and sc. 3 of Act III (3 meas. full score: OS, p. 197, meas. 2–p. 198, meas. 2).
Dedication: "à ma chère petite femme cette musique qui l'attendait. Claude Debussy. Avril 1908."

Former Coll. Arturo Toscanini: Photograph of Debussy with dedication to Arturo Toscanini, including 1 meas. music (Act III, sc. 2, meas. 1).
Dedication: "au Maestro Toscanini, que je ne pourrais jamais assez remercier! Claude Debussy. Juillet/1908." On reverse, first meas. of Act III, sc. 2 and "d'où Toscanini sortit tout de même victorieux."
Facsimile: Barblan, *Toscanini e la Scala*, opp. p. 97.

Notes

Introduction

1. OCexp and BNexp, respectively.

2. LL, p. xv. Lesure's views on the larger subject of the transcription and publication of archival documents are contained in his article "Archival Research: Necessity and Opportunity" (1972), pp. 67–70.

3. Pierre Lalo, " 'Pelléas et Mélisande' à l'Opéra-Comique (Mai 1902)," in Lalo, *De Rameau à Ravel* (1947), p. 391; Friedrich Spigl, "Wagner et Debussy" (1902), p. 518; Edwin Evans, Jr., "Debussy's 'Pelléas et Mélisande' " (1909), p. 363.

4. Wenk promises to pursue this line of analysis in greater detail in his forthcoming book on the opera, *Debussy's Prism: An Approach to 'Pelléas et Mélisande.'*

Chapter 1

1. "Debussy Discusses Music and His Work," *New York Times,* 26 June 1910, pt. 3, p. 5. The interview was dated 17 June 1910, Paris.

2. "Pelléas" was spelled with two *accents aigus* in both the 1892 and 1898 editions of Maeterlinck's play, though the first accent was dropped before the play's 1893 première and in the 1902 edition of the collected plays. Although the editions of Debussy's opera also spelled it without the first accent, the composer himself typically included both when writing the opera's title, preserving the spelling of the first edition. The differences among Maeterlinck's editions and the differences between these editions and Debussy's libretto are discussed at length in chapter 6.

3. The date of publication was 4 May 1892 according to OCexp, p. 39.

4. Jacques Robichez, *Le Symbolisme au théâtre* (1957), p. 159.

5. Ibid., p. 158.

6. Ibid.

7. Aurélien-François Lugné-Poe, *Le Sot du tremplin* (1930), p. 225.

8. Léon Vallas reported seeing Debussy's setting of a scene from the play, but the manuscript has since disappeared (VAL, p. 140). See ORL, pp. 14–17.

9. Robichez, p. 162.

10. Ibid., p. 165.

11. Lugné-Poe, p. 225.

12. Jean Warmoes, ed., *Maurice Maeterlinck: Le Centenaire de sa naissance* (1962), p. 57.

13. Robichez, p. 168.

14. Ibid., p. 166.

15. Ibid., p. 163.

16. Ibid., pp. 163–66. See also Lugné-Poe, pp. 226–27 and 236–39.

17. Lugné-Poe, p. 238.

18. OCexp, p. 40.

19. Lugné-Poe, p. 229. Debussy's subscription ticket is reproduced in facsimile in LPm, p. 10.

20. Robichez, p. 170.

21. Ibid., pp. 170–71.

22. Ibid., p. 171.

23. Lugné-Poe, p. 229.

24. Lugné-Poe, "La Parade de la baraque. Souvenirs de Lugné-Poe," *Cahiers de "Bravo,"* No. 7 (Supplément au numéro de septembre 1930), p. 45. The article was intended as a preview of Lugné-Poe's book.

25. Louis Laloy, "Pelléas et Mélisande," in *Essays on Music,* ed. Felix Aprahamian (1967), p. 75. The article originally appeared in the 19 May 1937 issue of *The Listener.*

26. Robert Godet, "En marge de la marge" (1926), p. 174.

27. Facsimile in TIE, p. 83.

28. OCexp, no. 130, p. 40.

29. VAL, p. 143. Maeterlinck remarked in the same letter (23 June 1891) that he had often been asked to authorize music for *Princesse Maleine.* Among those who had made such requests were Maurice Lefèvre and Xavier Carlier. In both cases, Maeterlinck, who neither knew nor cared for music, consulted his friend Grégoire Le Roy. A letter to Le Roy of 23 September 1890 asked about Lefèvre and another, this one undated, about Carlier: "Yet another note grinder ("croque-notes") has just pestered me for the Princess: Xavier Carlier. Do you know him?" (Van Nuffel, ed., *Pelléas et Mélisande . . . Catalogus* [1977], p. 8). According to Jean Cocteau, Erik Satie also toyed with the idea of an opera based on *La Princesse Maleine.*

30. Louis Laloy, *Claude Debussy* (1909), p. 28.

31. Laloy, "Pelléas et Mélisande," p. 75. In this 1937 account, the "friends" are not named. In the 1909 version of the same events, only one, Pierre Louÿs, was mentioned.

32. TIE, p. 69; facs. between pp. 56–57. Although announced for performance on 29 May 1894 by the *Société des grandes auditions musicales* at the *Jardin d'Acclimatation* (DIE, p. 95), the *Marche écossaise* was not performed until 19 April 1913 (LCat, p. 76).

33. LCat, pp. 83–84. It is significant that Debussy's attraction to the prose libretto of *Pelléas* coincided with his composition of the *Proses lyriques,* settings of his own free verse poems. Furthermore, the first songs that he wrote after the completion of the opera were the

Chansons de Bilitis, to prose poems of Pierre Louÿs. In April 1898, the month in which he returned to verse with settings of two of the *Trois chansons de Charles d'Orléans,* he wrote to Louÿs and explained why, for musical settings, he preferred "rhythmic prose" to "verse": "music and verse are two songs ('chansons') which seek in vain to achieve congruence; even in the very rare cases where they are in accord, it has the effect of a bad pun." (US-NYp: Music Division, Astor, Lenox & Tilden Foundations)

34.   Paul Dukas, *Correspondance de Paul Dukas* (1971), p. 21.

35.   LOC, I: 99.

36.   LCat, p. 71. The manuscript of Act I is dated 1891, those of Acts II and III, 1892.

37.   LL, p. 63.

38.   Alfred Cortot, "Un Drame Lyrique de Claude Debussy," in *Inédits sur Debussy* (1942), pp. 14–15. According to Carolyn Abbate, "*Tristan* in the Composition of *Pelléas*" (1981), p. 119, Cortot obtained Act I from Gabrielle Dupont and Acts II and III from the estate of Emma Debussy.

39.   Georgette Leblanc, *Souvenirs: My Life with Maeterlinck,* trans. Janet Flanner (1932), p. 168.

40.   André Boucourechliev et al., *Debussy* (1972), p. 111 (facsimile of letter). Debussy was not the first composer who requested permission to write music based on *Pelléas.* On 11 September 1892 Maeterlinck wrote to Grégoire Le Roy, asking if he knew Henri Quittard, "who would like to write music for *Pelléas*" (Van Nuffel, p. 4).

41.   Godet, "En marge de la marge," p. 174.

42.   Letter to Laloy of 25 July 1907 (LAL, p. 26).

43.   CHA1, p. 117, gives the date as "Sunday (6 September 1893)," but 6 September was a Wednesday that year, not a Sunday. If 6 September appeared as a postmark, the letter could have been started on Sunday the 3rd, but completed and mailed on the 6th. In fact, the letter's postscript seems to follow the body of the letter by several days: it seems unlikely that Debussy would have written in a single sitting that he was composing furiously and then announce in the postscript as "Latest News" the fact that he had completed two works.

44.   The letter is dated "Monday evening," probably 11 September, since it is in answer to Debussy's letter, which we may assume was mailed a few days after 3 September (see previous note).

45.   "The New Music Cult in France and Its Leader: Claude Achille Debussy Tells of His Present and Future Works," *New York Times,* 16 May 1909, pt. 5, p. 9.

46.   "Debussy Discusses Music and His Work," *New York Times,* 26 June 1910, pt. 3, p. 5. In an article "Debussy and Nationality in Music," *Musical Standard,* 34 (26 November 1910), 337, Debussy's English friend and biographer Mrs. Franz (Louise) Liebich commented that the composer was often misquoted in interviews: "His words ... are turned and twisted; they are used by writers as pegs upon which to hang their surmises of what they imagine he thinks; and if an interviewer fails to get answers from the composer to his questions he invents them forthwith." She quotes Debussy's complaint:

> Quite lately an interviewer asked me at what moment of the day I felt most inspired to write. Mon Dieu! the next time such a one asks me such a question I will tell him that I feel most disposed to compose when I am blacking my own boots.... People sometimes come

here who interest me as little as that navvy walking down there on the railroad; they spring upon me all kinds of queries: on the most far-fetched subjects and the most banal. I try to say something to the point when probably I am not in the least in the mood for the discussion of the given question. The next day I see what are supposed to be my sentences in print.... Ah Mon Dieu!

Some interviewers, though, were applauded by Mrs. Liebich: "Occasionally, however, a subject is sprung upon him which gives him instantly keen interest: as when a clever man discussed one day with him the theory of unconscious intellection applied to the composition of music. The reserved, intelligent countenance brightened with pleasure as he explained to us how it interested him to think that inspiration came in that logical, orderly way; built up of a great mass of impressions stored in the brain, linked together and suddenly finding outlet." One can only guess as to whether Debussy considered the *New York Times* interviewers uninteresting or "clever."

47. Raymond Bonheur, "Souvenirs et impressions d'un compagnon de jeunesse" (1926), p. 103.

48. Debussy's setting of a scene from Villiers de l'Isle-Adam's *Axël* may have been a similar kind of experiment to test the suitability of that play as an opera libretto.

49. The playwright's own work schedule provides an interesting parallel with the composer's. Anne Schillings, in her "La Genèse de *Pelléas et Mélisande*" (1970), a study of Maeterlinck's notebooks for the play, comments that he began with Act IV, scene 4 and Act V, scene 2 (Debussy's Act V) and returned to those scenes periodically throughout the notebooks, whereas secondary scenes were written at specific points (p. 122).

50. LCr, p. 12.

51. The letter is postmarked "24 October 1893" but is dated "Monday," which suggests that it was written on the 23rd.

52. Charles Oulmont, "Deux amis: Claude Debussy et Ernest Chausson. Documents inédits" (1934), p. 268.

53. Bonheur, p. 102.

54. Gustave Doret, *Temps et Contretemps* (1942), p. 95.

55. "Petite chronique," *L'Art Moderne*, 13 (12 November 1893), 367.

56. *L'Art Moderne*, 13 (26 November 1893), 379.

57. *L'Art Moderne*, 13 (29 October 1893), 345. The publicity granted the Libre Esthétique in *L'Art Moderne* was probably due, in large part, to the fact that Octave Maus, the head and director of expositions for the former, served on the editorial board of the latter.

58. Antoine Ysaÿe and Bertram Ratcliffe, *Ysaÿe: His Life, Work and Influence* (1947), p. 190.

59. Antoine Ysaÿe, *Eugène Ysaÿe* (1974), p. 111. In his letter to Chausson of 23 October 1893, Debussy wrote that he had sold his Quartet to Durand ("Barbarians of the Place de la Madeleine") for 250 francs: "They had the impudence to confess that they didn't pay me an amount commensurate with the effort that went into this 'work'" (LL, p. 59).

60. Ibid., p. 112; Lev Ginsburg, *Ysaÿe* (1980), p. 157. The eventual dedication of *Pelléas* was to the memory of Georges Hartmann (whose support of the composer had not yet begun) and to André Messager (whom Debussy barely knew in 1893). Dietschy believed that Debussy, in the letter to Ysaÿe, was referring to the dedication of the Quartet, and not of *Pelléas*. He attributed the confusion to an error of syntax (DIE, p. 130). This explanation seems

unlikely. In a letter to Debussy of 18 December 1893, Chausson still referred to the work as "my quartet," and it was not until early February 1894 that Debussy considered withdrawing the Quartet's dedication to Chausson. Deeply hurt by the latter's criticisms of the work, Debussy wrote to Chausson that he would compose "another quartet, which will be for you—really for you" (CHA1, p. 126). The dedication was then transferred to the Ysaÿe Quartet. Debussy's original intention of dedicating *Pelléas* to Ysaÿe is also confirmed in a letter of 13 October 1896 to the violinist in which the latter is referred to as the "Godfather" of Pelléas and Mélisande.

61. Ysaÿe and Ratcliffe, p.190.

62. Pierre Louÿs, who accompanied Debussy on this trip, gave his version of the meeting with Maeterlinck in a letter to his brother Georges dated 20 April 1914:

   Your postcard from Ghent arrived today. Thank you for having written me from there. I was back there only once, in 1892 or 93, accompanying Debussy, who, in a famous visit, went to ask Maeterlinck for permission to set *Pelléas* to music. I had to speak for Debussy, because he was too timid to express himself, and since Maeterlinck was even more timid than he and didn't reply at all, I also answered for Maeterlinck. I will never forget this scene.... (LOU1, p. 30)

63. According to Georgette Leblanc, Maeterlinck did not understand music at all (*Souvenirs: My Life with Maeterlinck*, p. 169), and in a letter of 14 May 1932, Maeterlinck wrote to Gabriel Astruc: "I hear nothing, absolutely nothing, in music" (Emile Vuillermoz, *Claude Debussy*, p. 156).

64. Debussy's final version of the scene omitted one large section and several short lines. A number of short, repeated exclamations were also trimmed. These cuts, however, were made long after Debussy's visit to Ghent. (See chapter 6.)

65. This letter is dated "Tuesday," and if indeed in reply to Chausson's letter of Monday night, 18 December, it was probably written on Tuesday, 26 December 1893, or perhaps 2 January 1894.

66. Thierry Bodin sale catalogue (14 December 1979), frontispiece and No. 32.

67. US-Wc; excerpt in LPm, p.13.

68. LPm, p. 12. It was not just *Pelléas*; Chausson also refused to attend a private performance of d'Indy's *Fervaal* on 18 December 1893, explaining in a letter written on that date to Debussy that it was not from lack of interest that he didn't want to hear it at the moment. In fact he hoped for a complete report on the audition (CHA3, p. 58).

69. The letter is published in LPm, p. 15, where it is mistakenly dated 19 December 1894. (The same wrong date is given in TIE, p. 86.) The correct date, given by Dietschy (p. 104), is corroborated by a letter that Chausson wrote to Debussy on the previous day (CHA3, pp. 58–59). Barricelli and Weinstein, in *Ernest Chausson* (1955), give the correct year but the wrong month in dating the letter 19 October 1893 (p. 36).

70. The name of Charles Bordes is included in the invitation list in quotations of the letter in DIE, p. 104, and Barricelli and Weinstein, p. 35; it does not appear in the quotations in LPm, p. 15, or TIE, p. 86. Bordes is not mentioned elsewhere in the letter.

71. Lerolle must have had trouble with his watch on this occasion; if Debussy began at quarter to twelve, he could not have finished at eleven-thirty! *Twelve*-thirty would have allowed about the right amount of time for performances of Act IV, scene 4 and Act I, scene 1 (the

music that it seems might have been completed by this date) and for a brief discussion of that music. For some reason, Dietschy concluded that Debussy played "for about an hour" (p. 104).

72. François Lesure, "Debussy à travers le journal de Madame de Saint-Marceaux (1894–1911)" (1976), p. 5.

73. So titled in a review of the concert in *L'Art Moderne*, 14 (4 March 1894), 67.

74. In February 1894, Debussy announced his engagement in a letter to Pierre de Bréville (LL, p. 63). The engagement was broken off the following month.

75. *L'Art Moderne*, 14 (25 February 1894), 64.

76. Henry Lesbroussart, "Pelléas et Mélisande," *L'Art Moderne*, 27 (13 January 1907), 9. Maurice Kufferath, music critic of the *Guide Musical*, and Guillaume Guidé became codirectors of the Théâtre de la Monnaie (Brussels) on 4 September 1900 and held those positions until 1914. *Pelléas* was given its first performance outside of the Paris Opéra-Comique at the Monnaie in January 1907.

77. *L'Art Moderne*, 14 (4 March 1894), 67. No trace of this second quartet has survived, although Debussy did publish the G minor Quartet as his "First Quartet" and even assigned it the opus number 10, making it his only work bearing an opus number.

78. VAL, p. 125.

79. LOC, I: 241–42.

80. A piano needed to be moved in for the occasion since the keyboard instrument that Louÿs owned was a Mustel harmonium. Jacques-Emile Blanche recalled, not this particular gathering, but similar ones, when he wrote: "It was at Pierre Louÿs's—not at the piano, but at Pierre's harmonium—that every day in the late afternoon, Debussy played and sang for us the scenes which he had just finished" (*La Pêche aux souvenirs*, pp. 221–22).

81. LER, pp. 29–30. This letter opens with an apology for not having written sooner and contains a report of a 27 July dinner with André Gide. (See Debussy's letter of that date to Louÿs: LOU1, p. 39.)

82. LPm, p. 13. It is presumably this translation that is meant by "a copy of *Lucien de Samosate*," as the book is described by Lesure. The printing of the book was accomplished on 30 April 1894, but the "millésime de public" was given as 29 June 1894 in the 7 July 1894 issue of *Bibliographie de France*. Therefore, Louÿs's presentation could have taken place even before the composer announced his decision to set the second scene of Act III; the inscription does not specify, after all, that Debussy had completed Act III in 1894, merely that he had worked on it. Of course, the dedication could have been written at any point after the book's publication, perhaps following Louÿs's return to Paris from Algeria in late August.

83. Debussy's initial musical idea for *La Chute de la Maison Usher*, his unfinished opera based on the Poe story, may also have been a particular orchestral sonority rather than specific melodic, harmonic, or rhythmic materials. (See Abbate, "*Tristan* in the Composition of *Pelleas*," pp. 124–25, and an important comment on this point in ORL, p. 124.)

84. LCat, p. 86.

85. The contract is photographically reproduced in Jean Barraqué, *Debussy* (1962), p. 93.

86. LCat, p. 88.

87. The second piece, "Sarabande," appeared in the *Grand Journal* supplement of 17 February 1896. All three were published by Presser in 1978 as "Images (oubliées)." At the end of the third piece, "Quelques aspects de 'Nous n'irons plus au bois' parce qu'il fait un temps insupportable," Debussy introduced a figure marked "Une cloche qui ne garde aucune mesure," which resembles the Golaud motive.

88. VAL, p. 178. The "Valse" has apparently not survived, if indeed it was ever written.

89. LPm, p. 14, reproduces a letter of 8 December 1894 from Jacques-Emile Blanche to Louÿs: "If Debussy is kind enough to give us a little music on Tuesday, tell me what I should prepare. Could you bring me the text of *Pelléas?*"

90. Louÿs left for Spain on 6 January 1895, arriving in Seville on the 10th and staying there for exactly two months. His subsequent travels took him to Cadiz, Tangier, Nemours, Oran, and Algiers, where he met Gide around the 23rd of March. He returned to Paris on 1 April, having spent his entire inheritance. See LOU1, p. 49, and Fleury, *Pierre Louÿs et Gilbert de Voisins* (1973), p. 204.

91. The plans for the project can be chronicled through the Debussy-Louÿs correspondence. See especially LOU1, pp. 20, 49–60, and 185–89; LOU2, pp. 62–64, LOU3, pp. 29–32; and ORL, pp. 261–62 and 312–13.

92. The letter is known only from an excerpt in an autograph catalogue, where it was assigned to April; on the basis of its contents, it could have been written as late as June.

93. LOU1, p. 55.

94. Reproduced in facsimile in LER, p. 31; Oscar Thompson, *Debussy: Man and Artist* (1967), p. 126; and André Gauthier, *Debussy. Documents iconographiques* (1952), pl. 46. The ending of Act V was further revised and expanded to six measures by the time Debussy drafted the vocal score.

95. This inscription was incorrectly reproduced in Emmanuel Winternitz, *Musical Autographs,* I, p. 135, where "Juin" ("June") was read as "Paris." LCat, p. 89, apparently following Winternitz, omits the June date for Act II.

96. The letter, dated "Saturday," was assigned in LER to "1894?" though it probably dates from June-July 1895.

97. Godet, "En marge de la marge," p. 175.

Chapter 2

1. LOU1, p. 59.

2. Ibid., pp. 59–60.

3. LL, p. 51.

4. Robichez, p. 388.

5. Gertrude R. Jasper, *Adventure in the Theatre* (1947), pp. 53–55, 61–62, and 254.

6. Robichez, pp. 514–15.

7. Jasper, p. 246.

8. Robichez, p. 386.

9. *Mercure de France,* 15 (August 1895), 256.

10. LPm, p. 8.

11. Robichez, p. 388.

12. Camille Mauclair, *Servitude et grandeur littéraires* (1922), p. 106. Mauclair gave a slightly different account of these events ten years later in the article "Claude Debussy et les poètes," which appeared in the *Programme et Livre d'or des souscripteurs du festival 1932,* the program booklet for the festival on the occasion of the dedication of the Debussy monument in the Bois de Boulogne. In this later version Mauclair recalled receiving an express letter from Louÿs:

> "Debussy has just completed a score based on Maeterlinck's *Pelléas et Mélisande,* which you produced. He is prepared to play it for you and me alone. Come."
>
> And the same mail, by a happy coincidence, brought me a letter from Maeterlinck, with whose works I was once again amicably occupied in Paris.
>
> "Dear Friend," he wrote me from Ghent, "I have received from a M. Debussy, whom I do not know at all, a request for authorization concerning my *Pelléas.* You know that, unfortunately, I am not only incompetent [to judge], but that music is no more intelligible to me than if I were deaf. You who are a fervent music lover, do me the favor of going to listen to this score, and if you judge it good, I will authorize it."

The discrepancies between the two versions suggest that Mauclair had not preserved the letter from Maeterlinck and was reconstructing it from memory. Errors in the 1932 account—quoting Maeterlinck as saying that Debussy was somebody of whom he knew nothing when the two had met in November 1893, and giving Debussy's address as rue Cardinet when he did not move there until 1898—suggest that the story had become "embroidered" during the intervening decade and that the 1922 account is probably more accurate.

13. Camille Mauclair, "Le Souvenir de Claude Debussy" (1936), p. 66.

14. Mauclair, *Servitude et grandeur littéraires,* p. 106.

15. Robichez, pp. 326–31.

16. *Mercure de France,* 16 (November 1895), 272.

17. Mauclair, *Servitude,* p. 106. Mauclair's 1932 version differs slightly:

> Louÿs and I were pale with emotion. When it was finished, Debussy said to me, with his sarcastic smile, "What are you going to say to M. Maeterlinck?" "This," I replied, taking a piece of paper on which I drafted this dispatch: "I have just heard one of the most beautiful masterpieces in all of music; be proud and happy at having inspired it; send your authorization immediately."
>
> I ran to take the telegram to the nearest post office and returned.

18. Maurice Dumesnil, "Personal Conferences with Debussy" (1935), p. 5. This letter was included in the 1933 sale of manuscripts, letters, books, and scores which had belonged to Debussy. From the description of the letter in the sale catalogue (AND, p. 40, no. 213), it is clear that Dumesnil's quotation is in part a paraphrase. According to the catalogue description, Maeterlinck expressed " 'an extreme reluctance' to renew relations with a person that he names, and consequently, with his representatives." Both the sale catalogue and Dumesnil diplomatically withheld the identification of the directors named by Maeterlinck, but it may be assumed that he was referring to Antoine and Larochelle, the former and current directors of the Théâtre Libre. Maeterlinck had indeed been mistreated by the Théâtre Libre and might have wished to have nothing more to do with the company.

In late October 1890, at the urging of Henry Bauër and Octave Mirbeau, Antoine, then director of the Théâtre Libre, requested Maeterlinck's permission to allow his play *La Princesse Maleine* to be performed by that company. Maeterlinck happily accepted the offer, having recently had a similar proposal from Albert Carré's Théâtre du Vaudeville fall through and having just rejected an offer from the Théâtre Mixte when his Parisian friends reported unfavorably on the quality of their productions. Maeterlinck's letter of approval to Antoine was published in *L'Echo de Paris* of 30 October 1890:

> *La Princesse Maleine* belongs to you and, to my way of thinking, has always belonged to you. You must not feel yourself in the least bit liable to me. You will present the *Princesse* either this year or in ten years or never, as you like. She will wait and will be yours alone. And whatever you do with her, I thank you from the bottom of my heart for your good intentions.... (Robichez, p. 85)

Princesse Maleine was announced among the plans of the Théâtre Libre throughout 1891, although Antoine, in his memoirs, claimed to have decided on 20 February 1891 to take Maeterlinck at his word and abandon the project, feeling that the play was unsuitable for his theater. Apparently there were repercussions from this decision; Antoine noted: "Now this is being used against me in Brussels, and it is said that the naturalist clique at the Théâtre Libre dissuaded me from the experiment" (*Memories*, p. 171). The Théâtre Libre did not perform *Princesse Maleine* or any other play by Maeterlinck in this or any other season. Evidently the disappointment of this situation made the Belgian playwright unwilling to renew connections with Antoine's company. (From the catalogue paraphrase of the letter it appears that Maeterlinck may have been under the impression that Antoine was still director of the Théâtre Libre and that Larochelle was his deputy.)

Maeterlinck's apology for not coming to Paris in August suggests that Debussy had written to him in that month concerning *Pelléas*, presumably to announce his completion of the opera.

19. Mauclair, *Servitude*, pp. 106–7.

20. This unpublished letter is mentioned in Robichez, p. 388, and LPm, p. 8. In his published accounts of the visit with Debussy, Mauclair made no mention of Larochelle nor did he suggest any interest on the part of the Théâtre de l'Oeuvre. The idea of performances at the Pavillon des Muses may have been nothing more than an idle thought of the composer (or perhaps an invention of Mauclair's?); no other reference to that possibility has emerged. From Mauclair's letter of 14 October 1895 to Lugné-Poe, we know that the former had discussed the Larochelle offer with Debussy. Would the composer have rejected an apparently concrete offer from an established company in favor of the mere possibility of one performance (or possibly two, according to Mauclair's 1932 recollection of the conversation) at the private estate of a rich amateur? Perhaps Debussy was attracted to this plan as a realization of his "Society of Musical Esotericism." He may well have been willing to sacrifice some measure of popular success for greater artistic control and a more sympathetic setting.

21. Debussy's testimony before the Société des Auteurs, 14 February 1902 (DIE, p. 117).

22. LPm, p. 8; Catalogue A. Blaizot et fils, October–November 1936, no. 2047.

23. Jasper, pp. 144–46.

24. Ibid., p. 216.

25. Marie-Jeanne Viel, "Une grande bataille à l'Opéra-Comique" (1957), p. 98.

26. The "Symphonic Suites" from *Pelléas* later devised by John Barbirolli, Pierre Monteux, and Erich Leinsdorf do make use of these expanded interludes.

27. The Théâtre de la Monnaie, then under the codirection of Stoumon and Calabresi, presented the première of only one new opera during the 1896–97 season—Vincent d'Indy's *Fervaal,* which had its first performance on 12 March 1897.

28. *L'Art Moderne,* 16 (11 October 1896), 326.

29. Dumesnil, p. 6.

30. OCexp, p. 43, no. 152; DIE, p. 124. Debussy advanced some of the same arguments a decade later when he rejected the request of the Royal Philharmonic Society that he conduct a concert performance of *Pelléas* in London; see his letter to the Society of 24 September 1906 in Edward Lockspeiser, *Debussy,* 5th ed., ed. Richard Langham Smith (1980), pp. 288–89 (GB-Lbm, Dept. of MSS, Loan 48.13/10, fols. 91^v-92^r).

31. Surely Alfred Bruneau was confusing Maeterlinck dramas when he wrote in June 1897: "Hitherto no theatre has extended hospitality to M. Debussy who has in his portfolio a score composed for Maeterlinck's *Princesse Maleine*" (LOC, I: 149). Lockspeiser took this quote at face value, but the opera in question was surely *Pelléas.*

32. Godet, "En marge de la marge," p. 175.

33. GOD, p. 100.

34. DIE, p. 129.

35. GOD, p. 184.

36. Gustave Samazeuilh, *Musiciens de mon temps* (1947), p. 118.

37. LCat, p. 93. The *Nocturnes* for violin and orchestra may be related to the earlier *Trois scènes au crépuscule* (1892–3) or the later *Nocturnes* for orchestra (1897–9); see LCat, pp. 82 and 96. On 13 October 1896, Debussy told Ysaÿe that the *Nocturnes* for violin and orchestra would be completed by December. The fact that no manuscript has survived does not necessarily mean that nothing was written; Vallery-Radot recalled often hearing the composer say: "After my death one will not find a single note of mine. I destroy everything which does not satisfy me" ("Claude Debussy: Souvenirs" [1938], p. 401). This claim, of course, is contradicted by the survival in manuscript of numerous unpublished and uncompleted works, the opera *Rodrigue et Chimène* among them.

38. See ORL, pp. 261–65.

39. LCat, p. 94. See Debussy's letters to Louÿs of 24 December 1897 and 27 March 1898 in LOU1, pp. 105 and 108–10.

40. LCat, p. 97.

41. DIE, pp. 120 and 127.

42. Robert Cardinne-Petit, *Pierre Louÿs inconnu* (1948), p. 176.

43. Albert Carré, *Souvenirs* (1950), p. 207.

44. Henri Heugel, "Le Nouveau Directeur de l'Opéra-Comique: M. Albert Carré" (1898), p. 19.

45. TIE, p. 103.

46. VAL, p. 180.

47. Lesure, "Debussy à travers le journal de Madame de Saint-Marceaux (1894-1911)," p. 7.

48. LL, p. 56; letter in the Lake Collection, US-AUS.

49. Carré, p. 275.

50. Ibid.

51. Lake Collection, US-AUS.

52. LOU1, p. 113.

53. HAR, pp. 112-13; LL, pp. 91-92. The letter was not immediately sent "due to neuralgia, which stupefied my fine intelligence for eight days," as the composer explained in a postscript dated 23 July. He continued with a description of a nightmare: "I attended a rehearsal of *Pelléas*, in which Golaud was suddenly transformed into a bailiff and performed his duties to the musical formulas which characterize his part."

54. Robert Orledge, *Gabriel Fauré* (1979), p. 124.

55. *L'Art Moderne*, 18 (30 October 1898), 353.

56. DIE, p. 129.

57. LCat, pp. 93, 95, and 98-100. The latter two works, *La Saulaie* and *Nuits blanches,* are mentioned in Debussy's letters to Hartmann of 3 July and 24 September 1899 (LL, pp. 98 and 100). In a letter to Godet of 5 January 1900 the composer also mentioned working on *La Saulaie* (GOD, p. 101).

58. Debussy announced the event to Godet in a letter of 5 January 1900: "Mlle Lilly Texier has exchanged her inharmonious name for that of Lilly Debussy, much more euphonious, as everyone will agree" (GOD, p. 101). This turn of phrase echoes the way in which Louÿs announced to Debussy his own marriage: "Out of a love for the rich rhyme which no doubt comes from her father, Mlle Louise de Hérédia exchanges her name for that of Louise Louÿs, which is more symmetrical and more balanced" (LOU1, p. 129; letter of 15 May 1899).

59. Date inscribed in NEC MS, IV, fol. 33.

60. This assumption is confirmed by the physical appearance of the manuscript short score (the NEC MS); see the discussion of this manuscript in chapter 7.

61. Dumesnil, p. 6. The same letter is "quoted," with a rather different wording in Dumesnil's "novelized" biography of the composer, *Claude Debussy: Master of Dreams* (1940), p. 205.

62. VAL, p. 256.

63. Of these, only *La Fille de Tabarin* and *L'Ouragan* were actually mounted, with premières on 20 February 1901 and 29 April 1901 respectively. *La Troupe Jolicoeur* was not performed until the next season, having its première on 30 May 1902, exactly one month after the first performance of *Pelléas*. *William Ratcliff* was never performed at the Opéra-Comique and had its première on 26 January 1906 in Nice. So much for definite plans!

64. Léon Vallas, *Claude Debussy: His Life and Works* (1933), p. 119.

65. Jean Barraqué, *Debussy* (1962), p. 114 (facsimile); F-Pn, 1.a. Carré (A), 50.

66. LAL, p. 26.

67. *L'Art Moderne,* making a similar announcement in its issue of 2 June 1901, gave the correct spelling of the title of its countryman's play.

68. Choudens published *Ballade slave* (later issued as *Ballade*), *Tarantelle styrienne, Valse romantique,* and *Marche des anciens comtes de Ross* (for piano, four hands–later published as *March écossaise sur un thème populaire*). Choudens also engraved, but did not publish, the *Fantaisie pour piano et orchestre.*

69. F-Pn, I.a. Choudens (P. de), 5; the letter is dated 13 May 1901. In his memoirs (*De Pelléas aux Indes Galantes,* p. 114), Henri Busser described a conversation with Choudens which took place during one of the intermissions of the *Pelléas* première (30 April 1902): Choudens did not share the unfavorable opinion of his house composers (Hüe, Leroux, and Hillemacher) and expressed regret at not having been the one to publish the work, stating that, if he had, "*Pelléas* would travel around the world, like *Faust* and *Carmen.*"

70. On 5 July 1902 Fromont paid Général Bourgeat 8000 francs for all of the Debussy works the latter inherited upon the death of his uncle, Georges Hartmann (DIE, p. 136). These included the rights and either the engraved plates or the manuscripts of the *Marche écossaise, Ballade slave, Tarantelle styrienne, Valse romantique, Proses lyriques, Chansons de Bilitis, Nocturnes* for orchestra, *Prélude à L'Après-midi d'un faune, Suite Bergamasque, Rêverie, Mazurka,* and a solo piano arrangement of Schumann's "Am Springbrunnen" (VAL, p. 256). Fromont also seems to have "inherited" from Hartmann the role of moneylender, a fact revealed in a letter from Debussy to Fromont dated 28 April 1901:

    I thought I had no more bills and, curses, I have another one this month. Rescue me again: it will be the last time, I assure you.

    Have the piano pieces [probably *Pour le piano*] engraved quickly to recoup all of these amounts. (Coll. Jobert-Georges)

71. VAL, p. 295.

72. Ibid., p. 228.

73. Coll. Jobert-Georges. Debussy's remarks in this letter relative to the proofs of the cover for *Pour le piano* reveal his careful attention to the appearance of editions of his music:

    With regard to "Pour le piano," the title page barely satisfied me, the trefoils are too big and the lettering did not look elegant enough on the plate. The printing is so light that one would think that Dupré waters down his ink. Aside from all of this, it's perfect.

Chapter 3

1. OCexp, p. 56, no. 247.

2. R. O. J. Van Nuffel, *Pelléas et Mélisande, Het drama van Maeterlinck* (1977), p. 8, no. 3.

3. Stéphane Wolff, *Un Demi-siècle d'Opéra-Comique* (1953), p. 25.

4. Leblanc, *Souvenirs: My Life with Maeterlinck* p. 124. At the première, on 27 November 1897 at the Opéra-Comique, the role of Fanny Legrand was sung by Emma Calvé. In 1903 Leblanc made an unpublished recording of a scene from *Sapho,* with the composer at the piano; a copy is preserved in the Historical Sound Recordings collection at Yale University (Harding, *Massenet,* pp. 128–29 and 207).

5. Wolff, p. 38. The program for the official inauguration, given the day before (7 December 1898), included a scene from *Carmen* (Carré, pp. 231–33).

6. LCD, p. 72, pl. 59.

7. In her *Souvenirs,* Leblanc described Saint-Saëns rushing up to her after a performance of *Sapho* in 1897: "He sputtered frantically, 'You are the Proserpine of my dreams.' . . . It was at once decided with the director of the theatre that I would sing Proserpine. But the opera was never produced" (p. 124). In fact, *Proserpine* was revived on 29 November 1899, with Mme de Nuovina in the title role; for the last performance of the season, the part was sung by Charlotte Wyns.

8. Arsène Alexandre, "Mlle Georgette Leblanc de l'Opéra-Comique" (1899), p. 17.

9. Although Leblanc recalled that this meeting occurred late in 1901, Maeterlinck, in his testimony given on 7 February 1902 before the Société des Auteurs (see note 45), placed it in the spring of that year, and Debussy, in *his* testimony the following week, claimed that it took place in the summer! Leblanc's recollection is probably erroneous (see note 15).

10. Leblanc, p. 169.

11. Ibid., p. 170. A more literal translation of Leblanc's French original would be: "I desired the role ardently. Maeterlinck expressed his desire to have me play Mélisande."

12. DIE, p. 156: excerpts from the testimony given before the Société des Auteurs on 7 and 14 February 1902. Leblanc recalled Debussy saying that he would be "delighted," a recollection that is at variance with the more contemporary testimony of both Debussy and Maeterlinck.

13. Leblanc, p. 170. Debussy was not alone in objecting to Leblanc's interpretation of *Carmen.* On 27 January 1899, E. Jaël, writing on behalf of "several Opéra-Comique regulars," complained to the management about Leblanc's performance, using the most insulting terms: he questioned her right to call herself a singer and dismissed her as a "street walker" who was "nothing but disgusting." In his years as director of the Opéra-Comique, Carré surely received many crank letters like this one. What is perhaps unusual about this letter is the fact that Carré kept it; it must have struck a responsive chord. (The letter is in the collection of the Association de la Régie Théâtrale.)

14. Dumesnil, "Personal Conferences with Debussy," p. 6; the second and fourth paragraphs are translated from excerpts from the letter printed in OCexp, p. 56, no. 248.

15. There is a chronological inconsistency in Leblanc's *Souvenirs:* she placed Debussy's reading of *Pelléas* at the end of 1901 (p. 168), yet reported that the subsequent coaching sessions occurred during the summer of 1901 (p. 177). If these sessions did take place as early as the summer, it was probably after the composer's vacation in Bichain, where he stayed during August and early September.

16. Leblanc, pp. 170–74.

17. Carré, p. 277.

18. Ibid., pp. 255–56.

19. PET, p. 172.

20. Ibid., p. 169.

21. Carré, pp. 279–80. Carré may be transposing events: from Debussy's correspondence, we know that Clément was discussed as a possible Pelléas in 1906.

22. Ibid., p. 280. From the earliest sketches, Debussy seems to have considered Pelléas a tenor's role, notating the part in treble clef and adhering to a range from middle C (Meyer MS, LPm, p. 58, sys. 2, meas. 3) to a high B flat (Bréval MS, fol. 15ᵛ; LPm, p. 118, sys. 3, meas. 1–4). In the published score, the part has the same lower limit and goes up to a high A. This

difference hardly represents an adaptation for a high baritone. The modifications made in the part to accommodate Périer, which were entered by hand in the proof set from which he learned the part (F-Pn, Rés. Vma. 237), were purely for his own use and were not incorporated into the published score. There is no reason to believe that Debussy came to regard Pelléas as a baritone. In fact, that character is specifically described as a tenor in the cast list found in the opening pages of the arrangement of the opera for solo piano, published by Durand in 1907. The tessitura of the role is, of course, problematic, and was discussed at some length by one famous Pelléas in an interview with Jean-Louis Dutronc: "Jacques Jansen: 30 ans de Pelléas" (1977). Jansen pointed out that Périer was actually more a true baritone than a *baryton Martin* and felt that, in granting the role to Périer, Debussy must have "attached primary importance to phrases in the middle and low range." Jansen felt that the first three acts belonged to the normal *baryton Martin,* but that the fourth called for a tenor who, in view of the weight of the orchestral accompaniment, was capable of great power. He pointed out, for example, that in Acts I and II, Pelléas has to sing entire phrases on low C's and D's, but that in Act IV he moves into the tenor range: his melodic lines include high G sharps and he has to hit a high A.

23. Claude Baignères, "Le Cinquantenaire de *Pelléas*" (1952), p. 6.

24. Dufranne's name was sometimes spelled Dufrane, as in the cast list included in the opening page of the *Pelléas* score.

25. *Ménestrel,* 67 (29 December 1901), 414–15. Massenet's *Grisélidis* had been given its première at the Opéra-Comique on 20 November 1901. Messager conducted and Dufranne sang the role of the Marquis de Saluces (Harding, p. 208).

26. André Messager, "Les Premières Représentations de *Pelléas*" (1926), p. 206.

27. DIE, p. 156.

28. F-Pn, 1.a. Carré (A), 51.

29. A notice in *L'Art Moderne,* 22 (19 January 1902), 23, reported: "*Pelléas et Mélisande* . . . has just entered into rehearsals at the Opéra-Comique and will be performed in April. The reading of it which was given last week produced a great impression on the artists." Since rehearsals began on Monday, 13 January, one could suppose that the reading took place during the previous week—the second week of January.

30. Messager, p. 206.

31. Baignères, p. 6.

32. Mary Garden and Louis Biancolli, *Mary Garden's Story* (1951), pp. 61–62. Here and elsewhere, Garden is not trustworthy regarding dates. She placed this reading "just after *La Reine Fiamette* . . . late in 1902." Since the première of *Pelléas* was on 30 April 1902 and that of *La Reine Fiamette* on 23 December 1903, Garden's chronology is hopelessly confused.

33. Baignères, p. 6.

34. Henri Busser, *De Pelléas aux Indes Galantes* (1955), p. 109. Landry's first name was Louis, and not Albert, which is how he was mistakenly identified on the cast page of the *Pelléas* vocal score in the first printing of the original 1902 Fromont edition.

35. The practice of keeping such records was instituted in 1848 by Emile Perrin (Carré, p. 213; see M. Elizabeth C. Bartlet, "Archival Sources for the Opéra-Comique and its *Registres* at the Bibliothèque de l'Opéra," [1983], pp. 121–22). The somewhat sketchy entries in the *livre de bord* reveal who was present at rehearsals and when the rehearsals began; they rarely indicate how long they lasted or what parts of the work were rehearsed.

36. Carré, p. 279. If Messager was involved in the coaching sessions, it was not noted in the *livre de bord.*

37. Garden and Biancolli, pp. 65–66.

38. Carré, p. 279.

39. Garden and Biancolli, pp. 66–67. In Carré's account, the composer's praise was even more extravagant: "Debussy went towards her, took her hands and said, with tears in his eyes, 'You came from the mists of the north to create my music. I feel now that you alone could be my Mélisande'" (p. 279). In a 1943 interview, Mary Garden gave a somewhat different version of her audition: "I auditioned at Carré's. Debussy said nothing. He was seated on a divan, his head in his hands. When I had finished, he did not budge. Then he left." The rest of the story is essentially the same, although the quoted conversations differ in wording (Vaillant, "Deux fois cent ans: Maeterlinck et Debussy" [1962], p. 78).

40. Leblanc, p. 173.

41. Maeterlinck's testimony before the Société des Auteurs, 7 February 1902.

42. US-AUS.

43. Maeterlinck's testimony before the Société des Auteurs, 7 February 1902.

44. Garden and Biancolli, p. 69.

45. The testimony relevant to this case from the meetings of 7, 14, and 21 February 1902 is recorded in the Procès Verbaux of the Society's Committee meetings, Vol. 8 (4 January 1901–8 May 1903), pp. 208–9, 215–17, and 220.

46. PET, p. 174.

47. DIE, p. 140.

48. Leblanc, pp. 174–75.

49. Henry Russell, *The Passing Show* (1926), pp. 208–9.

50. W. D. Halls, *Maurice Maeterlinck: A Study of His Life and Thought* (1960), p. 78.

51. Louis Laloy, *La Musique retrouvée: 1902–1927* (1928; rpt. 1974), p. 99.

52. Halls, p. 77.

53. VAL, p. 223.

54. Aurélien-François Lugné-Poe, *Sous les étoiles* (1933), p. 50.

55. G. and D.-E. Inghelbrecht, *Claude Debussy*, p. 111. In her *Souvenirs*, p. 26, Leblanc dismissed the incident as a simple manifestation of the playwright's hatred for cats!

56. Maurice Maeterlinck, *Le Temple enseveli* (1902), pp. 295–97.

57. Leblanc, p. 167.

58. René Peter noted that "Debussy never mentioned this meeting to me" (PET, p. 175).

59. See chapter 6 for a detailed discussion of the relationship between Debussy's libretto and Maeterlinck's various revisions of his play.

60. Leblanc, p. 176. Was Leblanc really as self-sacrificing as she appears in her memoirs? Lugné-Poe described her very much in control of Maeterlinck during this period: "I hear that the sly

dog is collared, that his bearing has changed, and the new manner that one wants him to adopt suits him as well as ruffles do a piglet!... During the times when I meet him and shake his hand while he is under the control of Mme Leblanc, he is no longer the man that I knew" (*Sous les étoiles*, p. 48). We know that Maeterlinck's actions were entirely on her behalf and wonder to what extent they were also on her instructions.

61.   Godet, "En marge de la marge," p. 179.

62.   On the same day, Carré wrote to Debussy that he had received "an excellent letter from Mirbeau about his friend Maeterlinck" (F-Pn, 1.a. Carré (A), 52).

63.   The role of Monna Vanna was a kind of "consolation prize" for Leblanc after she lost the part of Mélisande. As Lugné-Poe wrote of the production: "In reality, I didn't understand until much later that it was not my friend's work that I had to put on stage, it was his sweetheart!" (*Sous les étoiles*, p. 51).

64.   Octave Mirbeau, "Maurice Maeterlinck," *L'Art Moderne*, 22 (1 June 1902), 188; reprinted from the original article of 27 April. In his closing line of this paragraph, Mirbeau slightly misquotes Arkel's line from the end of Act IV, scene 2.

65.   The program is reproduced in facsimile in André Gauthier, *Debussy. Documents iconographiques* (1952), pl. 76; its text is given in PET, pp. 182–84.

66.   Garden and Biancolli, p. 71.

67.   G. and D.-E. Inghelbrecht, p. 157.

68.   Carré claimed to have been delighted to offer her the role, saying that it was not her talent that he had doubted, merely her suitability for the role of Mélisande (Carré, p. 277). Leblanc recalled the matter differently: "As soon as he [Dukas] asked that I be given the rôle, he met with unyielding opposition from the Opéra-Comique. But with his energetic and loyal nature, everything was simplified; he insisted on me, threatening the management with the withdrawal of his work if I were not the creator of Ariane" (Leblanc, p. 174). The production of *Ariane* represented a temporary reconciliation of Maeterlinck and Carré; after one of the performances, the playwright wrote to the director, thanking him with all his heart for the joy he felt, thanks to Carré, in seeing a text he thought unrealizable come to life (US-AUS).

In 1908, Maeterlinck was again at odds with opera administrations in what was almost a repetition of his conflict with the Opéra-Comique over *Pelléas*. This time the opera was *Monna Vanna*, with music by Henri Février. Again Maeterlinck insisted that Leblanc create the title role, but no opera house would agree to that condition. Carré (on behalf of the Opéra-Comique), the directors of the Théâtre de la Monnaie in Brussels, and Messager and Louis Broussan of the Paris Opéra all refused to present the opera if they were required to accept Leblanc as well; the Paris Opéra claimed it could not use any artists outside of its own company. Février finally decided to give the work to the Paris and Brussels Operas without insisting on Leblanc, and Maeterlinck tried to stop the former production by suing the company. His suit made no mention of Leblanc, but claimed that the Paris Opéra House was too large for his work (*New York Times*, 6 December 1908, pt. 3, p. 2). *Monna Vanna* opened at the Paris Opéra in January 1909, and Maeterlinck failed in his attempt to stop the production by injunction. In its decision, the court sided with neither composer nor librettist, but decided that the agreement both had made with the publisher Heugel gave the latter complete authority (story dated 25 March in *Musical America*, 3 April 1909, p. 18).

69.   Carré, p. 274.

70. Russell, pp. 160–65. Russell described Leblanc's artistry in rather unflattering terms: "... never at any time was she a great actress, and I am compelled to say that her singing was pitiable. The quality of her voice was harsh, her intonation defective, and she knew nothing whatever about music" (p. 207). Olin Downes, writing of her Boston Mélisande, was more tactful: "Mme Maeterlinck would probably not profess to be a singer. As she happily phrases it, she 'intones' the text of her husband.... She 'intoned' in the most beautiful and finished French, and often with an eloquence denied those of greater vocal ability. Her impersonation was conspicuous for its novelty, its decorative and atmospheric quality" (*Musical America*, 20 January 1912, p. 2). Ironically, Leblanc may not have been Russell's first choice for the role of Mélisande; an August 1911 magazine article reported: "Boston hopes to receive a visit from Debussy next season, when his *Pelléas et Mélisande* will be produced by Manager Russell. An attempt is being made also to secure Mme. Carré for the part of Mélisande" (*Metronome*, 26, no. 8 [August 1911], p. 55). Marguerite Carré had assumed the role at the Opéra-Comique in the 1910–11 season, replacing Maggie Teyte.

71. The rest of the cast included Alfred Maguenat (Pelléas), Hector Dufranne (Golaud), Gustave Huberdeau (Arkel), Maria Claessens (Geneviève), Dora de Phillippe (Yniold), and Constantin Nicolay (the Doctor); Marcel Charlier conducted.

72. Garden and Biancolli, p. 116.

73. VAL, p. 223.

74. *New York Sun*, 28 January 1920.

75. Halls, p. 78. According to Mary Garden, she and Georgette Leblanc had long since reconciled their differences. (After all, Leblanc's conflict had been primarily with Carré.) Garden told a reporter in 1908: "Mme Leblanc is charming. She came to see me many times as Mélisande, and we are the best of friends." (*New York Times*, 10 February 1908, p. 9). Leblanc, in her second volume of memoirs (*La Machine à courages: Souvenirs* [1947], pp. 41–43), described hearing Garden sing *Monna Vanna* in New York; while their backstage meeting was very cordial, it is clear that Leblanc still harbored some lingering resentment.

Chapter 4

1. The only Sunday rehearsal was on 26 January at 3:30 p.m., when Gerville-Réache worked with Landry. Perhaps this exception was necessary due to her late start; she began her "lessons" only three days earlier, on Thursday, 23 January, while the other had begun on the 13th.

2. Messager, p. 207.

3. Garden and Biancolli, p. 66.

4. Carré's mise-en-scène for *Pelléas* has been published by Durand; a copy was exhibited in the 1942 Exposition Debussy (OCexp, p. 57, no. 259). Several manuscript copies of the mise-en-scène are in the Bibliothèque de l'Association de la Régie Théâtrale (formerly l'Association des Régisseurs des Théâtres français), housed in the Bibliothèque Historique de la Ville de Paris: P.4.II appears to be Carré's original mise-en-scène and contains lighting and curtain cues and other instructions that are missing from P.4.I and P.4.III, both of which appear to be fair copies made from P.4.II; P.4.III seems to be equivalent to the mise-en-scène published by Durand. Rec. fact. Mes 4 is a copy of the printed libretto (Paris, Fasquelle, n.d.) but with the mise-en-scène handwritten on interleaved pages; it was included in the 1962 Debussy exhibition (BNexp, p. 44, no. 142), and a page of it was reproduced as plate 6 in Cohen, "Les livrets de mise en scène et la Bibliothèque de l'Association de la Régie Théâtrale" (1978).

5. Garden and Biancolli, p. 68.

6. Carré, p. 277.

7. Busser, *De Pelléas aux Indes Galantes*, p. 111.

8. Busser, "La Création de *Pelléas et Mélisande*" (1966), p. 275.

9. Busser, *De Pelléas*, p. 109.

10. DIE, p. 139; a different reading of the same letter is given in LOU1, p. 167.

11. *New York Times*, 26 June 1910, pt. 3, p. 5.

12. Henry Prunières, Robert Godet, and Léon Vallas, "Autour de Debussy" (June 1934), p. 24.

13. Godet, "En marge," p. 177.

14. Prunières, Godet, and Vallas, p. 24.

15. GOD, p. 185. A copyist supplied the text and vocal parts in portions of the manuscript full score: F-Pn, MS 964 (Act IV), fols. 55–87 and MS 965 (Act V), all fols. except 19 and part of 41. This evidence supports Godet's recollection that Debussy was racing to meet a deadline.

16. Messager, p. 207.

17. Godet, "En marge," p. 178.

18. Maurice Emmanuel, *Pelléas et Mélisande de Debussy* (1950), p. 45.

19. Busser, "Souvenirs de jeunesse sur Claude Debussy" (1942), p. vii.

20. Messager, p. 207.

21. Busser, *De Pelléas*, p. 111.

22. Ibid.

23. Carré, p. 276.

24. Apparently Jusseaume was famous for his forests; see LCr, p. 85.

25. Photographs of the décors are reproduced in LCD, pl. 62–71; *Le Théâtre*, No. 84 (June 1902), pp. 1–21; and *L'Art du Théâtre*, 2 (July 1902), 139–40, and (August 1902), 155–59 (pp. 156 and 159 contain sketches of three décors by Ronsin). The photographs in these publications illustrate all of the décors except "the vaults beneath the castle" (Act III, scene 2); however, photographs of this set were listed in two Debussy exhibition catalogues: OCexp, p. 59, no. 283, and BNexp, p. 45, no. 147; it is in the latter that the décor is attributed to Ronsin. Bianchini's drawings of some of the costumes are reproduced in Maurice Boucher, *Claude Debussy* (1930), pl. 30, and others appeared in the program book for the Royal Opera (Covent Garden) production of *Pelléas* (1978). Photographs of the original cast in costume are also contained in Boucher (pl. 31–32) and in the three publications listed at the beginning of this note.

26. Margaret G. Cobb, "Debussy in Texas" (1977), p. 46, and LL, p. 114 (the latter with a serious omission).

27. Carré, p. 277.

28. PET, p. 180.

29. The sketch is reproduced in PET, opp. p. 184, and in Gauthier, *Debussy. Documents iconographiques* (1952), pl. 82.

30. The *livre de bord* does not actually specify *Pelléas* for 27 March; the entry merely indicates that décors were brought on stage and that Messrs. Ronsin and Marteau were supervising.

31. Carré, p. 229.

32. Pierre Lalo, *La Musique 1898–1899* (n.d.), pp. 66–67.

33. Messager, p. 207. Although it is not conclusive evidence that this was his original intention, as Messager claimed, the vocal score of *Pelléas* does not contain the curtain cues that later appeared in the published full score. (These cues were, in fact, added by Messager in the manuscript full score.)

34. Ibid., pp. 207–8. Mary Garden recalled that during rehearsals, Debussy "was always making changes in those interludes" (Garden and Biancolli, p. 68). In a letter to René Peter (PET, p. 194), Carré stated: "Since it seemed risky to me to present the twelve tableaux [actually, thirteen] separated by intermissions necessary for changing the sets, I proposed to Debussy that he combine the tableaux into groups of three, linked by musical interludes, and with only four intermissions. It was during rehearsals that I asked him to write these interludes, and it was then that he composed them." Carré's recollection is only partially correct. Debussy's acts were not arbitrary groupings of three tableaux each (Acts III and IV have four scenes each, while Act V has only one); rather, they followed the act structure of Maeterlinck's play. Furthermore, Debussy decided very early, long before there was a question of performances at the Opéra-Comique, to connect the scenes within an act with orchestral interludes. These interludes are evident in the earliest surviving draft of Act II (Meyer MS), which dates from June–July 1895. Debussy even wrote above the interlude that connects the second and third scenes: "pour enchaîner (?) avec la S[cène] 3" ("to link up with scene 3") (Act II, fol. 17; LPm, p. 45).

35. Busser, *De Pelléas,* pp. 112–15, 119, and 123–24.

36. In his article "La Création de *Pelléas et Mélisande,*" p. 275, Busser assigned the events here ascribed to 6, 7, and 9 April to the 2nd of that month. According to the *livre de bord,* the first run-through with the sets was on 8 April!

37. Samazeuilh, "La Première Version inédite de 'En sourdine'" (1942), p. 34.

38. Raymond Bouyer, "'Pelléas et Mélisande' ou le Crépuscule du drame musical" (1902), pp. 278–79. Another critic, August Mangeot, provided this confirmation in *Le Monde Musical* (15 May 1902): [The orchestra] did not even seem to perceive that the curtain had fallen and continued to play while the décor was changed, smoothly and without sudden stops" (VAL. p. 236).

39. M.-D. Calvocoressi, "Pelléas et Mélisande" (1902), p. 157.

40. Busser, *De Pelléas,* p. 103.

41. Ibid., pp. 112–13.

42. *Le Ménestrel,* 68 (23 March 1902), 95, and (6 April 1902), 111.

43. DIE, pp. 141–42.

44. Garden and Biancolli, p. 68, mention forty orchestra rehearsals, but no more than twenty can be accounted for in the *livre de bord.*

45. "Bone for Critics in Next New Opera," *New York Times,* 10 February 1908, p. 9.

46. Garden and Biancolli, p. 68.

47. Dated January 1909, in "Original Autograph Letters, Poems, Manuscript Music, etc., written by some of the world's most illustrious people as expressions of their sympathy with Italy in the terrible calamity that befell her by the earthquakes at Messina and Reggio, December 1908" (US-CAh, fMS Ital 75, fol. 105; cited by permission of the Houghton Library).

48. Adolphe Aderer, "A propos des Répétitions générales" (1902), p. 4.

49. DIE, p. 143. A ticket to the dress rehearsal issued to Mme Ernest Chausson, the composer's widow, was included in the 1962 Debussy exhibition (BNexp, p. 44, no. 137).

50. Busser, *De Pelléas*, p. 113.

51. Messager, p. 208.

52. Carré, pp. 280–81.

53. René Peter, "Ce que fut la 'Générale' de *Pelléas et Mélisande*" (1942), p. 9.

54. Busser, *De Pelléas*, p. 113.

55. Messager, p. 208.

56. Camille Bellaigue, "Revue musicale. Théâtre de l'Opéra-Comique: *Pelléas et Mélisande*" (1902), p. 451.

57. Jean Marnold, "*Pelléas et Mélisande*" (1902), p. 802.

58. Godet, "En marge," p. 179.

59. Carré, p. 281.

60. Busser, "La Création de *Pelléas*," p. 277.

61. Baignères, p. 6.

62. Messager, p. 208.

63. Garden and Biancolli, p. 70.

64. Pasteur Vallery-Radot, "Claude Debussy: Souvenirs" (1938), pp. 390–91.

65. Carré, p. 281.

66. Messager, pp. 208–9.

67. Baignères, p. 6.

68. Carré, p. 281.

69. Ibid., p. 282.

70. Busser, *De Pelléas*, p. 114.

71. Busser, "La Création de *Pelléas*," p. 276.

72. Busser, "A propos du cinquantenaire de 'Pelléas et Mélisande' de Claude Debussy: Souvenirs" (1952), p. 536.

73. Paul Souday, "Revue musicale. Opéra-Comique. *Pelléas et Mélisande*" (1902), p. 482.

74. Camille Mauclair, "*Pelléas et Mélisande*" (1902), p. 331. Mauclair misquoted Golaud's line, "Je n'attache aucune importance à cela," as "Au reste, tout cela est sans importance."

75. PET, p. 191.

76. DIE, pp. 151–52.

77. Prunières, Godet, and Vallas, p. 24.

78. ORL, p. 82. This letter, dated "Monday," was kindly communicated to me by both Margaret G. Cobb and Robert Orledge. It may be in reply to Adolphe Jullien's review of *Pelléas* in the 16 May 1902 issue of *Journal des Débats,* and may thus date from 19 May.

79. Adolphe Jullien, "Revue musicale. Opéra-Comique: *Pelléas et Mélisande*" (1902), p. 937.

80. Souday, p. 482.

81. Carré, p. 282.

82. Prunières, Godet, and Vallas, p. 24.

83. PET, p. 166.

84. Ibid., p. 186.

85. Peter, "Ce que fut la 'Générale' de *Pelléas*," p. 9.

86. Prunières, Godet, and Vallas, p. 24.

87. Godet, "En marge," pp. 180–81. Mary Garden told yet a third story: that Debussy, having left the hall, was found late at night at the Café Riche, sitting sadly, with a beer and an ashtray overflowing with half-smoked cigarettes in front of him (Garden, *Souvenirs de "Mélisande"* [1962], p. 8).

88. Laloy, *La Musique retrouvée,* p. 100. The entire practice of having public dress rehearsals for the benefit of critics was being questioned in Paris during the 1901–02 season, and in May, shortly after the première of *Pelléas,* the directors of Paris theaters, with the approval of the "Société des Auteurs," decided to abolish them. This action apparently had nothing to do with the *Pelléas* incident (which seemed to be an isolated occurrence), but was rather an attempt to curb the high failure rate of new productions during that season, which the directors blamed on these events. (See Aderer, "A propos des Répétitions générales.")

89. DIE, p. 149.

90. BNexp, p. 44, no. 138.

91. Busser, *De Pelléas,* p. 114.

92. Vallery-Radot, *Tel était Claude Debussy* (1958), p. 48.

93. DIE, p. 149.

94. Emmanuel, p. 64.

95. According to the *livre de bord,* the usual starting time for evening performances was 8:15; that of the *Pelléas* première was listed as 8:30, but 8:35 (presumably the actual starting time) was added in parentheses.

96. Busser, *De Pelléas,* p. 114.

97. Messager, p. 209.

98. Carré, p. 281.

99. Claude Abravanel, *Claude Debussy: A Bibliography* (1974), p. 111, offers an index to some of the reviews of the première. Excerpts from some of these reviews are found in VAL, pp. 228–41, and DIE, pp. 150–52. Minkoff has announced a forthcoming volume of reviews and articles pertaining to the *Pelléas* premières (in various countries) in a series titled "Dossiers de Presse" (*Musique et Musicologie,* Septième Catalogue général, 1983, pp. 5–6).

100. Emmanuel, p. 64.

101. Messager, p. 209.

102. Busser, *De Pelléas,* p. 115.

103. Emmanuel, p. 64.

104. Busser, *De Pelléas,* p. 115.

105. Messager, p. 209. By mistakenly assigning to 1902 a letter from Messager to Carré of 9 March 1919, Henri Borgeaud wrongly assumed that Messager was actually in London on 9 March 1902, in the middle of the *Pelléas* rehearsals, and concluded, again mistakenly, that Messager was not sure that he would be able to conduct the première (Messager, "Lettres d'André Messager à Albert Carré" [1962], p. 101).

106. Busser, *De Pelléas,* p. 110.

107. Marguerite Long, *At the Piano with Debussy* (1972), p. 4.

108. Busser pasted the "bulletin" on the inside cover of the copy of the *Pelléas* vocal score given him by Debussy (F-Po, Rés. 2156).

109. Busser, *De Pelléas,* p. 116.

110. In this letter, Debussy mistakenly ascribed the rehearsal to Thursday and the performance to Friday, causing editor Jean André-Messager to assign the events of 7 and 8 May to the 1st and 2nd of that month.

111. Busser, *De Pelléas,* p. 116.

112. Emmanuel, p. 64.

113. Busser, *De Pelléas,* pp. 116–17.

114. Ibid., p. 117. The score is in the Bibliothèque de l'Opéra, Rés. 2156.

115. Carlton Lake, *Baudelaire to Beckett* (1976), pp. 64–65, no. 159.

116. OCexp, p. 58, no. 275.

117. DIE, p. 158.

118. F-Pn, l.a. Debussy (C), 13. Number 40, rue d'Anjou was the address of Fromont's shop. The postscript of this letter ("My best wishes to Madame, your mother") indicates that Debussy was already acquainted with the woman who was to become his second wife—Emma Bardac.

119. Prunières, Godet, and Vallas, p. 191.

120. See James J. Fuld, *The Book of World-Famous Music: Classical, Popular, and Folk* (1967), pp. 18–19. The Durand archival records reveal that the date of the copyright deposit sometimes coincided with the printing date; more usually, though, the copyright deposit followed the printing, often by about a month. Of course, the practice at Fromont may have differed from that at Durand.

121.   RLS, p. 82.

122.   Arthur Pougin, "Semaine théâtrale. Opéra-Comique. *Pelléas et Mélisande*" (1902), p. 139.

123.   DIE, p. 158.

124.   Emmanuel, p. 64.

125.   Though misdated by the editor, the correct date was determined on the basis of the letter's contents.

126.   Busser, *De Pelléas*, p. 118.

127.   Debussy expressed his gratitude privately as well as publicly. Thus he wrote on 8 May 1902 to Henry Bauër, critic for *Le Figaro:* "Thank you for your fine article on *Pelléas.* You can never know what a mighty relief it was for me amidst so much hateful stupidity" (LL, p. 114). On 13 May he thanked Dukas for the latter's review in *Chronique des Arts et de la Curiosité* of 10 May: "I thank you with all my heart—may I say, fraternally? Someone once said, 'to understand is to equal.' Never has this found itself to be more completely justified than in your 'essay' on *Pelléas!* It was, besides, purely natural, but I find in it the renewed opportunity for a joyous and sincere pride" (*Autographes musicaux,* sale of 20 June 1977 [Paris: Pierre Berès], no. 96).

128.   LCr, p. 9.

129.   DIE, p. 151.

130.   Pierre Lalo, " 'Pelléas et Mélisande' à l'Opéra-Comique (Mai 1902)," in *De Rameau à Ravel* (1947), p. 401. Lalo's article began: "The Opéra-Comique has presented a work of singular novelty and beauty. It has been received, as it naturally had to be, with surprise, scandal, raillery, and hostility." He compared the criticisms made of *Pelléas* to those made previously of *Tannhäuser, Carmen, Don Giovanni,* and *Hippolyte et Aricie,* and bluntly declared Debussy's opera superior to the recent operas of d'Indy and Charpentier: "Precious in and of itself: it is more novel than *Fervaal* and more beautiful than *Louise,* also more novel. Precious for its impact on our music: because, although I do not desire that others imitate the method of M. Debussy, the performance of his work could encourage young composers to emancipate themselves from the tyranny of Wagnerism, to conceive and to create with greater freedom" (pp. 401-2).

131.   Emmanuel, p. 64.

132.   This singer's name is variously spelled Delorn, Deloru (?), and Delory in the *livre de bord,* Deloris in OCexp, p. 59, and Delory and Delorn-Caire in Busser's copy of the *Pelléas* vocal score (handwritten annotations by Busser).

133.   A notice in *L'Art Moderne,* 22 (15 June 1902), 206, reported that more than one hundred people had to be turned away from the sold-out performance of 6 June.

134.   Messager, "Lettres d'André Messager à Albert Carré," p. 102 (F-Pn, l.a. Messager (A), 12). This letter contains the following unpublished passage: "We have had the good luck to come upon an extraordinary Italian tenor—Caruso. What a pity that he doesn't sing in French. His is certainly the most beautiful voice that I have ever heard." Even if Caruso had sung in French, it is doubtful that Messager would have considered him for the role of Pelléas!

135.   Ibid. (F-Pn, l.a. Messager (A), 13).

136.   DUR, p. 6 (letter, in Coll. Durand, published with some omissions).

137. Messager, "Lettres d'André Messager à Albert Carré," p. 103 (F-Pn. l.a. Messager (A), 14). Albert Vizentini was stage director of the Opéra-Comique.

138. Calvocoressi, "Pelléas et Mélisande," p. 157. The suppressed scene was Act IV, scene 3: Yniold's scene with the little sheep.

139. Messager,"Lettres d'André Messager à Albert Carré," p. 103 (F-Pn, l.a. Messager (A), 14).

140. Paul Dukas, "Opéra-Comique: reprise de *Pelléas et Mélisande*" (1902), p. 273. Act IV, scene 3 was not retained by the Opéra-Comique for very long. Lawrence Gilman, in his *Debussy's Pelléas et Mélisande* (1907), p. 39, noted that the scene was no longer included in their performances. The cut was eventually marked in later printings of the 1907 Durand vocal score.

141. Coll. Maurice Gendron. The letter is undated, but since the stationery bears the printed address "80, avenue du Bois de Boulogne," it could not have been written before 1908. Gheusi, the addressee, assumed the directorship of the Opéra-Comique (in conjunction with the Isola brothers) in January 1914, and *Pelléas* was performed during his directorship only between 3 and 26 June 1914. The first paragraph of the letter is as follows:

> In spite of my willingness, I cannot find the proper wording for the letter that you have asked me to write. Besides, let me assure you that I would have to combine the sureness of Pascal with the ingenuity of M. de Talleyrand, and I would still be wrong! It is a fact which is as certain as it is melancholy.

A remark in Gheusi's memoirs may help to explain this somewhat obscure paragraph. In his *Cinquante ans de Paris: Mémoires d'un témoin (1889–1938)* (1939), p. 221, Gheusi wrote of his revival of *Pelléas*, "where the poor and great Debussy went through mortal agony without daring to give me grounds publicly against the female lead. His notes, confidential and despairing, were my compensation for it, and I did not hand them over to the press." Perhaps the letter to Gheusi quoted above is one of those very letters in which Debussy expressed his inability to make a public statement against the female lead—presumably Marguerite Carré, wife of Albert Carré, who had sung the part of Mélisande at the Opéra-Comique since the 1910–11 season, including the performances of June 1914. In his *Souvenirs* (pp. 360 and 401–2), Carré recounted how, in leaving the Opéra-Comique to become director of the Comédie-Française, he had requested that Gheusi serve as codirector with the Isola brothers, who had already been appointed as his successors. Carré's only condition was that his wife maintain her position in the company, and Gheusi agreed to this. However, starting in February 1914, Gheusi began taking away her roles and eventually forced her to resign.

Although Debussy had written Mme Carré a highly complimentary letter on 19 February 1911, the day after her first public appearance as Mélisande ("Permit me to join the public which honored you last night. Thanks to you, the touching and fleeting charm of poor little Mélisande has recovered its power"), he had more recently been quite critical of her portrayal, writing to Robert Godet on 18 January 1913: "Madame Carré brings to bear a fierce zeal to make Mélisande a sort of melancholy laundress" (GOD, p. 134). Did Gheusi try to get Debussy to issue a public statement to that effect in order to justify his own actions against her? Was Debussy unable to satisfy Gheusi's request out of loyalty to Albert Carré? Or was Gheusi perhaps merely trying to use the composer in his intrigue against Mme Carré?

After the June 1914 performances of *Pelléas*, the opera was not performed at the Opéra-Comique until 9 May 1919, towards the end of the first postwar season. By this time, Debussy was dead and Albert Carré had returned as director of the Opéra-Comique; not surprisingly, Mélisande was sung by Marguerite Carré.

142. In the album notes for his recording of *Pelléas* (CBS, M3 30119), Pierre Boulez justified his decision to cast a child as Yniold on both vocal and dramatic grounds, even though "on two or three occasions the voice risks being submerged in the sonority of the orchestra." Naturally this problem is easily corrected on records, but in the performances of *Pelléas* that I attended at the Metropolitan Opera (James Levine conducting, 27 February 1978) and the New York City Opera (Julius Rudel conducting, 8 October 1978), both of which featured young Robert Sapolsky as Yniold, there was no danger of the boy being drowned out; Sapolsky's voice proved more penetrating than some of his elders'.

Chapter 5

1. The 1898 *Petit Dictionnaire Guide* published by Paris Hachette gave the following cost estimates for publishing music (p. 859):

    Cost of Setting Up: The engraving done on tin plates generally costs 2 to 3 fr. per plate for piano scores and 2 fr. 25 to 3 fr. 25 per plate for vocal scores. These prices vary according to the size of the engraving style used and the difficulty of the work; the tin costs between 0 fr. 90 and 2 fr. per plate (varying with the market price).

    The design of the title-page is done on stone or on zinc and costs generally between 20 and 25 fr., stone or zinc not included. A medium stone costs 3 fr.; zinc, 1 fr.

    Net Cost: A composition of 4 pages generally costs 60 fr. for 100 copies. Tin, engraving, paper, printing, 40 fr; title page and stone, 20 to 25 fr. An operetta score comes to 1500 or 2000 fr. for 500 copies; an opera score, 3000 fr., or in a deluxe edition, 4000 fr.

    Royalties: For dramatic works, the publisher does not receive any royalties; however, he rents out the orchestra parts, which are not sold.

    The figure of 3000 francs for printing 500 copies of an opera full score, aside from being four years out of date in 1902, does not include the cost of printing the parts, which Fromont included when he gave an estimate of 5500–6000 francs. Fromont's later estimate of 3500 francs for the score alone, however, is very close to that suggested in the *Guide*.

2. The new estimate, for the score alone, suggests that Debussy may have abandoned, for the time being, his original plan of publishing the parts as well. In any case, the present estimate enabled him to reduce the projected subscription price from 100 to 80 francs. When the score was finally published two years later, the cover price was 150 francs, slightly higher than the 125 franc nonsubscription price mentioned in the 9 June letter to Messager.

3. Debussy made allusion to the invitation in a letter to Messager dated "Wednesday, 8 July 1902." (Actually, Wednesday was the 9th.) In the letter Debussy described his plan to take the train on Saturday evening and arrive in London on Sunday, the 13th.

4. Debussy may actually have begun these activities the day before; the *livre de bord* entry for 17 September omitted the names of the coaches at the "lessons" of Dumesnil and Rigaux.

5. Dukas, "Opéra-Comique: reprise de *Pelléas et Mélisande*," p. 273.

6. Emmanuel, p. 65.

7. F-Pn, Mus W. 46 (78).

8. In an interview dated 17 June 1910 and published in the *New York Times* of 26 June 1910 (pt. 3, p. 5), Debussy stated that, although he could not compose regularly, "Of course, I can work out the instrumentation of a piece at almost any time. . . . " The conditions of June 1903 apparently put that claim to the test.

9. A correcting hand in addition to the composer's is apparent in those portions of the Lehman proofs (Lehman deposit, US-NYpm) that represent the first proofs (Acts III–V).

10. Called *Rapsodie orientale* in a letter of 8 June 1903 to Messager and *Rapsodie arabe* in a letter of early July 1903 to Louÿs, the work was titled *Rhapsodie mauresque pour orchestre et saxophone principal* in the draft dated 1901–8 in the Library of the New England Conservatory of Music; the work was commissioned by Elisa Hall of Boston. (See VAL, pp. 283–84.)

11. LOU3, p. 35.

12. In a closing paragraph, Debussy wrote in part: "it is raining and we are not very good at walking in wooden shoes, which makes strolling impossible." These meteorological conditions may have contributed to the inspiration of "Jardins sous la pluie," the third of the *Estampes,* which were written in July 1903. Gaby Dupont and J.-E. Blanche, however, have pointed to other instances of precipitation as the primary motivating factors. (See LCat, p. 105.)

13. In fact, the first performances of Debussy's opera outside of Paris did take place at the Monnaie in Brussels, but it was not until 9 January 1907 and the Mélisande was Mary Garden. Debussy remembered Lucy Foreau, however, when a cast was being chosen for the La Scala première of *Pelléas* (in Italian). He wrote to Durand on 20 July 1907, wondering why Giulio Gatti-Casazza, the director of La Scala, hadn't considered Lina Cavalieri for the part of Mélisande. He went on to recall that Madame Foreau-Isnardon had originally been chosen to sing the role in Brussels and thought that she could be considered for the Italian première (DUR, p. 49). If in fact she was considered, she again lost out, this time to Cesira Ferrani.

14. Emmanuel, p. 65.

15. See Margaret G. Cobb, *Discographie de l'oeuvre de Claude Debussy* (1975), pp. 23 and 80–81. The *Pelléas* excerpt has been reissued on French EMI "Hommage à Claude Debussy" (OVD 49.323) and in the U.S. on "Landmarks of Recorded Pianism, Vol. 1" (IPA/Desmar 117). Shortly before the première of *Pelléas,* René Peter made a wax cylinder recording of Debussy singing and playing the "Death of Mélisande"; repeated playing unfortunately wore out this precious document (PET, p. 198).

16. LOU1, p. 178.

17. Garden and Biancolli, p. 234.

18. The 1972 Coulet-Faure *Spectacles* sale catalogue listed (no. 1045, p. 175) proof pages 65–68 of the *Pelléas* full score, "containing some autograph corrections by the composer (in red ink)." These proofs have not surfaced since their sale, but it seems unlikely that they would have been part of a conductor's score, which would have been bound. Their very existence, however, suggests that Debussy's revisions of the *Pelléas* score were probably not quite as systematic as this reconstruction of events suggests.

19. LCat, p. 89, identifies these proofs as a corrected score, formerly owned by Pierre Monteux.

20. The date of the copyright deposit is indicated in the Durand archives: Livre de cotages, No. 3, entry for plate no. 6577.

21. A first edition of the full score, formerly belonging to the Opéra-Comique and currently in the Copyists' Office (Service de la Copie) of the Paris Opéra, may be the very score used for these and subsequent performances at the Opéra-Comique. This score, which shows signs of considerable wear, bears the annotations of many conductors and has clearly weathered numerous seasons of performances. The fact that the score is a first edition points to its early use; the original Fromont edition of 1904 was superseded the following year by the Durand edition of 1905.

22. LCat, pp. 107 and 109.

23. DUR, p. 19.

24. DIE, p. 179.

25. LCat, pp. 110–11 and 114.

26. The postscript reads: "You will have the *Suite bergamasque* on Saturday."

27. One copy is in the Durand archives and another belonged to the late Mme de Tinan. The latter appeared in BNexp, p. 46, no. 155.

28. Jacques Durand, *Quelques souvenirs d'un editeur de musique* (1924–25), vol. 1, pp. 4 and 121. The "contrat de cession" for *Ariane* had been signed by Dukas, Maeterlinck, and Durand seven weeks before, on 10 February 1905.

29. VAL, p. 295.

30. Victor I. Seroff, *Debussy: Musician of France* (1956), p. 233.

31. Oscar Thompson, *Debussy: Man and Artist* (1937; rpt. 1967), pp. 154–55. According to Thompson, Emma's annuity money "soon stopped flowing."

32. A letter written by Debussy on 27 July 1916 (less than two years before his death) mentions a lawsuit recently brought against him by Lilly, who is identified only by her initials, R.T., for Rosalie Texier (US-NYpm).

Chapter 6

1. See ORL for detailed accounts of these as well as Debussy's other theatrical projects.

2. A publication date of 4 May 1892 is given in OCexp, p. 39. Georges Hermans, *Les Premières Armes de Maurice Maeterlinck* (1967), p. 111, gives June 1892, but elsewhere (p. 91) cites a letter dated May 1892 in which the painter Maurice Denis mentions reading the play.

3. Unable to locate a copy of the fifth edition, M.G. Lorphèvre, Director of the Centre National de Bibliographie (Mundaneum), suggested that it was printed, but without an edition number (Hermans, *Les Premières Armes*, p. 50). If this were the case, the first and fifth editions would be indistinguishable.

4. Joseph Hanse, "Bibliographie," in *Maurice Maeterlinck: 1862–1962*, ed. Joseph Hanse and Robert Vivier (1962), p. 527.

5. Maurice Maeterlinck, *Théâtre*, vol. 1 (1901), pp. I–II.

6. Aurélien-François Lugné-Poe, *Le Sot du tremplin* (1930), pp. 238-39. The published letter mistakenly cites page 12 instead of 72.

7. Georges Hermans, "Les Cinq Chansons de Mélisande" (1971), p. 68.

8. *La Plume,* no. 100 (15 June 1893), pp. 282-83.

9. For the differences among the readings, see Hermans, *Les Premières Armes,* p. 50, or Hermans, "Les Cinq Chansons de Mélisande," p. 68.

10. Lugné-Poe, p. 239.

11. See LCr, pp. 61 and 267-68.

12. OCexp, p. 40, no. 130.

13. In the case of a subsequent operatic project, *La Chute de la Maison Usher,* such an annotated printed source survives: Debussy's copy of Baudelaire's translation of Poe's short story (Paris, Bibliothèque Nationale, Rés. Vmd. 41). Here, of course, the translation itself was not Debussy's libretto, but rather served as the basis for it. For a commentary on the annotations, see ORL, pp. 319 and 355.

14. Debussy's replacement of "au bord *au* clair de lune" with "au bord *du* clair de lune" was the correction of an obvious error in Maeterlinck's text, one which the playwright himself corrected in the 1898 edition of his play (p. 116).

15. LL, p. 60.

16. Anne Schillings's study of Maeterlinck's notebooks for *Pelléas* ("La Genèse de *Pelléas et Mélisande*" [1970]), shows that the playwright also eliminated characters in writing the play: he considered including a number of secondary characters—Mélisande's parents, her nurse, Pelléas's sisters, and his twin brother (who acts as an observer of his twin's actions)—but he abandoned them quickly (pp. 130-31).

17. Pierre Boulez, "*Pelléas* Reflected" (1970).

18. The handling of the servants and of elements of the external world has proved an area of experimentation in some recent productions of the opera. In Jorge Lavelli's 1977 production for the Paris Opéra, the servants appeared throughout the opera to change the scenery during the musical interludes which separate the scenes. According to the director, they function as "silent and distant witnesses to situations which they ritually prepare." André Delvaux, in his 1984 production for the Brussels Opera, went even further, and introduced a team of "operatives" who acted throughout as agents of destiny and witnesses of fate, "setting Mélisande on her course" and "collecting" her at its close. Delvaux also eliminated one "outsider" by having Yniold sing the Shepherd's line (Act IV, scene 3), as if playing a game. See Alain Lanceron, ed., "Jorge Lavelli: 'Pour échapper à la loi du Château,'" (1977), p. 106, and Paul Griffiths, "Maeterlinck's bluff is called at last," *London Times,* 26 January 1984, p. 9.

19. Translations of passages from *Pelléas* are my own adaptations of Richard Hovey's translation of the play in Maurice Maeterlinck, *The Plays of Maurice Maeterlinck* (Chicago, 1896).

20. LOC, I: 191. Debussy's delight at the prospect of the reinstatement of the scene is revealed in a letter of 29 August 1902 from Messager to Carré. See chapter 4 above.

21. For more complete descriptions of these and other sources of *Pelléas,* see chapter 7, the Appendix, and ORL, pp. 309-12.

22. Virgil Thomson, *The Musical Scene* (1945), p. 165. Thomson's analysis of the character of Mélisande, in this review of a 1944 performance of *Pelléas,* is at once witty and profound.

23. James R. McKay, in his article "The Bréval Manuscript: New Interpretations" (1977), pp. 9–15, discusses possible textual and musical motivations for Debussy's revisions of Pelléas's monologue.

24. In the NEC MS, Debussy first wrote "Nous sommes venus ici il y a de longs mois," obviously confusing it with Pelléas's line in the next speech, "Oui... oui... il y a de long mois." He realized his mistake and corrected it.

25. RLS, p. 80.

26. The fact that Act IV, scene 3 was omitted during the first season is immaterial to the present discussion. Debussy's instructions for the transition between scenes 1 and 2 were not followed in Albert Carré's mise-en-scène (Bibliothèque de l'Association de la Régie Théâtrale, mise en scène, lyrique, P.4.I–III [three copies]; another volume, Rec. fact. Mes 4, a copy of the printed libretto [Paris: Fasquelle, n.d.] with the mise-en-scène handwritten on interleaved pages, was not available for comparison). Carré directed Pelléas and Mélisande to exit through separate doors at the end of scene 1 and had Mélisande and Arkel enter (through the former's exit door) at the start of scene 2; the curtain was not lowered between the scenes, which constituted a single tableau. Only one copy of the mise-en-scène (P.4.II) adopted the settings listed in Debussy's score for Act IV; the other two divided the act into three tableaux: "Un corridor dans le château" (scenes 1–2), "Une terrasse dans la brume" (scene 3), and "Une fontaine dans le parc" (scene 4). The same division is found in the first edition of the libretto: *Pelléas et Mélisande. Nouvelle édition, modifiée conformément aux représentations de l'Opéra-Comique. Edition spéciale pour la France.* (Brussels: Paul Lacomblez, 1902).

27. The submission of plays and livrets to the Commission of Censorship and the Director of Fine Arts (in his capacity as inspector of theaters) was a formal procedure in this era, and the Archives Nationales in Paris conserve some of the livrets of operas, ballets, and pantomimes (manuscript, typed, or published) that the Opéra-Comique submitted between 1802 and 1906 (F^{18} 690–702). Unfortunately, the libretto of *Pelléas* was not among those preserved. However, other records in the Archives (F^{18}* I 52, no. 3925) indicate that the *Pelléas* libretto was submitted for inspection on 22 April 1902 and was authorized as acceptable on 30 April, the date of the première, presumably after Debussy had accepted the cut or cuts that Roujon demanded. The appearance of the thirty-one Opéra-Comique livrets from the years 1897–1906 preserved in the Archives (F^{18} 702) might suggest that approval was pro forma: for example, parts of Puccini's *La Bohème* (Opéra-Comique première on 28 May 1898) were not even read (some pages of the printed libretto were not cut apart) and Georges Boyer and Lucien Lambert's *La Marseillaise* (première on 14 July 1900) appears not to have been read at all. Only one livret shows signs of the censor's intervention—Gustave Charpentier's *Louise* (première on 2 February 1900)—and the few small changes imposed on this libretto provide a valuable point of comparison with the modifications in *Pelléas* which Debussy was forced to accept. In both cases the censor objected to passages which were risqué. In the following excerpts from *Louise,* the censored portions are in brackets and the substitutions which the censor accepted are in italics:

> Act II, scene 1
> Le Noctambule (à la fillette):
> Ou bien un frais désir
> [Fait-il ouvrir] *fait-il bondir*
> [Les seins amoureux?] *ton coeur d'amoureuse?*

Act III, scene 1
Julien: [Ton cher corps me désire?] *ton cher coeur me désire?*
Louise: [Je veux du plaisir!] *toujours du plaisir!*
Julien: [Prends-moi!] *à moi!*

Act III, scene 2
La Foule: N'en mangez pas, jeun's filles, ça fait [grossir]! *mourir*

Roujon was concerned to eliminate, not just suggestive words, but suggestive actions as well. This fact is revealed in a letter of 15 February 1901 to Pedro Gailhard, director of the Paris Opéra, in connection with a performance of Xavier Leroux's *Astarté*. Roujon insisted that the singers adhere rigorously to the approved text and that they eliminate all suspect gestures (Archives Nationales, F^{21} 4635). Obviously he was not content merely to read the librettos; he must have attended rehearsals and performances to ensure that public morals were upheld.

28. Garden quoted the line this way in her memoirs (Garden and Biancolli, p. 69). Carré's mise-en-scène (P.4.1–III) gives yet another version of this line: "Je suis bien malheureuse... ". The Lacomblez edition of the libretto (1902), like the published scores, retained the original reading of the line. It also observed just one of the seven cuts which were apparently made in the aftermath of the dress rehearsal: it suppressed only the discussion of the bed, the first of the two definitive cuts.

29. François Lesure, *Paul Dukas* (1965), p. 8.

30. *Musical Standard*, 30 (12 December 1908), 384. In this interview, Debussy also reveals that he was composing two operas based on Poe's short stories—"The Fall of the House of Usher" (one act) and "The Devil in the Belfry" (two parts connected by an intermezzo)—and was planning a "Tristan and Isolda" ("Four acts, at least"). With regard to the last, however, he noted: "Feeling as I do the danger of boring one's audiences with long works, I hesitate."

Chapter 7

1. The terms "preliminary" and "developed drafts" were borrowed from the Wagner literature by Carolyn Abbate to discuss the *Pelléas* manuscripts; see her article "*Tristan* in the Composition of *Pelléas*," pp. 124–25.

2. The omission of the text from the sketches is not exclusive to *Pelléas*; it is also true of some of the song sketches, for example, that of the nearly contemporary "De soir" from the *Proses lyriques* (Thierry Bodin sale catalogue, *Manuscrits musicaux*, 14 December 1979, no. 30).

3. Garden and Biancolli, p. 88; Misia Sert, *Misia and the Muses* (1953), p. 37. The Meyer draft of Act IV begins with Pelléas's "song," one-third of the way into the scene. The previous page would have included the mutual declaration of love, and perhaps Lilly kept the earlier part of the draft, which contained this precious moment.

4. Abbate, p. 128.

5. See the partial facsimile and transcription in Abbate, pp. 130–31 and 140.

6. Abbate, p. 129.

7. Lawrence Gilman, *Debussy's "Pelléas et Mélisande." A Guide to the Opera* (1907), p. 78; Emmanuel, *Pelléas et Mélisande de Debussy* (1950), pp. 196–97.

8. Boulez, "*Pelléas* Reflected," n.p.

9. The theme is so named in ORL, p. 88; Gilman (p. 58) called it "The Forest" and Emmanuel (p. 135), "distant times" ("les temps lointains").

10. M.-D. Calvocoressi, "Debussy and the Leitmotive" (1925), p. 696.

11. For a detailed analysis of the *Pelléas* prelude, see Jean-Jacques Nattiez and Louise Hirbour-Paquette, "Analyse musicale et sémiologie à propos du Prélude de *Pelléas*" (1973).

12. See ORL, pp. 73–75.

13. Wallace Goodrich, "The New England Conservatory of Music" (1947), p. 19. The dating is inferred from an inscription inside the front cover of the manuscript: "Transferred to this library from the office safe (Sept. 1911?)."

14. Russell, pp. 160–63.

15. John Grand-Carteret, *Papeterie et papetiers de l'ancien temps* (1913), gives the history of these Parisian paper makers: Maison Gazet (2, rue de Colonnes, later 92, rue de Richelieu), founded in 1795, became Esnault-Gazet in 1811, when Gazet was succeeded by his son-in-law, E. Esnault. Maison Esnault subsequently went through various mergers and name changes—Lard-Esnault (1837–66) and Henri Lard (1866–87)—and was known as H. Lard-Esnault when it subsequently became the property of Edmond Bellamy. On the basis of information contained in the *Annuaire de commerce* (Paris, 1892), Jean-Michel Nectoux concluded that Bellamy acquired the firm in 1891–92. (See Marie Rolf, "Orchestral Manuscripts of Claude Debussy: 1892–1905" [1984], p. 541.) In any case, it seems that Bellamy did not add his name to the firm (and to the company embossment) until 1898; he is listed in the Paris-Hachette *Petite Dictionnaire Guide* for that year but was not listed in the 1897 edition.

16. LAL, p. 26.

17. Folio 17 of Act II, which was only recently restored to the manuscript, was not examined.

18. The dates written in the MS may apply to scene 4 only. We do not know precisely when scenes 1–2 were composed, but the date of composition of scene 3, August 1894, is not listed.

19. Debussy inscribed her copy of the first edition of the *Pelléas* vocal score (no. 7 of the deluxe copies on "papier Japon") with a quotation from Act IV, scene 4: "To Lucienne Bréval, whose voice had passed over the sea in spring... the humble homage of Claude Debussy. February 1903" (F-Pn, Rés. F.1106).

20. LPm reverses the order of these two portions of the manuscript, placing fols. 18–19 before fols. 2–17. The relationship of rectos and versos has been preserved in the facsimile with a single exception: the versos of fols. 16 and 17 (pp. 119 and 120) are both blank; the facsimile prints the two rectos back to back.

21. See McKay, pp. 6–9, and Abbate, pp. 121–22.

22. The Basel MS may be the otherwise unknown manuscript of the beginning of Act IV mentioned by Estrade-Guerra in a note on p. 19 of his article "Les Manuscrits de *Pelléas et Mélisande*" (1957).

23. Stéphane Mallarmé, "Lettres et Autographes" (1952), pp. 102–3. The transcription of the letter erroneously gives the date as "19/3/36"! The actual date is clear from the facsimile of the letter which accompanies the transcription.

24. In FVS, p. 272, sys. 3, meas. 1, Mélisande's fifth note appears as $b\natural^1$ in the first two printings and was subsequently corrected to $c\natural^2$.

25. Abbate, p. 121, expressed, without explanation, the belief that the sketch belongs to *La Chute de la Maison Usher*.

26. This correction also appears in the revised edition of the score, Durand study score (1950) and full score (1966).

27. Two changes, both in Act V, restored the original text of Maeterlinck's play: the word "peux" in Mélisande's "C'est étrange... je ne peux pas lever les bras pour la prendre... " (FVS, p. 271) was corrected to the equivalent "puis" (OS, p. 395), and Golaud's textless sobs (FVS, p. 281) were given the words "oh! oh!" (OS, p. 406). Neither correction was adopted by later editions of the vocal score (see VS, pp. 298 and 307). Debussy also introduced two small changes that caused his text to deviate from the Maeterlinck original: Pelléas's exclamation in Act II, scene 3, "Ah!... voici la clarté!... " (FVS, p. 98) was changed to "Oh!... voici la clarté... " (OS, p. 144), and the word "plus" in Pelléas's "Il me dit que je puis arriver avant elle si je veux, mais qu'il n'y a plus de temps à perdre" (Act I, scene 2; FVS, p. 32) was changed to "pas" (OS, p. 42), changing the end of the sentence from "there is no more time to lose" to "there is no time to lose." In these two cases, the new versions were accepted by later editions of the vocal score (see VS, pp. 111 and 36). Another change altered the verb tense in Arkel's "Pourras-tu choisir entre le père et l'ami?... " (Act I, scene 2; FVS, p. 33); the full score, p. 43, changed the verb to "pourrais," the conditional rather than the future tense, making the question "Could you" and not "Will you choose between father and friend?" Later vocal scores retained the reading of the original, which followed the Maeterlinck play (see VS, p. 36).

28. Pelléas's "Oui, oui, là-bas... " on p. 87 was omitted, as was "Vos che-" from the beginning of Pelléas's line "Vos cheveux ont plongé dans l'eau... " on p. 81—the line was reduced to the nonsensical "Vous ont plongé dans l'eau." On p. 62, meas. 1, the second syllable of "ici" is missing (the note is present), and on p. 200, an extraneous "Ah!" appears in the line "Ah! je respire enfin!... ". Erroneous word substitutions are: "suis" instead of "vis" in Geneviève's "Il y a presque quarante ans que je vis ici" (p. 48), and "la mer" instead of "le mur" in two lines of Pelléas, "C'est là ce que je vois sur le mur?" (p. 155) and "Je ne vois que les branches du saule qui dépasse[nt] le mur... " (p. 162).

29. 10 February 1905 was the date of the "contrat de cession" of Dukas's *Ariane et Barbe-Bleue*. Is the date of the *Pelléas* printing erroneous, somebody at Durand having confused the two Maeterlinck-based operas? A copy of the first Durand edition of *Pelléas*, formerly owned by Nadia Boulanger, is in the Bibliothèque Nationale, Rés. Vma. 221.

30. See Samazeuilh's essay "L'Art de la transcription pianistique" in his *Musiciens de mon temps* (1947), pp. 415–18, for his views on the subject of piano transcriptions. A catalogue of Samazeuilh's transcriptions appears on pp. 419–24 of the same book.

31. This fact did not prevent Erich Leinsdorf from arranging, performing, and recording—with the Cleveland Orchestra on Columbia MM 845 (78 RPM) and ML 4049 (LP), reissued on Columbia Special Products P 14141—a "Suite from *Pelléas et Mélisande*," consisting of prelude, interlude, and postlude materials. Pierre Monteux and John Barbirolli also arranged concert suites drawn principally from these instrumental portions of *Pelléas*. Monteux conducted his suite with the Boston Symphony on 18–19 January 1957, and Barbirolli led his with the New York Philharmonic-Symphony Orchestra on 8–9 December 1938. Barbirolli justified his arrangement: "In the theatre, as soon as the curtain goes down for these interludes people start talking, and you hear the scene-shifters at work.

It struck me that it would be a good thing if people *heard* the music for once in a way."
Lawrence Gilman, reviewing the performance, praised it, noting the advantage of hearing
the music played by a top symphony orchestra rather than the usual opera orchestra. (See
Charles Reid, *John Barbirolli: A Biography,* pp. 184–86.)

32. The dates of the printings were June 1905 (500 copies), April 1907 (300), September 1909
(200), July 1911 (200), June 1915 (100), May 1919 (100), November 1920 (200), and July
1939 (200).

33. Pages 401–9 may also have been reprinted, perhaps for reasons of binding. If so, their
contents were unaffected.

34. A copy of the score, which was sold to Alphonse Catherine, conductor at the Paris Opéra
and Opéra-Comique, is in the Bibliothèque Nationale (Cons. X.346). Durand maintains a
list of those to whom full scores were sold.

35. Since the Fromont vocal score of *Pelléas* was assigned plate number 1416, and the full
score, 1418, one may wonder if number 1417 had been reserved for the parts. However,
there is some confusion in Fromont's sequence of plate numbers at this point, since the
three movements of Debussy's *Nocturnes* (published in 1900) had already been assigned
the plate numbers 1415, 1416, and 1417.

36. Could this J[?]LR have been Léon Roques, Durand's head reader ("correcteur en chef")?

37. The *dépôt légal* of the orchestra parts was on 11 November 1905. The schedule of the
printing of the parts was as follows: "Harmonie": July 1905 (25 copies), February 1909 (50),
January 1922 (100), October 1966 (100); Violin I: July 1905 (100 copies), September 1908
(100), January 1924 (200), November 1966 (300); Violin II: July 1905 (100 copies), July
1911 (100), November 1925 (100), November 1966 (200); Viola, Cello, Contrabass: July
1905 (100 copies), July 1918 (100), August 1950 (100), November 1966 (200).

   This information was drawn from the "livre de cotages" in the Durand archives. There is
a slight discrepancy in that the most recent flute part is dated September 1966 in the part,
but the "livre de cotages" indicates an October printing; the other wind, brass, and
percussion parts are not dated. Similarly, the recent string parts are dated October 1966, a
month earlier than the archives indicate.

   The schedule of the printing of the chorus parts was as follows: Men: May 1905 (200
copies), December 1907 (300), May 1911 (300), December 1945 (500), November 1966
(1000); Women: May 1905 (400 copies), December 1907 (300), May 1911 (300), November
1921 (300), July 1947 (500), April 1966 (1000).

38. An in-house note in the Durand files, dated 25 March 1966, remarks that the full scores of
Pelléas contain many manuscript changes and inquires as to whether these changes had
been made in the plates. Durand was apparently anticipating the reprinting of the full score
and accepted the manuscript changes as authoritative, even if the basis of that authority
had been forgotten. 1966 was the year in which all of the performance parts of *Pelléas*—full
score, orchestra and chorus parts—were reprinted.

39. The catalogue of Debussy's works appended to Léon Vallas, *Claude Debussy et son temps*
(1932), gives, as the thematic incipit for *Pelléas* (on p. LIX), the first page of the full score.
This is not a facsimile of the published score, but it does include (with some differences) the
corrections of August 1905. Apparently Vallas was aware of the changes even though they
had not yet appeared as part of any published score.

40. A reprint of the original edition, with some modifications, is available as a study score from
International Music Company (New York, 1962).

41. For example, on p. 294, meas. 4, Debussy struck the *arco* marking in both violin parts; *arco* was added to these parts four measures later, p. 295, meas. 1 (Bibl. Lang score only). Also, the string chords in meas. 2 and 4 of p. 368 and meas. 7 of p. 369 were redistributed and assigned to violas and cellos only: c¹ was deleted from violins 1 and 2 and was given to the violas; d was deleted from the violas and was given to the cellos (Bibl. Lang score only).

42. Examples of pedals are the added second horn part in meas. 3–4 and 7–8 of p. 379 (material identical to meas, 5–6 and 9–10 on the same page) and the clarinets' written d¹-e¹, sustained throughout meas. 5–8 of p. 380 (Bibl. Lang score only).

43. Leitmotif additions are: Pelléas theme in English horn, p. 108, meas. 4; Mélisande theme in second violin, p. 179, meas. 1–2; and Golaud theme in horns, p. 326, meas. 3–4. Grace notes added to the oboe and clarinet parts on p. 154, meas. 6 and the repetition of this material in the following measure produce a resemblance to a theme associated with the Fountain (see p. 71, meas. 6–7). The first three additions are found in both annotated scores, the second in Bibl. Lang only—the Durand score repeats the oboe-clarinet chord of p. 154, meas. 6, but does not add the grace notes.

44. For example, the addition of the violas on p. 28, meas. 1–4, producing a string of first-inversion chords with the divided second violins (both scores).

45. Instances are: p. 41, meas. 6, *pizzicato* d-minor chord (violins 1 and 2) on the first beat, dramatizing Pelléas's "une autre lettre"; and p. 320, meas. 2, violas and cellos double clarinets and bassoons, playing *pizzicato* on beat 2, setting off Pelléas's "Il faut que tout finisse... ". These two revisions are found only in the Bibl. Lang score.

46. The cut in Act II is from the end of the first measure on p. 93 to the beginning of the first measure on p. 94 (eight measures suppressed). The cut is indicated by circled plus signs; the appearance of such a sign, subsequently erased, at figure 16 on p. 97, suggests that this cut was at one time intended to extend to this point. This large cut would have made the interlude even shorter than its original form (i.e., before the expansion). The cut in Act IV begins at rehearsal letter B on p. 303, where the instruction "*cut*: Go to D" is written (referring to rehearsal letter D on p. 306). This cut eliminated nineteen measures. An additional cut, designed to eliminate Act IV, scene 3, is marked by plus signs and extends from the end of the second measure on p. 306 to the beginning of the fifth measure on p. 319. This cut is slightly different from the "traditional" one used at the Opéra-Comique and marked in later editions of the Durand 1907 vocal score. (It is possible that these cuts were marked, not by Debussy, but by Pierre Monteux, who conducted from this score.)

47. *New York Times*, 16 February 1935, p. 8.

48. André Boll, "Reprise de *Pelléas* à l'Opéra-Comique" (1959), p. 49.

49. The annotations in Monteux's study score of *Pelléas* are the subject of Marian Liebowitz's "Debussy's *Pelléas et Mélisande*. Monteux Score #40" (Master's thesis, Smith College, 1980). In a biographical work on her husband (written from the point of view of their dog Fifi), Doris Monteux mentioned this score when she described a discussion of *Pelléas* that Monteux had had with Charles Munch:

> One evening they perused the score of Debussy's *Pelléas et Mélisande* together, and Maître was very happy all the way home. This is the music he truly adores, and he had excessive pleasure showing his colleague certain changes Debussy had made in the score, which he possesses. (Doris Monteux, *Everyone is Someone*, p. 22)

Did Monteux actually own a score annotated by Debussy? The *New York Times* report of 16 February 1935 suggested that he did, as it commented that the score used in the Amsterdam performances was "in the possession of Monteux, to whom it was presented by Debussy's widow." The reporter was probably in error. If Debussy's widow had given Monteux an annotated score it obviously could not have been the same one that she sold at auction in 1933 (and that was purchased by François Lang), and if Monteux had possessed such a score, he would not have needed to borrow the one from Lang. A search of Monteux's library (Hancock, Maine) uncovered only the study score described above, whose annotations are not in Debussy's hand.

50. Felix Aprahamian, "Debussy's *Pelléas et Mélisande"* (1970), n.p. According to Aprahamian, the score used for the Boulez recording was emended on the basis of the Désormière list.

51. D.-E. Inghelbrecht, *Le Chef d'orchestre parle au public* (1957), p. 26. The Bibliothèque Centrale Musicale of the Office de Radiodiffusion-Télévision Française (ORTF) contains a study score (AA 801) into which Inghelbrecht's emendations were copied. In his book *The Conductor's World* (1954), p. 57, Inghelbrecht mentions "glaring mistakes" in the published score of *Pelléas,* the most important being on p. 210: in the final beat of the page, the first horn should be an E natural, and the last grace note in the glockenspiel should be A natural.

52. Some examples are: (1) p. 99, meas. 5—printed clarinet part deleted and replaced by clar. 1 and 2 doubling violin 2 for the entire measure, tied to eighth notes on the first beat of the next measure (like horns); (2) p. 119, meas. 3—horn adds written e^2 dotted half note for the second half of the measure; horn 2 changes its written $g\sharp^1$ whole note to $g\sharp^1$-c^2 half notes (i.e., horns double violin 2 for the first half of the measure, and viola for the second half); in meas. 4, the horns have written $d\flat^2$ and f^2 eighth notes (doubling violin 2); (3) p. 262, meas. 8—second violin part transferred to divided violas for the entire measure; in succeding measure, second violins resume and violas double them on first sixteenth note of measure (notated in flats); (4) p. 391, meas. 4—viola part extended from quarter notes to whole notes and slurred to f^1-$a\flat^1$ quarter notes in next measure (doubling clarinets).

53. Inghelbrecht, *Comment on ne doit pas interpréter Carmen, Faust, Pelléas* (1933), p. 58.

54. Some examples are: p. 216, meas. 11–13–cellos double bassoon 3; and p. 352, meas. 4—harp 1 has sixteenth note arpeggios on beat 3: upper stave—$a\natural^1$-b^1-$d\sharp^2$-$f\sharp^2$, lower stave—$f\sharp$-b-$d\sharp^1$-$f\sharp^1$.

55. Some examples are: p. 48, meas. 1—fifth eighth note of second viola corrected from g to a, as in the vocal score; and p. 191, meas. 1 and 3—all written e-flats (concert a-flats) in English horn, trumpets, and horns corrected to written e-naturals (concert a-naturals), as in the vocal score.

56. Aside from some details in the notation of dynamics and the order of the instruments on the page, this MS differs from the published score in only one respect: at fig. 34, the clarinets are not in octaves, but play the upper octave in unison. This page also lacks the fourth horn part which was added in Debussy's annotated score and in the Durand corrected score in the two measures before fig. 34.

57. Another score which belonged to Debussy was listed in an exhibition catalogue, *Musiciens d'Ile de France,* ed. Georges Poisson (1973), no 162: "*Pelléas et Mélisande,* ed. ayant appartenu à Cl. Debussy. Musée municipal de Saint Germain en Laye." The catalogue does not specify whether it is a full, study, or vocal score, nor does it say whether the score is signed or annotated.

58. Robert Chesterman, ed., *Conversations with Conductors* (1976), p. 87.

59. Robert Godet, "Cinq Lettres de Robert Godet à Claude Debussy" (1962), p. 92.

60. Doret, *Temps et Contretemps,* p. 190, and LL, p. 250.

61. There was also the possibility of performances in Vienna, as Debussy noted in a letter to Laloy of 10 September 1906: "the most distressing adventures are being planned in the form of agreements to present *Pelléas* in Brussels, Vienna, etc. Why not Singapore or Peking!" (LAL, p. 21).

62. Coll. Durand. Partially published in DUR, p. 44.

63. An earlier German translation by George Stockhausen had been published in 1897 by F. Schneider, Berlin.

64. John W. Freeman, "Swiss Timekeeper" (1962), pp. 24–25.

65. Vincent Sheean, *Oscar Hammerstein I. The Life and Exploits of an Impresario* (1956), pp. 194–202.

66. The printings of the score were as follows: Oct. 1907 (1000 copies), Feb. 1909 (1000), Sept. 1910 (1000), Nov. 1912 (1000), May 1917 (1000), July 1919 (1000), March 1921 (1000), March 1923 (1000), Jan. 1925 (1000), Apr. 1928 (1000), June 1928 (1000), July 1930 (1000), Sept. (?) 1934 (500), Sept. (?) 1938 (1000), Feb. 1943 (500), March 1946 (500), Feb. 1947 (2000), Jan. 1952 (2000), Apr. 1959 (2000), June 1966 (2000), Nov. 1973 (1000), Dec. 1976 (1000).

67. Two measures of the original interlude between scenes 2 and 3 of Act III, present in the full score, have never been added to the vocal score of the opera. The measures fall between meas. 6 and 7 of VS, p. 148. (See OS, pp. 197–98.)

68. The Kalmus vocal score (No. 6252) is a reprint of the original 1907 edition.

69. BNexp includes a copy of the *Pelléas* vocal score (Fromont, 1902) bearing a dedication by Jean Périer and containing changes in the part of Pelléas made by Francell (no. 165-bis, p. 48).

70. "Gatti talks of 'Pelléas' as sung in Milan and New York," *New York Times,* 15 March 1925, pt. 8, p. 6.

71. Harvey Sachs, *Toscanini* (1978), p. 101; Guglielmo Barblan, *Toscanini e la Scala* (1972), p. 343.

72. Barblan, p. 161.

73. Sachs, p. 101.

74. Barblan, p. 146 and plate opp. p. 97.

75. See Barblan, p. 239.

76. According to the Durand *Catalogue de l'oeuvre de Claude Debussy* (1962), the four excerpts were also published in separate English and Italian versions.

Chapter 8

1. Romain Rolland, *Musicians of To-day,* trans. Mary Blaiklock (1915), pp. 239–40. The article originally appeared in *Morgen,* 29 November 1907.

2. Debussy, "Lettres inédites de Debussy à divers," ed. Pasteur Vallery-Radot and James N.B. Hill (1964), p. 111.

3. Joseph Kerman, *Opera as Drama* (1956), p. 180.

4. Virgil Thomson, *A Virgil Thomson Reader* (1981), p. 441. Paul Landormy, *La Musique française: De Franck à Debussy* (1943), p. 224.

5. Pierre Boulez, "*Pelléas* Reflected" (1970), n.p.

6. Louis Laloy, "Le Drame musical moderne. IV: Claude Debussy" (1905), pp. 239–41.

7. ORL, p. 83; see James R. McKay, "The Bréval Manuscript: New Interpretations" (1977), p. 13: meas. 2 of musical example.

8. See, for example, the changes in the NEC MS, Act I, fol. 4, which are signalled in the right margin by blue pencil proofreaders' marks.

9. Hector Dufranne, who sang the part of Golaud in the première of *Pelléas* in 1902, recorded portions of this role in February-March 1928. (The recordings have been reissued on Pearl records, GEMM 145.) Dufranne apparently learned his role so thoroughly for the première that twenty-six years later, he still sang this passage in its original form, with an $E\flat$ instead of an $A\flat$.

10. The revised edition of the full score, presumably in an effort to restore the original reading of the passage, "corrected" the wrong note. That score has the following (p. 384):

11. In this example, the full score perpetuates the reading of the manuscript short score (NEC MS, V, fol. 1ʳ), and the vocal scores represent the revision.

12. The full score preserves the reading found in the manuscript short score and the manuscript vocal score; the revision was evidently made in the proofs of the 1902 vocal score.

13. The full score seems to preserve the ambiguously notated reading of the manuscript short score (NEC MS, II, fol. 10ʳ); the vocal scores thus represent the revision.

14. This phenomenon was noticed and discussed in D.-E. Inghelbrecht, *Le Chef d'orchestre parle au public* (1957), pp. 154–55.

15. The full score reading differs from the printed example in one detail: "moi" is written as an eighth note tied to a quarter note, not another eighth.

Chapter 9

1. Vallas devoted one chapter of his *Theories of Claude Debussy* (1929), pp. 112–29, to a summary of the composer's critical comments on the works of Wagner. The anthologies of Debussy's critical writings (LCr in French and RLS in English) include the complete articles which were quoted and summarized by Vallas.

2. François Lesure, "Claude Debussy, Ernest Chausson et Henri Lerolle" (1968), I: 341–42.

3. Martine Kahane and Nicole Wild, *Wagner et la France* (1983), pp. 158–61.

4. *Gil Blas* (10 June 1903) in RLS, p. 212.

5. *Gil Blas* (6 April 1903) in LCr, p. 140, and RLS, p. 167.

6. Erik Satie, *Ecrits* (1981), p. 69.

7. Henry Prunières, "A la Villa Medici" (1926), p. 135.

8. Arthur Hoérée, "Entretiens inédits d'Ernest Guiraud et de Claude Debussy" (1942), p. 33. The September 1889 date for the letter was suggested in DIE, p. 79, n. 12.

9. RLS, p. 74. Does this document really date from early April 1902, as Georges Ricou recalled in his preface to its publication in *Comoedia* (18 October 1941)? Internal evidence suggests that its writing followed, rather than preceded, the première. In the fourth paragraph, Debussy remarked: "That is why the reproach has been made concerning my so-called taste for monotonous declamation, where nothing seems melodic...." This comment sounds like a reply to the opera's critics and would logically postdate the early reviews.

10. *Mercure de France* (January 1903) in RLS, p. 83.

11. *S.I.M.* (1 November 1913) in RLS, p. 297.

12. See Debussy's remarks on his preference for setting prose texts in chapter 1, note 33.

13. Lalo, *De Rameau à Ravel*, pp. 391–92.

14. "Chronique parisienne," *Bibliothèque Universelle et Revue Suisse*, ser. 4, 26 (June 1902), 614.

15. Raymond Bouyer, " 'Pelléas et Mélisande' ou le Crépuscule du Drame musical" (1902), p. 279.

16. Camille Bellaigue, "Revue musicale" (1902), p. 452.

17. Vallas, *Claude Debussy: His Life and Works* (1973), p. 131.

18. Adolphe Jullien, "Revue musicale" (1902), p. 936.

19. Jean Marnold, "Musique" (1902), p. 808.

20. "The Curtain Falls on Claude Debussy," *New York Times,* 5 May 1918, pt. 4, p. 7.

21. Edwin Evans, Jr., "Debussy's 'Pelléas et Mélisande' " (1909), p. 361.

22. Jullien, "Théâtre National de l'Opéra-Comique" (1902), p. 11.

23. Friedrich Spigl, "Wagner et Debussy" (1902), pp. 518 and 530.

24. Louis Laloy, "Le Drame musical moderne. IV: Claude Debussy" (1905), pp. 241–44.

25. Ibid., p. 250.

26. Mrs. Franz Liebich, *Claude-Achille Debussy* (1908), pp. 70–71.

27. Lawrence Gilman, *Debussy's "Pelléas et Mélisande"* (1907), pp. 56–84.

28. Maurice Emmanuel, *Pelléas et Mélisande de Debussy* (1950), p. 135. Other important thematic analyses or discussions of leitmotifs in *Pelléas* are: Etienne Destranges, "*Pelléas et Mélisande*: étude analytique et critique" (1910); M.-D. Calvocoressi, "Debussy and the Leitmotive" (1925); Jacques Chailley, "Le Symbolisme des Thèmes dans *Pelléas et Mélisande*" (1942); Jules van Ackere, *Pelléas et Mélisande ou la rencontre miraculeuse*

d'une poésie et d'une musique (1952); Antoine Goléa, *Pelléas et Mélisande: Analyse poétique et musicale* (1952); and René Terrasson, *Pelléas et Mélisande ou l'Initiation* (1982).

29. Gilman, p. 53.

30. Gilman, "Wagner and Debussy" (1908), pp. 364–65.

31. Godet, "En marge," p. 174.

32. Ex. 2a illustrates the first appearance of the theme in the opera, in Act I, scene 2 (VS, p. 33, meas. 10–11). In the Meyer and Legouix MSS drafts of Act IV, scene 4, the initial interval is almost invariably a minor, rather than a major, second.

33. Note, for example, how it precedes his entrances in Act I, scene 2, and in Act IV, scene 2 (VS, pp. 25 and 197) and his first speech in Act I, scene 2 (VS, p. 29). It appears in diminuted form throughout these two scenes and recurs in Act V, where he says, "You do not know what the soul is" (VS, p. 303). Oddly enough, Example 4 seems to be precisely the kind of leitmotif use that Debussy ridiculed in his 1903 review of the *Ring,* a use which he compared to "those silly people who hand you their visiting cards and then lyrically recite key information they contain." Understandably, Debussy introduced the themes in this manner (i.e., coinciding with the first mention of the names of Golaud and Arkel) in order to establish the identification of the themes with those characters. Note, however, that later in the scene, when Mélisande finally reveals her name, her theme is not heard in the orchestra (VS, p. 19). The Arkel theme was ignored by Gilman and Destranges and was labeled "Fate" by Emmanuel (p. 135) and van Ackere (p. 36). Calvocoressi (pp. 696-97) called it the "Wisdom-motive" and noted its close connection with Arkel. Both Chailley (p. 889) and Goléa (p. 26) identified it with Arkel.

34. Carl Dahlhaus, *Richard Wagner's Music Dramas* (1979), pp. 61–62.

35. A further strengthening of the motivic link between these two moments was accomplished in a later revision of the latter passage, in which the figure just before Pelléas's "Je t'aime" was altered rhythmically and melodically to resemble more closely the parallel figure at the end of Pelléas's opening speech (VS, p. 235, meas. 9–p. 236, meas. 1):

(a) Bréval MS, fol. 7ʳ (LPm, p. 101);

(b)   VS, p. 244, meas. 2-3.

36.   Calvocoressi (p. 696) called this the Threat motive and pointed out its appearances in, among other places, Act I, scene 2 (VS, p. 36, meas. 3-4), when Arkel comments that they do not yet know how Golaud's return will affect them, at several points in the scene in the underground vaults (Act III, scene 2) and the scene of Golaud's interrogation of Yniold (Act III, scene 4), and again in Act IV, scene 2, as Golaud is about to brutalize Mélisande (VS, p. 214). Of course, all of these uses of the theme postdate the composition of the Legouix MS.

37.   At an earlier compositional stage, Debussy had considered but then rejected the use of the second Golaud theme in this passage (see Bréval MS, fol. 4ʳ, meas. 17; LPm, p. 95).

38.   This revision is discussed in ORL, pp. 78-81.

39.   The technique of thematic recollection, it will be recalled, was already employed in the scene's earliest drafts: the "proto-Mélisande" theme was used both in Pelléas's opening monologue and in the dialogue preceding the declaration of love, the original Golaud motive was fashioned into parallel four-measure phrase groups to mark the moments when Mélisande first hears Golaud and then when she spots him, and a triadic "love" theme marked the passionate aftermaths of two embraces.

40.   In the full score (p. 2, meas. 7-8) this augmented second is notated as a minor third.

41.   This use of the Arkel theme is not found in the Meyer MS, V, fol. 15ʳ (LPm, p. 80), but is in the NEC MS, fol. 14ʳ.

42.   Joseph Kerman, *Opera as Drama* (1956), p. 186.

43.   Terrasson, p. 26.

44.   Kerman, pp. 183-88.

45. This theme, which Emmanuel called "The Fountain," is not the same as the theme given that title by Gilman.

46. Another revision of this scene added the Mélisande motive to her opening lines; the addition was made in the NEC MS, I, fol. 18ʳ and appears in the full score (p. 47, meas. 4–6), but not the vocal score (p. 39, meas. 8–p. 40, meas. 2).

47. Gilman, *Debussy's "Pelléas,"* p. 68; Richard Langham Smith, "Debussy and the Pre-Raphaelites" (1981), p. 107.

48. An earlier version of the prelude is found in the Basel MS; it is longer than the published version but is based on the same materials.

49. Abbate, pp. 138–39. Pierre Boulez, in his "*Pelléas* Reflected," also commented on the resemblance of some of the interludes to the music of *Parsifal.* The subject of Wagnerian reminiscence in the *Pelléas* interludes is exhaustively treated by Robin Holloway in *Debussy and Wagner* (1979), pp. 76–95.

50. See, for example, Gilman, *Debussy's "Pelléas,"* p. 53.

51. Thomson, *A Virgil Thomson Reader* (1981), p. 437.

52. "Praise from Debussy. Composer Congratulates Campanini for Directing 'Pelléas et Mélisande,' " *New York Times,* 19 March 1908, p. 7.

Bibliography

Abbate, Carolyn. "*Tristan* in the Composition of *Pelléas*." *19th Century Music*, 5 (Fall 1981), 117–41.

Abravanel, Claude. *Claude Debussy: A Bibliography*. Detroit Studies in Music Bibliography, 29. Detroit: Information Coordinators, 1974.

Ackere, Jules van. *Pelléas et Mélisande ou la rencontre miraculeuse d'une poésie et d'une musique*. Publications de la Société Belge de Musicologie, ser. 2, no. 2. Brussels: Librairie Encyclopédique, 1952.

Aderer, Adolphe. "A propos des répétitions générales." *Le Théâtre*, no. 82 (May 1902), p. 4.

Albrecht, Otto E. *A Census of Autograph Music Manuscripts of European Composers in American Libraries*. Philadelphia: Univ. of Pennsylvania Press, 1953.

Alexandre, Arsène. "Mademoiselle Georgette Leblanc de l'Opéra-Comique." *Le Théâtre*, no. 14 (February 1899), 16–18.

Andrieux, Georges. *Catalogue de Vente... Collection Claude Debussy*. Paris: 30 November–8 December 1933.

Antoine André. *Memories of the Théâtre-Libre*. Trans. Marvin A. Carlson. Ed. H.D. Albright. Coral Gables, Fla.: Univ. of Miami Press, 1964.

————. *Mes souvenirs sur le Théâtre Antoine et sur l'Odéon*. Paris: Grasset, 1928.

Appledorn, Mary Jeanne van. "A Stylistic Study of Claude Debussy's Opera *Pelléas et Mélisande*." Ph.D. thesis, Univ. of Rochester, Eastman School of Music, 1966.

Aprahamian, Felix. "Debussy's *Pelléas et Mélisande*." In booklet accompanying recording *Boulez Conducts Debussy, Pelléas et Mélisande*. CBS M3 30119. New York: CBS, 1970.

Austin, William W. "Debussy, Wagner, and Some Others." *19th Century Music*, 6 (Summer 1982), 82–91.

Baignères, Claude. "Le Cinquantenaire de *Pelléas*." *Journal Musical Français*, (10 April 1952), 6.

Barblan, Guglielmo. *Toscanini e la Scala*. Milan: Edizioni della Scala, 1972.

Barksdale, A. Beverly. *Composer Portraits and Autograph Scores*. [Catalogue of an exhibition at the Toledo Museum of Art, 3 October–7 November 1954.] Toledo: Toledo Museum of Art, 1954.

Barraqué, Jean. *Debussy*. Collections microcosme solfèges, 22. Paris: Seuil, 1962.

Barricelli, Jean Pierre, and Leo Weinstein. *Ernest Chausson: The Composer's Life and Works*. Norman: Univ. of Oklahoma Press, 1955.

Bartlet, M. Elizabeth C. "Archival Sources for the Opéra-Comique and its *Registres* at the Bibliothèque de l'Opéra." *19th Century Music*, 7 (Fall 1983), 119–28.

Bauer, Harold. *His Book*. New York: Norton, 1948.

Bellaigue, Camille. "Revue musicale. Théâtre de l'Opéra-Comique: *Pelléas et Mélisande*." *Revue des Deux Mondes*, ser. 5, 9 (15 May 1902), 450–56.

Benda, Julien. "A propos de *Pelléas et Mélisande.*" *Revue Blanche,* 28 (July 1902), 391–94.

Blanche, Jacques-Emile. "Au dessus de son temps..." In *Le Tombeau de Pierre Louÿs,* pp. 87–97. Paris: Editions du Monde Moderne, 1925.

———. *La Pêche aux souvenirs.* Paris: Flammarion, 1949.

Boll, André. "Reprise de *Pelléas* à l'Opéra-Comique." *Musica-Disques,* no. 61 (April 1959), 49–53.

"Bone for Critics in Next New Opera." *New York Times,* 10 February 1908, p. 9.

Bonheur, Raymond. "Souvenirs et impressions d'un compagnon de jeunesse." *Revue Musicale,* 7, no. 7 (1 May 1926), 99–105 (3–9).

Boucher, Maurice. *Claude Debussy (Essai pour la connaissance du devenir).* Maîtres de la musique ancienne et moderne, 4. Paris: Rieder, 1930.

Boucourechliev, André, et al. *Debussy.* Collection Génies et Réalités. Paris: Hachette, 1972.

Boulez, Pierre. "*Pelléas* Reflected." In booklet accompanying recording *Boulez Conducts Debussy, Pelléas et Mélisande.* CBS M3 30119. New York: CBS, 1970.

Bouyer, Raymond. "'Pelléas et Mélisande' ou le Crépuscule du drame musical." *Nouvelle Revue,* new ser., 16 (15 May 1902), 276–80.

Brucher, Roger. *Maurice Maeterlinck: L'oeuvre et son audience. Essai de bibliographie: 1883–1960.* Brussels: Palais des Académies, 1972.

Bruneau, Alfred. "La Musique dramatique." *La Grande Revue,* 23 (1 July 1902), 212–24.

Brussel, Robert. "Claude Debussy ou le nouveau Prophète livré aux Bêtes." *Revue d'Art Dramatique,* 17 (15 May 1902), 226–28.

———. "Debussy (Claude). *Pelléas et Mélisande.*" *L'Art Dramatique et Musical,* 2 (December 1902), 450–53.

———. "*Pelléas et Mélisande.*" *L'Art Dramatique et Musical,* 2 (April 1902), 153–54.

Bugeanu, Constantin. "La Forme musicale dans le *Pelléas* de Debussy." *Revue Roumaine d'Histoire de l'Art,* 6 (1969), 243–60.

Busser, Henri. "A propos du cinquantenaire de 'Pelléas et Mélisande' de Claude Debussy: Souvenirs." *Revue des Deux Mondes,* 122 (1 April 1952), 534–40.

———. "La Création de *Pelléas et Mélisande.*" *Revue des Deux Mondes,* 136 (15 March 1966), 274–78.

———. *De Pelléas aux Indes Galantes:... de la flûte au tambour.* Paris: Arthème Fayard, 1955.

———. "Souvenirs de jeunesse sur Claude Debussy." In *Claude Debussy: Chronologie de sa vie et de ses oeuvres,* ed. Auguste Martin, pp. vi–viii. Paris, 1942.

Cadieu, Martine, et al. *Pelléas et Mélisande. L'Avant-Scène Opéra,* no. 9 (March–April 1977).

Cahn, Peter. "Der Szenenaufbau in Debussys *Pelléas et Mélisande.*" In *Bericht über den Internationalen Musikwissenschaftlichen Kongress Bonn 1970,* ed. Carl Dahlhaus, et al., pp. 207–12. Kassel: Bärenreiter, 1971.

Calvocoressi, Michel-Dimitri. "Debussy and the Leitmotive." *Musical Times,* 66 (1 August 1925), 695–97.

———. "Pelléas et Mélisande." *L'Art Moderne,* 22 (4 May 1902), 156–57.

Cardinne-Petit, Robert. *Pierre Louÿs inconnu.* Paris: Editions de l'Elan, 1948.

Carré, Albert. "La Bataille de *Pelléas.*" *Figaro littéraire,* (23 September 1950), 1, 6.

———. *Souvenirs de théâtre.* Ed. Robert Favart. Paris: Plon, 1950.

Catalogue de l'oeuvre de Claude Debussy. Paris: Durand, 1962.

Chailley, Jacques. "Le Symbolisme des Thèmes dans *Pelléas et Mélisande.*" *L'Information Musicale,* 2 (3 April 1942), 889–90.

Chausson, Ernest. "Dix lettres d'Ernest Chausson à C. Debussy (1893–1894)." Ed. François Lesure. *Revue de Musicologie,* 48 (July–December 1962), 49–60.

Chennevière, Daniel. *Claude Debussy et son oeuvre.* Paris: Durand, 1913.

Chesterman, Robert. "Ernest Ansermet." In *Conversations with Conductors,* ed. Robert Chesterman, pp. 75–99. London: Robson, 1976.

Clive, H. P. *Pierre Louÿs (1870–1925): A Biography.* Oxford: Clarendon Press, 1978.

Cobb, Margaret G. "Debussy in Texas." *Cahiers Debussy,* nouv. sér., no. 1 (1977), 45–46.

————. *Discographie de l'oeuvre de Claude Debussy.* Publications du Centre de Documentation Claude Debussy, 1. Geneva: Minkoff, 1975.

————. *The Poetic Debussy: A Collection of His Song Texts and Selected Letters.* Boston: Northeastern Univ. Press, 1982.

Cogeval, Guy, and François Lesure. *Debussy e il Simbolismo.* [Catalogue of an exhibition at the Villa Medici, Rome, April–June 1984.] Rome: Fratelli Palombi, 1984.

Cohen, H. Robert. "Les livrets de mise en scène et la Bibliothèque de l'Association de la Régie Théâtrale." *Revue de Musicologie,* 64 (1978), 253–67.

Cone, John Frederick. *Oscar Hammerstein's Manhattan Opera Company.* Norman: Univ. of Oklahoma Press, 1966.

Cortot, Alfred. "Un Drame lyrique de Claude Debussy [*Rodrigue et Chimène*]." In *Inédits sur Debussy,* ed. Arthur Hoérée, pp. 12–16. Collection Comoedia-Charpentier. Paris: Publications Techniques, 1942.

"The Curtain Falls on Claude Debussy." *New York Times,* 5 May 1918, pt. 4, p. 7.

Dahlhaus, Carl. *Richard Wagner's Music Dramas.* Trans. Mary Whittall. Cambridge: Cambridge Univ. Press, 1979.

Debussy, Claude. "Claude Debussy à Eugène Isaye. Lettres inédites." Ed. Gustave Samazeuilh. *Les Annales Politiques et Littéraires,* 101 (25 August 1933), 225–26.

————. "Correspondance de Claude Debussy et de Louis Laloy (1902–1914)." Ed. François Lesure. *Revue de Musicologie,* 48 (July–December 1962), 3–40.

————. *Debussy on Music.* Ed. and trans. Richard Langham Smith. New York: Knopf, 1977.

————. "Deux lettres de Debussy à Ernest Chausson." *Revue Musicale,* 7, no. 7 (1 May 1926), 183–84 (87–88).

————. "Un Document inédit: Mes raisons de choisir 'Pelléas.'" *Comoedia,* (18 October 1941), 1.

————. "Due Lettere di Debussy." *Rassegna Musicale,* 21 (January 1951), 56–59.

————. *L'Enfance de Pelléas. Lettres de Claude Debussy à André Messager.* Ed. Jean André-Messager. Paris: Dorbon-Aîné, 1938.

————. *Esquisses de 'Pelléas et Mélisande' (1893–1895).* Ed. François Lesure. Publications du Centre de Documentation Claude Debussy, 2. Geneva: Minkoff, 1977.

————. *Lettres 1884–1918.* Ed. François Lesure. Paris: Hermann, 1980.

————. *Lettres à deux amis. Soixante-dix-huit lettres inédites à Robert Godet et G. Jean-Aubry.* Ed. Georges Jean-Aubry. Paris: Librairie José Corti, 1942.

————. *Lettres de Claude Debussy à sa femme Emma.* Ed. Pasteur Vallery-Radot. Paris: Flammarion, 1957.

————. *Lettres de Claude Debussy à son éditeur.* Ed. Jacques Durand. Paris: Durand, 1927.

————. "Lettres de Debussy à divers." Ed. Pasteur Vallery-Radot and James N. B. Hill. *Revue Musicale,* no. 258 (1964), 109–11.

————. "Lettres de Debussy à l'éditeur Hartmann." Ed. Pasteur Vallery-Radot and James N. B. Hill. *Revue Musicale,* no. 258 (1964), 111–15.

————. *Lettres inédites à André Caplet (1908–1914).* Ed. Edward Lockspeiser. Monaco: Editions du Rocher, 1957.

————. "Lettres inédites de Claude Debussy à Pierre Louÿs." Ed. François Lesure. *Revue de Musicologie,* 57 (1971), 29–39.

————. "Des Lettres inédites et étonnantes de Debussy." Ed. François Lesure. *Le Nouveau Candide,* no. 60 (21–28 June 1962), 18.

————. *Monsieur Croche et autres écrits.* Ed. François Lesure. Paris: Gallimard, 1971.

————. "Trois lettres inédites." Ed. Jean Roy. *Revue Musicale,* no. 258 (1964), 117–20.

Debussy, Claude, and Ernest Chausson. "Correspondance inédite de Claude Debussy et Ernest Chausson." *Revue Musicale,* 7, no. 2 (1 December 1925), 116–26.

Debussy, Claude, and Pierre Louÿs. *Correspondance de Claude Debussy et Pierre Louÿs (1893–1904).* Ed. Henri Borgeaud. Paris: Librairie José Corti, 1945.

Debussy, Claude, and Paul-Jean Toulet. *Correspondance de Claude Debussy et P.-J. Toulet.* Ed. Henri Martineau. Collection Saint-Germain-des Prés, no. 10. Paris: Le Divan, 1929.

"Debussy Discusses Music and His Work." *New York Times,* 26 June 1910, pt. 3, p. 5.

Denis, Maurice. *Henry Lerolle et ses amis, suivi de quelques lettres d'amis.* Paris: Duranton, 1932.

Destranges, Etienne. "*Pelléas et Mélisande:* étude analytique et critique." *Revue Musicale de Lyon,* 8 (13, 20, 27 November, 4, 11, 18 December 1910), 137–44, 176–81, 207–11, 240–44, 269–73, 302–6.

Dietschy, Marcel. *La Passion de Claude Debussy.* Neuchâtel: La Baconnière, 1962.

Doret, Gustave. *Temps et contretemps.* Fribourg: Librairie de l'Université, 1942.

Downes, Olin. "Marvelous Stage Pictures in Boston Opera's First 'Pelléas.'" *Musical America,* 20 January 1912, p. 2.

Dukas, Paul. *Correspondance de Paul Dukas.* Ed. Georges Favre. Paris: Durand, 1971.

————. "Opéra-Comique: reprise de *Pelléas et Mélisande.*" *Chronique des arts et de la curiosité* (supplément à la *Gazette des Beaux-Arts*), no. 34 (8 November 1902), 272–73.

————. "Théâtre de l'Opéra-Comique: *Pelléas et Mélisande.*" *Chronique des arts et de la curiosité* (supplément à la *Gazette des Beaux-Arts*), no. 19 (10 May 1902), 148–50.

Dumesnil, Maurice. *Claude Debussy: Master of Dreams.* New York: Ives Washburn, 1940.

————. "Personal Conferences with Claude Debussy," *Etude,* 53 (January 1935), 5–6.

Duquesnel, Félix. "La Quinzaine théâtrale." *Le Théâtre,* no. 84 (June 1902), 2–3.

Durand, Jacques. *Quelques souvenirs d'un editeur de musique.* 2 vols. Paris: Durand, 1924, 1925.

Dutronc, Jean-Louis, ed. "Jacques Jansen: 30 ans de Pelléas." In *Pelléas et Mélisande,* pp. 90–92. *L'Avant-Scène Opéra,* no. 9 (March-April 1977).

Eaton, Quaintance. *The Boston Opera Company.* New York: Appleton-Century, 1965.

Emmanuel, Maurice. *Pelléas et Mélisande de Debussy: Etude et analyse.* Les Chefs-d'oeuvre de la musique expliqués. 3rd ed. Paris: Mellottée, 1950.

Estrade-Guerra, Oswald d'. "Les Manuscrits de *Pelléas et Mélisande.*" *Revue Musicale,* no. 235 (1957), pp. 5–24.

Evans, Edwin. "Debussy's 'Pelléas et Mélisande.'" *Musical Standard,* ill. ser., 31 (5 June 1909), 361–64.

Fabre, Gabriel. "Pelléas et Mélisande (Chanson chantée au 3ᵉ acte)." *La Plume,* no. 100 (15 June 1893), 282–83.

Flat, Paul. "Théâtres. Opéra-Comique: *Pelléas et Mélisande.*" *Revue Politique et Littéraire: Revue Bleue,* ser. 4, 17 (10 May 1902), 590–93.

Fleury, Robert. *Pierre Louÿs et Gilbert de Voisins: une curieuse amitié.* Archives et Documents, ed. Ferdinand Teulé. Paris: Editions Tête de Feuilles, 1973.

Fogel, Susan Lee. "L'originalité de *Pelléas et Mélisande:* les inventions orchestrales." Trans. Béatrice Vierne. In *Pelléas et Mélisande,* pp. 84–89. *L'Avant-Scène Opéra,* no. 9 (March–April 1977).

Fontainas, André. *Mes souvenirs du symbolisme.* Essais critiques, 10. Paris: La Nouvelle Revue Critique, 1928.

Freeman, John W. "Swiss Timekeeper." *Opera News,* 27, no. 8 (29 December 1962), 24–25.

Fuld, James J. *The Book of World-Famous Music: Classical, Popular, and Folk.* Rev. ed. New York: Crown, 1967.

Garden, Mary. *Souvenirs de "Mélisande."* Brimborion, no. 98. Liège: Editions Dynamo, 1962.

Garden, Mary, and Louis Biancolli. *Mary Garden's Story.* New York: Simon and Schuster, 1951.

Gatti-Casazza, Giulio. *Memories of the Opera.* New York: Charles Scribner's Sons, 1941.

"Gatti Talks of 'Pelléas' as Sung in Milan and New York." *New York Times,* 15 March 1925, pt. 8, p. 6.

Gauthier, André. *Debussy. Documents iconographiques.* Visages d'hommes célèbres. Geneva: Pierre Cailler, 1952.

Gerstenberg, Walter, and Martin Hürlimann. *Composers' Autographs.* Trans. Ernst Roth. 2 vols. Madison: Farleigh Dickinson Univ. Press, 1968.

Gevaert, M. "Figures d'artistes: Mme Georgette Leblanc." *Revue Théâtrale,* 1 (October 1902), 7-8.

Gheusi, P.-B. *Cinquante ans de Paris: mémoires d'un témoin (1889-1938).* Paris: Plon, 1939.

Gilman, Lawrence. "Concerning an Epoch-making Score." *Harper's Weekly,* 52 (21 March 1908), 25.

_____. "Debussy's 'Pelléas et Mélisande.'" *Harper's Weekly,* 52 (7 March 1908), 25.

_____. *Debussy's "Pelléas et Mélisande." A Guide to the Opera.* New York: Schirmer, 1907.

_____. "Wagner and Debussy." *Musical Standard,* ill. ser., 30 (28 November, 5 December 1908), 347-48, 363-65.

Ginsburg, Lev. *Ysaÿe.* Ed. H. R. Axelrod. Trans. X. M. Danko. Neptune City, N.J.: Paganiniana Publications, 1980.

Godet, Robert. "Cinq lettres de Robert Godet à Claude Debussy (1917-1918)." Ed. François Lesure. *Revue de Musicologie,* 48 (July-December 1962), 77-95.

_____. "En marge de la marge." *Revue Musicale,* 7, no. 7 (1 May 1926), 147-82 (51-86).

Golea, Antoine. *Claude Debussy.* 1966; rpt. Paris and Geneva: Slatkine, 1983.

_____. *Pelléas et Mélisande: Analyse poétique et musicale.* Paris: Imprimerie du Château-Rouge, 1952.

Goodrich, Wallace. "The New England Conservatory of Music." TS dated 17 May 1947.

Grand-Carteret, John. *Papeterie et papetiers de l'ancien temps.* Paris: Georges Putois, 1913.

Grayson, David. "The Libretto of Debussy's 'Pelléas et Mélisande.'" *Music and Letters,* 66 (January 1985), 34-50.

Grover, Ralph Scott. *Ernest Chausson: The Man and His Music.* Lewisburg: Bucknell Univ. Press; London: Associated University Presses, 1980.

Hallays, André. *"Pelléas et Mélisande."* *Revue de Paris,* ser. 9, 3 (15 May 1902), 411-20.

Halls, W.D. *Maurice Maeterlinck: A Study of his Life and Thought.* Oxford: Oxford Univ. Press, 1960.

Hanse, Joseph. "Bibliographie." In *Maurice Maeterlinck: 1862-1962,* ed. Joseph Hanse and Robert Vivier, pp. 521-47. [Brussels]: La Renaissance du Livre, 1962.

Harding, James. *Massenet.* New York: St. Martin's Press, 1970.

Harrison, Jay S. "Maggie Teyte Recalls 'Fiery' Debussy." *New York Herald-Tribune,* 25 April 1954, pt. 4, p. 8.

Hermans, Georges. "Les Cinq Chansons de Mélisande." *Annales de la Fondation Maurice Maeterlinck,* 17 (1971), 67-76.

_____. *Les Premières Armes de Maurice Maeterlinck.* Ledeberg-Gand: Erasmus, 1967.

Heugel, Henri. "Le Nouveau Directeur de l'Opéra-Comique: M. Albert Carré." *Le Ménestrel,* 64 (16 January 1898), 19.

Hill, Edward Burlingame. "Debussy's 'Pelléas et Mélisande': An Inquiry." *Musical Standard,* ill. ser., 29 (6 and 13 June 1908), 359 and 371.

Hirsbrunner, Theo. "Richard Wagner's Influence on French Opera: Towards an Invisible Theatre." In *Report of the Twelfth Congress: Berkeley 1977,* ed. Daniel Heartz and Bonnie Wade, pp. 492-97. Kassel: Bärenreiter, 1981.

Hoérée, Arthur. "Entretiens inédits d'Ernest Guiraud et de Claude Debussy notés par Maurice Emmanuel (1889-1890)." In *Inédits sur Debussy,* ed. Arthur Hoérée, pp. 25-33. Collection Comoedia-Charpentier. Paris: Publications Techniques, 1942.

Holloway, Robin. *Debussy and Wagner.* London: Eulenburg, 1979.

Inghelbrecht, Désiré-Emile. *Le Chef d'orchestre parle au public.* Paris: René Julliard, 1957.

————. *Comment on ne doit pas interpréter Carmen, Faust, Pelléas.* Paris: Heugel, 1933.

————. *The Conductor's World.* Trans. G. Prerauer and S. Malcolm Kirk. New York: Library Publishers, 1954.

Inghelbrecht, Germaine and Désiré-Emile. *Claude Debussy.* Musiciens d'hier et d'aujourd'hui, 1. Paris: Costard, 1953.

Irvine, David. "Wagner and Debussy." *Musical Standard,* ill ser., 31 (12 June 1909), 379–80.

————. "'Wagner and Debussy.' A Reply." *Musical Standard,* ill. ser., 30 (19 December 1908), 392–93.

Jardillier, Robert. *Pelléas.* La Musique moderne, 4. Paris: Editions Claude Aveline, 1927.

Jarocinski, Stefan. *Debussy: Impressionism and Symbolism.* Trans. Rollo Myers. London: Eulenburg, 1976.

Jasper, Gertrude R. *Adventure in the Theatre: Lugné-Poe and the Théâtre de l'Oeuvre to 1899.* New Brunswick: Rutgers Univ. Press, 1947.

Jean-Aubry, G. "Some Recollections of Debussy." *Musical Times,* 59 (1 May 1918), 203–9.

Jullien, Adolphe. "Revue musicale. Opéra-Comique: *Pelléas et Mélisande." Journal des Débats,* no. 434 (16 May 1902), 934–37.

————. "Théâtre National de l'Opéra-Comique. *Pelléas et Mélisande." Le Théâtre,* no. 84 (June 1902), 5–15.

Kahane, Martine, and Nicole Wild. *Wagner et la France.* Paris: Bibliothèque Nationale and Théâtre National de l'Opéra de Paris, 1983.

Kerman, Joseph. *Opera as Drama.* New York: Knopf, 1956.

————. "Sketch Studies." *19th Century Music,* 6 (Fall 1982), 174–80.

Knowles, Dorothy. *La Réaction idéaliste au théâtre depuis 1890.* Bibliothèque de la société des historiens du théâtre, 4. Paris: E. Droz, 1934.

Koechlin, Charles. *Debussy.* Paris: Renouard, 1927.

Lake, Carlton. *Baudelaire to Beckett: A Century of French Art and Literature. A Catalogue of Books, Manuscripts, and Related Material Drawn from The Collections of the Humanities Research Center.* Austin: Humanities Research Center—Univ. of Texas at Austin, 1976.

Lalo, Pierre. *La Musique 1898–1899.* Paris: Rouart, Lerolle & Cie, n.d.

————. *De Rameau à Ravel. Portraits et souvenirs.* Paris: Albin Michel, 1947.

Laloy, Louis. *Claude Debussy.* Paris: Dorbon Ainé, 1909.

————. *Debussy.* Paris: Aux Armes de Frances, 1944.

————. "Le Drame musical moderne. IV: Claude Debussy." *Mercure Musical,* 1 (1 August 1905), 233–50.

————. *La Musique retrouvée: 1902–1927.* 1928; rpt. [Paris]: Desclée de Brouwer, 1974.

————. "*Pelléas et Mélisande.*" In *Essays on Music: an anthology from "The Listener,"* ed. Felix Aprahamian, pp. 74–77. London: Cassell, 1967.

Lanceron, Alain, ed. "Jorge Lavelli: 'Pour échapper à la loi du Château.'" In *Pelléas et Mélisande,* pp. 104–6. *L'Avant-Scène Opéra,* no. 9 (March–April 1977).

Landormy, Paul. *La Musique française: De Franck à Debussy.* Paris: Gallimard, 1943.

Lastret, Louis. "Autour de la Pièce." *Le Théâtre,* no. 84 (June 1902), 17–22.

Leblanc, Georgette. *La Machine à courages: Souvenirs.* Paris: J. B. Janin, 1947.

————. *Souvenirs (1895–1918).* Pour mon plaisir, 9. Paris: Bernard Grasset, 1931.

————. *Souvenirs: My Life with Maeterlinck.* Trans. Janet Flanner. New York: Dutton, 1932.

Lecat, Maurice. *Bibliographie de Maurice Maeterlinck: Littérature, science, philosophie.* Brussels: Castaigne, 1939.

————. *Maeterlinck en pantoufles.* Brussels: Castaigne, 1939.

Lesbroussart, Henry. "Pelléas et Mélisande," *L'Art Moderne,* 27 (13 January 1907), 9.

Lesure, François. "Archival Research: Necessity and Opportunity." Trans. Rita Benton. In *Perspectives in Musicology,* ed. Barry S. Brook, Edward O. D. Downes, and Sherman Van Solkema, pp. 56–71. New York: Norton, 1972.

_____. *Catalogue de l'oeuvre de Claude Debussy.* Publications du Centre de Documentation Claude Debussy, 3. Geneva: Minkoff, 1977.

_____. *Claude Debussy.* [Catalogue de l'exposition, Galerie Mansart à la Bibliothèque Nationale de juin à septembre 1962.] Paris: Bibliothèque Nationale, 1962.

_____. *Claude Debussy.* Iconographie musicale, 4. Geneva: Minkoff, 1975.

_____. "Claude Debussy after his Centenary." Trans. Denis Stevens. *Musical Quarterly,* 49 (July 1963), 277-88.

_____. "Claude Debussy, Ernest Chausson et Henri Lerolle." In *Humanisme actif: Mélanges d'art et de littérature offerts à Julien Cain,* vol. 1, pp. 337-44. Paris: Hermann, 1968.

_____. "Debussy à travers le journal de Madame de Saint-Marceaux (1894-1911)." *Cahiers Debussy,* ser. 1, no. 3 (1976), 5-10.

_____. *Paul Dukas.* [Catalogue de l'exposition à la Bibliothèque Nationale.] Paris: Bibliothèque Nationale, 1965.

Lesure, François, and Nanie Bridgman. *Collection Musicale André Meyer.* 2 vols. Abbeville: F. Paillart, 1961, 1973.

Liebich, Louise Shirley (Mrs. Franz). *Claude-Achille Debussy.* Living Masters of Music. London: John Lane, 1908.

_____. "Claude Debussy's 'Pelléas et Mélisande.'" *Musical Standard,* ill. ser., 27 (12 January 1907), 20-22.

_____. "Debussy and Nationality in Music." *Musical Standard,* ill. ser., 34 (26 November 1910), 337-38. (Corrections on p. 364.)

_____. "An Englishwoman's Memories of Debussy." *Musical Times,* 59 (1 June 1918), 250.

_____. "A Few Thoughts on 'Pelléas et Mélisande.'" *Musical Standard,* ill. ser., 31 (29 May 1909), 340-41.

_____. "An Impressionist Composer: Claude Debussy and his Music of Legend and Dream." *Musical Standard,* ill. ser., 21 (20 February 1904), 119.

Liebowitz, Marian. "Debussy's *Pelléas et Mélisande.* Monteux Score #40." Master's thesis, Smith College, 1980.

Lockspeiser, Edward. *Debussy.* 5th ed. Ed. Richard Langham Smith. The Master Musicians Series. London: Dent, 1980.

_____. *Debussy: His Life and Mind.* 2nd ed. 2 vols. Cambridge: Cambridge Univ. Press, 1978.

_____. *The Literary Clef.* London: John Calder, 1958.

Long, Marguerite. *At the Piano with Debussy.* Trans. Olive Senior-Ellis. London: Dent, 1972.

Louÿs, Pierre. "Neuf lettres de Pierre Louÿs à Debussy (1894-1898)." Ed. Edward Lockspeiser. *Revue de Musicologie,* 48 (July-December 1962), 61-70.

_____. "Quatre lettres inédites de Pierre Louÿs." In *Le Souvenir de Pierre Louÿs,* pp. 7-10. Lille: Mercure de Flandre, 1928.

Lugné-Poe, Aurélien-François. *Acrobaties.* La Parade, 2. Paris: Gallimard, 1931.

_____. "La Parade de la Baraque. Souvenirs de Lugné-Poe." *Les Cahiers de "Bravo,"* no. 7 (Supplément au numéro de septembre 1930).

_____. *Le Sot du tremplin.* La Parade, 1. Paris: Gallimard, 1930.

_____. *Sous les étoiles.* La Parade, 3. Paris: Gallimard, 1933.

Macdonald, Hugh, Roger Nichols, Alan Raitt, and Nicholas John. *Pelléas et Mélisande, Claude Debussy.* English National Opera Guide Series, ed. Nicholas John; 9. London: John Calder, 1982.

Maeterlinck, Maurice. *Pélléas et Mélisande.* Brussels: Paul Lacomblez, 1892.

_____. *Pélléas et Mélisande.* 6th ed. Brussels: Paul Lacomblez, 1898.

_____. *Pelléas et Mélisande, Alladine and Palomides, and Home.* Trans. Richard Hovey. New York: Dodd, Mead and Co., 1918.

_____. *Le Temple enseveli.* Paris: Bibliothèque-Charpentier, 1902.

————. *Théâtre.* 3 vols. Brussels: Paul Lacomblez; Paris: Per Lamm, 1901–2.

"Maeterlinck Sues in Defense of Wife." *Musical America,* 12 December 1908, p. 19.

Mallarmé, Stéphane. "Lettres et autographes." Ed. B. Dujardin. *Empreintes,* nos. 10–11 (September–October 1952).

Marnold, Jean. *"Pelléas et Mélisande." Mercure de France,* 42 (June 1902), 801–10.

————. "Reprise de *Pelléas et Mélisande." Mercure de France,* 44 (1 December 1902), 794–98.

————. "Théâtre de l'Opéra-Comique: *Pelléas et Mélisande." Mercure de France,* 55 (1 May 1905), 132–34.

Martin, Auguste. *Claude Debussy: Chronologie de sa vie et de ses oeuvres. Catalogue de l'exposition organisée du 2 au 17 mai 1942 au foyer de l'Opéra-Comique.* Paris, 1942.

Mauclair, Camille. "Claude Debussy et les poètes." In *Programme et livre d'or des souscripteurs.* Paris: Théâtre des Champs-Elysées, 17 June 1932.

————. *"Pelléas et Mélisande," Revue Universelle,* no. 65 (1 July 1902), 331–33.

————. *Servitude et grandeur littéraires.* Paris: Librairie Ollendorff, 1922.

————. "Le Souvenir de Claude Debussy." *Terres Latines,* 4 (March 1936), 66–67.

Maus, Octave. *"Pelléas et Mélisande." L'Art Moderne,* 22 (25 May 1902), 177–78.

McKay, James R. "The Bréval Manuscript: New interpretations." *Cahiers Debussy,* nouv. sér., no. 1 (1977), 5–15.

Meltzer, Henry. "Recalling an interview he had with Claude Debussy . . ." *Musical Standard,* ill. ser., 30 (12 December 1908), 384.

Messager, André. "Lettres d'André Messager à Albert Carré." Ed. Henri Borgeaud. *Revue de Musicologie,* 48 (July–December 1962), 101–4.

————. "Les Premières Représentations de *Pelléas." Revue Musicale,* 7, no. 7 (1 May 1926), 206–10 (110–14); reprinted in *Revue Musicale,* no. 258 (1964), 57–60.

Mirbeau, Octave. "Maurice Maeterlinck." *L'Art Moderne,* 22 (1 June 1902), 188–89.

"'Monna Vanna' Goes on: Maeterlinck loses Suit in Endeavor to stop Opera's Production." *Musical America,* 3 April 1909, p. 18.

Monteux, Doris G., [pseud. Fifi Monteux]. *Everyone is Someone.* New York: Farrar, Straus and Cudahy, 1962.

————. *It's All in the Music.* New York: Farrar, Straus and Giroux, 1965.

Nattiez, Jean-Jacques, and Louise Hirbour-Paquette. "Analyse musicale et sémiologie à propos du Prélude de *Pelléas." Musique en jeu,* no. 10 (March 1973), 42–69.

Nectoux, Jean-Michel. "Debussy et Fauré." *Cahiers Debussy,* nouv. sér., no. 3 (1979), 13–30.

"The New Music Cult in France and Its Leader: Claude Achille Debussy Tells of His Present and Future Works." *New York Times,* 16 May 1909, pt. 5, p. 9.

O'Connor, Garry. *The Pursuit of Perfection: A Life of Maggie Teyte.* New York: Atheneum, 1979.

Orledge, Robert. *Debussy and the Theatre.* Cambridge: Cambridge Univ. Press, 1982.

————. *Gabriel Fauré.* London: Eulenburg, 1979.

Ouellette, Fernand. *Edgard Varèse.* Trans. Derek Cottman. New York: Orion, 1968.

Oulmont, Charles. "Deux amis: Claude Debussy et Ernest Chausson. Documents inédits." *Mercure de France,* 256 (1 December 1934), 248–69.

————. *Musique de l'Amour.* 2nd ed. Strasbourg: Istra, 1969.

"Pelléas et Mélisande." *L'Art du Théâtre,* 2 (July and August 1902), 139–40, 155–59.

Peter, René. "Ce que fut la 'Générale' de *Pelléas et Mélisande."* In *Inédits sur Debussy,* ed. Arthur Hoérée, pp. 3–10. Collection Comoedia-Charpentier. Paris: Publications Techniques, 1942.

————. *Claude Debussy.* 2nd ed. Paris: Gallimard, 1944.

Photiadès, Constantin. "M. Claude Debussy et la centième de 'Pelléas et Mélisande.'" *Revue de Paris,* ser. 20, 2 (1 April 1913), 513–38.

Poisson, Georges. *Musiciens d'Ile de France. Musée de l'Ile de France, Orangerie du Château de Sceaux (31 mai–27 juin 1973).* Sceaux: Musée de l'Ile de France, 1973.

Pougin, Arthur. "Semaine théâtrale. Opéra-Comique. *Pelléas et Mélisande.*" *Le Ménestrel,* 68 (4 May 1902), 138–40.

"Praise from Debussy. Composer Congratulates Campanini for Directing 'Pelléas et Mélisande.'" *New York Times,* 19 March 1908, p. 7.

Prunières, Henry. "A la Villa Médicis." *Revue Musicale,* 7, no. 7 (1 May 1926), 119–38 (23–42).

Prunières, Henry, Robert Godet, and Léon Vallas. "Autour de Debussy." *Revue Musicale,* 15, pt. 1 (May 1934), 349–58; 15, pt. 2 (June, September–October 1934), 21–26, 189–94.

Reid, Charles. *John Barbirolli: A Biography.* New York: Taplinger, 1971.

Rivière, Jacques. "Reprise de *Pelléas et Mélisande* (Opéra-Comique)." *Nouvelle Revue Française,* no. 28 (1 April 1911), 623–25.

Robichez, Jacques. *Le Symbolisme au théâtre: Lugné-Poe et les débuts de L'Oeuvre.* Paris: L'Arche, 1957.

Rohozinski, Ladislas. *Cinquante ans de musique française de 1874 à 1925.* 2 vols. Paris: Librairie de France, 1925.

Rolf, Marie. "Debussy's *La Mer:* A Critical Analysis in the Light of Early Sketches and Editions." Ph.D. thesis, Univ. of Rochester, Eastman School of Music, 1976.

――――. "Orchestral Manuscripts of Claude Debussy: 1895–1905." *Musical Quarterly,* 70 (Fall 1984), 538–66.

Rolland, Romain. *Musicians of To-day.* Trans. Mary Blaiklock. New York: Henry Holt, 1915.

Rorem, Ned. "Pelléas and Pierre." In *Pure Contraption,* pp. 51–55. New York: Holt, Rinehart and Winston, 1974.

Russell, Henry. *The Passing Show.* Boston: Little, Brown and Co., 1926.

Sachs, Harvey. *Toscanini.* Philadelphia and New York: Lippincott, 1978.

Samazeuilh, Gustave. *Musiciens de mon temps. Chroniques et souvenirs.* Paris: La Renaissance du Livre (Editions Marcel Daubin), 1947.

――――. "La Première Version inédite de 'En sourdine.'" In *Inédits sur Debussy,* ed. Arthur Hoérée, pp. 34–38. Collection Comoedia-Charpentier. Paris: Publications Techniques, 1942.

Satie, Erik. *Ecrits.* Ed. Ornella Volta. 2nd ed. Paris: Editions Champ Libre, 1981.

Schaeffner, André. "Debussy and the Theatre." In booklet accompanying recording *Boulez Conducts Debussy, Pelléas et Mélisande.* CBS M3 30119. New York: CBS, 1970.

Schillings, Anne. "La Genèse de *Pelléas et Mélisande.*" In *Souvenir du Symbolisme,* pp. 120–31. *Audace* (1970).

Schneider, Louis. "Echos de théâtres." *Revue Illustrée,* 17, no. 11 (15 May 1902), n.p.

Seebass, Tilman. *Musikhandschriften in Basel aus verschiedenen Sammlungen. Ausstellung im Kunstmuseum Basel vom 31. Mai bis zum 13. Juli 1975.* Basel, 1975.

Sermet, Julien. "Théâtres. Opéra-Comique. *Pelléas et Mélisande.*" *Courrier Français,* 19, no. 18 (4 May 1902), 10.

Seroff, Victor I. *Debussy: Musician of France.* New York: G. Putnam's Sons, 1956.

Sert, Misia. *Misia and the Muses: The Memoirs of Misia Sert.* Trans. Moura Budberg. New York: John Day, 1953.

Sheean, Vincent. *Oscar Hammerstein I: The Life and Exploits of an Impresario.* New York: Simon and Schuster, 1956.

Smith, Richard Langham. "Debussy and the Pre-Raphaelites," *19th Century Music,* 5 (Fall 1981), 95–109.

Souday, Paul. "Revue musicale. Opéra-Comique. *Pelléas et Mélisande.*" *La Revue,* 41 (15 May 1902), 481–82.

Spigl, Friedrich. "Wagner et Debussy." *Revue Blanche,* 29 (December 1902), 517–33.

Stanley, May. "Debussy, the Man, as Maggie Teyte knew him." *Musical America,* 13 April 1918, pp. 5–6.

Stoullig, Edmond. *Les Annales du theatre et de la musique (1902).* Paris: Librairie Paul Ollendorff, 1903.

Taubman, Howard. *The Maestro: The Life of Arturo Toscanini.* New York: Simon and Schuster, 1951.

Terrasson, René. *'Pelléas et Mélisande' ou l'Initiation.* Paris: EDIMAF, 1982.

Teyte, Maggie. "Maggie Teyte corrects some False Ideas about Debussy." *Musical America,* 11 October 1913, p. 2.

————. "Reflections on 'Pelléas.'" *The Music Magazine (The Musical Courier),* 13, no. 164 (August 1962), 14.

Thompson, Oscar. *Debussy: Man and Artist.* 1937; rpt. New York: Dover, 1967.

Thomson, Virgil. *The Musical Scene.* New York: Knopf, 1945.

————. *A Virgil Thomson Reader.* Boston: Houghton Mifflin, 1981.

Tiénot, Yvonne, and Oswald d'Estrade-Guerra. *Debussy: l'homme, son oeuvre, son milieu.* Paris: Lemoine, 1962.

Turner, J. Rigbie. "Nineteenth-Century Autograph Music Manuscripts in The Pierpont Morgan Library: A Check List." *19th Century Music,* 4 (1980), 49–69, 157–83.

————. *Nineteenth-Century Autograph Music Manuscripts in The Pierpont Morgan Library: A Checklist.* New York: The Pierpont Morgan Library, 1982.

Turner, J. Rigbie, Robert Kendall, and James Parsons. *Four Centuries of Opera: Manuscripts and Printed Editions in The Pierpont Morgan Library.* New York: The Pierpont Morgan Library and Dover, 1983.

Vaillant, Annette. "Deux fois cent ans: Maeterlinck et Debussy." *Preuves,* no. 141 (November 1962), 76–78.

Vallas, Léon. *Claude Debussy et son temps.* Paris: Alcan, 1932.

————. *Claude Debussy et son temps.* 2nd ed. Paris: Albin Michel, 1958.

————. *Claude Debussy: His Life and Works.* Trans. Maire and Grace O'Brien. 1933; rpt. New York: Dover, 1973.

————. *The Theories of Claude Debussy, Musicien français.* Trans. Maire O'Brien. 1929; rpt. New York: Dover, 1967.

Vallery-Radot, Pasteur. "Claude Debussy: Souvenirs." *Revue des Deux Mondes,* ser. 8, 45 (15 May 1938), 390–418.

————. *Tel était Claude Debussy, suivi de lettres à l'auteur.* Paris: René Julliard, 1958.

Van Nuffel, R. O. J. *Pelléas et Mélisande: Het drama van Maeterlinck als bron van inspiratie de muziek en de grafische kunst. Catalogus.* Ghent: Kabinet Maurice Maeterlinck, Museum Arnold Vander Haeghen, 1977.

Van Vechten, Carl. *Interpreters and Interpretations.* New York: Knopf, 1917.

Viel, Marie-Jeanne. "Une grande bataille à l'Opéra-Comique: La Générale de *Pelléas et Mélisande* (28 avril 1902)." In *La Belle Epoque,* ed. Gilbert Guilleminault, pp. 95–114. Paris: Denoël, 1957.

Vuillermoz, Emile. *Claude Debussy.* Les Grands Compositeurs du XXᵉ Siècle, ed. Bernard Gavoty. Geneva: René Kister, 1957.

Warmoes, Jean. *Maurice Maeterlinck: Le Centenaire de sa naissance.* [Catalogue of an exhibition at the Bibliothèque Albert I, 20 September–31 December 1962.] Brussels: Bibliothèque Albert I, 1962.

Wenk, Arthur B. *Claude Debussy and Twentieth-Century Music.* Twayne's Music Series, edited by Chris Frigon and Camille Roman. Boston: Twayne, 1983.

Winternitz, Emanuel. *Musical Autographs from Monteverdi to Hindemith.* 2 vols. 2nd ed. New York: Dover, 1965.

Wolff, Stéphane. *Un Demi-siècle d'Opéra-Comique (1900–1950).* Paris: André Bonne, 1953.

Ysaÿe, Antoine. *Eugène Ysaÿe (1858–1931). Etude biographique et documentaire illustrée sur sa vie, son oeuvre, son influence.* 2nd ed. Brussels: Editions Ysaÿe, 1974.

Ysaÿe, Antoine, and Bertram Ratcliffe. *Ysaÿe: His Life, Work and Influence.* London: Heinemann, 1947.

Index

DATE DUE

DEMCO 38-297